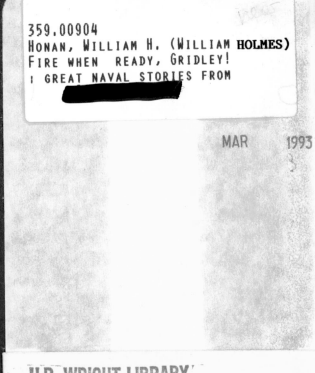

San Buenaventura
"Friends of the
Library"

"FIRE WHEN READY, GRIDLEY!"

"Fire When Ready, Gridley!"

Great Naval Stories from Manila Bay to Vietnam

Compiled and Edited by
William H. Honan

St. Martin's Press

New York

Design by Richard Oriolo

Library of Congress Cataloging-in-Publication Data

Honan, William H.
    Fire when ready, Gridley! : great naval stories from Manila
Bay to Vietnam / William H. Honan.
        p.   cm.
    ISBN 0-312-08778-0
    1. Naval history, Modern—20th century.   I. Title.
D436.H66   1993   92-21571
359′.009′04—dc20   CIP

First Edition: January 1993

10 9 8 7 6 5 4 3 2 1

FOR NANCY, BRADLEY, DANIEL, AND EDITH

To keep peace, study war.

—A SAGE

CONTENTS

ACKNOWLEDGMENTS

I am grateful to Robert Weil, my friend and editor at St. Martin's Press, who helped greatly in refining the concept for this book, and proved himself an expert pilot in guiding it through the rocky shoals of publishing.

Joshua Marwell of St. Martin's Press was also involved from the very beginning, and contributed much. One evening, over a glass of wine, he looked up and said: "We could call it '*Fire When Ready, Gridley!*" What a good idea!

My agent, Roslyn Targ, was an effective booster, as always. By now, she deserves to wear admiral's braid.

Edwin C. Finney, Jr., of the photographic section of the Naval Historical Center in Washington, D.C., was of great assistance in helping to find illustrations for the book. Who but he would know where to lay hands on a picture of a World War I Italian *Motobarche Anti-Sommergibili*?

In researching copyrights, I am grateful for assistance and advice from Lotte Meister, associate general counsel of St. Martin's Press; Bob Simpson of the Roslyn Targ Literary Agency; Cathy Cabana of the U.S. Copyright Office in Washington, D.C.; Ingeborg Godenschweger of the German Information Center; Janet Bacon of the British Information Services; and Karl Meyer, my friend and colleague.

Daniel T.B. Honan served as my managing editor, keeping track of manuscripts, permissions, and many other details. To him, hugs and kisses.

I would also like to extend the aforementioned signs of affection to Daniel's mother, brother, sister, dog, goats, and cats in gratitude for their wholehearted support throughout the long months of *Gridley*'s gestation.

INTRODUCTION

By William H. Honan

These stories are drawn from a lifetime of reading naval history. A few are new acquaintances, but most have long stood out in this sailor's memory like constellations on a starry night.

They are tales of astounding heroism, or, if you prefer, a reckless disregard for self-preservation. Either way, they reveal human qualities outside the frame of ordinary experience. For that reason, they are enthralling, impossible to lay down once started.

Take Rudyard Kipling's tale of a fearless British destroyer crew that deliberately rammed a German battleship at the Battle of Jutland—and pulled away with 20 feet of her side plating mounted on their forecastle.

Or the steel-nerved Lieutenant Luigi Rizzo of the Italian Navy, creeping his bantam sub chaser up to point-blank torpedo range of the monstrous Austrian battleship *Wien*.

Or the American carrier pilots who move at two and a half times the speed of sound, in unearthly states of gravitational distortion, dodging enemy missiles that look like flying telephone poles.

Or Commander Georg von Hase peering through a gunnery periscope on the largest and most heavily armed German battle cruiser at Jutland, muttering *"Gut schnell!"* ("Salvo fire!") and then gasping in horror as the *Queen Mary* blows up before his eyes, snuffing out 1,025 lives in an instant.

Or, at the beginning of an era, Commodore Dewey calmly telling Captain Gridley to discharge the main battery. He didn't say: "Give them a taste of our steel!" That was someone else. Dewey, always a gentleman, said: "You may fire when you are ready, Captain Gridley!" He was surely no phrasemaker; what made Dewey's plain words stick in the public mind is that they broke with the tradition of high-blown exhortation to battle, substituting the new, cool-headed vocabulary of the engineer. Swashbuckle had given way to science—and courtesy.

The stories in this anthology cover roughly a century of modern naval history, beginning with the Spanish-American War in 1898 and closing with Vietnam and the late Cold War. Commodore Dewey's victory over the Spanish squadron at Manila Bay is an appropriate starting point, because it was one of the first occasions when high-speed warships, precision artillery and high-explosive shell were tested in actual combat.

There was a grim splendor to these weapons as they became perfected. Contemplating a sleek, new battleship, knifing the sea at 26 knots, naval writers in the early years of the century used to say: "The three most beautiful things in the world are a fighting ship, a nubile woman and a fast racehorse—in that order!"

The big ship with the biggest guns reached the zenith of its power at the Battle of Jutland in 1916, and thereafter began to be superseded by naval aviation which culminated in the Pearl Harbor attack, and later the guided missile which gained supremacy during the Cold War.

Throughout this century, warships attracted interest at least partly because they are the largest of all moveable man-made objects. That was true in Commodore Dewey's day, and it remains so today. Present-day news commentators like to use superlatives when describing the Saturn rocket and spacecraft assemblies used to hurl American astronauts into orbit around the earth, but the fact is that *three* such contraptions could be laid end to end along the flight deck of the aircraft carrier *Enterprise*—with 31 feet to spare! Even when compared to the greatest stationary structures, the nuclear-powered aircraft carrier inspires awe. If stood on end, such a vessel would come within a few feet of being as tall as the World Trade Center in Manhattan.

Naval combat is thus a game of giants. But it fascinates, also, because it is both intellectual and sanguinary—a chess game played in a slaughterhouse. More so, on both counts, than a land battle.

The authors selected for this volume are a mixture of master storytellers like Kipling and C. S. Forester; major participants in the fighting like Captain Tom Moore who dive-bombed a Japanese aircraft carrier at the Battle of Midway, and Sir Roger Keyes who commanded the daring St. George's Day raid on German U-boat pens in 1918; and distinguished journalists and historians like Hanson W. Baldwin, Samuel Eliot Morison and Joseph L. Stickney. Stickney was the New York *Herald* reporter who stood on the bridge of the *Olympia* beside Commodore Dewey at the Battle of Manila Bay.

The mixture is important because each of these writers has something special to offer, while none can entirely satisfy the reader individually. Rudyard Kipling, for example, who was his country's first winner of the Nobel Prize for Literature, is one of the most magnetic authors of the twentieth century, yet his reports must not be taken literally word for word. Writing in wartime, he had to rely on still-incomplete and often contradictory action reports, and also was obliged to mollify the censor by disguising the ships he mentioned. Still, when it comes to capturing the sense of actually being there, who better than Kipling?

More detached authors—those who write with what John Richard Hale calls the celestial vision of the historian—knew more about the battles described than did the commanders who staged them, yet they may lack the ability to convey some of the heart-in-mouth excitement experienced by the participants. Consequently, a variety of authors has been tapped in order to represent the best writing and widest perspective.

Has an American bias crept into the selection? Some readers may find it so, although I have conscientiously tried to prevent it. For example, while the Imperial Japanese Navy is seen to suffer mightily in the latter chapters of the book as the climactic battles of World War II are recounted, the IJN is shown triumphant at the beginning of the book. The daring Japanese torpedo-boat attack at Port Arthur set a precedent that reverberated down through the century, not the least at Pearl Harbor. And Japan's victory over Czarist Russia at Tsushima is surely one of the greatest naval victories of all time.

Germany and Spain do not come off so well in these pages, yet how is one to compensate for the fact that these nations consistently came out on the losing side in the period covered? I chose Hale's account of the Battle of Santiago partly because he seems to have gone out of his way to be fair to the Spaniards, and I attempted to do justice to German valor on the high seas by including the report by Commander von Hase.

Finally, when all these stories are viewed together in one volume charting the naval history of the century, what general observations are possible? Was the U.S. Navy the deterrent its promoters claimed it would be? Or did its existence—as its critics predicted—tempt America into foreign adventures?

Without detracting from the heroism of those who served the guns, the honest answer is that the United States had no sound justification for building a huge, ocean-going naval force in the late nineteenth century. Great Britain and Japan could well argue that their national survival depended upon the regular comings and goings of freighters from across the sea, and that they required brawny navies to protect the sealanes, but no such argument could be made for the virtually self-sufficient United States. Furthermore, unlike Italy and France, the United States could not maintain that she needed an enormous navy to protect extensive coastlines from nearby potential aggressors.

Our ocean-going navy was constructed—like the navies of Germany and Czarist Russia—as an imperialist toy, and, some will say, it was a toy we might have done better without. Without it, we would not have mugged the Spanish Empire in 1898 and then rifled its pockets, making off with the Philippines and Guam. And had we not owned those territories in the far reaches of the Western Pacific, it seems hardly likely that Admiral Yamamoto would have disturbed Pearl Harbor in December 1941.

Nevertheless, once Japan attacked, America had no choice but to fight back—and thank Providence for every seaworthy bottom in her fleet. In fact, it is when we come to World War II and the late Cold War that the U.S. Navy's contribution to our national security is beyond argument. World War II showed the Navy to be remarkably resourceful when in a position of inferiority (Coral Sea and Midway) and strikingly flexible and efficient after achieving superiority (Leyte Gulf, etc.). Moreover, throughout the 40 years of Cold War, the great American armada of nuclear submarines was the mainstay of our doctrine of massive retaliation. And the Sixth Fleet in the Mediterranean and the Seventh Fleet in the Pacific, among other deployments, also held back the advance of communism.

But enough philosophizing! This book is not about soft-handed policymakers and politicians; it deals with men of action and gritty courage, men who *had* to take part, men who *had* to be there. Like the dying sailor who greeted his commander after the Zeebrugge raid in 1918, these men would say with beaming pride: "Sir, I wouldn't have missed it for anything!"

Mason's Island,
Connecticut,
August 1992

THE SPANISH– AMERICAN WAR

American sailors on the *Iowa* watch a Spanish
warship burn in the Battle of Santiago.
(U.S. Navy photo)

Manila Bay: "Fire When Ready, Gridley!"

Joseph L. Stickney

The New York Herald *reporter Joseph L. Stickney got the scoop of a lifetime when Commodore George Dewey invited him to stand at his side on the bridge of his flagship* Olympia *during the Battle of Manila Bay. This was the first engagement of the Spanish–American War in 1898. The stunning American victory would demonstrate that the United States had become a world power, with imperial ambitions equal to those of Britain, France, and Germany, and with the industrial might and engineering skill to back it up.*

Stickney had graduated from the U.S. Naval Academy during the Civil War and served on the Franklin *with Admiral Farragut, but when peace came he drifted into journalism. In 1898, when war broke out between the United States and Spain, Stickney happened to be in Japan. Quickly, he made contact with Dewey's squadron which was then assembled at Hong Kong. He asked permission to join the fleet. The commodore cabled: "Yes. Come immediately."*

At Hong Kong, Stickney boarded the Olympia *just before the fleet weighed anchor and departed in search of the Spaniards. Dewey must have taken a liking to Stickney (or thought it providential to have a publicist readily available) because when Stickney asked the commodore "if I might be allowed a position on the forward bridge, if a battle should be fought," the taciturn Dewey mumbled something like, "I think you will be satisfied."*

Soon, Stickney was summoned to the quarterdeck.

"Mr. Caldwell has volunteered for duty on the guns," said Dewey, referring to his secretary, "and I have decided to appoint you as my aide. You will take station with me on the forward bridge." Dewey paused, then added with a wink: "Satisfied?"

Not only would Stickney be at Dewey's elbow throughout the action, but, as we shall see, at one point he actually directed the Olympia's *fire.*

The sea fastenings of the guns were hastily cast loose, the training levers shipped, the sights uncovered, the elevating screws worked and the sponge and rammer placed ready for use. In the powder division the magazines were opened, the hatches of the shell rooms taken off, the electric battle lanterns turned on and put in their proper places, the division tubs filled with water, and the ammunition hoists set at work whipping up powder and shell. The master's division went to the wheel and the lead, hung up the battle lanterns and swiftly swung the search lights around to be sure that they were in easy working condition. The signalmen cleared away the Ardois lights and got out the Coston signals, ready to communicate with the other ships of the fleet as occasion might require. The engineer's division gathered at their stations in the fire rooms and engine rooms, ready to fire up under all boilers and put on any pressure of steam up to the maximum limit as called upon, at the same time closing the watertight compartment doors and starting the forced-draft air blowers. Throughout the ship there was continuous movement and preparation, carried forward in silence and generally in darkness, the only noises being those caused by the working of the machinery and the guns.

Suddenly, out of the silent gloom, the voice of the executive officer, Lieutenant Rees, was heard: "Man the starboard battery! Pivot to starboard!" The heavy turrets swung around on their centers till their guns pointed off to starboard, and the men quickly took their places at the guns on the starboard side of the ship. When each division officer had satisfied himself that not one small detail of preparation had been overlooked, he went to the upper deck where the executive officer was standing and reported his division. The ship's writer, acting as clerk for the executive—in the absence of naval cadets in the *Olympia*—took note of the time when each division officer made his report, thus keeping a record by which the captain could judge the promptitude of his crew in all its departments.

In just seven minutes from the first note on the bugle, Lieutenant Rees reported to the captain: "The ship is cleared for action, sir." A rapid drill at the guns—"going through the motions" of loading and firing at an imaginary enemy, first on one side and then on the other—kept the men on the jump for twenty minutes, and then came the order: "Secure!" With a rapidity like to that with which the guns had been cast loose, the crew returned to the magazines and shell rooms the ammunition that had been brought on deck, replaced the temporary fittings that had been removed and secured the guns for sea. Again the division officers had a brisk rivalry to be first in reporting their divisions secured, and when they had made their reports the executive officer sent word to the captain, "All secure, sir." This was followed by "Retreat!" sounded on the bugle, and the men left their battle stations to resume the usual routine of the night watches.

During the slow run across the China Sea, the men in our ships were exercised in all the duties pertaining to battle except the actual firing of the guns. There was never a moment after the time the "hands were turned to"—the navy phrase that indicates the waking up of every one aboard and the stowing of all hammocks in the nettings—when the crews were not busy about something that would be of use to them in the fight that was now so near at hand. When twilight hour came it was a fairly well tired-out lot of jackies that carried their hammocks below to get a night's rest, broken, of course, by the regular sea watches.

At the hour when the officers dined in the evening the band mustered on the deck just forward of the commodore's cabin and played popular airs, the selections being made usually from the light comic operas and stirring march movements of favorite composers; but on Thursday, the day after leaving Mirs Bay, Bandmaster Valifuoco selected the music with special reference to rousing the patriotism of the "boys in blue," choosing many of the airs that had been popular in the north during our civil war. These were all favorably received, but it was not till the band struck up "Yankee Doodle" that the boys cheered. When the concert closed with "The Star Spangled Banner," the voices of at least fifty men took up the words of each verse, the young apprentices being particularly noticeable in the lead, and the chorus spread through the ship from forecastle to cabin with an enthusiasm that carried with it the hearts of all on board.

Land was sighted Saturday morning, April 30, the squadron having arrived off Cape Bolinao, near the north end of Luzon, the largest of the Philippine islands. That forenoon the *Boston* and the *Concord* were sent ahead of the rest of the fleet to enter Subig Bay, which is about thirty miles north of the entrance to Manila Bay. As it was thought that perhaps the Spanish squadron might have moved up to this bay, the *Baltimore* was sent to reinforce the other two vessels a little before noon.

As the remaining ships came down the coast at easy speed, several small schooners were sighted along the shore and the commodore ordered the *Zafiro* to overhaul one of them to see whether she could give us news concerning the Spanish defenses at Manila. When the *Zafiro* returned from this duty signal was made to her to come within hail of the flagship. Her captain, misgauging his speed as he came close alongside the *Olympia,* shot ahead and then made the mistake of putting his helm the wrong way. In consequence, the *Zafiro* swung straight across the flagship's bow, and a collision seemed inevitable. Lieutenant Strite, the officer of the deck—that is, the officer having charge of the handling of the *Olympia* during that watch—was equal to the emergency. He quickly put the *Olympia's* helm over also, and the two vessels glided past each other without touching. As the *Olympia's* bow just cleared the *Zafiro's* stern by a distance of not more than three or four feet, the commodore said to Captain Gridley:

"Who has the deck, Captain Gridley?" and then, when informed, he added: "Give my compliments to Lieutenant Strite and tell him that I noticed and appreciated his coolness and skill in handling the ship so as to avoid a collision."

It was not a matter of much moment in itself, since Strite did no more than his duty, but the incident was illustrative of Dewey's way of dealing with his officers.

When we arrived off the entrance to Subig Bay, early in the afternoon, the *Boston*, the *Baltimore*, and the *Concord* came out of the bay and reported that the Spaniards had neither ships nor shore guns in the harbor. Our course for Manila was resumed. Now the final preparations for battle were made. All woodwork that could be removed without injury to the working of the vessels was thrown overboard, and it was interesting to see the men coming on deck in a steady stream, carrying in their arms tables, chairs, doors, and bulkheads, which they would pitch into the sea as though they were enjoying the opportunity to dismantle the interior of their ship. In fact, the seamen were glad to get rid of everything that might endanger their lives by fire. In the *Olympia* the men had a number of board tables, made to swing from the beams above the berth deck, upon which they served their meals. The executive officer gave an order that these mess tables should be "put over the side," meaning that they should be hung outside the ship by ropes in a position where, even if they should catch on fire, they would endanger nothing else. But the seamen chose to interpret the order to mean that the tables should go overboard, and the result was that, after the battle, the jackies had to eat either standing or lying down, since they had no tables.

A few miles north of the entrance to Manila Bay, Commodore Dewey stopped his flagship and made signal for commanding officers to repair on board. When every gig had been called away, and the captain of each ship was steering in solitary state toward the *Olympia*, no one needed to be told that we were on the eve of battle.

"They're comin'," said one of the old seamen, "to hear the 'old man's' last word before we go at the Dons."

"Not his last word," said one of the younger men.

"Perhaps not his," was the reply, "but it's near our last words some of us are. There'll be many an eye will look at that sunset tonight that'll never see another."

But such prophets of sorrow were rare. As a rule our men went into the action of Manila Bay with their minds more set upon revenge than foreboding.

The sun went down on a sea as calm as if storm were unknown, the deep sapphire surface being unruffled by even a ripple. Heaps of clouds in the southeast were colored in all the gorgeous pageantry of a tropical brilliancy, and some of the more imaginative minds were able to see cloud-shapes that resembled the *Maine*.

The war council was of short duration. Commodore Dewey had decided on his plans before it met, and he took little time in giving to each captain his duties for the night and next day. By seven o'clock the gigs were all hoisted at their davits, the flagship was again under way, and long before dark every vessel had taken her station, ready to run by the batteries at the mouth of the bay or to fight her passage, as circumstances might require. Aside from one light at the very stern of each ship, intended as a guide for the next in line, not a glimmer was to be seen aboard any craft in the fleet. As I looked astern from the *Olympia's* taffrail, I could just get a faint suggestion of a ghostly shape where the *Baltimore* grimly held her course on our port quarter, while the *Raleigh*, somewhat farther away on our starboard quarter, could be seen by only the sharpest eyes when the moon was wholly unobscured by cloud.

The commodore decided to waste no time in useless delay; but, regardless of hidden mines and shore batteries, led the way into the harbor. With all lights out, and the crews at the guns, the warships in their gray war paint turned silently toward the Boca Grande, the larger entrance to the bay, the flagship, *Olympia,* leading. Following closely, in the order that was retained during the battle of the succeeding day, came the *Baltimore*, the *Raleigh*, the *Petrel*, the *Concord,* and the *Boston.*

As the fleet approached the entrance it moved as slowly as was compatible with keeping the formation of the line. Half of the crew of each gun were allowed to sleep alongside their stations in order that they might be better fitted for what was to come. Except for the sleepless eye on the bridge of the *Olympia,* and the alert gaze of the officers on watch, the ships seemed to slumber, as did the city and the forts.

It was at 9:45 that the men were sent to their guns, but there was little needed in the way of preparation for battle. On the shore north of the other channel—Boca Chica, as it is named—we had seen a bright light, but there was no stir perceptible to indicate that we had been discovered by the Spaniards. Opposite the middle of Corregidor—the island that lies in the entrance to the bay—another light now began to flash at intervals, as if making signals, and soon the flight of a rocket from this island told us that we had been discovered.

"We ought to have a shot from Corregidor very soon now," said the commodore; and having been already sighted, our ships were permitted to increase their speed to 8 knots. The *Olympia* could have moved at a 15-knot gait without any unusual effort, and all the warships could have made about 12 knots; but it would not have been safe for the fighting craft to run away from the noncombatant column led by the revenue cutter *McCulloch,* and as the *Nanshan* and the *Zafiro* were not capable of doing much better than eight knots that speed was never exceeded.

Into the yawning blackness between Corregidor and the lone

rock that is called El Fraile—the Monk—we passed, and still no hostile demonstration from the Spanish guns and torpedoes. The moon was now hidden in the western clouds, and the solemn stillness of the *Olympia,* as we steamed along in the complete darkness, made the passage of the entrance probably the most oppressive time of our whole operations.

On, on crept the mighty engines of war, but the batteries on shore gave no sign. Suddenly when the flagship had passed a mile beyond Corregidor Island, a gun boomed out, and a shell went screaming over the *Raleigh* and the *Olympia,* soon followed by a second. Three ships, the *Raleigh,* the *Concord,* and the *Boston,* replied, apparently with effect, for the firing ceased, and again the batteries lay silent.

As Commodore Dewey had planned, the fleet arrived within five miles of Manila at daybreak. With what must have been the astonishment in the Spanish lines when the sun rose, they looked out on the American ships that had come in during the night.

While, as yet, the fleet retained the appearance of calm that had characterized its approach, now many eyes on board lighted with the fire of war, as they sighted the Spanish fleet, under command of Rear Admiral Montojo, lying off Cavite, and realized that the battle was at hand. During most of the battle the Spanish vessels were moving about at full speed. The Spaniards had a well-equipped navy yard called Cavite Arsenal, which had put the ships in first-rate fighting trim.* And on Sangley Point they had two strong batteries containing three 6.2-inch and one 4.7-inch guns; so that, when we take into account the advantages that the Spaniards had in position, in their opportunities to lay mines, and in their knowledge of the bay, it may be seen that it was no trifling task that confronted the fleet.

With the American flag flying from all mastheads, the ships moved on. No excitement was visible; the quiet man on the bridge of the *Olympia* was as unmoved, apparently, as though he were sailing into a peaceful harbor. For the first time in many years the stars and stripes were being borne aggressively into a foreign port. It was an epoch in history. The rapid changes of scene and the whole picturesque effect was something never to be forgotten. The underlying meaning of it all was too great to be readily understood.

---

*In fact, Montojo's fleet was decrepit and markedly inferior in heavy guns. Dewey's squadron had ten 8-inch guns while Montojo had none. Moreover, in lesser major-caliber weapons the Americans had 53 to Spain's 31. *(Editor)*

Nineteenth-century civilization and fifteenth-century medievalism lay confronting each other.

As the ships passed in front of Manila, action was begun by the Spaniards. Three batteries, mounting guns powerful enough to send shells to the distance of five miles, opened fire. The *Concord* replied, but Commodore Dewey, after two shots, made signal to stop firing, since there was danger of the shells carrying destruction and death into the crowded city beyond.

At six minutes past five o'clock, when nearing Cavite, there was a splash and roar, and two great jets of water were thrown high in the air ahead of the flagship. The fleet had come upon the first of the submarine mines. Of course it was possible and probable that the whole harbor was filled with torpedoes. At any moment they were liable to explode beneath the ships; but Commodore Dewey had foreseen this when he entered the bay, and it did not now cause him to change his plans. Moreover, he had fought with Farragut at New Orleans and at Mobile, and submarine mines had no terrors for him. Contrary to expectation no more mines exploded, and it is believed that no others had been placed by the Spaniards. We regarded these explosions as a sort of "bluff," intended to make us imagine that there might be other mines in front of Cavite.

"They ain't so good at blowing up ships that come with their fighting clothes on as they are at murdering a crew in time of peace," said one of the Olympia's petty officers, as he saw the column of water and smoke subsiding ahead of us; and this reference to the *Maine* showed what was uppermost in the minds of our men as they were moving on for their first chance to avenge the crime perpetrated in Havana last February.

Steaming at the comparatively slow speed of eight knots, our ships approached Cavite. From the peak of each vessel and from every mast-head floated the "stars and stripes"—the largest regulation ensign being displayed. In the lead was, of course, the *Olympia*, followed by the *Baltimore*, the *Raleigh*, the *Petrel*, the *Concord*, and the *Boston*, in the order named. The revenue cutter *McCulloch* and the merchant steamers attached to the squadron as coal carriers were ordered to keep well out of range in the bay, and they naturally did not try to come nearer. The warships had closed up to an interval of about two cables' lengths—say, 300 yards—and they held their respective positions with an accuracy that must have astonished Don Basilio Augustin Davila, the Spanish governor, who had told his people that our vessels were manned by men without training or discipline.

Drawing on at this slow speed toward the enemy's line, I could not help recalling the lines of—I believe it's Southey:

Like leviathans afloat lay our bulwarks on the brine,
While the sign of battle flew down the lofty British line—
      It was ten of April morn by the chime.
As we drifted on our path,
There was silence deep as death,
And the boldest held his breath,
      For a time.

Presently, we came near enough to distinguish the Spanish ships in the Bay of Cavite. Most prominently in view at first was a sort of cream-colored vessel, apparently at anchor. This we recognized as the *Castilla.* She was moored, head and stern, with her port battery to seaward, just outside the point of low land that makes out like a lobster's claw and protects the inner anchorage. Behind the *Castilla,* with all steam up and moving to and fro in the back bay, were the *Reina Christina,* flagship, the *Isla de Luzon,* the *Isla de Cuba,* the *Don Juan de Austria,* the *Don Antonio de Ulloa,* the *Marques del Duero,* the *General Lezo,* the *Argos,* several torpedo boats, and the transport *Isla de Mindanao.* The latter steamed away as fast as she could and was beached some distance up the coast, where she was burned by the *Concord* later in the day.

When we were at a distance of about 6,000 yards a puff of very white cloud arose from a clump of bushes on shore. It was a pretty sight, for the smoke floated away in fantastic shapes above the red clay shore and the bright green foliage. But for whom aboard our ships did that apparently harmless pillar of white mean death or mutilation? Within four seconds we heard the scream of the shot, as it passed far over us, and we knew that the first gun in the battle of Manila Bay had failed to do us any damage. Then the Spanish flagship, taking a lesson probably from the excessive elevation given to the shore gun, fired several times in quick succession, with an aim as much too short as the battery's had been too high. Yet one or two of her projectiles passed between our masts on the rebound from the water. More puffs of flame from the shore in different places showed that the Spaniards were better protected than we had supposed. Soon all the Spanish vessels were aflame with rapid gun fire. Shell after shell flew close over our superstructure or skimmed past the head of our commodore and his staff on our forward bridge.

Still our courtly chief made no sign. In the usual service white uniform, wearing, however, a gray traveling cap on his head, having been unable to find his uniform cap after the guns in his cabin had been cleared for action, the commodore paced the bridge, watching the enemy's hot fire as if he were a disinterested spectator of an unusual display of fireworks.

"Take her close along the five-fathom line, Mr. Calkins," he said to the navigator, "but be careful not to get her aground."

The 5 fathom line is the curve of the coast outside of which the water is five fathoms deep. As the *Olympia* was drawing more than four fathoms, it was not safe to take her in closer. We had been approaching the Spanish line at an angle of about fifteen degrees and soon the shoaling of the water, as shown by repeated casts of the lead, called for a change of course. As the helm was put to port and the *Olympia's* men at the port battery began to get a view of their still-distant enemies, they felt that the moment for which they so long had waited was at hand. No order to open fire had been given, but the experienced petty officers saw that the ship was nearing a range at which all our guns would be effective.

Although at first the Spanish shots flew wild, after a time the gunners got a better range and the shells from both the batteries and the Spanish vessels began to strike near or burst close aboard the American ships.

All this time, with the exception of the shots from the *Concord,* the guns of the American fleet had remained inactive. The strain on our men was fearful, but they had confidence in their commodore and submitted willingly to his judgment. The heat was intense, and stripped of all clothing except their trousers, the gunners stood silent and obedient at their posts. The *Olympia* might have been empty if the whir of the blowers and the throb of the engines had not told of pulsating human life. On the forward bridge of the *Olympia* stood Commodore Dewey surrounded by his staff. In this little group were Commander Lamberton, fleet captain; the executive officer, Lieutenant Rees; Lieutenant Calkins, the navigator, who conned the ship admirably all through the battle, and the commodore's aide, myself. It was considered unwise to run the risk of losing all the senior officers by one shell, and therefore Captain Gridley was in the conning tower.

Suddenly a shell burst directly over the center of the ship. As the projectile flashed over the head of the man who held the destiny of the fleet in his grasp, it became evident that the moment of activity had come. Even the powerful will of their leader could no longer restrain the surging war fever of the crew. A boatswain's mate, who had been bending over, looking eagerly ahead with his hand on the lock string of the after five-inch gun, sprung up and cried out: "Boys, remember the *Maine!*" Instantly the watchword was repeated by the two hundred men at the guns. The hoarse shout was caught up in the turrets and fire rooms. It echoed successively through all the decks of the silent ship, till finally, in a sullen whisper, "Remember the *Maine*" stole up through the ventilators from the lowest parts of the hold to the officers on the bridge. There seemed to be no premeditation in the cry, but the explosion that wrecked the gallant *Maine* in Havana Harbor was the spark that fired the first gun in Manila Bay, as it was the flame that set blazing the righteous indignation of the American nation against the cruelty of Spain to her oppressed colonies.

"You may fire when you are ready, Captain Gridley," said the commodore. This order sufficed, and at 5:41 in the morning, at a distance of three miles, America roared forth her first battle cry to Spain from the starboard eight-inch gun in the forward turret of the *Olympia.*

The *Baltimore* and the *Boston* were not slow in following the example of the flagship, and almost immediately their 8-inch guns were sending 250-pound shells toward the *Castilla* and the *Reina Cristina.* The battle now began to rage fierce and fast. Encouraged by the fact that the range was too great for accuracy, and that the American gunners were obliged to guess the distance, the Spaniards fired more rapidly. Shots from their ship and shore guns came through the air in a screaming shower; time-fuse shells were constantly bursting about the American fleet, and their fragments, scattering in all directions, would strike the water like shrapnel or cut the hull and rigging of the ships.

The *Olympia* was the target for most of the Spanish guns, because she was the flagship and because she steered directly for the center of the Spanish line. One shell struck close by a gun in the ward room. The signal halyards were cut from Lieutenant Brumby's hand, as he stood on the after bridge. One great projectile, with almost human intuition, came straight toward the forward bridge, but burst less than a hundred feet away. A fragment cut the rigging directly over the heads of Commander Lamberton and myself. Another struck the bridge railings in line with us, and still another, about as large as a flat iron, gouged a hole in the deck a few feet below the commodore.

The *Baltimore's* crew had several narrow escapes. One shot struck her and passed through her, but fortunately hit no one. Another ripped up her main deck, disabled one 6-inch gun, and exploded a couple of three-pounder shells, wounding eight men. This shell is worthy of special notice on account of its eccentric actions. It came undoubtedly from the Cañacao battery and entered about two feet above the upper deck, on the starboard side, between the after 6-inch gun and the 3-pounder mounted on the rail. After piercing two plates of steel, each one-quarter of an inch thick, it struck the deck and penetrated till it cracked one of the heavy deck beams clear through. Bounding upward it tore its way through the steel combing of the engine room skylight, and again passed through two quarter-inch plates. Leaving the skylight, it ranged forward, struck the recoil cylinder of the port 6-inch gun on the quarterdeck and disabled the carriage. It at last met the steel shield curved in front of the gun. This was strong enough to resist the attack, and the shell followed the curve of the shield until it was traveling in exactly the opposite direction to what had been its former course. It again crossed the ship to the starboard side, where it struck a ventilator and stopped. This shell was the cause of wounding two officers and six men by exploding the two 3-pounder shells mentioned; but directly, it injured no one, and its course was one of the most remarkable on record.

The *Boston* received a shell in her port quarter. It burst in Ensign Doddridge's stateroom and caused a hot fire, as did also one that burst in the port hammock netting; but both these fires were quickly extinguished. One shell passed through the *Boston*'s foremast, just in front of Captain Wildes on the bridge. The entire battle was a series of incidents of this sort and the wonder is that they were no more than incidents.

Even now, when the Spaniards had brought all their guns into action, the Americans had not yet responded with all their strength. Commodore Dewey was reserving his force. The men naturally chafed at this continued restraint, but they laughed and joked good-naturedly among themselves. Sometimes, when a shell would burst close aboard or would strike the water and pass overhead, with the peculiar sputtering noise characteristic of the tumbling of a rifled projectile, some of the more nervous would dodge mechanically.

At a distance of 4,000 yards, owing to her deep draught, the commodore was obliged to change his course and run the *Olympia* parallel to the Spanish column. At last, as she brought her port broadside toward the foe, Commodore Dewey said:

"Open with all the guns," and the roar that went forth shook the vessel from end to end. The battle was indeed on. Above the snarling of the *Olympia*'s 5-inch rapid-firers was heard the prolonged growl of her turret 8-inchers. The other ships joined in, and Cavite Harbor was no longer comfortable for the Spaniards.

It is almost impossible to describe the situation at this moment. War has been always fearful, but the confusion and horror of modern warfare can only be understood by an eye witness. The roar of the guns of today and the horrors resulting from their powerful shells can best be left to the imagination of those who have not actually been in battle and seen the effects of their deadly work. And even to those aboard the American fleet that day, the fearful event was not known to its limit till later; for the scenes of carnage and death were upon the Spanish side.

During the first hour of the fight, as I stood near Commodore Dewey on the bridge, I saw a torpedo boat come creeping out from behind Sangley Point and called his attention to her.

"You look after her," he answered; "I have no time to bother with torpedo boats. Let me know when you've finished her."

Her commander must have been ignorant of modern guns or utterly indifferent to death, for not till twice hit by the secondary battery did this daring craft turn back and reach the beach just in time to save her crew from drowning.

The American fleet had made four runs along the Spanish line, when, finding the chart incorrect, Lieutenant Calkins told the commodore he believed he could take the ship nearer the enemy. Carefully watching the depth of the water, as shown by the lead, the *Olympia* started over the course for the fifth time and ran within 2,000 yards of the Spanish vessels, a range so close that now even the 6-pounders were effective. A storm of shells poured upon the Spaniards, but, as far as the Americans could see, they had not yet been crippled to any great extent. Matters were not particularly cheerful on board the *Olympia*. Many of our projectiles had seemed to go too high or too low, as had those of the Spaniards, and several times the Admiral had expressed dissatisfaction. He now gave the order to haul off into the open bay, in order to take stock of ammunition, which was in danger of running short, and to plan a new attack. It would never have done to admit this state of affairs to the men, so the scheme was devised of making breakfast the cause of the cessation of hostilities.

The interruption was not welcomed joyfully, however. As the ships drew away, the temper of the men was well shown by the almost tearful appeal of one gun captain to Commander Lamberton:

"For God's sake, Captain," he cried, "don't stop now! Let's finish 'em up right off."

As the action ceased the other ships passed the flagship and cheered lustily. The fight had now lasted about two hours and a half, when for about four hours hostilities were suspended and the fleet lay inactive in the center of the bay. During this time it was found that there remained in the magazines of the *Olympia* only 85 rounds of 5-inch ammunition, and that the stock of 8-inch charges was sufficiently depleted to make another two hours' fighting impossible. The *Baltimore* was discovered to have the best supply, so when, at 10:50 the signal for close action went up again, she was given the place of honor in the lead, the *Olympia* following and the other ships as before. As the *Baltimore* began firing at the Spaniards at 11:16 she made a series of hits as if at target practice.

In this second attack the Spaniards replied very slowly, chiefly from their shore guns. The Americans now recognized the results of their morning's work, for the Spanish flagship and the *Castilla* were burning fiercely, and we had heard the explosion of the magazines on board the *Reina Cristina*. For some reason the *Castilla* did not blow up, although she burned fiercely as late as Monday night. This was undoubtedly due to the fact that her magazines had been flooded before she was abandoned by her crew. Commodore Dewey now signalled the *Raleigh*, the *Boston*, the *Concord*, and the *Petrel* to go into the inner harbor and destroy all the enemy's ships.

The work of the little *Petrel*, Commander E. P. Wood, commanding, is worthy of special mention. Her draught was so light that she was able to approach within 1,000 yards. From this close range she commanded everything flying the Spanish flag and fired with the greatest accuracy. Lieutenant E. M. Hughes, with an armed boat's crew, set fire to the *Don Juan de Austria*, the *Marques del Duero*, and the *Isla de Cuba*. The large transport *Manila* and many tugboats and small craft were also captured. The other ships did their duty as well, and soon not a red-and-yellow ensign remained aloft, except one fluttering from a battery far up the coast. The *Don Antonio de Ulloa* was the last vessel to be abandoned. She at last lurched over and sank. The Spanish flag on the arsenal was hauled down at 12:30, the white flag was hoisted in its place, and the power of the Spanish Dons in the Philippines was at an end.

Commodore Dewey closed the day by anchoring off the City of Manila, and sending word to the governor-general that the port was blockaded and that if a shot was fired at the American fleet from Manila, the city would be laid in ashes. He also sent word that he wished to use the cable to Hong Kong, but no reply to this demand was ever received.

The commodore had been ordered to capture or destroy the Spanish squadron, and instructions were never more effectively carried out. Within seven hours after arriving on the scene of action nothing remained to be done.

The only Americans wounded were on board the *Baltimore*—eight in number, all slightly, except two men, each of whom had a leg broken. As each captain reported on the flagship, he was eagerly asked: "How many killed?" And while each man could not conceal his satisfaction at the condition of his ship and crew, he was also desirous that this should be understood to be no proof that he had not been in danger. It was feared that some casualties might have taken place on the *Boston,* as she had been on fire, but her report was equally satisfactory, and the men on the *Olympia* cheered loudly.

Nevertheless, there was great suffering among our men during the fight, owing to the terrific heat, and some of those shut up below would undoubtedly have succumbed had it not been for the excitement of battle.

In the arsenal grounds a number of bodies of Spaniards were found unburied on Monday morning. A Roman Catholic priest was called in to read the burial service. The bodies presented a horrible sight. The head of one had been almost wholly carried away by a shell. Another had been struck in the stomach by a large projectile which had cut everything away to the backbone. One very large man, apparently an officer, was not only mangled but swollen out of all proportion to his real size. To add to the horror several lean, wolflike dogs had already visited the scene.

The victory in Manila Bay was one of the most remarkable in the history of the world. Not an American was killed, and at night, after the battle, every American ship was fit to go into a similar action on the succeeding day. The result was almost incomprehensible, but it is probably what may be expected in all the affairs of life, where coolness and wisdom hold the balance against bravado and inefficiency.

CHAPTER 2

Santiago: "Don't Cheer, Boys. Those Poor Devils Are Dying!"

John Richard Hale

D espite *Commodore Dewey's spectacular victory at Manila Bay and the national rejoicing it inspired, the United States still faced grave danger in its war against Spain.*

Congress, the press, and the public were demanding the immediate capture of Havana, the citadel of Spanish power in the Americas. But 80,000 Spanish regulars were guarding the city. Furthermore, it would take months to train an army, manufacture its equipment, and prepare transportation. Meanwhile, Admiral Cervera's powerful squadron was on the loose somewhere in the Atlantic or Caribbean. Cervera might attack the American invasion fleet, or bombard New York, Washington, Charleston, or any other Atlantic seaport.

In the following chapter, John Richard Hale tells how the war progressed, climaxing with a second American naval victory every bit as decisive as Dewey's.

Hale, it should be noted, is a figure shrouded in mystery. In fact, the name is probably a pseudonym used by a British naval officer—all of whom were prohibited from publishing anything about naval subjects while in the service, and many of whom resorted to writing anonymously.

Whatever the facts, the naval history attributed to John Richard Hale from which this chapter is drawn was regarded as a classic in its time, going through eight editions between 1911 and 1940.

The Spanish-American War in the Atlantic began several weeks after Dewey's exploit at Manila Bay when Admiral William T. Sampson's North Atlantic Fleet left its base at Key West in May 1898. Sampson promptly established the blockade of Western Cuba, reconnoitered the sea defenses of Havana, and exchanged some shells with them at long range. Also, in order to satisfy popular feeling in America, Sampson bombarded the batteries of San Juan, Puerto Rico, an operation that had no real effect on the fortunes of the war, and inflicted only trifling local loss on the Spaniards.

An army had been assembled at Tampa, Florida, and a huge fleet of transports was collected to ferry it over to Cuba. Its destination was supposed to be the western end of the island, where, in cooperation with the insurgents by land and the fleet by sea, it would besiege and capture Havana. But again and again the sailing of the fleet was delayed, and there was alarm in the cities of the Atlantic states, because the newspapers published wild reports of phantom armadas hovering off the coast. When news came that Admiral Pascual Cervera's Atlantic Squadron (four armored cruisers and three destroyers) had sailed from the Portuguese harbor of St. Vincent in the Cape de Verde Islands, and for many days there was no trace of his movements, there was a quite unnecessary alarm as to what the Spanish squadron might do.

For some days after the declaration of war (April 23) Cervera's squadron lay at St. Vincent. All the ships were repainted a dead black, some coal was taken on board, and quantities of ammunition transferred from the holds of the *Ciudad de Cadiz* to the magazines of the cruisers. At last, on April 29, Cervera sailed, leaving the torpedo boats and the armed liner in port, and taking with him only his high-speed ships, the four armored cruisers, and the three destroyers.

His course was westward, and it was conjectured that San Juan de Puerto Rico was his destination. The distance is about 2,400 miles, and supposing that he would proceed at a cruising speed of ten knots, in order to economize his coal, it was calculated that he would be across the Atlantic in ten days, reaching the West Indies about May 9. Two swift armed liners that had been attached to Commodore Schley's reserve fleet, officially known as the "Flying Squadron," at Hampton Roads, were sent out to sweep the Western Atlantic, and it was expected that by the end of the first week in May they would bring back news of the enemy, but May 7 came and brought no news. Ships arriving in ports on both sides of the ocean told of having seen the smoke of a squadron on the horizon in so many places that it seemed as if the Atlantic must be full of fleets. Look-out stations as far north as the New England states told of glimpses of warships seen far off in the morning twilight, or vaguely distinguished through mist and rain. But definite news of Cervera there was none. It seemed as if his squadron had vanished into space.

Then there were theories designed to account for his disappearance. It was suggested that he had altered his course and gone to the coast of South America, to intercept the battleship *Oregon,* which had come around from the Pacific to reinforce Sampson's fleet; or perhaps he was making for the Cape or the Horn, bound on a long voyage for Manila, to destroy Dewey's unarmored cruisers and restore Spanish supremacy in the Philippines; or he was ranging the oceans to prey upon American commerce.

Then came a strange report, worth remembering as a caution against too easily accepting the rumors of war-time. From Cadiz came American press dispatches, duly passed by the Spanish censor, stating that Cervera's squadron had steamed back into that port. The start westward from St. Vincent was said to be a mere feint. The Spaniards had hoped to draw some of the swifter American ships out into the Atlantic, and score a victory by fighting them in European waters. Naval experts gravely discussed Cervera's tactics. Correspondents described the position of his fleet in Cadiz harbor. Perhaps the Spanish censor helped the misleading rumors into circulation by letting Americans at Cadiz imagine that ships fitting out in the harbor were the missing fleet.

At last, on May 12, came definite news of one unit of the squadron. The night before the destroyer *Furor* had paid a flying visit in the dark to the French port of St. Pierre, in Martinique, probably calling for cabled information and orders. On the 12th the *Terror* visited the same port in broad daylight. That evening, from the hills of Martinique, four large cruisers were seen far out at sea, steering northwards, under easy steam. The cable from Martinique by St. Lucia to the United States was out of order, and it was not till the 15th that Admiral Sampson received the news. Several of his heavy ships were coaling at Key West. He hurried on the work, and sent his lighter ships to watch the Windward and Mona Passages. He sent off Schley with the Flying Squadron to the south of Cuba, with orders to sweep the island-fringed Caribbean sea and watch the Yucatan Channel with his cruisers. As soon as he had completed coaling he himself sailed for the waters north of Cuba.

Once more there was for a while no news of Cervera. After dark on May 12 he had altered his northern course and steered a little south of west, making for the Dutch island of Curaçao, where he expected to find some tramp steamers laden with coal and other supplies awaiting him. On Saturday, May 14, the *Maria Teresa* and the *Vizcaya* entered the port, the two other cruisers, accompanied by two destroyers, remaining outside. The expected colliers had not arrived; the Dutch authorities insisted on Cervera leaving Curaçao within twenty-four hours, and he sailed on the Sunday without being able to fill up his bunkers. Once more the United States cruisers failed to sight him, as he steamed slowly across the Caribbean Sea, husbanding his coal and steering for Cuba.

On Wednesday, May 18, three American warships were off Santiago de Cuba. They came so close in that the Morro battery at the entrance fired upon them. Before sundown they steamed away. They had missed Cervera by a few hours, for at sunrise next morning he brought his four cruisers and two destroyers into Santiago harbor.

Santiago is the oldest Spanish city in Cuba, and was its capital in the early days before Havana was founded.

The old city stands at the head of a landlocked arm of the sea, surrounded by forest-clad hills, and is approached through narrow ravine-like straits. Cervera had come there to obtain coal and supplies. If he had made it only a temporary base, and had been able to coal immediately, and put to sea to attack the American cruisers scattered over the Caribbean waters, he might have scored successes for a while. But he waited at Santiago till he was hopelessly blockaded.

For some days the Washington government, mindful of the *Cadiz* hoax, refused to believe reports that the Spanish fleet was hidden behind the headlands of Santiago harbor. It was not till May 27 that Admiral Schley obtained definite proof of the fact, and formed the blockade of Santiago with his squadron. Admiral Sampson then brought his fleet around, and took over the command.

Until he reached Santiago, Cervera had shown no lack of energy, but now he was strangely devoid of enterprise. He allowed an American armed liner to capture, off the port, a steamer that was bringing him 3,000 tons of much-needed coal, though he might have saved her by sending one of his cruisers outside the headlands. He allowed an inferior force to blockade the entrance for some days, without bringing out his cruisers by day to engage them, or sending out his destroyers by night to torpedo them. He waited until there was an overwhelming force assembled off the harbor.

Then came a month of deadlock. He was blockaded by a vastly superior force that watched the narrow pass through which, if he left the harbor, his fleet must come out one by one. But so long as he was within the headlands he was unassailable.

Admiral Sampson declined to risk his ships in an attempt to force the narrow entrance and destroy the Spanish squadron inside. An attempt to "bottle up" Cervera, by sinking a tramp steamer, the *Merrimac*, in the entrance, proved a failure. Long-ranging bombardments produced no effect on the Spaniards. All the plans formed at Washington for the Cuban campaign were disorganized. The blockade of the island had become the blockade of the one port of Santiago. If the United States Government had known how short of supplies were the city and garrison of Santiago and Cervera's fleet, it might have trusted to the blockade by sea and the operations of the insurgents by land, with the help of a few regulars, to force the Spanish admiral either to surrender or come out and fight. But it was decided to abandon for the present the projected attack on Havana, and send the army, collected for this purpose at Tampa, to attack Santiago by land, and so deprive Cervera of his refuge in the harbor.

Santiago was defended by lines of entrenchments with some improvised outworks, and garrisoned by a division under General Linares. The American transports from Tampa began to arrive on June 20, and the expeditionary force, under General Shafter, was disembarked during the following days some miles east of the city. There was then an advance over mere forest tracks through hilly country covered with dense bush. Cervera landed seamen gunners with machine guns and light quick-firers to strengthen the defense, and anchored one of his cruisers so that her heavy artillery could enfilade an attack on the entrenchments nearest the harbor.

On July 1, Shafter made his attack. The Spaniards defended themselves with such obstinate energy that after fighting through a long summer day only two outposts had been taken by the Americans, and at the cost of heavy loss. Next day there was desultory fighting along the front, but no progress. It was difficult to bring up supplies along the forest tracks, now sodden with tropical rains. Sickness had broken out in the American lines. The resistance of the Spaniards showed a dogged determination that was a surprise to the invaders.

Shafter himself was ill. Late on Saturday, July 2, he appealed to Admiral Sampson to help him by forcing the narrows at all costs, and in the early hours of Sunday, the third, he sent off to his Government a dispatch which was a confession of failure.

This discouraging report was cabled to Washington early on the Sunday morning, and caused deep dismay at the White House, but before evening news arrived of events that had changed the whole situation.

The evening before (July 2) Mr. Ramsden, the British consul at Santiago, had written in his diary:

> It seems incredible that the Americans with their large force have not yet taken the place. The defense of the Spaniards has been really heroic, the more so when you consider that they are half-starved and sick. It was affirmed today that the squadron would leave this evening, but they have not done so, though the pilots are on board. I will believe it when I see them get out, and I wish they would. If they do, they will fare badly outside.

On Saturday, July 2, Cervera had reembarked the seamen landed for the defense of the city, and had got up steam. He was going out because the presence of his crews now only added to the difficulty of feeding the half-starved garrison and population of the place. He had a short supply of inferior coal, and the most he hoped for was that some of his ships would elude, or fight their way past, the blockading squadron, and reach Havana. It is impossible to understand why, having decided to go out, he did not make the attempt in the darkness of Saturday night, instead of waiting for broad daylight next day.

In one respect he was fortunate. His coming out was a complete surprise for the Americans, and found them quite unprepared, with some of their best ships far from the scene of action. Admiral Sampson had steamed off to the eastward in his flagship, the *New York,* intending to land at Siboney for his interview with General Shafter. The battleship *Massachusetts* had gone with two of the lighter cruisers to coal at Guantanamo. But there were quite enough

ships left off the seaward opening of the narrows, where four battleships, an armored cruiser, and two light craft were keeping up the
blockade.

It was a bright summer day, with a light wind and a smooth
sea. Due south of the harbor entrance, and about 5½ miles from it,
lay the battleship *Iowa*. To the east of her lay the *Oregon*, with the
Indiana between her and the land, and about two miles nearer in,
west of the *Iowa*, was the battleship *Texas*, with the armored cruiser
Brooklyn, Commodore Schley's flagship, lying between her and the
land, and still nearer in the small armed revenue cruiser *Vixen*, lying
about three miles southwest of Morro Castle. On the other side of
the entrance, close in to the land, was a small armed steamer, the
Gloucester. She had been purchased by the Navy Department on
the outbreak of the war from Pierpont Morgan, the banker, and
renamed. Before this she had been known as the steam yacht *Gloucester*. She was commanded by one of the best officers of the United
States Navy, Captain Wainwright, who had been second in command of the *Maine* when she was blown up in Havana Harbor.
Wainwright was to show this day that even an armed steam yacht
may do good service in a modern naval action. All the ships except
the *Oregon* and the little *Gloucester* had let their fires burn low, and
had hardly any steam pressure on their boilers. At half-past nine the
order was given for the crews to fall in for general inspection. A
few minutes later an apprentice on board the *Iowa* called attention
to a mass of black smoke rising over the headlands of the harbor
mouth. And then between the cliffs of Morro and Socapa Points
appeared the bow of Cervera's flagship. An alarm gun rang out
from the *Iowa*, the signal, "Enemy escaping—clear for action," flut-
tered out from the halyards of the *Brooklyn* and on every ship the
bugles sounded, the men rushed to their battle stations, and the
stokers worked madly to get steam on the boilers.

Admiral Cervera, guided by a local pilot, Miguel Lopez, had
led his fleet down the harbor, the *Maria Teresa* being followed in
succession by the cruisers *Vizcaya*, *Cristobal Colon*, and *Oquendo*,
and the destroyers *Pluton* and *Furor*. As the flagship entered the
ravine of the narrows Cervera signalled to his captains, "I wish you
a speedy victory!" Miguel Lopez, who was with him in the conning
tower, remarked that the admiral gave his orders very deliberately,
and showed no sign of anxiety or excitement. He had asked Lopez
to tell him how soon he could turn to the westward. On a sign from
the pilot, he gave the order, "Starboard!" to the helmsman, put the
engine-room indicator to full speed, and told his captain to open

fire. As the guns roared out Cervera turned with a smile to Lopez and said, "You have done your part well, pilot; I hope you will come out of this safe and be well rewarded. You have deserved it."

The cruisers had run out with an interval of about 600 yards between the ships. There was a longer gap between the last of them and the destroyers, but the *Furor* was out within a quarter of an hour of the *Maria Teresa's* appearance between the headlands. That quarter of an hour had been a busy time for the Americans. The *Brooklyn* and the four battleships had at once headed for the opening of the harbor, the *Oregon* making the best speed till the steam pressure rose on the boilers of her consorts. They were no sooner moving than they opened fire with their forward guns, the Spanish cruisers and the batteries of Socapa and Morro replying with shots, every one of which fell short.

As Cervera turned westward the American ships also altered their course in the same direction. And now as the huge ships of the blockading squadron, each wrapped in a fog of smoke from her guns, converged upon the same course, there was a momentary danger of disastrous collision between them, a danger accentuated by an unexpected maneuver of Commodore Schley's ship, the *Brook-lyn*. The *Texas* and the *Iowa* just cleared each other in the smoke cloud. As they sheered off from each other, the *Oregon,* which had been following the *Iowa,* came rushing between the two ships, and the *Brooklyn* circled past their bows, suddenly crossing their course. Schley, in the first dash towards the Spaniards, had brought his great cruiser within 3,000 yards of the *Maria Teresa*, then, seeing the Spanish flagship turning, as if to ram, he swung around to starboard, bringing his broadside to bear on the enemy, but at the same time heading for his own battleships. He cleared them by completing a circle, coming back thus to the westward course, which had at the same time been resumed by the Spanish flagship. As the *Brooklyn* turned, the battleships swept up between her and the enemy, masking her fire, the *Oregon* leading, but the speed of Schley's ship soon enabled him to secure a forward place in the chase near the *Oregon*.

While the giants were thus maneuvering, the little *Gloucester* had come pluckily into action. Running in close under the Morro batteries, Commander Wainwright had fired some shots at the enemy's cruisers. Then realizing that his light guns could do them no vital harm, he almost stopped the way on his ship, and waited to engage the destroyers. Out came the *Furor* and *Pluton,* turning eastward as they cleared the entrance, and dashing for the *Gloucester* with a mass of foam piling up over their bows. The *Indiana,* the rearmost of the battleships, fired some long-range shots at them, but it was a stream of small shells from the *Gloucester*'s quick-firers that stopped their rush. The *Furor* was soon drifting towards the cliffs, enveloped in clouds of escaping steam. The *Gloucester*'s fire had killed her helmsman, wrecked her steering gear, and cut up several of her steam pipes, making her engine room uninhabitable. The *Pluton,* not so badly crippled, but with her hull penetrated in several places, was next turned back. The *New York,* hurrying up from the eastward at the sound of the firing, escorted by the torpedo boat *Ericsson,* fired on her at long range. The *Pluton* kept her engines going just long enough to drive her ashore under the Socapa cliffs. The *Furor* sank before she could reach the land.

There was now a running fight, the four Spanish cruisers steaming westward close to the wooded shore, the American ships following them up and pouring in a deadly fire from every gun that could be brought to bear. It was soon evident that the Spaniards could not get up anything like their trial speed, and their gunnery was so defective that there was small chance of their stopping any of their pursuers by well-aimed fire, or even of inflicting any appreciable loss or damage on them. The *Maria Teresa* was the first to succumb. As she led the line out of the harbor she had received the converging fire of the American ships, but she had not suffered any serious injury. Until the American ships got up full steam the Spaniards had gained a little on them. An Englishman, Mr. Mason, who watched the cruisers from a hill near Morro till at ten o'clock the curve of the coast westward hid them from view, thought they were successfully escaping. So far as he could see they had not been badly hit, and none of the Americans were yet abreast of them. But soon after the ships disappeared from the point of view near Morro, and when the *Maria Teresa* was only some six miles from the entrance, she suffered a series of injuries in rapid succession that put her out of action.

It was the secondary armament of the American ships, the guns of medium caliber, that proved most effective in the running fight. It appears that the big 13- and 12-inch barbette and turret guns only made two hits in the whole day. Two 12-inch shells fired simultaneously from a pair of guns struck the *Maria Teresa* just above the water-line on the port side, aft and below her stern turret. They burst in the torpedo room, killing and wounding every one there, blowing a jagged hole in the starboard side, and setting the ship on fire. An 8-inch shell came into the after battery and exploded between decks, causing many casualties. A 5-inch shell burst in the coal bunkers amid-ships, blew up the deck, and started a second fire. Another destructive hit was made by an 8-inch shell a few feet forward of the point where the pair of 12-inch shells had come in. The official report thus describes its course:

> An 8-inch shell struck the gun deck just under the after barbette, passed through the side of the ship, and exploded, ranging aft. The damage done by this shell was very great. All the men in the locality must have been killed or badly wounded. The beams were torn and ripped. The fragments of the shell passed across the deck and cut through the starboard side. This shell also cut the fire main.

Shells from the lighter artillery of the American ships riddled the funnels, and cut up the deck houses. One of these shells, bursting near the forward bridge, wounded Admiral Cervera slightly in the arm. He had come outside the conning tower the better to watch the progress of his squadron. The armor belt had kept the water line of the ship intact, and her barbettes and heavy guns were also protected efficiently by the local armor, but the enemy's shell fire had told on the unarmored structure, inflicted heavy loss, and started two serious fires. All efforts to get these put out failed. The blazing tropical heat had scorched the woodwork of the ship into tinder, the movement of the vessel produced a draft that made the burning bunkers and decks roaring masses of flame. The men were driven by the heat from battery and engine room. The *Maria Teresa,* with silent guns and masses of black smoke ascending to the sky, was headed for the land. At a quarter past ten she drove ashore at Nimanima, 6½ miles west of Morro Castle. Some of the men swam ashore, others were taken off by the boats of the *Gloucester,* which came up just in time to help in saving life. Commander Wainwright had to land a party to drive off a mob of Cuban guerillas, who came down to the shore, and were murdering the hapless Spaniards as they swam to the land. One of the *Gloucester*'s boats took out of the water Admiral Cervera and his son, Lieutenant Cervera. They were brought on board the yacht, where Wainwright chivalrously greeted the unfortunate admiral with the words: "I congratulate you, sir, on having made as gallant a fight as was ever witnessed on the sea."

At half-past ten another of the Spanish cruisers was a helpless wreck only half a mile westward of the stranded and burning flagship. This was the *Almirante Oquendo,* whose station had been last in the line. This drew upon her a converging fire from the guns of the pursuing battleships and cruisers. The destruction was terrible. Two guns of the secondary battery were disabled. A shell came through the roof of the forward turret, killed and wounded all the gun crew, and put the gun permanently out of action. Ventilators and deck fittings were swept away, the funnels cut up, and the unarmored part of the sides repeatedly pierced by shells that started several fires amidships. It was these that made further effort to keep up the fight hopeless. After her captain, Juan Lazaga, had been killed by a bursting shell, the *Oquendo,* now on fire in a dozen places, was driven ashore to save life. She blew up on the beach, the explosion of her magazines nearly cutting the wreck in two.

Of the Spanish squadron only the *Cristobal Colon* and the *Vizcaya* still survived. The *Colon,* best and newest of the cruisers, was making good speed, and was furthest ahead. The *Vizcaya* lagged behind her, hard pressed by several American ships, led by the *Iowa.* The *Vizcaya* had suffered severely from the fire of the pursuit. Her coal bunkers were ablaze on one side, and there was another fire making steady progress in the gun deck. Schley, in the *Brooklyn,* urging his engines to the utmost, rushed past the *Iowa,* and attempted to head off the *Vizcaya.* Her gallant captain, Antonio Eulate, realized that the *Brooklyn* was the swiftest ship in the pursuit, and that her destruction would materially increase the chance of the *Colon* escaping. So he made a last effort to ram or torpedo the *Brooklyn* before his own ship succumbed. He headed for Schley with a torpedo ready in his bow over-water tube. A shell from the *Brooklyn's* battery struck it fair, exploded the torpedo in the tube, and blew up and set fire to the fore-part of the *Vizcaya.* Eulate then headed his ship for the land, and she struck the shore under the cliffs at Asseradores, fifteen miles west of Morro, at a quarter past eleven. The *Brooklyn,* the *Iowa,* and the *Oregon* were pouring their fire into her as she ran aground. Another explosion blew up part of her burning decks, and Eulate hauled down his flag. The Americans cheered as they saw the flag come down amid the clouds of smoke, but Captain Robley Evans, of the *Iowa,* called out from the bridge to stop the cheers of his men. "Don't cheer, boys. Those poor devils are dying," he said. Evans, with the *Iowa,* stood by the burning ship to rescue the survivors.

The *Colon* alone remained. She had a lead of a good six miles, and many thought she would escape. The *Brooklyn* led the pursuit, followed closely by the battleships *Oregon* and *Texas,* and the small cruiser *Vixen,* with Sampson's flagship, the *New York,* far astern, too far off to have any real share in the action. On her trials the

Colon had done 23 knots. If she could have done anything like this in the rush out of Santiago, she would have simply walked away from the Americans, but she never did more than 14. For some time, even at this reduced speed, she was so far ahead that there was no firing. It was not until ten minutes past one that the *Brooklyn* and *Oregon* at last got within range and opened fire with their forward heavy guns. The *Colon,* with her empty barbettes, had nothing with which to reply at the long range. In the earlier stage of the fight she had been hit only by an 8-inch shell, which did no material damage. As the pursuers gained on her she opened with her secondary battery. Even now she received no serious injury, and she was never set on fire. But her captain, Moreu, realized that lack of speed had put him at the mercy of the enemy. As they closed in upon him and opened fire with their heaviest guns, he turned his ship into the creek surrounded by towering heights amid which the little Tarquino River runs into the sea, forty-eight miles west of Morro Castle. He hauled down his flag as he entered the creek. Without his orders the engineers opened the Kingston valves in the engine-room, and when the Americans boarded the *Colon* she was rapidly sinking. She went down by the stern under the cliffs on the east side of the inlet, and lay with her bow above water and her after decks awash. It was twenty minutes past one when she surrendered.

The men of the *Iowa* and *Gloucester* had meanwhile rescued many of the survivors of the *Vizcaya,* not without serious risk to themselves, for there were numerous explosions, and the decks were red-hot in places. Some of the Spaniards swam ashore, made their way through the bush to Santiago, and joined the garrison. Captain Eulate was brought on board the *Iowa,* and received by a guard of marines, who presented arms as he stepped from the gangway. He offered his sword to Robley Evans, but the American captain refused to take it. "You have surrendered," he said, "to four ships, each heavier than your own. You did not surrender to the *Iowa* only, so her captain cannot take your sword."

Never in any naval action was there such complete destruction of a fleet. Of the six ships that steamed out of Santiago that summer morning, the *Furor* was sunk in deep water off the entrance; the *Pluton* was ashore under the Socapa cliff. At various points along the coast columns of black smoke rising a thousand feet into the sunlit sky showed where the burning wrecks of the *Maria Teresa,* the *Oquendo,* and the *Vizcaya* lay, and nearly fifty miles away the *Colon* was sunk at the mouth of the Tarquino River.

And never was success obtained with such a trifling loss of the victors. The Spanish gunnery had been wretchedly bad. The only ships hit were the *Brooklyn* and the *Iowa*, and neither received any serious damage. The only losses by the enemy's fire were on board the *Brooklyn*, where a signalman was killed and two seamen wounded. Nine men were more or less seriously injured by the concussion of their own guns.

It must be confessed that the gunnery of the Americans was not of a high order. Some 6,500 shells were expended during the action. The Spanish wrecks were carefully examined, and all hits counted. Fires and explosions perhaps obliterated the traces of some of them, but so far as could be ascertained, the hits on the hulls and the upper works were comparatively few. And of hits by the heavy 13-inch and 12-inch guns, only two could be traced anywhere.

The Spanish squadron had 2,300 officers and men on board when it left Santiago. Of these 1,600 were prisoners after the action. It was estimated that in the fight 350 were killed and 150 wounded. This leaves some 200 to be accounted for. Nearly 150 rejoined the garrison of Santiago after swimming ashore. This leaves only 50 missing. They were probably drowned or killed by the Cuban guerillas. The fact that three of the Spanish cruisers had been rendered helpless by fires lighted on board by the enemy's shells accentuated the lesson already learned from the battle of the Yalu as to the necessity of eliminating inflammable material in the construction and fittings of warships. The damage done to the *Vizcaya* by the explosion of one of her own torpedoes in her bow-tube proved the reality of a danger to which naval critics had already called attention. Henceforth the torpedo tubes of cruisers and battleships were all made to open below the water line.

The result of the victory was a complete change in the situation at Santiago. The destruction of Cervera's fleet was the "beginning of the end" for the Spanish power in Cuba.

PART TWO

THE
RUSSO-
JAPANESE
WAR

The Japanese torpedo boat *Sazanami* during
the Russo-Japanese War.
(*Yarrow Public Limited Company*)

Port Arthur:
The First Pearl
Harbor

William H. Honan

During the latter part of the nineteenth century, the leading industrial nations of the world invested lavish amounts of time, treasure, and talent in the construction of great fleets of ocean-going warships. To help defray the cost of these armadas, they sold warships to the less-industrialized nations.

Germany did a brisk business selling men-of-war, and its new Krupp guns to China; the United States and France sold to Czarist Russia; and Great Britain dominated the Japanese market, especially in the sale of torpedoes and torpedo boats—"speciality items" in which many nations held little interest.

The Japanese put these Whitehead torpedoes and Yarrow and Thornycroft boats to effective use in the Sino–Japanese War of 1894, and then astounded (and terrified) the world with their unorthodox use of these new weapons one evening in the winter of 1904.

Night had fallen. The sea off Port Arthur lay flat and gleaming like an enormous field of coal. The only disturbance for miles around was a foaming path, slowly being plowed across this black waste by a column of eleven torpedo boats bearing the insignia of Imperial Japan.

The boats were small steamers roughly the displacement of present-day Coast Guard cutters, but much longer and narrower—about 215 feet in length and a sleek 20 feet in beam. Each was fitted with four tall funnels that pumped up volumes of soot and steam. Captain Shojiro Asai, the officer in command of the squadron, stared intently ahead, searching the chill night for an unseen enemy. His fellow officers did likewise, gripped with the knowledge that they were embarked on a historic mission.

But others in the crew gazed dreamily overhead. It was the kind of deeply peaceful night that tempts sailors at sea to think of their loved ones far away.

The date was February 8, 1904. Czarist Russia and Imperial Japan, long in contention for mastery of East Asia, were finally on the brink of war. Ambassadors had been recalled from Moscow and Tokyo. The world waited with a thrill of horror for the news that a state of war existed—but, as yet there was no declaration.

Russian naval might in this quarter of the globe was represented by its powerful Asiatic Squadron based at Port Arthur, a sheltered bay on the north China coast. This squadron, if combined with its sister fleet stationed in the Baltic, would constitute a much larger and more powerful naval force than all the warships Japan could muster. Consequently, when negotiations broke down between the two countries, Vice Admiral Heihachiro Togo, the feisty British-trained Japanese naval commander, sought the permission of Imperial General Headquarters in Tokyo to offset his disadvantage by attacking the Russian armada even before a declaration of war had been issued. Permission was granted.

Thus, by the night of February 8, a Japanese surprise-attack fleet consisting of six of the world's heaviest and most modern battleships, 6 first-class cruisers, 4 second-class cruisers, and 18 torpedo boats lay off Round Island, 60 miles east of Port Arthur. At precisely 1815, Togo signaled the torpedo boats to leave the main fleet and attack the Russian warships in their anchorages. "Blow up the enemy squadron," his message concluded. "I wish you success!" A wild cheer went up throughout the flotilla. There were hoarse cries of "Banzai!" Swords cleaved the air, and champagne and sake were quaffed with great gusto.

The torpedo boat flotilla formed into two squadrons. The first Squadron, made up of the First, Second, and Third divisions—11 boats in all, under Captain Asai's command—was to proceed to Port Arthur and attack any Russian warships it found there. The Second Squadron, consisting of the eight boats of the Fourth and Fifth divisions, would shape a course for nearby Talien Bay where they, too, hoped to "blow up the enemy."

It was a daring plan. Although a prototype of the modern torpedo had been in naval arsenals since the 1870s and fast steamers for delivering these missiles had been developing rapidly, the weapons were disparaged as erratic and unseaworthy in most naval circles at the turn of the century. The first attempts to use the so-called automobile torpedo to sink an armored warship could hardly inspire confidence. At the start of the war between Chile and Peru in 1879, for example, the Peruvian man-of-war *Huascar* fired a torpedo at a Chilean ironclad. Halfway to its target, the torpedo abruptly turned around and bore down on the *Huascar*. An intrepid officer in the *Huascar* averted disaster by leaping overboard, swimming to the torpedo, and wrestling with it like an alligator until it lay still in the water.

But if most navies had little use for the torpedo boat, that was not the case in Japan. In 1894, following the great Japanese naval victory over China at the battle of the Yalu River, the survivors of the Chinese fleet, including the flagship *Ting Yuen*, took shelter in the well-defended harbor of Wei-hai-wei. The Japanese battle fleet, commanded by the brilliant and daring Admiral Ito, then blockaded the harbor, standing just outside the range of Chinese shore batteries. During the next several nights, Admiral Ito hurled wave after wave of torpedo boats into the harbor until he had sunk or driven ashore four Chinese combatants, including the mighty *Ting Yuen*, thus obliging Admiral Ting, the Chinese commander, to surrender.

In the following decade, the Japanese Navy devoted itself diligently to perfecting the torpedo boat as an offensive weapon. Naval maneuvers invariably stressed torpedo-boat exercises. Japan purchased a large flotilla of these craft from the leading French, British, and German manufacturers and, after extensive testing and analysis, bought the best—those built at the British yards Thornycroft and Yarrow—in quantity. By 1901 Japan launched from its yard at Yokosuka five copies of the Yarrow boat. These were succeeded by 25 boats of an improved design that were given a name that would echo through Japanese naval history: "kamikaze" boats.

The Japanese also purchased, tested, and studied all available torpedoes, from the British Whitehead to the German Schwartzkopff. Imperial Navy observers were sent as far afield as Boston, Massachusetts, to witness the trials of the Sims–Edison torpedo—an ungainly, cable-guided 31-foot-long copper canoe that carried an explosive device suspended beneath its hull. Apart from other difficulties, the Sims–Edison device had to be launched by a crane whose weight would capsize any existing torpedo boat. Another contender that was considered and rejected by the Japanese, but adopted for a time by the U.S. Navy, was the Howell torpedo. It was driven through the water by a rapidly rotating 100-pound flywheel that spun the torpedo's propeller shaft. Before being launched, the flywheel had to be cranked up to speed of 150 revolutions per second by a hulking and thunderous auxiliary steam engine—hardly ideal for making a stealthy approach to the enemy.

Japanese agents saw the impracticality of many such inventions and chose instead the silent and efficient British Whitehead torpedo, which was propelled by a compressed-air-powered engine.

Seen from a distance, the torpedo boats that Captain Asai led to Port Arthur in February 1904 had a fierce, leonine look to them—puffed up in front and tapering to a long, slim stern. The first quarter of the topside was sheathed with a rounded, umbrella-like covering called the turtle back. This protection was needed, since when making good speed in rough weather the bow would frequently pierce an onrushing wave. The forward part of the boat would then be underwater and would have to struggle from under the crest of the wave, shrugging off several tons of water, just before the boat came down with a violent, shuddering whack in the trough before the next wave.

Mounted on pivots, which from a distance looked like heavy-caliber guns, the torpedo tubes were placed on the low-slung after deck. In earlier models, fixed forward torpedo tubes were mounted on top of the turtle back, or enclosed within it, but by 1904 most navies were abandoning the forward placement of tubes.

Many accidents had occurred in which these fast boats, which could make an amazing thirty-one knots, had caught up with and overrun torpedoes they had just fired. Consequently, the pivoting tubes were placed amidships and at the stern so that the newer boats fired only a broadside or an over-the-stern shot. Characteristically, the torpedo boat would have to charge its target, then wheel around sharply and, like a scorpion, strike with its tail.

The risk of attacking an armed ship in such a bantam steamer was fearful to contemplate. As effective as the 18-inch Whitehead torpedo was, it had the shortest range of any ship-to-ship weapon in the naval arsenal. At best, the torpedo could travel 1,500 yards, but it could be fired accurately at not much more than 500 yards. Therefore, to press home her attack, the torpedo boat had to expose herself to the possibility of being hit with virtually any weapon her adversary might choose to exercise. According to a British Admiralty study in 1897, a torpedo boat under fire by a battleship had a life expectancy of two minutes. An authority on the subject expressed the danger this way: "The average torpedoman," he wrote matter-of-factly, "expects to get killed when he attacks."

The torpedoman of course, did have a few things in his favor. His boat was swift and small and, bobbing between waves, she could be difficult to hit. Furthermore, a squadron of torpedo boats attacking simultaneously might rattle and confuse an adversary. Better yet, the torpedo boat might use the cover of darkness to advantage. The torpedoman could steal up on his enemy while asleep, and, in effect, slit his throat.

Soon after departing from Admiral Togo's main fleet, the two squadrons cut through the sea like long knives in single line-ahead formation. The names on the boats had been blacked out, and each showed only a single, screened stern light. The crews had been instructed to speak only when absolutely necessary, and then only in whispers, and to avoid dropping metal objects or otherwise producing noise. The boats' furnaces were carefully stoked with picked coal so as not to show a telltale flame at the tops of their funnels or to emit sparks.

Shortly, the Second Squadron broke off for Talien Bay, 20 miles north of Port Arthur. To the disappointment of the crews of these eight boats, they found no Russian ships present when they reached their destination just after midnight. Between their intense frustration and night blindness, they came within a hair's breadth of blowing to kingdom come a British merchantman, the *Foo Chow*.

At approximately 2230, as a light snow was beginning to fall, Captain Asai in the lead boat of the First Squadron, *Shirakumo*, spotted lights 1,000 yards off his port bow. The lights came closer until he was able to recognize them as the searchlights of two Russian torpedo boats on patrol. The Japanese quickly put out their stern lights and, not knowing what to expect, trained their quick-firing guns on the Russians as they closed. Amazingly, the Russian boats passed straight through the Japanese column 200 yards astern of the *Akatsuki*, the fourth boat in line, without firing a shot. The Russians then turned and headed back to Port Arthur. Their increase in speed, however, warned Captain Asai that they must have caught sight of at least one or two of his boats and were now racing home to report this strange encounter.

The Japanese column was thrown into disarray. To avoid being seen, all boats behind the *Akatsuki* scattered. Some throttled down their engines. Others veered out of line in different directions. Two boats—the *Oboro* and the *Ikazuchi*—actually collided, although damage to both was minor. In time, all but one of these seven boats re-formed into a column and proceeded to Port Arthur, but they never regained contact with Captain Asai and the four boats of the First Division.

Meanwhile, Captain Asai increased speed and made for Port Arthur almost directly behind the Russian patrol. At exactly 0012, he saw through the snowy haze the lights at the entrance to the harbor. He leaned forward and said softly into a speaking tube: "Ready the torpedoes."

Armorers slid firing cartridges into sleeves in the breechblocks of the torpedo tubes, loosened propeller clamps, removed safety pins, and connected electrical circuits to firing mechanisms.

As they were preparing to fire, Captain Asai pondered his situation. On the one hand, the Russian torpedo boats might sound the alarm and spoil his chance of making a surprise attack. But on the other hand, it might be a stroke of good fortune to be guided to his targets by escorts so familiar with the harbor. According to the charts prepared by Japanese intelligence agents and given to each torpedo boat captain, about 14 warships of the Imperial Russian Asiatic Squadron lay at anchor in the outer roadstead, or mouth of the harbor of Port Arthur. The Russians had not even taken the precaution of moving these naval prizes into the more protected inner harbor. Even so, the anchorage was close to shore and, amid the confusion of a life-or-death struggle in the middle of the night, these unfamiliar waters could prove treacherous.

As Captain Asai weighed his prospects, he suddenly caught sight of the outline of a large vessel dead ahead that seemed to be flashing powerful electric searchlights back and forth. In another minute, he could make out two more ships signaling to each other with colored masthead lamps. And then, all at once, he felt as though he had entered a vast city on the sea, with fantastic, shadowy shapes and glistening lights all around. On the horizon in every direction were huge black blotches, surmounted with a row of twinkling lights, and higher still, a row of funnels as tall as factory chimneys. Some enemy ships were fully lighted. Others were dark.

The two returning Russian torpedo boats had dashed into the channel leading to the inner harbor and, although they were still signaling frantically with their searchlights, there seemed to be no response on the great ships at anchor in the outer harbor.

Captain Asai selected as his target the biggest dark blotch he could make out through the falling snow. At a distance of 1,000 yards from this vessel, he reduced speed to dead slow so that the seemingly dozing enemy might not be alerted by a sparkling bow wave or the dull red flames that were apt to spout from a speeding boat's funnels. No one spoke. The engines were almost soundless. There was only the soft creak of the steering wheel and the swish of water hissing around the long, sleek hull. Apparently, the Japanese had not lost the advantage of surprise.

Indeed, the Russian ships were woefully unprepared. Two-thirds of the Russian officers had been given leave on this particular night. Many were guests of the Russian fleet commander, the elderly Vice Admiral Oscar Victorovich Stark, who was throwing a party on shore in honor of his wife's birthday.

As the *Shirakumo* crept ahead, Captain Asai started to adjust and tighten clamps on a brass instrument that looked like a large protractor fastened to a shelf in the conning tower. This was the torpedo director. On one graduated bar, he tightened a clamp at 29 knots—the speed of the torpedoes he was planning to launch. Another clamp was tightened at four knots—his own present speed. There would have been other adjustments to make if the target had been moving, but since she was anchored, Captain Asai now sighted across two notches on the instrument and, whispering into the speaking tube, instructed the coxswain to turn slightly to port.

Before him lay the 6,630-ton cruiser *Pallada*—an enormous warship for her time. Launched in 1899, the *Pallada's* armament consisted of 6 six-inch quick-firing guns and 20 three-inch repeaters that could lay down a hail of fire that might chew to bits the *Shirakumo* and all her cousins in a matter of seconds.

At 600 yards from the *Pallada*, Captain Asai signaled the coxswain, this time by telegraph, to turn to port, away from the target. As the *Shirakumo* swung parallel to the *Pallada*, Captain Asai depressed another telegraph key before him that closed an electric circuit. A platinum wire inside a cartridge in the breech of a torpedo tube flashed and set off a four-ounce charge of cordite. The resulting explosion did not go off with a sharp crack like a gun; instead, much of its force was absorbed by the cushion of air surrounding the tapered tail end of the torpedo. As this compressed air expanded, it briskly heaved the torpedo out of its tube with a clatter and a deep-throated *poof!* The missile flew a few yards through the air and dove into the water like a fish returning to its element. Captain Asai pressed another telegraph key and fired a second torpedo.

Next, he ordered hard-right rudder and full steam. The doors of the furnaces in the stokehold were flung open, crewmen shovelled in coal frantically, and electric blowers whirred to life, forcing a draft of air into the furnaces. A shower of sparks and thick black smoke burst from all four funnels, and within seconds flames shot into the air and turned the funnels so hot the fresh black paint on them rose up in blisters. The throb of the engines quickened, causing everything on board to dance. Now the sea started to rush by and boil in the wake.

Suddenly, there was a terrific explosion in the distance. Looking back at the *Pallada*, Captain Asai saw a tall pillar of water rise in front of the great cruiser. The Russian warship had been struck amidships. The torpedo had knocked a hole in her side large enough for three Cossack cavalrymen to gallop through, riding abreast and with sabers flying. The blast ignited a coal bunker and smashed an engine room, twisting boiler tubes into grotesque shapes. Almost at once, the huge ship began to list to port.

The *Asahiwo* and the *Kasumi*, second and third in line of the Japanese torpedo boats, had also selected targets and were making their stealthy approaches. Like the *Shirakumo*, they had cut their speed to four knots. Before launching their missiles, they crept even closer to the Russian warships than had Captain Asai's boat—close enough so that the Japanese sailors could dimly make out figures on the enemy warships. Then the torpedo boats wheeled away, fired, and disappeared into the darkness.

The most gallant performance of the action was that of the *Akatsuki*, the fourth Japanese torpedo boat, commanded by Lieutenant Suyetsuga. He got as close as 400 yards to the first-class cruiser *Askold*, but held fire, hoping to find a battleship. As the *Akatsuki* slinked forward, he soon spied the gigantic *Retvizan*, a first-class battleship nearly 400 feet long with three gigantic funnels placed directly amidships. Soon Lieutenant Suyetsuga could see the *Retvizan*'s fore and aft free-standing, round turrets, each bearing a monstrous brace of 12-inch guns. Launched only two years before by the William Cramp and Son Ship and Engine Building Company of Philadelphia, this warship embodied the latest thinking on resistance to attack by mine and torpedo.

Whether or not such sophisticated engineering could protect

the ship from underwater attack was about to be tested as the *Akatsuki*, one of the older Japanese boats still fitted with a forward tube, bore down on her prey. At 0032 precisely, Lieutenant Suyetsuga fired his right-ahead tube. "A great explosion followed," he later reported, "a huge column of water being thrown up alongside the battleship, and all ships threw their searchlights everywhere." Several Russian ships now opened fire and half a dozen heavy projectiles shrieked over the mast of the *Akatsuki*. Fearlessly, Lieutenant Suyetsuga held his course and speed of four knots until, at precisely 0034, he fired his bow tube at a ship he thought must be the stricken *Pallada*.

His second discharge, Lieutenant Suyetsuga reported, was followed by "a high column of flames rising at the vessel's side, which seemed quite solid and to tremble before it vanished." At last, the *Akatsuki* turned south and steamed rapidly away.

Pandemonium broke throughout the roadstead. Everywhere, ships' guns fired wildly. Thick, acrid smoke—from torpedo explosions, gunfire, and the funnels of the torpedo boats as well as the Russian warships, which were frantically building up heads of steam—was billowing and curling everywhere, wreathed in the glare of searchlights. Vessels that had been hit were struggling to make for the beach or shallow water before sinking. Searchlights swept back and forth, now catching the dull black hull of a racing torpedo boat, now losing it. Then, suddenly, all searchlights were turned upward, seeming to some witnesses to form an immense St. Andrew's cross of light, as if imploring heaven to chase away this dreadful nightmare. It was, in reality, a signal of distress, but of course much too late to be of any use.

Approximately eight minutes after the *Shirakumo* had loosed her first torpedo, the seven boats of the re-formed Second and Third Divisions came pounding at full speed in a single line-ahead formation down the length of the outer roadstead a little to the east of where the First Division had made its attack. Then, all together, this second wave turned sharply to port so as to form a single line abreast charging the whole length of the enemy anchorage. As soon as within firing range of the Russian ships, each boat turned, discharged two torpedoes, and dashed out to sea.

In such a melée, it was impossible to tell which boats had scored a hit and which had not. It was certain, however, that if they had not been struck before, two Russian battleships, the *Retvizan* and the *Czarevich* (an even heavier and more modern first-class battleship of French construction) were now rocked by torpedo explosions. A hole measuring 220 square feet was torn through the port side of the *Retvizan*. The *Czarevich* was struck aft on her port side and suffered a wound nearly as large. In both cases, the blast of 200 pounds of wet gun cotton in the Japanese torpedoes was great enough to shatter the side plus the armored lateral bulkhead (the second bottom) behind it. In addition, watertight doors were blown off their hinges and portions of the highly touted cellular construction were crushed, as if by giant's fingers. Seawater poured in, drowning trapped seamen and, in the case of the *Czarevich*, flooding the steering compartment. The shock of the explosions was so great that the *Retvizan*'s engines were thrown out of line and her boilers began to leak. The *Czarevich* lost her rudder.

Although sinking, both battleships and the cruiser *Pallada* managed to get up a head of steam, cast off their moorings, and make for the channel into the harbor. The *Pallada* grounded close to a lighthouse on the west side of the harbor entrance. The *Retvizan* and the *Czarevich* sank in the gullet of the channel, leaving only a narrow passage around them.

Despite the tremendous volume of fire from the Russian ships, no Japanese torpedo boat had been hit or sustained a casualty. And thus, as Captain Asai led his squadron to meet Admiral Togo's main fleet, the results were clear. Although war had not yet been officially declared, three colossal Russian fighting ships lay stuck in the harbor mud while triumphant and unscathed Japanese raiders rumbled home to receive the personal congratulations of the Emperor of Japan.

"Treacherous!" was the word the Czar's spokesman used to denounce the Japanese surprise attack. One might expect, in the light of worldwide outrage aroused by a similar attack by a Japanese naval force a generation later, that in 1904 most neutral powers would have joined Russia in castigating Japan for having struck without warning. But only France, a close ally of the Czar's, regarded the Japanese action as an offense against international law.

Most other powers, including the United States and Great Britain, saw nothing infamous about the way in which Japan had commenced hostilities. *The New York Times* spoke for many in the West when it observed, "The Russophile publicists of Paris who have been so absurd as to base a claim of 'treachery' upon Japan's promptitude . . . find no countenance either in the writings of the authorities or in the practice of nations." A few days later, this newspaper applauded the heroism of the crews of the Japanese torpedo boats: "The [Japanese] exploit commands wonder and admiration. These are the sort of men Nelson would have loved to lead on a cutting-out expedition."

At Harvard, Japanese flags were displayed in student dormitories with honor and esteem, and the handful of Japanese students on campus were lionized and invited to make speeches about the nobility of Japanese manhood. At Yale, Professor Theodore S. Woolsey, an authority on international law, stated: "There was nothing treacherous or improper in the Japanese attack upon the Russian ships. . . . Not only is a declaration of war not essential to a lawful war, but even when made it does not necessarily set the date of its commencement."

These sentiments were echoed in Britain and on the Continent. Two Oxford law professors, for example, published a thick volume that solemnly intoned: "A declaration of war is convenient, but by no means necessary. Japan broke no law in striking before a declaration was made." In Germany, an article in the *Neue Freie Presse* twitted Russia over the fact that in 1877 it had invaded Turkey without having declared war.

One of the most interesting contemporary commentators on the Port Arthur attack was Major General Sir Frederick Maurice of the British Army. "Those who have attacked the action of Japan," he stated in an article in *Nineteenth Century*, a British periodical, "are either ignorant of history or reckless about the extent to which they besmirch their own countries by the mud they fling at Japan."

Sir Frederick knew whereof he wrote. In 1882, as a young brevet-lieutenant colonel in the Intelligence Department of the British War Office, he had become remarkably well informed on the subject of undeclared wars as a result of having been given an unusual assignment. The chief of the Intelligence Department had asked him to study the record of history—going back to 1700—to learn how prevalent surprise attacks had been. In a debate in Parliament about the possible danger of constructing a tunnel under the English Channel, a prominent member had wondered whether or not there was any historical basis to fear that "war would be declared against us, as we might say, out of a clear sky, without any previous strain," and Maurice's chief wanted to set him straight on the facts.

Maurice recalled in 1904,

"I started under the general impression that normally every power, before taking any overt action of hostility against another, conformed to something like the old duelling laws: [it] presented its challenge in due form, received its counter challenge, and then both, stepping into their places, after a few passes came duly to business."

But Maurice was in for a shock.

"I could during the two centuries trace no case which justified the assumption that modern nations considered themselves under any obligation to send a foreign court a warning of coming war, delivered as a declaration of war at the foreign court, in any instance in which a surprise advantage was to be gained. Even the U.S. Constitution, which treats the declaration of war with greater solemnity than any other national charter, requires a vote by Congress only to declare that a state of war actually exists. . . . It formally announces the fact of preceding acts of war."

Maurice's report, entitled "Hostilities without Declaration of War," came to 79 pages of extremely fine print when published in 1882 by Her Majesty's Stationery Office. It is as remarkable a document today as then. Although his research may not have included all the niceties of modern scholarship, his general conclusions may not be doubted. Maurice analyzed 107 wars between 1700 and 1870. He found that since a maritime state has greater facilities for a sudden strike than a land power, maritime states carried out these strikes most often. In other words, attacking without a declaration of war appeared to be a function of opportunity rather than moral scruple. France and Britain, he determined, had delivered more surprise attacks during the years studied than any other nation. France had struck 36 of these blows, Britain 30, Austria 12. Russian 7 (not including its habitual practice toward Turkey, China, and other bordering states), Prussia 7, and the United States at least 5.

In most of these cases, the openly avowed or obvious motive in making a surprise attack was simply to gain an advantage over an unprepared enemy. In 12 cases, the failure to make a declaration apparently proceeded from a desire to pin the responsibility for the war on an opponent by making it the first to declare war, or from mere indifference to a formal declaration. Among "the most scathing pages that could be imagined for all lovers of parchment security," according to Maurice, were the U.S. invasion of Mexico in 1846 and Admiral Horatio Nelson's unannounced attack on Copenhagen and destruction of the Danish fleet in 1801.

More than just the moral and historical implications of the attack on Port Arthur stirred interest throughout the world. There were lessons in the art of war to be considered as well. Indeed, it became commonplace to find soldiers, sailors, and statesmen ardently discussing ways in which they, like the Japanese, might employ the latest military and naval technology to get the jump on their opponents.

The riskiness of this sort of talk became evident in 1905 when a British statesman blurted out a remark that brought Great Britain and Germany perilously close to war. During the previous year, the British fleet had engaged in what were seen on the Continent as provocative maneuvers, and there had been jingoist statements in the British press as well—all of which had aroused fear and antagonism in Germany. Then, on February 8, 1905, Arthur Lee, the First Lord of the Admiralty, was heard to say that in the event of war with Germany the Royal Navy "would get its blows in first, before the other side had time even to read in the papers that war had been declared." Quite obviously, Lee had Port Arthur in mind, and it was particularly unfortunate that his ill-considered remark was uttered almost exactly on the first anniversary of the Japanese surprise attack. When Kaiser Wilhelm got wind of what Lee had said, he mobilized the German fleet and recalled his ambassador from London. Tense days followed. In a few months the crisis simmered down, and yet this incident—the so-called Anglo-German war scare of 1905—is remembered today as one of the first fateful steps leading to World War I.

Despite these and similar ripples, the spectacular Japanese offensive at Port Arthur began to fade from world consciousness before what might have been wisely learned from it was generally grasped. There are at least two reasons for this sudden, widespread amnesia. First, as brilliant a stroke as was the initial Japanese attack, the torpedo service was never able to repeat its success despite many attempts and much sacrifice. Subsequent Japanese torpedo boat attacks against the Russian fleet produced indifferent results, and then, at the great battle of May 1905 at Tsushima, where Admiral Togo's main fleet annihilated the Russian Baltic Squadron, torpedo boats did no more than administer the coup de grâce to disabled Russian warships. Consequently, by the war's end a widely held view was that the Port Arthur attack had been little more than a lucky stunt.

Second, even at the start of the war, the torpedo boat did not prove itself a decisive weapon. Only three out of the fourteen Russian warships at Port Arthur on February 8, 1904, were sunk. Within a week, the *Czarevich* and the *Pallada* were refloated and towed into the inner harbor for repair, and eventually returned to service. As the struggle wore on, it became increasingly clear that, except in unusual circumstances, the only reliable way to destroy a first-class battleship was with another first-class battleship. Togo drove home that point at Tsushima. And thus, the lessons of Port Arthur became lost amid the thunder of the big guns from the biggest ships at Tsushima and at those cataclysmic soon-to-follow naval engagements of World War I.

CHAPTER 4

Tsushima: A Whirlwind of Fire and Iron

Captain Vladimir Semenoff

The climactic battle of the Russo–Japanese War—one of the most decisive actions in the annals of naval history—took place in May 1905 in the Straits of Tsushima, a narrow sea which separates Japan from Korea.

Since the Japanese surprise attack at Port Arthur the year before, Admiral Heihachiro Togo had kept the Russian Asiatic Squadron bottled up inside the harbor. Once, the Russians tried to escape, but the result was disastrous. Consequently, there seemed no alternative for the Russians but to dispatch their Baltic Fleet on an epic journey halfway around the world to relieve the squadron at Port Arthur.

When the Russian fleet under the command of Admiral Zinovi Rojestvensky finally arrived in Japanese waters, the crews were weary and their ships heavily laden with coal for long-distance steaming. And Togo was waiting for them.

As the two fleets approached from opposite directions, Togo ordered a daring single-file turnabout so that the adversaries would be moving in the same direction in two parallel columns. Then, with his greater speed, Togo forged ahead and swung to starboard so as to cross the T— facing his broadsides against the more lightly-armed bows of Rojestvensky.

The historic result was that the 38 vessels of the Russian fleet were, in a naval sense, annihilated. Of this entire armada, only three reached the safety of Vladivostock; 34 were sunk, captured, or interned at a neutral port. In contrast, the Japanese lost three torpedo boats.

The story of this extraordinary engagement has been told many times from the victor's point of view, but here is an account by Captain Vladimir Semenoff, a Russian naval officer who served aboard the 13,500-ton battleship Suvoroff. *Rojestvensky had chosen Semenoff to take notes and record what he thought would be his great victory.*

Far ahead of us in the distance could be dimly seen approaching through the mist the Japanese main force. "There they are, sir—*all six,*" I said triumphantly.

But Rojestvensky, without turning, shook his head.

"No, there are more—they are all there," and he went down into the conning tower.

"To your stations, gentlemen," said the flag captain quickly, as he followed the admiral.

And there, sure enough, following after the first six ships, and slowly appearing out of the mist, came the *Idzumo, Yakumo, Asama, Adzuma, Tokiwa,* and *Iwate.*

"Now the fun will begin," thought I to myself, going up to the after bridge of the *Suvoroff.* This seemed the most convenient place for carrying out my duty of seeing and noting down everything, since from there I could see both the enemy and our own fleet.

"Hullo! Look! What *are* they up to?" said Lieutenant Reydkin, and his voice betrayed both delight and amazement.

I looked and looked, and, not believing my eyes, could not put down my glasses. The Japanese ships had suddenly commenced to turn "in succession" to port, reversing their course! This maneuver made it necessary for all the enemy's ships to pass in succession over the point on which the leading ship had turned; this point was, so to speak, stationary on the water, making it easy for us to range and aim. Besides—even with a speed of 15 knots, the maneuver must take about fifteen minutes to complete, and all this time the vessels, which had already turned, would mask the fire of those which were still coming up.

The maneuver was undoubtedly risky, but, on the other hand, if Togo found it necessary to reverse course, there was no other way of doing it. He might have ordered the fleet to turn "together," but this would have made the cruiser *Iwate* the leading ship, which he evidently did not wish. Togo accordingly decided to turn "in succession," in order that he should personally lead the fleet, and not surrender that honor to a junior flag officer.

My heart beat furiously. If we succeeded! God grant it!

Meanwhile Rojestvensky hastened to avail himself of this favorable opportunity.

At 1:49 P.M., when the maneuver had been performed by the *Mikasa* and *Shikishima* (two only out of the twelve), the *Suvoroff* fired the first shot at a range of 32 cables, and the guns of the whole fleet thundered forth. I watched closely through my glasses. The shots which went over and those which fell short were all close, but the most interesting, i.e. the hits, could not be seen. Our shells on bursting emitted scarcely any smoke, because the fuses were adjusted to burst inside after penetrating the target. A hit could only be detected when something fell—and nothing fell! In a couple of minutes, when the *Fuji* and *Asahi* had turned also and were following the first ships, the enemy began to reply.

The first shells flew over us. At this range some of the long ones turned a complete somersault, and could clearly be seen with the naked eye curving like so many sticks thrown in the air. They flew over us, making a sort of wail, different from the ordinary roar.

"Are those the portmanteaus?" asked Reydkin, smiling.

"Yes. Those are they." Indeed, what else could you call a shell, a foot in diameter and more than 4 feet long, filled with explosive?

But what struck me most was that these "portmanteaus," curving awkwardly head over heels through the air and falling anyhow on the water, exploded the moment they touched its surface. This had never happened before.

After them came others short of us—nearer and nearer. Splinters whistled through the air, jingled against the side and superstructure. Then, quite close and abreast the foremost funnel, rose a gigantic pillar of smoke, water, and flame. I saw stretchers being carried.

The next shell struck the side by the center 6-inch turret, and there was a tremendous noise behind and below me on the port quarter. Smoke and tongues of fire leapt out of the officers' gang-

way; a shell having fallen into the captain's cabin, and having penetrated the deck, had burst in the officers' quarters, setting them on
fire.

And here I was able to observe, and not for the first time, the
stupor which seems to come over men who have never been in
action before when the first shells began to fall. A stupor which
turns easily and instantaneously, at the most insignificant external
shock, into either uncontrollable panic which cannot be allayed, or
into unusually high spirits, depending on the man's character.

The men at the fire mains and hoses stood as if mesmerized,
gazing at the smoke and flames, not understanding, apparently,
what was happening. I went down to them from the bridge, and
with the most commonplace words, such as "Wake up! Turn the
water on!"—got them to pull themselves together and bravely to
fight the fire.

I was taking out my watch and pocketbook to make a note of
the first fire, when something suddenly struck me in the waist, and
something large and soft, though heavy, hit me in the back, lifting
me up and hurling me onto the deck. When I again got up, my
notebook and watch were in my hands as before. My watch was
going; but the second hand was slightly bent, and the glass had
disappeared. Stupefied by the blow, and not quite myself, I began
carefully to hunt for the lens on the deck, and found it unbroken.
Picking it up, I fitted it into my watch—and, only then realizing
that I had been occupied with something of no importance, I looked
around.

I had probably been unconscious for some time, as the fire had
been extinguished, and, save for two or three dead bodies on which
water was pouring from the torn hoses, no one was to be seen.
Whatever had struck me had come from the direction of the deck
house aft. I looked in the direction where the flag officers, with a
party of poop signalmen, should have been. The shell had passed
through the deck house, bursting inside. Of the ten or twelve signalmen, some seemed to be standing by the starboard 6-inch turret,
others seemed to be lying in a huddled group. Inside was a pile of
something, and on the top lay an officer's telescope. In all seri-
ousness, I had intended to note the times and the places where we
were hit, as well as the damage done. But how could I make detailed
notes when it seemed impossible even to count the number of
projectiles striking us? I had not only never witnessed such a fire
before, but I had never imagined anything like it. Shells seemed to
be pouring upon us incessantly. Shimose and melinite explosive

powder were to a certain extent old acquaintances, but this was something new. It seemed as if these were mines, not shells, which were striking the ship's side and falling on the deck. They burst as soon as they touched anything—the moment they encountered the least impediment in their flight. Handrails, funnel guys, topping lifts of the boats' derricks, were quite sufficient to cause a thoroughly efficient burst. The steel plates and superstructure on the upper deck were torn to pieces, and the splinters caused many casualties. Iron ladders were crumpled up into rings, and guns were literally hurled from their mountings. In addition to this, there was the unusual high temperature and liquid flame of the explosion, which seemed to spread over everything. I actually watched a steel plate catch fire from a burst. Of course, the steel did not burn, but the paint on it did. Such almost non-combustible materials as hammocks, and rows of boxes, drenched with water, flared up in a moment. At times it was impossible to see anything with glasses, owing to everything being so distorted with the quivering, heated air.

By now the enemy had finished his risky turning maneuver described earlier. His twelve ships were in perfect order at close intervals, steaming parallel to us, but gradually forging ahead. No disorder was noticeable. It seemed to me that with my Zeiss glasses (the distance was a little more than twenty cables), I could even distinguish groups of men. But with us? I looked around. What havoc!—Burning bridges, smouldering debris on the deck—piles of dead bodies. Signalling and range-finding stations, gun-directing positions, all were destroyed. And astern of us the *Alexander* and *Borodino* were also enveloped in smoke.

The enemy, steaming ahead, commenced quickly to incline to starboard, endeavoring to cross our T. We also bore to starboard, and again we had him almost on our beam.

It was now 2:05 P.M.

Demchinsky appeared, supporting Flag Lieutenant Sverbeyeff, who could scarcely stand.

He was gasping for breath, and asked for water. Ladling some out of a bucket into a mess kettle, I gave him some, and, as he was unable to use his arms, we had to help him. He drank greedily, jerking out a few words—"It's a trifle—tell the flag captain—I'll come immediately—I am suffocated with these cursed gases—I'll get my breath in a minute." He inhaled the air with a great effort through his blue lips, and something seemed to rattle in his throat and chest. On the right side of his back his coat was torn in a great rent, and his wound was bleeding badly. Demchinsky told a couple of men to take him down to the hospital, and we again went on deck.

After steering on their new course for a quarter of an hour, the enemy had again forged a considerable distance ahead, and now Togo's flagship, the *Mikasa*, at the head of the column, gradually inclined to starboard to cross our T. I waited for us to incline to starboard also, but the admiral held onto the old course for some time longer. I guessed that by doing this he hoped to lessen the distance as much as possible, which would naturally have assisted us, since, with our wrecked range-finders and gun-directing positions, our guns were only serviceable at close quarters. However, to allow the enemy to cross our T and to subject ourselves to a raking fire was not acceptable. Counting the moments anxiously, I watched and waited. The *Mikasa* came closer and closer to our course. Our 6-inch starboard turret was already preparing to fire, when—we sharply inclined to starboard. Breathing freely again, I looked around.

Demchinsky was hard at work, apparently moving the cartridge boxes of the 47-millimeter guns off the deck into the turret, so that there should be less risk of their exploding in the fire and causing greater damage. I went to ask him what he was doing, but before I was able to say anything the captain appeared at the top of the ladder just behind me. His head was covered with blood and, staggering convulsively, he clutched at the handrail. At that moment a shell burst quite close to us and, losing his balance from the sudden explosion, he fell, head foremost, down the ladder. Luckily we saw it coming and were able to catch him.

"It's nothing—only a trifle," he said in his ordinary quick way of speaking. He tried to force a smile and, jumping up, endeavored to go on. But as to go on to the hospital meant another three ladders, we put him, in spite of his protests, on a stretcher.

Meanwhile, though we were unable to see the enemy on account of the smoke, they had a good view of us, and concentrated their fire on the battered battleship in the hope of sinking us. Shells simply poured upon us—a veritable whirlwind of fire and iron.

Suddenly a shell whistled past us, quite close. Everything seemed to start up, and splinters rained upon us. "That must have hit the 6-inch turret," thought I to myself, closing my eyes, and holding my breath so as not to swallow the gas. Sure enough, as the smoke cleared away, only one helpless-looking gun stuck defiantly out of the turret, while out of the armored door of the latter came its commander, Lieutenant Danchich.

"Mine's done for; the muzzle of one has been carried away, and the elevating gear of the other is smashed."

Going to the door I looked in. Of the gun's crew two lay huddled up in a curious manner, while one sat motionless, staring with wide-open eyes, holding his wounded side with both hands. A gun captain, with a worried, businesslike look, was extinguishing some burning cloths.

At this moment there was another explosion quite close to me, and something from behind hit me in the right leg. It was not hard, and I felt no pain. I turned around to look, but none of my men were to be seen. Were they killed, or had they gone below?

"Haven't we any stretchers?" I heard Danchich ask anxiously.

"For whom?" I said.

"Why! For you. You're bleeding."

Looking down I saw that my right leg was standing in a pool of blood, but the leg itself felt sound enough.

It was 3 P.M.

"Can you manage to go? Stop—I'll order someone to go with you," said Danchich, making what seemed to me an unnecessary fuss.

I was annoyed, and angrily said: "Who wants to be accompanied?" and bravely started to go down the ladder, not realizing what had happened. When a small splinter had wounded me in the waist at the beginning of the fight, it had hurt me; but this time I felt nothing.

Later, in the hospital, when carried there on a stretcher, I understood why it is that during a fight one hears neither groans nor shouts. All that comes afterwards. Apparently our feelings have strict limits for receiving external impressions. A thing can be so painful that you feel nothing, so terrible that you fear nothing.

Having passed through the upper and lower batteries, I descended to the mess deck (under the armored one), to the hospital, but I involuntarily went back to the ladder.

The mess deck was full of wounded. They were standing, sitting, lying—some on mattresses made ready beforehand—some on hastily spread tarpaulins—some on stretchers—some just anyhow. Here it was that they first began to feel. The dreadful noise of deep sighs and half-stifled groans was audible in the close, damp air, which smelled of something sour and disgustingly sickly. The electric light seemed scarcely able to penetrate this stench. Ahead somewhere, in white coats stained with red splotches, busy figures were moving about, and towards them all these piles of flesh, clothes, and bones turned, and in their agony dragged themselves, expecting something from them. It seemed as if a cry, motionless, voiceless, but intelligible, a cry which reached to one's very soul, a request for help, for a miracle, for relief from suffering—though at the price of a speedy death—rose up on all sides.

I did not stop to wait my turn, and, not wishing to put myself before others, quickly went up the ladder to the lower battery, where I met the flag captain, who had his head bandaged. From him, I learned that the steering gear had been damaged by a shell which had caused the *Suvoroff* to veer out of formation. Also, he told me that Admiral Rojestvensky and Vladimirsky had both received head wounds when a shell hit the conning tower. The latter had gone below to have his wound dressed, but the admiral had not done so. Rojestvensky, although badly wounded in the head, back, and right leg, was taking it all most cheerfully.

"Portmanteaus" were still raining on us. Word had been received from the engine room that the men were being suffocated and rapidly passing out, as the ventilators were bringing down smoke instead of air; soon there would be no men left to work the engines! Meanwhile, the electric light grew dim, and it was reported from the dynamo engines that steam was scarce.

"Torpedo boats ahead!"

We rushed to our only gun (the other had been found to be past repair), but it turned out to be the *Buiny*, one of our torpedo boats which happened to be passing us, and was on her own initiative coming alongside the crippled battleship to inquire if she could be of assistance.

Kruijanoffsky was ordered by the flag captain, who was standing on the embrasure, to semaphore to her (with his arms) to "Take off the admiral."

I ought to mention here that Admiral Rojestvensky had not been to the dressing station, and none of us knew how badly he was wounded because, to all inquiries when he was hit, he angrily replied that it was only a trifle. At times he would look up to ask how the battle was progressing, and then would again sit silently, with his eyes on the ground. Considering, however, the state the ship was in, what else could he do? His conduct seemed most natural, and it never occurred to us that these questions were merely momentary flashes of energy—short snatches of consciousness from a man whose skull had been fractured.

On the arrival of the torpedo boat being reported, he pulled himself together, and gave the order to "collect the staff" with perfect clearness, but afterwards, he only frowned, and would listen to nothing.

The *Buiny* kept close alongside, dancing up and down. Her captain, Kolomeytseff, shouting through his speaking trumpet, asked: "Have you a boat in which to take off the admiral? We haven't!" To this the flag captain and Kruijanoffsky made some reply.

The Admiral was sitting huddled up, with his eyes on the ground; his head was bandaged in a blood-stained towel.

"Sir, the torpedo boat is alongside! We must go," I said.

"Call Filipinoffsky," he replied, without moving.

Kursel, with the boatswain and two or three sailors, had got hold of some half-burned hammocks and rope from the upper battery, and with these had begun to lash together something in the shape of a raft on which to lower the admiral into the water and put him on board the torpedo boat. It was risky, but nothing else was at hand.

The raft was ready. Filipinoffsky appeared, and I hurried to the Admiral.

"Come, sir! Filipinoffsky is here."

Rojestvensky gazed at us, shaking his head.

"I don't want to. No," he said.

We were at a loss how to proceed.

"What are you staring at?" said Kursel suddenly. "Carry him; can't you see he is badly wounded?"

There was a hum of voices and much bustling about. Some took hold of the Admiral by his arms and raised him up, but no sooner had he put his left leg to the ground than he groaned and completely lost consciousness. It was the best thing that could have happened.

"Bring him along! Bring him along! Splendid! Easy now! The devil! Take him along the side! Get to the side, can't you? Stop—something's cracking! What? His coat is being torn! Carry him along!" were the anxious shouts one heard on all sides.

"Hurrah! the Admiral is on board!" shouted Kursel, waving his cap.

"Hurrah!" cheered everyone.

How I, with my wounded legs, boarded the *Buiny*, I don't remember. I can only recollect that, lying on the hot engine-room hatch between the funnels, I gazed at the *Suvoroff*, unable to take my eyes off her. It was one of those moments which are indelibly impressed upon the mind.

This is how a Japanese report describes the last moments of the *Suvoroff*:

> In the dusk, when our cruisers were driving the enemy northwards, they came upon the *Suvoroff* alone, at some distance from the fight, heeling over badly and enveloped in flames and smoke. The division of torpedo boats, which was with our cruisers, was at once sent to attack her. Although much burned and still on fire, although she had only one serviceable gun— she still opened fire, showing her determination to defend herself to the last moment of her existence—so long, in fact, as she remained above water. At length, about 7 P.M., after our torpedo boats had twice attacked her, she went to the bottom.

PART THREE

WORLD
WAR I

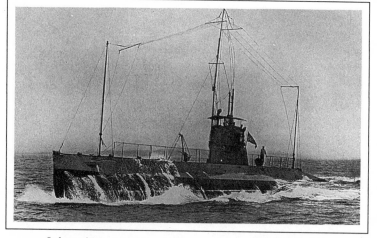

Submarines were the terror weapons of World War I,
but played only a minor role in naval combat.
Above, the American sub *K-1* in 1918.
(U.S. Navy Photo)

Indian Ocean: *Sydney* vs. *Emden*

Hector C. Bywater

The most dramatic naval action during the first year of World War I was not the Battle of Heligoland Bight, in which British warships sank three German light cruisers and a destroyer. It was not the loss of the British battleship Audacious, which struck a German mine off Lough Swilly and sank while being towed to port. It was, instead, the 30,000-mile rampage of the German commerce raider Emden, which finally came to an end with her historic duel against the Australian cruiser Sydney.

At one point during the Emden's three-month-long reign of terror, no fewer than 70 Allied warships were pursuing her. Reports of the chase, and of the Emden's surprise and always deadly visits throughout the Indian Ocean, were avidly followed by millions of newspaper readers around the world.

No one was better equipped to tell the story of the Emden than

Hector C. Bywater, an English journalist who became the world's leading authority on naval affairs in the period between the two world wars. Apart from being a gifted storyteller, as this and other selections here will testify, Bywater knew about the Emden *from her earliest days. He had been present at her launching at Danzig in 1908. From that moment on, he well understood the lethal purpose for which this extraordinary ship had been created.*

To compress into a single chapter the adventures of a ship whose career has inspired a whole library of books is an impossible task. I shall therefore give the merest outline of the *Emden*'s activities previous to her famous duel with the *Sydney*, though her dramatic raid on Penang deserves more particular notice. Launched at Danzig in 1908, she was a sister to the *Dresden*. Although completed only a few months before the "Kolberg" class (*Mainz, Cöln*, etc.) began to appear, the *Emden* was a much smaller ship, displacing only 3,650 tons as against 4,350 tons. Her length was 387 feet, her beam 44½ feet, and she was driven by turbine machinery of 13,500 horsepower, her maximum speed on trial in 1909 being 24.1 knots. Normally she carried 400 tons of coal, but with all reserve bunkers full she could stow 850 tons. Her complement consisted of 31 officers and 330 men.

She mounted what was, in pre–World War I days, the standard main armament of twelve 4.1-inch 35-pounder guns, two torpedo tubes, and a large number of machine guns. Her only armor protection was a steel deck, varying in thickness from 2 inches to ¾ inches, which covered the machinery, boilers, magazines, and steering gear. Such was the comparatively small and second-rate cruiser whose name was to become a household word all over the globe and a synonym for daring, chivalry, and good judgment in the conduct of naval warfare.

Here, as in every other great story of the sea, the ship was nothing, the human element everything. Under a mediocre commanding officer the *Emden* would probably have accomplished little and come to grief weeks if not months before she actually did. But in Captain Erich von Müller the German Navy was fortunate in possessing an officer of outstanding ability who would undoubtedly have distinguished himself in any command. Besides being a fine seaman, he was a zealous student of naval history, and it is a fair inference that his wide knowledge of sea warfare and stratagems derived from such reading were given practical application when he found himself in command of a cruiser ordered to operate against enemy trade.

On the outbreak of war in 1914, the *Emden* formed part of the German Asiatic Squadron, under Admiral Count Spee, with headquarters at Tsingtao, Shantung Province. She had been left behind at Tsingtao when Admiral Spee, with his armored cruisers *Scharnhorst* and *Gneisenau*, had sailed in June 1914, for a cruise to the South Sea Islands. When the telegram advising him that war was imminent reached the admiral he was on passage to Pagan in the Ladrone Islands, and it was there that he summoned by wireless the *Emden*.

That ship had left Tsingtao on July 31, and on August 3, while cruising in the Japan Sea, captured her first prize, the Russian ship *Ryasan*. This vessel was promptly fitted out as an auxiliary cruiser, armed with guns transferred from the old gunboat *Cormoran*, whose name she also took. On August 12 the *Emden* joined Admiral Spee's flag at Pagan. There, to Captain von Müller's great delight, he heard that his ship was to be detached on a special mission to the southward, to harass and capture enemy trade. Eleven days later he was passing through the Molucca Passage on his way to the Indian Ocean and the scene of his remarkable exploits.

On September 4 the *Emden* coaled from a tender off the north coast of Sumatra, where she narrowly missed being caught by the British armored cruiser *Hampshire*. Her next appearance was in the Bay of Bengal. Operating off the Hoogly she captured a number of prizes. Altogether, during her three months' cruise as a commerce raider, the *Emden* captured and sank 16 British vessels totalling 70,825 tons, and took, but afterwards released, seven other vessels.

It is true that later in the war many a German submarine accounted for a much larger aggregate of tonnage than this. But whereas the U-boats had the advantage of comparative invisibility and, in the beginning at least, had little to fear from enemy counter-measures, the *Emden* was a conspicuous object, cruising in waters constantly traversed by hostile men-of-war which were looking for her. At the height of the pursuit no less than seventy British and Allied warships were on her trail.

Furthermore, while a submarine carried enough fuel to take it out and home again, the *Emden* had to depend for coal on the prizes she captured, and, when the coal was found, transfer it to her own bunkers, often in an open anchorage, where apart from the physical difficulties of the work she was liable to be surprised at any moment by superior forces. Captain von Müller was, in fact, operating under much the same circumstances as his famous predecessor, Captain Raphael Semmes, of the Confederate cruiser *Alabama*, though the pursuit of Semmes was nothing as vigorous or as formidable as that which the *Emden* had to evade.

Though Captain von Müller was invariably chivalrous to his captives, and as far as possible refrained from molesting noncombatants, he missed no opportunity of damaging the enemy to the utmost of his power. An example of this legitimate ruthlessness occurred on September 22. Shortly after 9 P.M., the *Emden*, with masked lights, appeared off the port of Madras and opened fire on the Burma Company's oil depot, which formed a conspicuous target on the sea front.

The shells started a great fire in which about half a million gallons of oil were destroyed. So sudden was the attack that the defenses were caught unprepared, but with commendable promptitude the batteries were manned and fire opened on the raider, whose position was revealed by the flash of her guns. She was soon driven off, but not before the oil tanks had been badly damaged, a British steamer hit, and about twenty people killed and wounded. Knowing from intercepted wireless signals that British and Japanese cruisers were hot on his track, von Müller doubled back to the southward and was next heard of on the west coast of Ceylon.

His next destination was the Maldives, where he coaled from a tender, and then proceeded to Diego Garcia in the Chagos group. No news of the war having reached this remote outpost of the British Empire, the residents gave the German raider a hospitable reception under the impression that she was paying a courtesy visit. Von Müller did not disabuse his hosts, who gave him every facility for coaling and assisted him in cleaning the bottom of his ship which had become foul with much steaming in tropical seas. This important task accomplished, the *Emden* sailed from Diego Garcia to the accompaniment of good wishes and friendly cheers from the deluded British inhabitants.

Crossing the Indian Ocean she steered for Penang, where von Müller was about to bring off his most daring and sensational exploit. Information had reached him pointing to the presence there of the French cruiser *Dupleix* and other enemy warships, and he had made up his mind to strike a stunning blow. To appreciate the courageousness of his decision it must be remembered that the *Dupleix* was an armored cruiser of twice the *Emden*'s tonnage, mounting eight 6.4-inch guns which were far more powerful than the German ship's armament. But von Müller was counting on the element of surprise to equalize matters, and not without reason, as the event was to show.

Penang at that time had no shore batteries, and as a German surprise visit was considered not improbable British cruisers visiting the port invariably anchored in such a position as would allow them quickly to bring their broadsides to bear on the entrance. So much had been learned from the fate of the *Pegasus*, which had been caught unawares at Zanzibar by the German cruiser *Königsberg* and shot to pieces. As it happened the *Dupleix* was not at Penang. In her place was the small Russian cruiser *Jemtchug*, weighing 3,180 tons, mounting eight 4.7-inch guns, an opponent much less formidable than the *Dupleix*. In spite of warnings by the harbor-master, Commander McIntyre, R.N.R., and by a British naval officer who was attached to the *Jemtchug*, the Russian captain, either through fatalism or indolence, neglected all precautions.

Terrible was the penalty to be exacted. The *Emden* reached Penang before dawn on October 28. A dummy fourth funnel had been rigged, giving her an appearance not unlike that of British cruisers known to be in the Eastern seas, while the deception was further aided by her dark gray paintwork and the colors she was flying. The latter appeared to be the British White Ensign, but may have been some other flag made to resemble it. A picket boat patrolling off the entrance took her for a British cruiser and let her pass unchallenged. Boldly she steamed up the harbor towards the berth where the *Jemtchug* lay all unsuspecting and ripe for the slaughter. When the distance had closed to 900 yards a torpedo leaped from the *Emden*'s submerged tube and raced towards the Russian cruiser.

It caught her in the stern, detonated with tremendous violence, and put her engines out of action. An instant later the *Emden* increased speed and, running past her target, opened rapid fire with her full broadside of 4.1-inch guns. In a moment the *Jemtchug* was smothered with bursting shell. At point-blank range they crashed through her sides and transformed her into a spouting volcano. So complete was the surprise that not a shot was fired in reply. In less time than it takes to write these words the Russian cruiser was disabled and waterlogged, her decks a shambles. Two French destroyers and a French gunboat moored near at hand were equally taken by surprise, but for some reason the *Emden* did not fire at them. Instead she retraced her course, ran past the *Jemtchug* again, and gave her another torpedo and two more salvos. This completed the grim business, for the Russian ship, already on fire alow and aloft, blew up with a thunderous explosion, taking with her to the bottom two hundred officers and men out of a complement of three hundred and forty.

It had been not a battle but a massacre. Still the *Emden*'s work was not done. As she turned to leave the harbor she met the Glen liner, *Glenturret*, which had stopped to pick up a pilot. Well may the British official historian speak of the "fine effrontery" which inspired Captain von Müller at this critical moment to stop and lower boats in order to board the *Glenturret*. Folly it may have been, but it was magnificent folly.

At this moment, however, he was interrupted. In the half light there was seen coming up the fairway a vessel which appeared to be a light cruiser. Von Müller at once recalled his boats and stood out to meet the new enemy, which on closer inspection was found to be the small French destroyer *Mousquet*, weighing 303 tons, armed with small guns and two torpedo tubes. Suspecting nothing, this little ship steamed headlong into destruction. Holding his fire until the range was point-blank, the German captain blasted the *Mousquet* with his first broadside. The few Frenchmen that survived the tempest of shell gallantly stood to their weapons, but in seven minutes their boat had sunk beneath them, literally blown to pieces.

As might have been expected of him, von Müller stayed his course long enough to pick up the *Mousquet*'s survivors. Then he steamed out to sea, followed by another French destroyer, which with great courage hung on to his heels for four hours, till a rainstorm came down and ended the chase. It is surprising that the *Emden* did not turn on this puny pursuer and rend her.

By now von Müller's active career was drawing to a close. From Penang he proceeded northwest to the Nicobars, crossing the Rangoon–Singapore trade route, then turned to the south, his movements no doubt actuated by information conveyed to him by intercepted wireless. Arriving on the Sumatra–Colombo route he took what was to be his last prize, the British steamer *Newcastle*, transferred to her his French prisoners, and despatched her to Sabang. No other shipping was seen, and after having drawn blank for two days he headed southwest for the Cocos Islands. In so doing he sealed the fate of his ship, and it is therefore interesting to give his own explanation—written after the loss of his ship—of his motives in raiding this isolated British cable station.

My raid on the Cocos group was determined by the following considerations: Apart from the material damage the enemy would have suffered by the destruction of the cable and wireless stations and the temporary interruption of telegraphic communication between Australia on the one hand and England and other countries on the other, I hoped also to effect (1) a general unrest among shipping to and from Australia by creating the impression that the *Emden* would proceed to harry the steamer traffic south and west of Australia, and (2) a withdrawal from the Indian Ocean of at least some of the English cruisers which were taking part in the hunt for the *Emden*. My intention was, after carrying out the raid on the Cocos group, to make for Socotra and cruise in the Gulf of Aden, and then on the steamer route between Aden and Bombay.

After the destruction of the *Emden* her captain was criticized, not only abroad but in Germany as well, for what was held to be an ill-judged move—a move which, significantly enough, was to be repeated almost exactly a month later by Admiral Spee at the Falklands, and with the same result. But in fairness to Captain von Müller it must be stated that disaster overtook him less as the result of faulty judgment than of pure luck. On reviewing all the circumstances it seems that the chance of his being caught at the Cocos Islands was not more than one in a hundred. Ordinarily there would have been no British or Allied cruiser anywhere near that locality, and it was pure coincidence that von Müller timed his raid to take place just when the Australian convoy with its escorting cruisers was passing only fifty miles away to the east.

This enormous convoy of nearly forty ships, crowded with Australian and New Zealand troops, had, after many delays induced by a well-grounded reluctance to let it sail as long as Admiral von Spee's powerful squadron, or, indeed, any single German cruiser, was still at large and unlocated, finally set forth from King George's Sound, Albany, on November 1, 1914, escorted by the British armored cruiser *Minotaur*, the Australian cruisers *Sydney* and *Melbourne*, and the Japanese armored cruiser *Ibuki*. Once at sea the *Minotaur* took station five miles ahead; the Australian transports followed in three columns abreast, astern of which came ten New Zealand troopships in two parallel lines. To starboard of the convoy the *Ibuki* steamed abreast of the leading transports at a distance of four miles, while the *Sydney* kept station at a similar distance to port, and far astern came the *Melbourne*.

The official Australian history expressed the situation this way:

> So the great fleet, comprising four warships with thirty-eight transports in charge, voyaged towards its tiny enemy

(the *Emden*) like an elephant timidly approaching the dreaded mouse. No more conspicuous example could be given or imagined of naval power and its limitations, of the overwhelming need of warships to the Empire, and its defenselessness without their dominance throughout the oceans. One enemy cruiser, smaller and weaker than any of the four in the convoy's escort, could force not only the use of all the four, but the spreading over the Indian Ocean of nine more . . .

for at this moment six British, one Russian, and two Japanese cruisers were all being directed against the *Emden*.

What a single German cruiser such as the *Emden* might possibly have done against the convoy had she fallen in with it is indicated by a statement made later by one of von Müller's officers. "We should have got in among the transports from astern," he said, "and slipped into the first division astern of the third and fourth ship; then we should have done all possible damage with our guns and torpedoes, and we should certainly have sunk half a dozen ships— possibly twelve—before your escort could have come up and stopped us." While it is not necessary to accept this as an accurate forecast of what might have happened it is, as the Australian historian points out, "difficult to put limits to the ravaging that could be done at night among a number of defenseless transports by a single audacious cruiser, which could fire indiscriminately—since all other vessels would be enemies—while their escort must continually be considering the danger of sinking a transport by mistake."

Moreover in view of what the *Emden* had done at Penang the naval officers responsible for the convoy were fully justified in taking every precaution. To have underrated such a doughty and enterprising foe as von Müller would have been madness. A successful stroke against the Anzac convoy would have been, as regards moral effect, almost the worst catastrophe that could have befallen the Allied cause at that particular moment of the war. It was because of their perfect confidence in the sure shield provided by the British Navy that the Dominions had not hesitated to send the pick of their manhood across thousands of miles of ocean while hostile warships were still at large.

On November 8, when the *Emden* was, in fact, less than 250 miles from the convoy, the naval escort was seriously weakened by the recall of the *Minotaur*. News had reached the Admiralty of the Coronel disaster and it was feared that the victorious German squadron might set a course for Southwest Africa to aid the compatriots against whom General Botha was leading an expedition. As the British naval force in those waters was very weak the Admiralty radioed the *Minotaur* to detach itself from the convoy and proceed at once to the Cape. On receipt of this signal the *Minotaur* immediately altered her course, put on speed, and soon disappeared to south-westward, leaving Captain M. L'E. Silver, of the *Melbourne*, in charge of the convoy.

He at once took station ahead in the *Minotaur's* place and the great fleet of transports steamed steadily on, now bereft of a rear guard. Time passed without incident till 6:30 A.M. on November 9. Then the wireless operators in the escort cruisers and several of the transports intercepted a cryptic message; "Kativ Battav." The code was unknown, but it is a fact worth recording that several wireless experts in the convoy at once declared the signal to be from the *Emden*. They were right: von Müller, who had no idea of the presence of enemy ships, was instructing his collier, the *Buresk*, to meet him at Port Refuge in the Cocos group, where he proposed to coal.

Hardly had the strange message been taken in when the convoy heard a response from the Cocos radio station, asking "What is that code?" Ten minutes passed and then came a call from Cocos to the *Minotaur*, which was, of course, many miles away. It was promptly followed by a second call, "Strange warship approaching," and a repeat prefixed "SOS." At the same moment the Cocos telegraph operator was cabling to Australia that a three-funnelled warship was off the island and was putting a party ashore in boats.

The wireless appeal left no doubt in Captain Silver's mind as to what was happening. Instinctively he increased speed and swung around in the direction of the Cocos group, realizing that in all probability he had the notorious German raider in his grasp. Then, however, devotion to duty triumphed; as senior officer his place was with the convoy, and the privilege of dealing with the *Emden* must be delegated to another. The captain of the Japanese cruiser *Ibuki* begged hard for the honor, but since his ship was by far the most powerful unit of the escort his entreaties were in vain. Captain Silver ordered the *Sydney* to make for the Cocos at full speed. By seven o'clock she was off at 20 knots, gradually working up to full power, while the men were sent to breakfast on the excellent principle that it is bad to fight on an empty stomach.

At 9:15 the Australian cruiser, now driving through the calm sea at 25 knots, came in sight of the menaced island. Almost at the same instant the tall masts and funnels of a warship were seen.

Meanwhile, Captain von Müller, standing on the bridge of the *Emden* while his landing party under Lieutenant von Mücke was busy ashore smashing the radio and cable instruments, had for some time been watching a cloud of smoke on the horizon to northward. He took it to be the *Buresk* hurrying to the rendezvous. "But soon (in his own words) we began to doubt whether it could be the *Buresk*, as she was usually almost smokeless; but it was considered that the unusually dense smoke cloud might be attributed to her having had a fire in her bunkers the day before, which was probably causing her to use the partly burned coal; moreover she would certainly be running at top speed." From the crow's nest, too, the lookout at first incorrectly reported the oncoming ship to have one funnel and two masts.

But von Müller was growing uneasy. As the wrecking party ashore seemed to be taking their time he signalled to them at 9:15: "*Arbeiten beschleunigen*" ("Hurry up with the work"). All eyes in the *Emden* were now on the unknown ship. Soon the tall topmasts of an unmistakable warship were seen clearly. It could only be an enemy, but what enemy? Von Müller believed her to be the *Newcastle*, a ship of less formidable type than the *Sydney*, and not until the action was over did he discover his mistake. We have accounts from both sides of what happened in that brief period of tension before the duel began.

The official Australian chronicler describes the *Sydney* as rushing along at her full 25 knots towards the enemy, who had just been sighted at a distance of seven to eight miles. Captain J. C. T. Glossop was on the compass platform, his navigating officer lying on the armored hood of the conning tower taking bearings, the gunnery officer peering through his binoculars, listening to the ranges being called, and waiting for permission to open fire when his sights were on. On deck the paymaster sat upon the weighted box containing the ship's confidential papers, ready to hurl it overboard should disaster befall the ship. Elsewhere officers and men stood at their action stations—and then, literally, as a bolt from the blue, came the *Emden*'s first salvo, "dropping out of the sky."

At that date the extremely long range at which German naval guns, even of medium caliber thanks to their high-angle mountings, could shoot was still not realized. Von Müller had characteristically determined to get in the first blow, and, as we shall see, with better luck on his side it might have turned the odds in his favor. As soon as he had recognized the distant ship as a British cruiser his actions were swift and resolute. There was, indeed, no time to lose, for the

Sydney was racing up at 28 miles an hour. "I ordered steam in all boilers and repeated several times the recall for the landing party: then I gave the orders, 'Up anchor,' 'Clear ship for action,' 'Get up steam immediately for all possible speed.' "

"About 9:30 A.M. the landing party began to reembark, but with the enemy quickly approaching it was seen to be impossible to get them on board before the fight began. As soon, therefore, as the anchor was weighed, I ordered full steam ahead and set the ship on a north-northwest course so as to improve still further our advantageous position with regard to the wind until the actual beginning of the fight. My object was to attempt to inflict on the enemy such damage by gunfire that her speed would be seriously lessened, and I might be able to bring on a torpedo action with some chance of success." This is the point at which it becomes possible to coordinate the narratives of the duellists, which from now on coincide very closely as to time and incident.

It was exactly at 9:40 A.M. that the *Emden* began the action by opening fire at a range of 10,300 yards. The first salvo was very much of a "wide," but without waiting for correction by the spotters the second was fired—also an over. The third and fourth salvos were short, but out of the fifth several shells found the mark. In the British official history the *Emden* is credited with having "straddled the *Sydney* at once," but von Müller's own report shows this to be incorrect. The German tactics were eminently sound, for only by crippling or demoralizing her far more powerful opponent by a sudden hail of fire could the *Emden* hope to have the best of it. In a standup fight her 36-pounders had no chance against the *Sydney*'s broadside of 100-pounder guns.

Nevertheless it seemed for a few minutes that von Müller's terrific drum fire of 4.1-inch shells might decide the issue. During this time the *Sydney*, taken by surprise, steamed through a hurricane of shell, half hidden by the spouting columns of water that leapt up all around her. But she presented a very narrow target for what was virtually high-angle fire, and out of the hundreds of shells that spouted and burst in her immediate vicinity not more than fifteen actually hit her, and of these only five detonated. Creditable the German shooting certainly was, for the ships were closing at the rate of nearly a mile a minute, and as the *Emden* was firing at the extreme elevation of her guns, 30 degrees, gunnery control was complicated.

Very soon the *Sydney* began to suffer. Several shells from a closely bunched salvo hit the after control station, putting out of action everyone there. At the same instant a shell struck the range-finder on top of the fore bridge, killing the operator and smashing the instrument. Most fortunately this projectile was a "dud": had it burst it would probably have killed Captain Glossop, who was standing only a few feet away. Eight or nine shells burst on and below deck, causing casualties among the guns' crews and setting fire to some cordite charges lying nearby. This blaze looked alarming for a minute or so, but it was promptly put out by the fire parties.

Meanwhile, the *Sydney* had not been taking this punishment passively. As it happened Captain Glossop had arranged with his gunnery officer to open fire at 9,500 yards. The ship had accordingly been swung around to bring her full port broadside to bear at that range, and the order to fire was about to be given when the *Emdern*'s first salvo arrived. Apparently the destruction of the forward range-finder and the wrecking of the after control station caused a momentary delay in opening fire, but a few seconds afterwards the *Sydney*'s first 6-inch salvo thundered out. According to Captain von Müller's report, the Australian shooting was not very accurate at first, though all other accounts agree that the first hits on the *Emden* were made with the third salvo, which appears to be creditable enough. Until the precise range was found the *Sydney* fired deliberately, in contrast to the exceedingly rapid discharges from the German guns, which were firing ten rounds to the minute. Soon, however, the *Sydney* began hitting in grim earnest, and nearly every 100-pounder shell that crashed into the unarmored German cruiser caused widespread damage and loss of life.

From that moment the *Emden*'s own fire ceased to be effective. Not another hit was made on the *Sydney*, which now proceeded to pound her enemy into a mass of wreckage. Of this phase Captain von Müller wrote:

> As soon as the *Sydney* got our range a good deal of damage was done to the *Emden*, and this increased so quickly that I very soon got the impression that the *Sydney* had gained fire superiority over us. The *Sydney*'s guns after but a brief interval overwhelmed the *Emden*'s although we scored the first lucky hits and in the first phase of the fight had kept on our mark and displayed much greater speed in firing.

He attributes the speedy defeat of his ship to her opponent's heavier guns, better protection, and greater steadiness as a gun platform. The critical moment of the action came when the *Sydney* turned slightly away starboard to maintain her own range rather than accept a closer combat which would have suited the enemy's lighter artillery. As she turned, the *Emden* also veered to starboard, hoping to get astern of the Australian ship and to give her several raking broadsides. But Captain Glossop was not to be caught. He swung back to port and opened with every gun that would bear, the range now being considerably shorter.

Within the space of minutes the *Emden* was virtually overwhelmed. Shells disabled her steering gear, demolished all signal and fire-control apparatus, and brought down the forward funnel and the mainmast, the latter in its fall wrecking most of the fore bridge. The crews of the guns and men of the ammunition parties were suffering terribly as the 6-inch lyddite shell burst about them. "They seemed to drop on the deck in bunches," said a survivor, "and as each shell burst it sent a tornado of splinters hissing and clanging in every direction. So far did these razor-edged steel fragments travel that many people amidships were killed by shells bursting on the forecastle or the quarterdeck. There was no protection anywhere."

At the hottest phase of the duel, when the two ships were only 5,500 yards apart, the *Sydney* fired a torpedo, which missed. Captain von Müller, on his side, made several attempts to bring his torpedo tubes into action, but was always thwarted by the *Sydney*'s superior speed. By now the *Emden*'s two remaining funnels were down, yet she was still able to move at 19½ knots and was steered by her screws, the steering gear, both mechanical and manual, being wrecked.

It was now that von Müller decided to run his ship ashore. "In the meantime," he writes, "our gun fire had completely collapsed, so I swung away from the *Sydney* by stopping the starboard engine. Shortly afterwards I was informed from the torpedo room that it must be abandoned on account of a leak from a shot under water. As it was now impossible for me to damage my opponent in any way further, I decided to put my ship, which was badly damaged by gunfire and burning in many places, on the reef in the surf on the weather side of North Keeling Island and to wreck it thoroughly, in order not to sacrifice needlessly the lives of the survivors." This wise and humane decision was carried into effect at 11:20 A.M., one hour and forty minutes after the first shot of the action had been fired.

Just before the *Emden* struck the reef both her engines were stopped, then immediately after the impact they were put to full speed ahead again to drive her hard and fast ashore. This done, von Müller ordered all fires to be drawn and all engine and boiler rooms to be flooded. His one fear was that the enemy might salve his beloved ship, but the measures he took were so thorough that there was never any question of refloating her.

When Captain Glossop saw his opponent heading for the reef he gave her two more salvos. After making sure that she was firmly wedged on the rocks, he turned at full speed to catch the collier *Buresk*, which rather unwisely had remained hovering on the fringe of the battlefield. He overtook her at noon, but the German crew, finding escape impossible, had opened the sea cocks, and after the *Sydney* had put four shells into her to hasten her sinking she went to the bottom. Only then did Glossop feel free to return to the *Emden*.

Returning to North Keeling Island at 4 P.M., he found the wrecked cruiser with her colors still flying. No response being made to repeated signals asking whether she had surrendered, he fired two salvos at the wreck. At that the German ensign came down and a white sheet was waved from the quarterdeck, whereupon the *Sydney* ceased fire.

Subsequently Captain Glossop was severely criticized for his action in shelling the wreck, but on an impartial review of the evidence he must be acquitted of any suspicion of inhumanity. He had no proof that the Germans would not fire on his boats if he sent them in, and for many centuries a ship which has not lowered her colors has been considered an enemy still determined to resist.

All that evening and night the *Sydney* patrolled off the islands, for the captain half suspected that the German cruiser *Königsberg* might be in the vicinity, as there was a general impression—erroneous, as it proved to be—that she and the *Emden* had been hunting in couples. Moreover, Glossop knew that a German armed party had landed on Direction Island (the cable station), and not until the following morning did he learn that they had made good their escape in a small schooner. Only then did he feel free to turn his attention to the *Emden*.

When the *Sydney*'s boats reached the wreck they were faced with a gruesome state of affairs. Corpses and terribly wounded men lay everywhere. High explosives and numerous fires had done their work so well that the *Emden* barely retained the semblance of a ship. Wrote the *Sydney*'s surgeon:

> The transhipping of the wounded was an exceedingly dif-
> ficult and painful undertaking, as there was a large surf running
> on the beach where the *Emden* went ashore, and she was so

much of a shambles that the shifting, collecting, and lowering of the wounded into the boats was necessarily rough. Besides the seventy wounded received that day, there were over one hundred and ten prisoners, and twenty Chinamen from the sunken collier *Buresk*; so the crowding can be imagined, seeing that we were a crowded ship before.

Yet for all the inevitable "roughness" in handling the wounded, one of the captured German officers has volunteered the statement that the work was carried out "very cleverly and carefully." Once on board the *Sydney* the unfortunate Germans were treated as their gallantry deserved. Their worst cases were attended to before those of the *Sydney*. Captain von Müller added his own tribute in the following passage of his official report:

> The treatment of prisoners of war aboard her (the *Sydney*) was good and I must particularly recognize the great care that was taken of the wounded.

In view of the allegations against Captain Glossop, the following account of his conduct when the *Sydney* rejoined the Anzac convoy after her victory over the *Emden* is worth putting on record. As she steamed into Colombo harbor the troops in the transports lined the rails and were preparing to greet her with cheers. Glossop, however, signalled a request that there should be no cheering in deference to the feelings of the many wounded Germans on board his ship, whose lot was already hard enough. He made this request both in his own name and in that of his officers and men. On the *Sydney*'s arrival at Colombo the wounded were promptly landed and placed in hospital, while the unwounded prisoners were distributed among various steamers of the convoy, to be taken on to Malta.

According to Captain von Müller's own statement, the *Emden* went into action with 316 officers and men on board. Her casualties were 12 officers and warrant officers and 122 men killed or died of wounds, 65 wounded. One hundred and seventeen officers and men were unhurt. These figures attest the terrible effects of the *Sydney*'s lyddite shells. The Australian cruiser escaped serious structural damage and her casualties were only four killed and twelve wounded. She owed her comparative immunity less to armor protection, which was slight enough, than to her superior weight of gunfire.

With the *Emden*'s destruction a great burden was lifted from the minds of those responsible for the safety of the outer seas. During her three months' cruise, in which she covered a total distance of 30,000 miles, she exerted a moral effect out of all proportion to her actual fighting power. At one period no less than seventy British and other warships were engaged in the pursuit of the elusive raider, and the detachment of so many vessels necessarily weakened the Allied squadrons in other theaters of the war. Captain von Müller had every reason to be proud of the part he had played against his country's enemies. Moreover, he had consistently shown himself to be a chivalrous enemy and a clean fighter. Alike in England and Australia the most generous tributes were paid to his prowess, and the news of his untimely death, soon after the war, was received with genuine regret by his erstwhile foes.

In Australia, of course, the news of the *Sydney*'s victory evoked immense enthusiasm. It was the first time a ship of the young Australian Navy had been in action, and nobly had she acquitted herself. While the majority of the officers and men had been lent from the Royal Navy, a considerable part of the crew were Australian-born, "young hands and men under training," as they were officially described. Among them were thirty boys from the Australian training ship *Tingira*, whose average age was under seventeen. The conduct of these youths was beyond all praise. Under the *Emden*'s torrent of shell at the beginning of the fight they performed their duties with the steadiness of veterans. In short, the fierce duel off the Cocos Islands brought credit to all concerned, though the disparity between the size and armament of the contending ships was too marked to permit any useful technical conclusions being drawn.

CHAPTER 6

British Submarines: Little Tin Turtles

Rudyard Kipling

R udyard Kipling, Britain's poet laureate and first winner of the Nobel Prize for Literature, had celebrated the Royal Navy in verse and prose for years before the start of World War I. And thus, in 1916, after two years of war, he gladly accepted an invitation from the British Admiralty to visit the relatively new submarine service and read some of its official records.

The result is the following outpouring of song and story. Because the censor changed all of the boat numbers, and because the information Kipling was given was incomplete, the details here must not be accepted as fact. But when it comes to capturing the spirit of the enterprise, Kipling has no equal.

FAREWELL and adieu to you, Greenwich ladies,
Farewell and adieu to you, ladies ashore!

For we've received orders to work to the eastward
Where we hope in a short time to strafe 'em some more.

We'll duck and we'll dive like little tin turtles,
We'll duck and we'll dive underneath the North Seas,
Until we strike something that doesn't expect us,
From here to Cuxhaven it's go as you please!

The first thing we did was to dock in a minefield,
Which isn't a place where repairs should be done;
And there we lay doggo in twelve-fathom water
With tri-nitro-toluol hogging our run.

The next thing we did, we rose under a Zeppelin,
With his shiny big belly half blocking the sky.
But what in the—Heavens can you do with six-pounders?
So we fired what we had and we bade him good-bye.

Like the destroyer, the submarine has created its own type of officer and man—with language and traditions apart from the rest of the Service, and yet at heart unchangingly of the Service. Their business is to run monstrous risks from earth, air, and water, in what, to be of any use, must be the coldest of cold blood.

The commander's is more a one-man job, as the crew's is more teamwork, than any other employment afloat. That is why the relations between submarine officers and men are what they are. They play hourly for each other's lives with Death the Umpire always at their elbow on tiptoe to call them "out."

There is a stretch of water, once dear to amateur yachtsmen, now given over to scouts, submarines, destroyers, and, of course, contingents of fishing trawlers. We were waiting the return of some boats which were due to report. A couple surged up the still harbor in the afternoon light and tied up beside their sisters. There climbed out of them three or four high-booted, sunken-eyed pirates clad in sweaters, under jackets that a stoker of the last generation would have disowned. This was their first chance to compare notes at close hand. Together they lamented the loss of a Zeppelin—"a perfect mug of a Zepp," who had come down very low and offered one of them a sitting shot. "But what *can* you do with our guns? I gave him what I had, and then he started bombing."

"I know he did," another said. "I heard him. That's what brought me down to you. I thought he had you that last time."

"No, I was forty foot under when he hove out the big 'un. What happened to *you?*"

"My steering gear jammed just after I went down, and I had to go around in circles till I got it straightened out. But *wasn't* he a mug!"

"Was he the brute with the patch on his port side?" a sister boat demanded.

"No! This fellow had just been hatched. He was almost sitting on the water, heaving bombs over."

"And my blasted steering gear went and chose *then* to go wrong," the other commander mourned. "I thought his last little egg was going to get me!"

Half an hour later, I was formally introduced to three or four quite strange, quite immaculate officers, freshly shaved, and a little tired about the eyes, whom I thought I had met before.

Meantime (it was on the hour of evening drinks) one of the boats was still unaccounted for. No one talked of her. They rather discussed motor cars and Admiralty constructors, but—it felt like that queer twilight watch at the front when the homing airplanes drop in. Presently a signaller entered: "*V 42* outside, sir; wants to know which channel she shall use." "Oh, thank you. Tell her to take so-and-so." Mine, I remember, was vermouth and bitters, and later on *V 42* himself found a soft chair and joined the committee of instruction. Those next for duty, as well as those in training, wished to hear what was going on, and who had shifted what to where, and how certain arrangements had worked. They were told in language not to be found in any printable book. Questions and answers were alike Hebrew to one listener, but he gathered that every boat carried a second in command—a strong, persevering youth, who seemed responsible for everything that went wrong, from a motor cylinder to a torpedo. Then somebody touched on the mercantile marine and its habits.

Said one philosopher: "They can't be expected to take any more risks than they do. *I* wouldn't, if I was a skipper. I'd loose off at any blessed periscope I saw."

"That's all very fine. You wait till you've had a patriotic tramp trying to strafe you at your own back door," said another.

Someone told a tale of a man with a voice, notable even in a Service where men are not trained to whisper. He was coming back, empty-handed, dirty, tired, and best left alone. From the peace of the German side he had entered our hectic home waters, where the usual freighter shelled, and by miraculous luck, crumpled his periscope. Another man might have dived, but Boanerges kept on rising. Majestic and wrathful he rose personally through his main hatch, and at 2,000 yards (have I said it was still day?) addressed the freighter. Even at that distance she gathered it was a naval officer with a grievance, and by the time he ran alongside she was in a state of coma, but he managed to stammer: "Well, sir, at least you'll admit that our shooting was pretty good."

"And that," said my informant, "put the lid on!" Boanerges went down lest he should be tempted to murder; and the freighter affirms she heard him rumbling beneath her, like an inverted thunder storm, for fifteen minutes.

"All those freighters ought to be disarmed, and *we* ought to have all their guns," said a voice out of a corner.

"What? Still worrying over your 'mug'?" someone replied.

"He *was* a mug!" went on the man of one idea. "If I'd had a couple of twelves even, I could have strafed him proper. I don't know whether I shall mutiny, or desert, or write to the First Sea Lord about it."

"Strafe all Admiralty constructors to begin with. *I* could build a better boat with a 4-inch lathe and a sardine tin than—," the speaker named her by letter and number.

"That's pure jealousy," her commander explained to the company. "Ever since I installed—ahem!—my patent electric wash basin he's been intriguin' to get her. Why? We know he doesn't wash. He'd only use the basin to keep beer in."

However often one meets it, as in this war one meets it at every turn, one never gets used to the Holy Spirit of Man at his job. The "common sweeper," growling over his mug of tea that there was "nothing in sweepin'," and these idly chaffing men, new shaved and attired, from the gates of Death which had let them through for the fiftieth time, were all of the same fabric—incomprehensible, I should imagine, to the enemy. And the stuff held good throughout all the world—from the Dardanelles to the Baltic, where only a little while ago another batch of submarines had slipped in and begun to be busy. I had spent some of the afternoon in looking through reports of submarine work in the Sea of Marmora. They read like the diary of energetic weasels in an overcrowded chicken run, and the results for each boat were tabulated something like a cricket score. There were no maiden overs. One came across jewels of price set in the flat official phraseology. For example, one man who was describing some steps he was taking to remedy certain defects, interjected casually: "At this point I had to go under for a little, as a man in a boat was trying to grab my periscope with his hand." No reference before or after to the said man or his fate. Again: "Came across a dhow with a Turkish skipper. He seemed so miserable that I let him go." And elsewhere in those waters, a submarine overhauled a steamer full of Turkish passengers, some of whom, arguing on their allies' lines, promptly leaped overboard. Our boat fished them out and returned them, for she was not killing civilians. In another affair, which included several ships (now at the bottom) and one submarine, the commander relaxes enough to note that: "The men behaved very well under direct and flanking fire from rifles at about fifteen yards." This was *not*, I believe, the submarine that fought the Turkish cavalry on the beach. And in addition to matters much more marvellous than any I have hinted at, the reports deal with repairs and shifts and contrivances carried through in the face of dangers that read like the last delirium of romance. One boat went down the straits and found herself rather canted over to one side. A mine and chain had jammed under her forward diving plane. So far as I made out, she shook it off by standing on her head and jerking backwards; or it may have been, for the thing has occurred more than once, she merely rose as much as she could, when she could, and then "released it by hand," as the official phrase goes.

And who, a few months ago, could have invented, or having invented, would have dared to print such a nightmare as this: There was a boat in the North Sea which ran into a net and was caught by the nose. She rose, still entangled, meaning to cut the thing away on the surface. But a Zeppelin in waiting saw and bombed her, and she had to go down again at once—but not too wildly or she would get herself more wrapped up than ever. She went down, and by slow working and weaving and wriggling, guided only by guesses at the meaning of each scrape and grind of the net on her blind forehead, at last she drew clear. Then she sat on the bottom and thought. The question was whether she should go back at once and warn her confederates against the trap, or wait till the destroyers which she knew the Zeppelin would have signalled for, should come out to finish her still entangled, as they would suppose, in the net? It was a simple calculation of comparative speeds and positions, and when it was worked out she decided to try for the double event. Within a few minutes of the time she had allowed for them, she heard the twitter of four destroyers' screws quartering above her; rose; got her shot in; saw one destroyer crumple; hung around till another took the wreck in tow; said good-bye to the spare brace (she was at the end of her supplies), and reached the rendezvous in time to turn her friends.

And since we are dealing in nightmares, here are two more—one genuine, the other, mercifully, false. There was a boat not only at, but *in* the mouth of a river—well home in German territory. She was spotted, and went under, her commander perfectly aware that there was not more than five feet of water over her conning tower, so that even a torpedo boat, let alone a destroyer, would hit it if she came over. But nothing hit anything. The search was conducted on scientific principles while they sat on the silt and suffered. Then the commander heard the rasp of a wire trawl sweeping over his hull. It was not a nice sound, but there happened to be a couple of gramophones aboard, and he turned them both on to drown it. And in due time that boat got home with everybody's hair of just the same color as when they had started!

The other nightmare arose out of silence and imagination. A boat had gone to bed on the bottom in a spot where she might reasonably expect to be looked for, but it was a convenient jumping-off, or -up, place for the work in hand. About the bad hour of 2:30 A.M. the commander was waked by one of his men, who whispered to him: "They've got the chains on us, sir!" Whether it was pure nightmare, a hallucination of long wakefulness, something relaxing and releasing in that packed box of machinery, or the disgustful reality, the commander could not tell, but it had all the makings of panic in it. So the Lord and long training put it into his head to reply! "Have they? Well, we shan't be coming up till nine o'clock this morning. We'll see about it then. Turn out that light, please."

He did not sleep, but the dreamer and the others did, and when morning came and he gave the order to rise, and she rose unhampered, and he saw the gray, smeared seas from above once again, he said it was a very refreshing sight.

Lastly, which is on all fours with the gamble of the chase, a man was coming home rather bored after an uneventful trip. It was necessary for him to sit on the bottom for a while, and there he played a game of solitaire. Of a sudden it struck him, as a vow and an omen, that if he worked out the next game correctly he would go up and strafe something. The cards fell all in order. He went up at once and found himself alongside a German, whom, as he had promised and prophesied to himself, he destroyed. She was a mine-layer, and needed only a jar to dissipate like a cracked electric light bulb. He was somewhat impressed by the contrast between the single-handed game fifty feet below, the ascent, the attack, the amazing result, and when he descended again, his cards just as he had left them. . . .

No one knows how the title of "the Trade" came to be applied to the Submarine Service. Some say that the cruisers invented it because they pretend that submarine officers look like unwashed chauffeurs. Others think it sprang forth by itself, which means that it was coined by the lower deck, where they always have the proper names for things. Whatever the truth, the Submarine Service is now "the Trade"; and if you ask them why, they will answer: "What else could you call it? The Trade's 'the trade,' of course."

It is a closed corporation; yet it recruits its men and officers from every class that uses the sea and engines, as well as from many classes that never expected to deal with either. It takes them; they disappear for a while and return changed to their very souls, for the Trade lives in a world without precedents, of which no generation has had any previous experience—a world still being made and enlarged daily. It creates and settles its own problems as it goes along, and if it cannot help itself no one else can. So the Trade lives in the dark and thinks out inconceivable and impossible things which it afterwards puts into practice.

It keeps books, too, as honest traders should. They are almost as bald as ledgers, and are written up, hour by hour, on a little sliding table that pulls out from beneath the commanders' bunk. In due time they go to my Lords of the Admiralty, who presently circulate a few carefully watered extracts for the confidential information of the junior officers of the Trade, that these may see what things are done and how. The Juniors read but laugh. They have heard the stories, with all the flaming detail and much of the language, either from a chief actor while they perched deferentially on the edge of a mess-room fender, or from his subordinate, in which case they were not so deferential, or from some returned member of the crew present on the occasion, who, between half-shut teeth at the wheel, jerks out what really happened. There is very little going on in the Trade that the Trade does not know within a reasonable time. But the outside world must wait until my Lords of the Admiralty release the records. Some of them have been released now.

Let us take, almost at random, an episode in the life of H.M. Submarine *E 9*. It is true that she was commanded by Commander Max Horton, but the utter impersonality of the tale makes it as though the boat herself spoke. (Also, never having met or seen any of the gentlemen concerned in the matter, the writer can be impersonal too.) Some time ago, E 9 was in the Baltic, in the deeps of winter, where she used to be taken to her hunting grounds by an ice-breaker. Obviously a submarine cannot use her sensitive nose to smash heavy ice with, so the broad-beamed pushing chaperone comes along to see her clear of the thick harbor and shore ice. In the open sea apparently she is left to her own devices. In company of the ice-breaker, then, E 9 "proceeded" (neither in the Senior nor the Junior Service does any one officially "go" anywhere) to a "certain position."

Here—it is not stated in the book, but the Trade knows every aching, single detail of what is left out—she spent a certain time in testing arrangements and apparatus, which may or may not work properly when immersed in a mixture of block ice and dirty ice cream in a temperature well towards zero. This is a pleasant job, made the more delightful by the knowledge that if you slip off the superstructure the deadly Baltic chill will stop your heart long before even your heavy clothes can drown you. Hence (and this is not in the book either) the remark of the highly trained sailor man in these latitudes who, on being told by his superior officer in the execution of his duty to go to Hell, did insubordinately and enviously reply: "D'you think I'd be here if I could?" Whereby he caused the entire personnel, beginning with the commander, to say "Amen," or words to that effect. E 9 evidently made things work.

Next day she reports: "As circumstances were favorable decided to attempt to bag a destroyer." Her "certain position" must have been near a well-used destroyer run, for shortly afterwards she sees three of them, but too far off to attack, and later, as the light is failing, a fourth destroyer, towards which she maneuvers. "Depth-keeping," she notes, "very difficult owing to heavy swell." An observation balloon on a gusty day is almost as stable as a submarine "pumping" in a heavy swell, and since the Baltic is shallow, the submarine runs the chance of being let down with a whack on the bottom. Nonetheless, E 9 works her way to within 600 yards of the quarry; fires and waits just long enough to be sure that her torpedo is running straight, and that the destroyer is holding her course. Then she "dips to avoid detection." The rest is deadly simple: "At the correct moment after firing, 45 to 50 seconds, heard the unmistakable noise of torpedo detonating." Four minutes later she rose and "found destroyer had disappeared." Then, for reasons probably connected with other destroyers, who, too, may have heard that unmistakable sound, she goes to bed below in the chill dark till it is time to turn homewards. When she rose she met storm from the north and logged it accordingly. "Spray froze as it struck, and bridge became a mass of ice. Experienced considerable difficulty in keeping the conning-tower hatch free from ice. Found it necessary to keep a man continuously employed on this work. Bridge screen immovable, ice six inches thick on it. Telegraphs frozen." In this state she forges ahead till midnight, and any one who pleases can imagine the thoughts of the continuous employee scraping and hammering around the hatch, as well as the delight of his friends below when the ice slush spattered down the conning tower. At last she considered it "advisable to free the boat of ice, so went below."

In the Senior Service the two words "as requisite" cover everything that need not be talked about. E 9 next day "proceeded as requisite" through a series of snowstorms and recurring deposits of ice on the bridge till she got in touch with her friend the ice-breaker; and in her company ploughed and rooted her way back to the work we know. There is nothing to show that it was a close call for E 9, but somehow one has the idea that the ice-breaker did not arrive any too soon for E 9's comfort and progress. (But what happens in the Baltic when the ice-breaker does not arrive?)

That was in winter. In summer, quite the other way, E 9 had to go to bed by day very often under the long-lasting northern light when the Baltic is as smooth as a carpet, and one cannot get within a mile and a half of anything with eyes in its head without being put down. There was one time when E 9, evidently on information received, took up "a certain position" and reported the sea "glassy." She had to suffer in silence, while three heavily laden German ships went by; for an attack would have given away her position. Her reward came next day, when she sighted (the words run like Marryat's) "enemy squadron coming up fast from eastward, proceeding inshore of us." They were two heavy battleships with an escort of destroyers, and E 9 turned to attack. She does not say how she crept up in that smooth sea within a quarter of a mile of the leading ship, "a three-funnel ship, of either the *Deutschland* or *Braunschweig* class," but she managed it, and fired both bow torpedoes at her.

"Number one torpedo was seen and heard to strike her just before foremost funnel: smoke and debris appeared to go as high as masthead." That much E 9 saw before one of the guardian destroyers ran at her. "So," says she, "observing her I took my periscope off the battleship." This was excusable, as the destroyer was coming up with intent to kill and E 9 had to flood her tanks and get down quickly. Even so, the destroyer only just missed her, and she struck bottom in 43 feet. "But," says *E 9*, who, if she could not see, kept her ears open, "at the correct interval (the 45 or 50 seconds mentioned in the previous case) the second torpedo was heard to explode, though not actually seen." *E 9* came up twenty minutes later to make sure. The destroyer was waiting for her a couple of hundred yards away, and again *E 9* dipped for the life, but "just had time to see one large vessel approximately four or five miles away."

Putting courage aside, think for a moment of the mere drill of it all—that last dive for that attack on the chosen battleship; the eye at the periscope watching "Number one torpedo" get home; the rush of the vengeful destroyer; the instant orders for flooding everything; the swift descent which had to be arranged for with full knowledge of the shallow sea floors waiting below, and a guess at the course that might be taken by the seeking bow above, for assuming a destroyer to draw 10 feet and a submarine on the bottom to stand 25 feet to the top of her conning tower, there is not much clearance in 43 feet of salt water, especially if the boat jumps when she touches bottom. And through all these and half a hundred other simultaneous considerations, imagine the trained minds below, counting, as only torpedomen can count, the run of the merciless seconds that should tell when that second shot arrived. Then "at the correct interval" as laid down in the table of distances, the boom and the jar of the Number 2 torpedo, the relief, the exhaled breath and untightened lips; the impatient waiting for a second peep, and when that had been taken and the eye at the periscope had reported *one* heavy battleship in place of two on the waters, perhaps some floating debris, etc., while the destroyer sickled about at a venture overhead.

Certainly they give men rewards for doing such things, but what reward can there be in any gift of kings or peoples to match the enduring satisfaction of having done them, not alone, but with and through and by trusty and proven companions?

E 1, also a Baltic boat, her commander F. N. Laurence, had her experiences, too. She went out one summer day and late—too late—in the evening sighted three transports. The first she hit. While she was arranging for the second, the third inconsiderately tried to ram her before her sights were on. So it was necessary to go down at once and waste whole minutes of the precious scanting light. When she rose, the stricken ship was sinking and shortly afterwards blew up. The other two were patrolling nearby. It would have been a fair chance in daylight, but the darkness defeated her and she had to give up the attack.

It was *E 1* who during thick weather came across a squadron of battle cruisers and got in on a flanking ship—probably the *Moltke*. The destroyers were very much on the alert, and she had to dive at once to avoid one who only missed her by a few feet. Then the fog shut down and stopped further developments. Thus do time and chance come to every man.

The Trade has many stories, too, of watching patrols when a boat must see chance after chance go by under her nose and write— merely write—what she has seen. Naturally they do not appear in any accessible records. Nor, which is a pity, do the authorities release the records of glorious failures, when everything goes wrong; when torpedoes break surface and squatter like ducks; or arrive full square with a clang and burst of white water and—fail to explode; when the devil is in charge of all the motors, and clutches develop play that would scare a shore-going mechanic bald; when batteries begin to give off death instead of power, and atop of all, ice or wreckage of the strewn seas racks and wrenches the hull till the whole leaking bag of tricks limps home on six missing cylinders and one ditto propeller, *plus* the indomitable will of the red-eyed husky scare-crows in charge.

There might be worse things in this world for decent people to read than such records.

Coronel and the Falklands: Sweet Vengeance

Hector C. Bywater

W*hat drives men to do such things?*
The question is raised again and again throughout the annals of warfare. In the present instance, which concerns some extraordinary naval fighting in the early days of World War I, why would the British Admiral Cradock attack a German squadron which he knew with certainty to be overwhelmingly superior to the forces under his command? What made the captain of the Monmouth *refuse an opportunity to surrender when his ship could no longer reply to the guns of her adversary? And what made the sailors on the sinking cruiser* Nürnberg *defiantly wave a German ensign lashed to a staff as the freezing sea closed over them?*

In mortal combat, men will perform strange and seemingly superhuman acts. Hector C. Bywater, the British naval authority and prophet of the Pacific War, tells the story of these events.

"Coronel" is a word that will always conjure up memories both tragic and proud. On November 1, 1914, a British force under Admiral Sir Christopher Cradock was defeated off the Chilean port of that name by Admiral Count Spee, with the loss of the *Good Hope* and the *Monmouth* and all on board those ships, including the admiral himself. The German victory was due in part to a marked superiority in heavy guns and in part to the weather conditions, which were bad enough to render ineffective half the armament of the old and ill-designed British cruisers.

The *Scharnhorst* and *Gneisenau* each mounted eight 8.2-inch and six 5.9-inch guns. The *Good Hope* carried two 9.2-inch and sixteen 6-inch, while the *Monmouth* was armed with fourteen 6-inch. In both the British ships half the six-inch guns were mounted so near the waterline that they could not be worked in a seaway— and a very heavy sea was running at the time of the battle. Moreover, against such stoutly armored ships as the two *Scharnhorsts*, 6-inch gunfire availed little. Coronel, therefore, was essentially a heavy artillery duel, in which sixteen German 8.2-inch guns of modern type were opposed to two old British 9.2-inch guns, the total weight of metal fired at each discharge being 4,400 pounds from the German guns and only 700 lb. from the British. Given reasonably good markmanship—and no one has ever questioned the high standard of German naval gunnery—this six-to-one preponderance in weight of heavy shell was bound to be decisive.

Besides the *Good Hope* and *Monmouth,* Admiral Cradock had with his flag the light cruiser *Glasgow* and the armed liner *Otranto.* The *Glasgow* was a ship of 4,800 tons with a speed of 26 knots, completed in 1910. She carried a mixed armament of two 6-inch and ten 4-inch guns, with two torpedo tubes, and her complement was 376 officers and men. Her commanding officer was Captain John Luce.

With the German squadron were three light cruisers, *Dresden*, *Nürnberg*, and *Leipzig*. The *Dresden*, a sister ship to the *Emden*, weighed 3,650 tons, and her trial speed was 24½ knots. She mounted twelve 4.1-inch guns and two torpedo tubes. The *Nürnberg*, two years older and slightly smaller, was a 24-knot ship, carrying two 4.1-inch guns less than the *Dresden*. The *Leipzig* was nearly ten years old at the date of the Coronel action, her weight being 3,250 tons, her speed 23 knots, and her armament identical with that of the *Nürnberg*. In all three vessels the only armor protection was a 2-inch deck over the midship spaces, similar to the defensive system of the *Glasgow*.

November 1, 1914, found both squadrons off the Chilean coast in the latitude of Coronel. On the previous day the *Glasgow* had visited that port and there got wind of the *Leipzig*, which Admiral Cradock believed to be the only German ship in the neighborhood. News of the *Glasgow*'s visit was promptly radioed to Admiral Spee, who on his part had no suspicion of the presence of other British ships. Each squadron was, therefore, searching for what was thought to be a solitary unit of the other. At 2:30 P.M. on November I the *Glasgow* rejoined the squadron. It was blowing strong from the southeast and a heavy sea was running. Two hours later the *Glasgow* sighted smoke on the starboard bow and turned towards it to investigate. She was soon able to identify the *Scharnhorst*, *Gneisenau*, and a light cruiser, and reported them as such to Admiral Cradock.

He can have been under no illusion as to the odds now confronting him. Writes the official British historian:

> It is not without emotion that one contemplates the feelings of so fine an officer when suddenly he found himself face to face with the hopeless situation into which, against all his protests and better judgment, he clearly believed himself to have been forced. A cloud that can never be lifted has fallen on one of the most tragic moments in our naval history. All we can ever know is the silver lining. For whatever he thought and felt, Admiral Cradock did not flinch.

The German admiral, fully alive to the advantage on his side, determined to make the most of it. For more than two hours the opposing squadrons maneuvered without coming within gun range, for the Germans were waiting for sunset which, as the British squadron was on the western horizon, would leave it sharply silhouetted against the afterglow. The German ships, on the other hand, would then become mere smudges against a background of lowering night clouds.

At 7 P.M., when the lines were 12,500 yards apart, the Germans opened fire, which was promptly returned. In the conditions of light just described the British ships stood out as splendid targets in contrast to the German vessels, which were all but invisible. As was to be expected from their record, the *Scharnhorst* and *Gneisenau* shot with great accuracy. The former's third salvo destroyed the *Good Hope*'s forward 9.2-inch gun, and in three minutes the *Monmouth* was heavily on fire. So devastating was the German cannonade that the action may be said to have been decided in the first ten minutes, if not less.

Meanwhile, the *Glasgow* was receiving her full share of attention. By 7:10 she was being heavily fired on by the *Leipzig* and *Dresden*—the *Nürnberg* had not yet come into action—but the German 4.1-inch guns were less effective than their heavier metal and for half an hour the *Glasgow* remained practically untouched. Then she received her first and only serious hit. This was a 4.1-inch shell which burst on the water line and blew a hole about six feet square, but the explosion spent most of its force on a coal bunker and the seaworthiness of the cruiser was not seriously impaired. Altogether she was hit five times and had four men slightly wounded, yet she was under the fire of the *Dresden* and *Leipzig* for a full hour, and for ten minutes was a target for the infinitely deadlier guns of the *Gneisenau*. At least six hundred shots were discharged at her in the course of the action, a fact which renders her escape almost miraculous, though there is little doubt that her low freeboard and violent motion in the heavy seas made her a difficult target.

The *Glasgow*'s own gunners, firing from a reeling deck only eight feet above the water line, with spray continually obscuring their telescopes, did their best in difficult circumstances. The German ships at which they aimed were almost entirely hidden in the murk and only to be detected by the flash of their broadsides. Further, as the splash of the *Glasgow*'s shells could not be "spotted," fire control was impossible. In these circumstances it is not surprising that the German cruisers escaped damage.

The battle reached its climax at 7:14 P.M. Excepting the *Otranto*, which Admiral Cradock had ordered to keep out of range, all the British ships were still in action, though there is every reason to believe that by this time both the *Good Hope* and the *Monmouth* had received mortal injuries. Prior to this, the three British ships had been keeping excellent station, but now several full salvos struck the *Monmouth* and she sheered out to starboard, either because she was out of control or in an effort to throw off the enemy's aim. The *Glasgow*, however, kept her place astern of the *Good Hope*, a position which made her officers and men unwilling spectators of the tragedy that was being enacted ahead.

Shell after shell struck the British flagship, detonating in orange flashes against hull or upperworks, while the sea on either side continually spouted in geysers as other German salvos fell short of or over the target. The *Good Hope* was now ablaze in many places, and to the watchers in the *Glasgow* it seemed incredible that the flagship should still be able to keep under way and fight several of her guns when her decks and sides appeared to be glowing with heat. By this time the German ships were invisible. Their position could be detected only by the ripple of gun flashes, which were incessant.

At 7:45 the *Good Hope* perceptibly slowed down and turned out of line in the direction of the enemy, presumably in an attempt to attack them with torpedoes. But the maneuver was never completed, for a few minutes later a great explosion was observed just forward of the mainmast. Flames shot up to a height of two hundred feet, the sudden glare revealing a huge cloud of wreckage in which two lifeboats were clearly seen flying through the air. It was obvious that a magazine had exploded, probably blowing out the bottom of the ship and killing or stunning most of those on board, for thereafter the guns were silent and the ship gave no sign of life. Her actual sinking was not witnessed either from the *Glasgow* or the German squadron, but after 7:55 P.M. the glow of the numerous fires in the *Good Hope* was no longer visible and it is practically certain that she foundered at that time, with all hands.

The *Monmouth*, which was already down by the bow and listing badly to port, now became a target for the concentrated fire of the *Scharnhorst* and *Gneisenau*. The *Glasgow* closed toward her and made signals by flashing lamp, to which the *Monmouth* replied that she was trying to point her stern to the waves, as large quantities of water were entering forward. Meanwhile the German squadron was steadily approaching, and as the *Glasgow* could do nothing to assist her stricken consort and, by remaining on the scene, would invite certain destruction, her commanding officer, Captain Luce, had no alternative but to leave the *Monmouth* to her fate. He therefore worked up to full speed, and was soon out of sight of the enemy, whose searchlights were seen far astern vainly stabbing the night. Just before 9:15 numerous gun flashes were seen, and we know now that these denoted the passing of the hapless but indomitable British cruiser at the hands of the *Nürnberg*.

The last-named vessel had been too far astern of her squadron to take part in the main action, and when darkness fell, she was still many miles away from her flagship. Only the gun flashes gave her the position of her friends. When these ceased, she had nothing further to guide her. By now pale moonbeams occasionally pierced the cloud wrack, and by their dim light she suddenly came upon a large three-funnelled ship which was listing heavily to port, giving out great clouds of steam amidships.

Instantly identifying the stranger as the *Monmouth*, and realizing that with her heavy list she could not use her port guns, the *Nürnberg* approached on this side within very close range and opened rapid fire, aiming at the water line of the British ship which was, in fact, the unprotected underside of her hull. Thus every shell crashed into the *Monmouth*'s vitals, opening new gaps through which the sea poured in. Her end, therefore, was clearly a matter of minutes only, and realizing this the German ship ceased fire for several minutes to give the *Monmouth* an opportunity of surrendering. But such an act did not accord with British naval tradition, and when it was seen that the British colors were still flying, the *Nürnberg* reopened at point-blank range, her shells literally ripping the bottom out of the *Monmouth*. Under this frightful punishment her list rapidly increased, and in another minute she lay on her beam ends and then disappeared, her battle flags flying defiantly to the last.

Not a soul was saved, for the sea was much too rough to permit the *Nürnberg* to lower boats, and although the German ship remained on the scene for a few minutes longer, no survivors were sighted.

In the meantime the *Glasgow* was steaming south to warn the old battleship *Canopus*, which for several days had been plodding north at 13 knots, the best speed of which she was capable, to join Admiral Cradock. Frankly, he had not wanted her, for with her low speed and obsolete guns she promised to be more of a hindrance than a help, and most naval historians are satisfied that had she joined the squadron before the action of Coronel was fought she would have shared the fate of the *Good Hope* and the *Monmouth*. On November 2, the *Glasgow* got in touch by wireless with the old battleship and told her what had happened. Eventually both ships reached Port Stanley in the Falkland Islands, where they remained to coal and await further instructions.

On November 15, the *Glasgow* arrived at Rio de Janeiro, where thanks to the benevolent neutrality of the Brazilian authorities she was able to go into dock and have the damage to her hull repaired. It was while at Rio that Captain Luce received a confidential telegram acquainting him with the imminent arrival of the battle cruisers *Invincible* and *Inflexible*, under the command of Admiral Sturdee, at Abrolhos Rocks off the Brazilian coast, and ordering him to join the admiral there. When the *Glasgow* reached the rendezvous on

November 23, she found Rear Admiral Stoddart, with his flag in the *Carnarvon*, together with the other armored cruisers *Defence*, *Cornwall*, and *Kent*, her own sister ship *Bristol*, the armed liner *Orama*, and a whole fleet of colliers. Three days later the battle cruisers arrived, and conferences were held on board the *Invincible* to discuss the best way of catching the German squadron and avenging the defeat of Coronel.

The dramatic story of how Lord John Fisher, who had been appointed first sea lord only forty-eight hours before the disaster, took immediate and drastic steps to retrieve the situation has been told often. He at once detached the *Invincible* and *Inflexible* from the Grand Fleet, and had them brought to Devonport to refit and take in stores for a long voyage. Some delay threatened when the dockyard officials, on examining the *Invincible*, reported that she could not be made ready for sea until November 13. But Lord Fisher would have none of this. Both vessels, he insisted, must sail at latest on the eleventh, and if the work was not finished by that time a number of dockyard hands must sail with her and complete the job during the voyage.

Under this masterful urge all repairs were so speeded up that the squadron duly sailed on the afternoon of the eleventh, and after an uneventful voyage reached the Abrolhos Rocks on November 26. There Sturdee received revised orders from the Admiralty, instructing him to proceed with Admiral Stoddart to the Falklands and to use those islands as a base from which to carry out an intensive search for the German squadron, which was believed to be somewhere off the Chilean coast. He was told further that an Anglo–Japanese squadron, including the battle cruiser *Australia*, would reach the Galapagos Islands on December 2, after which it would steam south as far as Cape Horn if necessary, while at the same time a Japanese squadron would probably be moving eastwards from Fiji to the Marquesas Islands. Such was the impressive concentration of force which had been effected as a result of the Coronel disaster, and if, as seemed certain, Admiral Spee was still in the Pacific, there was little hope of his escaping the net which was closing around him from three different directions.

What his instructions were could only be surmised by the Admiralty, but it was inferred that he would either make for South Africa to create a diversion there, and incidentally bring aid and comfort to his countrymen who were fighting in German Southwest Africa, or would attempt to break through to Germany, possibly under cover of a sortie into the Atlantic by German battle cruisers.

We know now that he was under orders to return to Germany, though having regard to the immense distance from Cape Horn to the North Sea and the fact that during the latter part of his voyage he would be passing through waters closely patrolled by the British Navy, he must have realized the desperate character of his undertaking. But, in fact, the brief but brilliant war career of this German squadron was already nearing its close.

Admiral Sturdee sailed from the Abrolhos Rocks on November 28, steering for the Falklands. At the same time the German ships were heading for the same place, but encountering such heavy seas that their speed was sometimes reduced to five knots. This slow rate of progress due to bad weather was to have fateful results. Admiral Spee had decided on his own initiative to make a raid on the Falkland Islands, to destroy the wireless station and, if possible, capture, even if but temporarily, this southernmost outpost of the British Empire. Even though the military significance of such a coup might be negligible, he felt that it would be a severe blow to British prestige and therefore well worth the risks involved. Granting all that, it is nonetheless obvious that in deciding to break his voyage at the Falklands he committed a grave error of judgment. His only hope of breaking through to Germany lay in masking the movements of his squadron in secrecy for as long as possible, and above all, in giving a wide berth to British signalling stations.

Barely a month before, the German cruiser *Emden* had brought destruction upon herself by raiding the British cable station at the Cocos Islands, where the operators had been able to flash out a warning of her approach. Admiral Spee may not have known the circumstances which led to the destruction of the *Emden*, but he can hardly have failed to reckon with the probability that his arrival at the Falklands would be broadcast before he was able to put the wireless station out of action. It has since become known that at least one of his captains vainly attempted to dissuade the admiral from interfering with the Falklands.

Meanwhile, the inhabitants of this isolated colony, having heard on November 25 that the German force had rounded Cape Horn, were in daily expectation of an attack. Their only means of defense consisted of the old battleship *Canopus*, which had berthed herself on the mud at Port Stanley, the inner harbor, from which position her 12-inch turret guns commanded the approaches from either side. Further, a number of the ship's lighter guns were mounted in batteries ashore, where an observation station was also erected. As a final measure the entrance to Port William, the outer harbor, was defended by electric mines improvised out of oil drums. Despite these preparations it seemed only too probable that the colony would fall an easy prey to the expected invader, and it was therefore with profound relief that the inhabitants welcomed Admiral Sturdee's powerful squadron when it arrived off Port William on the morning of December 7.

It was the Admiral's intention to coal his ships without delay and leave again on the ninth to prosecute his search for the enemy in the Pacific. As coaling facilities were limited, the ships had to wait in line to fill their bunkers one after another. To further complicate matters, the *Cornwall* found it necessary to open up one engine for repairs. All through the day and night the work went on, but at dawn on December 8 only half the ships had coaled, and the squadron as a whole was by no means ready for sea.

This was the position when at 7:50 A.M. the signalmen from the *Canopus*'s shore station reported the approach of two strange warships from the southward. They proved to be the *Gneisenau* and the *Nürnberg*, which had been despatched by Admiral Spee to reconnoiter the islands and bombard the wireless station. It has often been argued since that had the German admiral pressed forward with his whole squadron he might have caught the British ships in a trap and inflicted heavy damage by concentrating his fire on the channel through which they must pass out of Port William. He, however, could not know the strength of the British force, and to have rushed, as it were, blindfold into action in these circumstances would have been culpably rash. Moreover, an incident now occurred that must have confused the Germans and left them in doubt as to what resistance they might encounter.

When the *Gneisenau* and *Nürnberg* had approached to within 11,000 yards, the *Canopus* fired both of her forward 12-inch guns. The shots pitched short, but the enemy ships, obviously taken by surprise, promptly turned away and steered to the southeast, followed by another salvo from the *Canopus*, which fell less than 200 yards astern. Apparently realizing that he was now out of range, the captain of the *Gneisenau* followed the coast at a discreet distance until he came within sight of Port William, where the many columns of smoke betrayed the presence of what was evidently a large number of ships. A few moments later an officer in the foretop, staring hard through his binoculars, discerned amidst the smoke what he took to be tripod masts, which at that date were carried almost exclusively by dreadnought battleships and battle cruisers. His report caused consternation on the bridge. Instantly realizing the danger, the captain turned sharply away and steamed off at full speed to join the rest of the squadron, signalling the ominous news to Spee as he went. On receiving the message, the German admiral acted with equal promptness. It was possible, of course, that the observers in the *Gneisenau* had been misled, and that the supposed tripod masts were shear legs or some other dockyard fittings ashore, but in the circumstances it would be madness to explore any further.

Consequently, as soon as the *Gneisenau* and *Nürnberg* rejoined him, Spee led his squadron southeast at its best speed. In the meantime the British sailors had worked furiously to get their ships ready for sea, and by ten o'clock the *Inflexible* and *Invincible* were moving out of the harbor, preceded or followed by the other vessels. It was one of those rare occasions during the First World War when the elements smiled on British arms, for after a long period of stormy weather December 8 had dawned as an almost perfect day, with blue skies, calm sea, and remarkably high visibility. As the squadron emerged from harbor the German ships, although at least fourteen miles away to the southeast with their hulls below the horizon, were easily visible by their masts. Admiral Sturdee, therefore, hoisted the signal "General Chase," and his ships settled down to a stern pursuit of the enemy who only five weeks previously had triumphed over the gallant Cradock at Coronel.

Volumes of black smoke gushing from the funnels of the battle cruisers bore witness to the manful efforts of the stokers, but as the murky clouds were interfering with vision Sturdee slightly reduced his speed and ordered the *Glasgow*, which was scouting ahead, to increase her distance from the flagship. The squadron was now in a somewhat ragged formation, for the old cruisers *Carnarvon* and *Cornwall* could not maintain the pace, and the latter soon signalled that 19 knots was her best speed. Although the presence of these two ships was not vitally necessary, since the battle cruisers alone had an immense all-around superiority over the enemy, Admiral Sturdee with characteristic chivalry slowed down to 20 knots to give them an opportunity of taking part in the impending action. He was the better able to do this because, in spite of his reduced speed, he was steadily gaining on the enemy, who according to a report from the *Glasgow* was steaming at not more than 15 knots.

The general position at about 11:30 A.M. was that the *Invincible* and *Inflexible* were steaming abreast at 20 knots, with the *Glasgow* some three miles ahead on the *Invincible*'s port bow, and the *Kent*, *Cornwall*, and *Carnarvon* astern of the *Inflexible* in that order. It will thus be seen that Sturdee had with him only a single light cruiser, the *Glasgow*, though three vessels of this type were with the German squadron. The *Bristol*, which thanks to a superhuman effort by her engineering staff had been able to get her machinery into working order and was now well outside the harbor, notified Sturdee that three strange ships had been sighted off Port Pleasant. While Sturdee believed them to be colliers which had accompanied Spee on his voyage around the Horn, the possibility of their being transports carrying German reservists from South American ports who were to garrison the Falklands after the islands had been captured could not be ignored. He therefore ordered the *Bristol* to chase the strange ships, instructions which prevented her from taking any part in the main action.

Except for certain alterations in course to conform with those made by the enemy, the pursuit continued uneventfully until nearly 1 P.M. Meanwhile the crews of the British ships had been piped to dinner, in accordance with the ancient and well-proven tradition that men fight best on full stomachs. Shortly after twelve noon Sturdee could see from the bridge of the *Invincible* that the enemy squadron was altering to starboard and apparently changing formation, a movement which might indicate an intention to scatter. He decided therefore that it was time to bring matters to a head, and as the *Carnarvon* was still lagging far astern he had no option but to leave her behind. He signalled down for full speed, and at 12:50 P.M. the battle cruisers were doing 25 knots, presenting a grand if awe-inspiring spectacle as they rushed through the water with dense smoke streaming from their funnels, their bows throwing up great waves and their wakes a tumbling mass of foam.

The enemy was now being rapidly overhauled and his rearmost ship, the *Leipzig*, whose boilers were in bad condition, was dropping so far astern that at 12:51 she was within 16,000 yards of the *Inflexible*. As Sturdee had signalled permission previously, the *Inflexible* trained her 12-inch guns on the *Leipzig* and fired a few ranging shots. These went wide, but as the range was closing every minute the British gunners were soon on the mark and great waterspouts arose ahead and astern of the small German cruiser, occasionally blotting her out of sight. Since at any moment she might receive her death blow, Spee, realizing her peril, promptly made a decision which as he well knew must seal his own fate.

He signalled his three light cruisers to scatter—"Proceed independently"—and try to escape, while he himself together with the *Gneisenau* held on to face the now inevitable combat. His decision must have been inspired by the reflection that the survival of these three small ships as potential commerce raiders was of more importance to Germany than the safety of his flagship and her immediate consort. It was a gesture entirely in keeping with what we know of this most gallant and able German leader, whose whole career, and not least his end, did honor to his country and her naval service.

But unfortunately for Spee this move had been foreseen by Sturdee and provided for in his battle orders. When, therefore, the *Dresden, Nürnberg,* and *Leipzig* were seen to detach themselves from the squadron and break away to the southward, the *Glasgow, Kent,* and *Cornwall* immediately turned in pursuit, leaving the battle cruisers to attend to the German armored ships.

At 1:20 P.M., when the range was down to about 14,000 yards, the British ships opened fire in earnest, the *Invincible* taking the *Gneisenau* as her target, and the *Inflexible* ranging on the *Scharnhorst.* Ten miles astern, Admiral Stoddart in the *Carnarvon* was doing his utmost to get into action by cutting corners, but his chance was yet to come.

At first the British gunners were seriously hampered both by the smoke of their own ships and that of the Germans, and for the first hour very few hits were made. The *Invincible* herself had received one hit when, shortly after 2 P.M., the range opened to nine miles and both sides ceased fire. With a view to renewing the action Sturdee turned in nearer to the enemy, who by this time was invisible in the smoke. When Spee came into sight again he was found to have turned sharp to starboard and to be steaming at full speed after his light cruisers. Once more, therefore, Sturdee worked up to full speed and by 2:50 P.M. he was again within range. Fire was opened with full salvos and drew an immediate reply from the Germans, who soon brought their secondary 5.9-inch batteries into action. Between 3 P.M. and 3:15 the combat reached its decisive stage.

The Germans were firing with the utmost rapidity, although those shells that struck the British ships had little effect, whereas the British twelve-inch projectiles were taking a heavy toll. Within a few minutes the *Gneisenau* was listing so badly to starboard that her secondary armament could not be used. The *Scharnhorst* was in a still worse plight; her third funnel had disappeared, fires were raging in several places, and for minutes on end she was almost hidden by the smoke from shell bursts and the fires burning in her interior. Even from the *Invincible,* seven miles away, the dull red glow of these fires could be plainly seen. The end came at 4:17 when the German flagship heeled over to starboard and sank with her flag still flying, taking with her Spee and every other soul on board, for with the *Gneisenau* still afloat and firing gamely it was impossible for the British ships to slow down for rescue work.

The *Gneisenau* herself continued the unequal action for nearly an hour and a half longer, during which she was at times under the fire not only of the *Invincible* and *Inflexible* but of the *Carnarvon* as well, the numerous alterations of course during the action and the reduced speed at which it was fought having at last enabled this ship to get within range. The *Gneisenau* sank at approximately 5:30 P.M. after an heroic resistance which the victors were the first to acknowledge. At least three-quarters of her complement of 850 had been killed or wounded. The British ships succeeded in picking up about two hundred survivors, but as the water was only a few degrees above freezing point many of the shipwrecked men succumbed to shock and were buried with full military honors.

Let us turn now to the fate of the three light cruisers, for whose sake Spee had sacrificed himself. To those on board at least two of these ships the prospects of escape must have seemed good, since the *Dresden* could steam considerably faster than her nominal 24 knots and the *Nürnberg* had on occasion proved capable of travelling at 24 knots. On the other hand, the *Leipzig* had become something of a lame duck through boiler trouble, and was not likely to average more than 20 knots on a protracted run. Of the British ships the *Glasgow*, with her 25 knots, was the swiftest. Both the *Cornwall* and the *Kent* could reach 23 knots on paper, but the last-named was notorious as a poor steamer whose machinery had a habit of giving trouble at awkward moments.

Everything depended on whether the British ships could draw within range of their quarry, for once this happened the issue would not be in doubt, thanks to the overwhelming weight of their fire as compared with that of the German cruisers. The *Cornwall* and *Kent* each mounted fourteen 6-inch guns behind armor protection, and even the *Glasgow* carried two of these relatively powerful weapons, to which none of the German ships could oppose anything heavier than 4.1-inch guns.

As we have seen, it was 1:25 P.M. when the three German light cruisers, in obedience to Spee's self-sacrificing signal, detached themselves from his flag and steered out into the ocean on divergent courses. At this time they were at least ten miles ahead of their foremost pursuer, the *Glasgow*, but it soon became evident that the British ships, not excluding the supposedly sluggish *Kent*, had a knot or two up their sleeves. The *Glasgow* was surprising her own people by racing through the water at 27 knots, while the *Kent*, as if determined to challenge her traducers, was actually bowling along at 24 knots, a speed she had rarely, if ever, attained before. At 2:53 P.M., the *Glasgow* opened fire on the *Leipzig* with her bow 6-inch gun at 12,000 yards, but apparently no hits were registered.

As the range shortened both the *Leipzig* and the *Nürnberg* replied with their 4.1-inch guns. They proved to have a greater range than the 4.1-inch secondary armament of the British ship, which soon found herself steaming through a forest of shell splashes. Captain Luce, therefore, opened the range by turning to starboard, whereupon the German ships ceased fire and again steered south. In this opening phase of the light cruiser action the *Glasgow* had been hit twice and suffered a few casualties. She herself had put a 6-inch shell into the after part of the *Leipzig*, where a fire broke out.

The *Leipzig*'s alteration of course to bring her full broadside to bear caused her to lose ground, and this enabled the two armored cruisers to creep up foot by foot until, shortly after 4 P.M., their range-finders began to record figures which were within the maximum reach of their guns. It had already been decided between the captains that the *Cornwall* would register on the *Leipzig* while the *Kent* attended to the *Nürnberg*, and as the *Glasgow* was nearer to the *Leipzig* she also made that ship her target. No sooner had firing begun than the *Nürnberg* broke away from her consort and made off to the eastward, with the *Kent* in hot pursuit.

For a time the *Cornwall*'s 6-inch guns, which were of an old model, were unable to reach the mark, but the *Glasgow* was more fortunate, and during the next fifty minutes she fought a fierce duel with the *Leipzig*. Both the 6-inch and 4-inch armament of the British light cruiser were now fully engaged and repeatedly hitting the enemy, who in reply sent two shells through the *Glasgow*'s foretop and a third into the foremast itself. The *Leipzig*'s fire was very rapid, but her gunners appear to have overestimated the range since most of the salvos flew well over the *Glasgow*. At this juncture the *Cornwall* was able for the first time to open an effective fire, and so good was her shooting that the *Leipzig* was straddled at almost every broadside.

The torpedo officer of the *Leipzig*, who was one of the few survivors, has vividly described scenes on board when the ship was under the concentrated fire of the *Cornwall* and the *Glasgow*. A lyddite shell burst full on Number 1 starboard gun, blowing several of the crew to pieces and setting fire to the deck on which lay the ready ammunition, but the flames were extinguished before they reached the powder. All this time the speed of the German ship had been gradually falling, for the boilers were in a bad way and long overdue for repair. She was making at most 20 knots and was thus being steadily overhauled by the *Cornwall*.

As for the *Glasgow*, her much greater speed gave her a freedom of movement of which she took full advantage. Undismayed by the overwhelming odds against her, the *Leipzig* stood up valiantly to the *Cornwall* and succeeded in hitting her nearly a dozen times in a few minutes, though the majority of the shells were stopped by armor and caused only superficial damage. Owing to a hit on the waterline, which flooded one of the boiler rooms, the German ship's speed now dropped to 18 knots. Shell after shell crashed into her, spreading death and destruction everywhere and starting new fires which could not be put out, as hoses and water mains were riddled with splinters.

By now so many officers and men had fallen that all the dressing stations were full, and dozens of badly wounded men lay on the stokers' halfdeck. Still the gallant ship's company did not abandon all hope. If only the *Leipzig* could keep afloat until nightfall and maintain even a moderate speed, she might still shake off her pursuers and find sanctuary in the nearest South American port. But this was not to be. Shortly after 6 P.M. it was reported to the captain that all the ammunition in the after magazines had been expended and that no more than 200 rounds remained in the ship. Shells were therefore passed by hand from the forward to the after guns. All orders were now communicated by writing pad, for the continual explosion of shells had rendered everybody on deck temporarily deaf.

So the hopeless struggle went on until a few minutes past seven, when the *Leipzig* fired her last shell. She was now doing only 15 knots, and as the range was down to less than 7,500 yards almost every salvo from the British ships took effect. Wreathed in smoke and flame, the dying ship still held on her course without evincing any sign of surrender, so that there was nothing for it but to keep her under fire.

We know now that she was still showing her teeth, for between 7 P.M. and 7:15 she fired three torpedoes from her starboard tube, the first two aimed at the *Cornwall* and the third at the *Glasgow*. All three missed, however, and were not even sighted from the British ships.

His last weapon having failed, the German captain at 7:20 gave the order: "Sink the ship. All hands on deck." In obedience to this, the seacocks were opened and men began to stream up from below. Most of them were from the engine and boiler rooms, for the greater part of the deck personnel had already fallen. Many of the survivors as well as the dead and wounded were stained yellow with the gases given off by exploding lyddite. By now the British ships had ceased fire. Both captains were anxious to avoid unnecessary bloodshed, but at the same time they could not risk losing sight of the enemy in the darkness that would soon descend on the sea.

The *Glasgow* made repeated signals to the *Leipzig* by flashlamp in the international Morse code, asking: "Do you surrender? Am anxious to save life." This signal was made again and again for over twenty minutes before more drastic action was taken. According to one of the few officers saved from the *Leipzig*, no one on board could read the signal, though this is difficult to credit. In any case no reply whatever was made, and at length the British captain felt compelled to reopen fire.

At this close range the shells took a frightful toll, particularly as the *Leipzig*'s survivors had crowded amidships, away from the heat of the fires raging at bow and stern. Whole groups were swept away, and in all probability the casualties inflicted in those few minutes were heavier than the total sustained earlier in the action. At length someone had the wit to burn two green flares, which the British ships accepted as a token of surrender and at once ceased fire. Boats were lowered as quickly as possible and approached to within 40 yards of the burning ship. Between 40 and 50 men, probably all that remained alive or able to move, were seen to leap overboard. Two minutes later the *Leipzig* turned gently on her side and disappeared in a cloud of smoke and steam.

The British boats did their utmost, but only five officers and thirteen men were alive when they were hauled on board, the rest having drowned in the rising sea or succumbed to the icy chill of the water. Among those lost was the gallant captain who had fought his ship with superb valor and had cheered his men on to the very end.

To this day German historians are inclined to write bitterly of the British action in reopening fire long after the *Leipzig* had discharged her last shot and was obviously a beaten ship. As to this, it can only be repeated that the Germans were given a respite of nearly half an hour, during which it would surely have been possible to make some form of signal denoting that resistance was at an end. This could have been done without incurring any shadow of dishonor or the risk of letting the ship fall into enemy hands, since the opening of the seacocks and the fires blazing below deck rendered it certain that the *Leipzig* could not be kept afloat.

If, as is conceivable, unyielding pride forbade the making of such a signal, then it is clearly unjust to blame the British captains for forcing the issue by gunfire. In the British ships there was nothing but admiration for the magnificent fight which the enemy had made, and the rescued officers and men, it is hardly necessary to add, were treated with the utmost consideration.

It is now time to return to the *Nürnberg*, which shortly after 4:30 P.M. had broken away to the eastward with the *Kent* in hot pursuit. Since then nothing had been heard from the *Kent* in spite of repeated wireless calls from other British ships, and for a time some anxiety was felt as to her fate. It came out later that her wireless room had been wrecked by a shell, so that she had to remain silent until visual contact was regained with the squadron.

When the chase began those on board the *Kent* had no great hope of catching their prey, which had gained a start of seven miles and appeared to be steaming well. The *Kent* herself had already been under full power for eight hours and her engineers were wondering how much longer their boilers and machinery, notorious for giving trouble, would stand the strain. A further cause for anxiety lay in the shortage of coal, for the alarm had sounded at Port William before the *Kent* had had time to replenish her bunkers. It was therefore clear that the *Kent* would burn her last ton of coal long before the chase was over, leaving her a helpless log on the sea.

But the excitement of pursuit left no time for such somber thoughts. The stokers, many of whom were naval reservists who had joined the ship little more than two months before, worked with superhuman energy, while wrecking parties with axes and crowbars stripped away all the woodwork they could find in the ship, including furniture and even boats, and sent it below to feed the furnaces. In the boiler rooms the needles of the pressure gauges gradually crept up to the red danger mark, where they remained, while the engines, responding to this unaccustomed pressure, increased their revolutions until the ship was making something over 24 knots, the highest speed she had ever achieved since her completion eleven years previously.

At 5 P.M. she was perceptibly gaining on the chase, for the range was down to 11,500 yards; but owing to a mist which had now descended the German ship was little more than a blur, and presented a hopeless target for the old-type guns mounted in the

Kent. It was now that the *Nürnberg* opened fire with her stern guns, which in spite of her smaller caliber considerably outranged those of her opponent. In any case accurate shooting at this range would have been impossible due to the excessive vibration of the *Kent*'s engines which rendered the range-finders practically useless.

From the first, the *Nürnberg*'s fire was rapid and accurate. Every salvo fell close to the *Kent*, but was so closely bunched that only one or two shells hit the ship. The *Kent* on her part fired occasional shots from the foremost 6-inch turret, and in spite of range-finding difficulties caused by vibration she succeeded in driving two shells home, one of which burst in the *Nürnberg*'s after steering flat below the waterline and killed all but one of the men assembled there.

It was, however, bad luck rather than the quality of the *Kent*'s gunnery at this stage that led to the undoing of the German ship. Her boilers were in poor condition, and shortly after the action began two of them burst, thereby reducing the speed of the ship to nineteen knots. Consequently the *Kent* was now coming up very fast, and at 5:45 P.M. was little more than 6,000 yards astern. Realizing that action could no longer be avoided, the *Nürnberg* starboarded her helm to bring her port broadside to bear, a movement to which the *Kent* immediately conformed.

The engagement that now ensued was exceedingly fierce, for Captain Allen of the *Kent* was determined to finish off the enemy as quickly as possible, and thanks to his superior speed he was able to maintain a position before the *Nürnberg*'s beam where he was safe from torpedo attack. He ordered rapid fire with lyddite shell, and ignoring the hail of projectiles which beat about his ship he steered a converging course which, in a quarter of an hour, brought him within 3,000 yards of the target. At this range the *Nürnberg* was literally smothered with shell, and to onlookers in the British ship she seemed to be melting away under the torrent of fire. The top mast collapsed across the bridge, two funnels leaned drunkenly over to starboard, upperworks assumed the semblance of scrap iron, and great fires broke out in several places. Under this merciless punishment she turned sharply away, but although this move momentarily threw off the British gunners' aim, they speedily found the mark again and continued to blast the doomed cruiser with full salvos of high explosives.

Having regard to the close range at which the action was fought it was inevitable that the *Kent* herself should sustain many hits, and in fact she was struck by about 35 shells, most of which were deflected by her armor. The only serious hit was from a shell that entered one of the 6-inches gun casemates, splinters from which killed one man and wounded nine. The explosion set fire to some cordite cartridges which had just come up the ammunition hoist, and for several seconds the ship was in grave danger. But disaster was averted by the presence of mind of Sergeant Mayes, who with great courage kicked and thrust the burning powder away, and closed the hatch over the hoist, thus cutting off access to the magazine below. A second shell burst in the wireless room and destroyed the transmitting instrument, though the receiver was undamaged.

Shortly after 6 P.M. the *Nürnberg* was firing only two guns of her port battery, and her speed was dropping every minute. This enabled the *Kent* to shoot ahead and cross her bow, a maneuver which the *Nürnberg* tried to counter by turning to port and bringing her starboard battery to bear. This, however, was a most ill-judged move, for at the moment when she came bow on to the *Kent* the latter's starboard guns thundered in unison, raking the unfortunate cruiser fore and aft. Two 6-inch shells crashed into her forecastle, wiping out the bow guns and their crews, while others ploughed deep into the vitals of the ship, and exploded with devastating force far below deck. This raking fire proved decisive, for the battered cruiser now lost way and lay almost motionless on the water, a shattered wreck whose guns were silent.

The whole forepart of the ship was glowing with the heat of internal fires, and for some minutes not a single man could be seen on deck. It was now 6:45 P.M., and what with the bad light and the clouds of smoke from the burning ship it was impossible to see whether she had surrendered by hauling down her colors. To satisfy himself on this point Captain Allen closed the range to little more than three thousand yards, only to observe that the *Nürnberg*'s ensign was still fluttering in the breeze. Being reluctant to cause further suffering, he held his fire for another ten minutes in the hope that the *Nürnberg* would strike her colors, but as this did not happen he had no choice but to open on her again. It needed only a few salvos to end the business, for a few minutes before seven o'clock the flag was lowered in token of submission, after a fight as gallant as any recorded in naval history.

The *Kent* at once prepared for rescue work, and the only two boats that were seaworthy were promptly lowered. But they were leaking badly, and could only be kept afloat by constant bailing. Before they could reach the *Nürnberg* she heeled over to starboard and sank quietly, under the glare of a searchlight from the *Kent*, which revealed a group of German sailors standing right aft and waving a German ensign lashed to a staff. They stood there still waving the colors till the cold sea closed over them, leaving on the minds of the British spectators an indelible impression of the courage that is faithful unto death.

In view of the appalling cannonade to which she had been exposed for an hour and a half, it is doubtful whether more than a handful of the *Nürnberg*'s company were still alive when she foundered. The *Kent*'s boats continued to search for survivors till 9 P.M. by which time it was quite dark. A number of corpses were found floating, but only seven men were picked up alive, and some of these had been viciously attacked by great albatrosses which swooped down soon after the *Nürnberg* disappeared.

The *Kent* emerged from this hard-fought action practically undamaged and with only 16 casualties, including 4 dead. There is no doubt that she owed her immunity to her armor protection, but for which the hurricane of German shell must have proved very destructive. The chase had taken her nearly 150 miles to the southeastward of the Falklands, and as she was no longer able to transmit by wireless, the rest of the squadron remained in ignorance of her fate until she steamed into Port Stanley some 20 hours later.

It will be recalled that shortly after the British flagship had left Port Stanley in pursuit of the German squadron, Sturdee was informed by signal that three strange ships, "probably transports or colliers," had been sighted off Port Pleasant. The British admiral at once directed the *Bristol* and the armed liner *Macedonia* to "destroy the transports." Consequently the *Bristol*, which had hurriedly completed her machinery repairs and was now catching up with the rest of the squadron, at once altered course and made off at high speed to the southeastward, where the German auxiliary ships had last been observed. They were soon sighted and proved to be the *Seydlitz*, *Santa Isabel*, and *Baden*, the former with a mixed cargo of supplies for the German squadron and the two latter ships with full loads of coal.

The *Seydlitz*, having a good turn of speed, managed to escape, but the *Baden* and *Santa Isabel* were soon overhauled and compelled to heave to by shots across their bows. It is noteworthy that in neither case did the crew attempt to scuttle their vessel to avoid capture. When boarded by boats from the British ships it was at once evident that they were most valuable prizes, filled as they were with thousands of tons of excellent coal. This notwithstanding, the captain of the *Bristol* considered himself bound to give literal effect to Sturdee's orders—though these had been issued in misapprehension of the character of the two vessels—and they were therefore sunk by gunfire after the crews had been removed. It is not surprising that this needless sacrifice subsequently gave rise to strong criticism in the squadron. The *Seydlitz* had disappeared into the blue and was not heard of for a week, when it became known that she had entered the Gulf of San Matias and had there been interned by the Chilean authorities.

From the British point of view, the one blemish on an otherwise complete and decisive victory was the escape of the *Dresden*. Several commentators on the action maintain that the *Glasgow* should have concentrated on the pursuit of this ship, leaving the *Leipzig* and *Nürnberg* to be dealt with by British armored cruisers. This argument, however, assumes that the *Cornwall* would have been able, by her own unaided efforts, to overhaul the *Leipzig* and bring her to action, a supposition not entirely warranted by the facts. On a general review of the situation as it presented itself on the morning of December 8, it is difficult to resist the conclusion that the British dispositions were the best that could be made. The *Dresden* owed her escape on the one hand to her high speed, and on the other to Sturdee's shortage of fast light cruisers, and for neither factor could the British admiral be held responsible. The escape had unfortunate results, in that it diverted to her pursuit a number of ships which were sorely needed elsewhere, but except for this it had no direct effect on the further course of the naval campaign. The subsequent adventures of the *Dresden* make an interesting story which can only be briefly summarized here.

Three days after the battle she put into Punta Arenas in the Strait of Magellan, and having coaled there put to sea again only a few hours before the *Bristol* arrived at the same port. For the next three months she played hide and seek with British ships in Chilean waters, and eventually dropped anchor at Juan Fernandez. There, on March 14, 1915, she was found by her old enemies, the *Kent* and *Glasgow*, who were accompanied by the armed liner *Orama*. Although the German ship was in neutral waters it was evident that she had not been interned, and equally clear that the local Chilean authorities, represented by the lighthouse keeper in Cumberland Bay, had no means of controlling her actions. Further, it was notorious that during her three months of freedom she had consistently violated Chilean neutrality, and although two wrongs do not make a right the British captains had no difficulty in presenting a good case for the action they now took.

When Captain Luce of the *Glasgow* caught sight of the *Dresden* he found smoke pouring from her funnels, as though she were about to make a dash for freedom. This could not be tolerated, so without hesitation he opened fire at 8,400 yards and hit her hard with his first salvo. His second broadside also went home, and just then the *Kent* also joined in. Although the *Dresden* promptly replied, she was overwhelmed almost from the start, and within three minutes her guns fell silent.

The evidence as to what now happened is conflicting. British eyewitnesses assert that she hauled down her colors and hoisted the white flag, while the *Dresden*'s commanding officer, Captain Lüdecke, stated in his report that his colors were shot away and rehoisted. In view of the stubborn resistance offered by other German ships when faced with heavy odds, no one will imagine that the *Dresden* did not make a gallant fight of it, or that her officers in any way fell short of the standard of courage and devotion established by their comrades elsewhere. What is beyond dispute is that the *Dresden*, which had suffered numerous casualties under the British fire, was blown up by order of her captain. Subsequently the British Government made full amends to Chile for the technical breach of neutrality.

CHAPTER 8

Jutland: Blind Man's Bluff

John Richard Hale

The Battle of Jutland in May 1916 was the last major two-dimensional fleet action. Submarines, although greatly feared by both the Germans and the British, played no role in the actual fighting, and the contributions made by airships were negligible.

But that did not make it simple. The Battle of Jutland was, in fact, the stupendous clash of 111 German warships manned by 45,000 officers and men against 150 British vessels with crews totalling 60,000. Each of the battleships and battle cruisers in action had more destructive capacity than a squadron of the Russian or Japanese capital ships that took part in the Battle of Tsushima only eleven years before.

Furthermore, neither the British commander, Admiral Sir John Jellicoe, nor his adversary, Admiral Reinhard Scheer, could really see what he was doing. In the fog and haze of a late summer afternoon, it was a game of blind man's bluff, ruled as much by serendipity as by strategy.

The British naval expert John Richard Hale describes the encounter as if he had been there, and—for all we know about his mysterious identity—maybe he was!

From the outset of the First World War, Englishmen had looked forward with patriotic and confident hope to a tremendous naval battle that might well be a rival to Trafalgar in its complete destruction of the enemy fleet and in its decisive results. And, in Germany as well as in England, there was a general expectation that in the earliest stage of the war the British "Grand Fleet" and the German "High Seas Fleet" would meet in full force and cleared for action in the North Sea. But nearly two years went by before this trial of strength came. For the German Admiralty had decided on a waiting policy. The main body of the fleet was to be kept at its bases behind the minefields of the Frisian coast, with Heligoland as its fortified outpost. Several "Super-Dreadnoughts" building in the shipyards would be completed, while a maritime guerilla warfare of torpedo craft, submarines, and mine layers would reduce the numbers of the British fleet, and attacks were to be made on the nearer British trade routes. Some British naval units, mostly light craft or old ships watching the Flanders coast, were sunk by mines and torpedoes, but new additions were made to the Royal Navy, and in the first months of the war British squadrons inflicted serious loss on the patrols of the enemy's fleet by daring raids into the German coast waters. As the war went on, submarine warfare against British commerce began on a limited scale, and German submarines appeared in the Mediterranean. But the High Seas Fleet still confined its activities to hurried bombardments of the English coast towns and operations in the Baltic by a detachment sent through the Kiel Canal. It was not till 1916 that a more enterprising policy was adopted in the North Sea upon Admiral Reinhard Scheer's taking over the command of the fleet.

The British Grand Fleet, besides keeping up a continual patrol of the waters between Scotland and Norway to maintain the blockade of Germany, and prevent commerce raiders running out into the Atlantic, had made repeated "sweeps" southward in the North Sea in the hope of the German fleet's coming out to risk an encounter. So far as one can gather from Admiral Scheer's memoirs his policy was to venture on cruiser sorties into the open sea, in the hope of drawing his opponents into prepared traps of submarines and newly laid minefields, and also to engage, if opportunity offered, not in a great battle fought out to the end, but in an engagement in which he might be able to bring a superior force into action against a detachment of Admiral Sir John Jellicoe's huge armada.

In April 1916, he showed a first sign of activity by sending his battle cruisers to bombard Lowestoft and Yarmouth. In May he planned an operation in the North Sea for the whole fleet. All available submarines were to be sent out to cruise off the British naval bases and ports from Scapa Flow to the Humber. They were to watch any British movements, and seize any opportunity of attacking British ships and squadrons as they came out. At the end of May, the German squadron of battle cruisers under Admiral Hipper was to start for the entrance of the Skagerrak (the strait between Jutland and Norway) and cruise in sight of the Norwegian coast, capturing any British shipping on the trade route to the Baltic. Admiral Scheer would follow with the main body of the fleet, keeping some 40 miles south of his cruisers. Hipper's appearance on the Norwegian coast was expected to lure out some large detachment of the British fleet, and Scheer counted on bringing off an encounter with his line of retreat to his base clear, in case he had to meet superior forces.

Thanks to the capture of a German signal book, a staff of experts highly skilled in deciphering coded messages, and the interception of German wireless, the Admiralty at Whitehall, though it did not secure complete information, picked up enough to be sure that the enemy was preparing for some exceptional activity in the North Sea about the end of May. It was rather a critical time. Plans were already being elaborated for a reorganization and redistribution of the Grand Fleet, for which some new units were lately available, and these changes were in progress and preparation when after the April raid on the east coast the British Government announced that steps were being taken to make such enterprises more difficult for the enemy. A feature of the new plans was to be that the Forth and the Humber were to become important naval bases. Admiral David Beatty's battle-cruiser squadron, reinforced with Admiral Thomas's 5th Battle Squadron (Dreadnoughts of the *Queen Elizabeth* type), was already in the Forth. But the main body of the Grand Fleet was still at Scapa Flow, with a battle squadron in Moray Firth. The 3rd Battle Squadron with a cruiser squadron was at the mouth of the Thames.

On the afternoon of May 30 the Admiralty was so convinced that the enemy was about to make an important move, that orders were sent to Admiral Jellicoe to take the Grand Fleet out to sea, to a position already selected to meet such an emergency. The Grand Fleet, picking up on the way the battle squadron from Moray Firth, was to proceed to a point north of the Dogger Bank and west of the opening of the Skagerrak. Beatty's force from the Forth was to steam eastward to a position northwest of the Dogger Bank, and then join the Grand Fleet early in the afternoon of the thirty-first. All these forces were at sea by midnight on the thirtieth.

The British and German fleets were thus converging on May 31 towards the waters west of the Skagerrak, and the result was the great battle of the naval war, known in England as the Battle of Jutland, in Germany as the Battle of the Skagerrak.

The battle has been the subject of a whole library of books, and numbers of shorter studies in the form of articles in popular and professional periodicals; and also of much acute controversy. All that can be done here is to outline its main course and select from the narratives of those who took part in it some incidents that throw light on the realities of a modern naval engagement on this tremendous scale.

On both sides, the general grouping of the forces to be engaged was based on the same principle. There was a main fighting force of battleship squadrons, with their due proportion of lighter craft, and to serve as its advanced guard there was a less numerous, but still exceptionally powerful, fleet of battle cruisers and their auxiliaries.

Counting only the ships that actually went to sea in the night of May 30–31, the British battle fleet was made up of 24 battleships, all of the Dreadnought type. Attached to this main force were two squadrons each of four armored cruisers, a squadron of the new battle cruisers (*Invincible, Inflexible,* and *Indomitable*), a light cruiser squadron, three flotillas of destroyers, and a mine-layer. The Commander in Chief, Admiral Sir John Jellicoe, flew his flag on the *Iron Duke.*

The "advance guard," officially the "battle-cruiser fleet," was under the command of Vice Admiral Sir David Beatty, whose flag flew in the battle cruiser *Lion.* Including the *Lion* there were six battle cruisers organized in two squadrons. Attached as a supporting force was Rear Admiral Evan-Thomas's squadron of four battleships. There were also 3 squadrons of light cruisers, 13 ships in all, 3 flotillas of destroyers, and a seaplane carrier, the armed liner *Engadine.*

There were 150 ships in all—28 battleships and 9 battle cruisers, 8 armored cruisers and 22 light cruisers, 81 destroyers, a mine-layer, and a seaplane carrier.

The German High Seas Fleet had for its main force 21 battle-ships, Admiral Scheer's flagship the *Friedrich der Grosse,* a squadron of 8 ships and two others of 6 each. Only 15 were Dreadnoughts. The six ships of the 2nd Squadron, the *Deutschland* and her consorts, were older ships, constructed before the new type was adopted. But the 3rd Squadron, under Rear-Admiral Behncke, was made up of the newest ships of the *König* class, the largest and most heavily armed in the whole fleet, several of them completed since the beginning of the war.

There were three cruiser squadrons. The first of these, officially the "first scouting group," was made up of 5 battle cruisers commanded by Vice Admiral Hipper, whose flag flew on the *Lützow,* a ship completed only a few months before; a squadron of light cruisers (11 ships in all); and 2 other light cruisers detailed as leaders of the destroyers. Of these torpedo craft there were seven squadrons, each of 11 units, but half of 1st Flotilla did not go out with the fleet.

In all there were 111 ships of all classes: 22 battleships, 5 battle cruisers, 11 light cruisers, and 73 destroyers. Sixteen submarines had been sent out some days before to cruise off the British naval bases. There were 10 Zeppelins attached to the fleet, but the cloudy weather of May 31 led to their not being sent out on that day.

When the British fleet put to sea at midnight on the eve of the battle, few of its officers and men expected that anything of exceptional importance was likely to happen in the next 24 hours. There had been so many "sweeps" of the fleet into the North Sea that ended without any incident of moment, that there was an impression that the German fleet had abandoned any idea of risking a trial of strength in full force.

The presence of submarines off the Scottish coasts had been known for some days, and as British fleets put to sea a sharp lookout for them was kept. In the early hours of the night more than one British ship reported that a torpedo had been loosed off at her from an unseen enemy, but there were no hits. The enemy's submarines sent some messages to Scheer through the wireless station at Wilhelmshaven, but they gave him little information. All they told was that here and there British ships had been seen, but there was nothing to show that a great concentration was in progress.

It was a dull cloudy night with a smooth sea. From Scapa Flow, Jellicoe was leading the main fleet eastwards, keeping the speed down to 14 knots so that, if a general action followed, his torpedo craft would have plenty of fuel still in hand. Away to the south

Admiral Jerram, with his battleships and their attendant light craft, was steaming from Moray Firth on a converging course to join up at the appointed rendezvous. Still further south Beatty, with the battle-cruiser squadron, and Evan-Thomas with the 5th Battle Squadron and their screen of light cruisers, were on the way from the Forth to their first post north of the Dogger Bank, this powerful contingent forming a flank guard for the main movement.

The night passed without incident, and the summer morning was fine, but with a good deal of low cloud in the sky and patches of mist on the sea. The German fleet came out that morning, and by 9 A.M. its main body was passing Heligoland, steering a little west of north with Hipper's battle cruisers, which had gone out at 2 A.M., scouting some 50 miles or more in advance. The British had long been taking in and decoding the German wireless signals, but on this eventful day, all through the morning hours, the wireless watch on the enemy gave a misleading result. How this happened is not quite clear, but during several hours of the morning such messages as Scheer sent out seemed to come from the powerful wireless station at his base, Wilhelmshaven, and Jellicoe far off in the North Sea was informed from London that the main enemy fleet was probably still at anchor in the Jade.

By 10 A.M. Jerram had joined up with Jellicoe, and at 3 P.M. the united battle fleet was close to the appointed rendezvous west of the Skaggerak. But by this time, further south, Beatty was already in touch with the enemy, believed at this stage of the operations to be only Hipper's cruiser force.

Until shortly after 2 A.M. Beatty's "battle-cruiser fleet" had been steaming westward, with the light cruisers thrown out some miles in advance, in a long curve. The four battle cruisers followed him. Beatty now altered his course to the northward to join Jellicoe, the light cruiser screen covering his movement on the east and south. Narratives of some of those in the cruiser squadron show that the general idea was that the "sweep" into the North Sea was over and the return home beginning.

Furthest east of the light cruisers was the *Galatea*, the flagship of the squadron attached to Beatty's force. A few minutes after 2 P.M. her lookout reported a German torpedo boat out east searching a merchant ship. The enemy had sighted the British ship and began to steam away. On board the cruiser the order for "Action Stations" was sounded. Her wireless operator tells how at first he imagined it was only the beginning of a drill already announced for that afternoon. It was the report of the 6-inch bow gun fired at the

German that told him something more serious than drill might be coming. This proved to be the first shot of the great day, fired at 2:20 P.M.

As the enemy destroyer raced away eastward there came in sight in that direction light cruisers and torpedo craft, obviously the covering screen of a fleet, and the *Galatea* was in action for a while with the nearest of the newcomers at 14,000 yards. Between the opponents with the shells flying over her a peaceful merchantman, with all sail set to catch the light wind, moved slowly across the field of fire. The *Galatea's* warning that the enemy was in sight had been radioed to Beatty and Jellicoe (now some 65 miles away). At 2:40 the main fleet was ordered to raise full steam and turned to join the cruiser fleet. Beatty had put his cruisers and Evan-Thomas's battleships on a south-southeast course to interpose between the enemy and their line of retreat southwards.

The *Engadine* (which was attached to Beatty's command) was directed to send up one of her seaplanes to reconnoiter the enemy. It got away just after 3 P.M. The clouds hung low at 1,000 feet or less, and the plane had to fly dangerously low to see anything. Haze also made visibility limited, and the plane had to fly within three miles of the Germans with shrapnel from their light guns bursting around her, but she was never hit. Despite persistent enemy attempts to jam her wireless, she was able to send back a useful report on the German dispositions and movements. The force facing the British was Hipper's squadron of five battle cruisers, with its vanguard and escort of light cruisers and torpedo craft. At 3:45 a leaking gas line forced the seaplane to return to the *Engadine*.

Some of the British and German light cruisers had been in action at long range, with little result. This preliminary skirmish ended towards 3:30 P.M., when Hipper, having discovered that the British were steaming southeast, promptly changed his own course and swung around to the southward to parry the menace to his own line of retreat and to join Scheer who was coming up some 60 miles away.

There was now the strange situation that neither the Germans nor the British knew that their opponents' main fleet was at sea. Beatty was preparing to engage Hipper and hold on to him until Jellicoe could come up, and then the German cruiser squadron would be crushed by overwhelming force. Hipper was expecting this would be the fate of Beatty if he could draw him on and hold his own against him until Scheer would come into action.

The two battle-cruiser fleets were at first steaming on converging lines, until about 4 P.M. they were both running south on parallel courses 6 or 7 miles apart. With both of them the battle cruisers were in line ahead, with their light cruisers and torpedo craft out ahead and right and left of leading ships. Beatty was leading his battle line in his flagship the *Lion*, followed (at five hundred-yard intervals between the ships) by the *Princess Royal*, *Queen Mary*, *Tiger*, *New Zealand*, and *Indefatigable*. Five miles away to the northwest were Evan-Thomas's four battleships.

At 3:48, while the fleets were still converging and the distance between them was some eight miles, the *Lion* opened fire, and the fight between the battle-cruiser squadrons began, the range shortening as their courses became parallel. Visibility eastward was poor under a clouded sky, but the British cruisers were easier targets, showing up well against the bright western sky. In this first stage of the action there were few hits on Hipper's big ships, though all around them short and long shots were sending up columns of water higher than the masts. Beatty's cruisers also were moving in a forest of these huge geysers, but there were some deadly hits on them, and for a while the German fire was terribly effective. Within a few minutes of the first shot Hipper's leading ship, the *Lützow*, put a salvo of three 12-inch shells first just over the *Lion*, another short, and then a third fairly on her fore part. The German shells had a delaying fuse which burst them after passing through armor or plating and a hit like this meant heavy damage. A shell burst inside one of the *Lion's* turrets, blew off the roof, killed or wounded most of those at the guns, and started a fire. The commander of the turret, Major Harvey, with both his legs shattered and only a few minutes of life left, gave the order to close magazine doors and flood the forward magazine, and thus saved Beatty's flagship from the fate that soon befell other ships of his squadron.

Just after 4 P.M., two officers of the *New Zealand* were watching their next astern, and the last in the line, the *Indefatigable*. A salvo of shells hit her aft and smoke rose from her astern. Her steering gear must have been damaged for she swung out of the line. Then two shells burst on her forecastle and fore turret, sheets of flame shot up first forward, then aft in a tremendous explosion, and an immense pillar of smoke rose into the sky. Among the flying debris was a 50-foot picket boat turning over and over high in the air. As the smoke cleared not a vestige of the great ship was to be seen. Of her officers and crew more than a thousand lost their lives and only five survived, picked up later on by a German light craft.

Twenty minutes later another battle cruiser was destroyed—

the *Queen Mary*. From the narratives of one of the few survivors of her 1,200 officers and men we know that she had received considerable damage from the enemy's shells before the end came. Those who watched from her next astern saw a salvo strike her amidships; at first it seemed no great damage had been done; but then came a burst of smoke and flame, and her funnels and masts seemed to fall inwards, everything forward had disappeared, but her after part kept afloat for a few minutes, and then turned over and sank, some of the men scrambling onto her side, and slipping into the sea. As the two following ships passed close on each side of her all that was left was a huge mushroomed column of smoke 600 feet high.

Beatty had now only four of his six cruisers left against Hipper's five, but Evan-Thomas had begun to help with very long-range fire from his leading battleships, and the enemy was turning away and sent his destroyer flotilla to attack. This was countered by Beatty's destroyers, which had been already ordered to intervene. There was an engagement of these lighter craft in the "No-Man's-Waters" between the main battle lines. On each side two were lost, but on the whole the British ships scored. Torpedoes fired at long range at Beatty's cruisers were easily evaded, but some British destroyers pressed on to closer range as the enemy's flotilla withdrew, and one of them made a hit on the starboard bow of the *Seydlitz,* the torpedo tearing a rent 13 feet long near the waterline. An inner bulkhead kept the German battle cruiser afloat.

Toward the close of this fight of the destroyers a new phase of the battle began. Four miles ahead of the British battle cruisers was the 2nd Light Cruiser Squadron, the *Southampton, Nottingham, Birmingham*, and *Dublin*. At 4:38 their leader, the *Southampton*, sent back the unexpected report that the enemy's main fleet was coming. In those later hours of the afternoon visibility had become very variable, the sun was often overclouded for a while, and summer haze gathered in wide patches on the sea. It was at a moment when the sun shone out that "suddenly" light cruisers were sighted some 8 miles away to the southeast, steaming north, and in a few minutes more there appeared behind them the head of a line of big ships. The news told Beatty he was in danger of being caught between hammer and anvil, and he ordered (at 4:46) a retirement northwards to close on the Grand Fleet, still far out of sight. It was then about 40 miles away.

As the British battle cruisers swung around to port to take the new course, Hipper turned inward to starboard to hold on to them. Evan-Thomas with his four battleships had just joined up with

Beatty; holding on southward before turning he interposed between him and Hipper, engaging the German battle cruisers with good effect and then turned and followed up the retirement, a couple of miles astern. As the two advanced fleets moved northwards on parallel lines their guns kept in action, though at times they were almost hidden from each other by smoke and mist.

The light cruisers had held on, nearing the enemy for a few minutes in order to get a good look at Scheer's main fleet. The *Southampton* was able to make out sixteen or seventeen battleships coming up in line ahead, the big *Dreadnought* squadron of the *König* class leading, the older pre-Dreadnoughts of the second division next to them. The light cruisers were in range of the enemy but were not fired at till they turned northwards. Till then perhaps the Germans in the doubtful misty light took them for some of Hipper's light craft. Then the leading enemy ships kept firing on them, but made no serious hits. British ships fired a few shots in reply but the range was at first too long for their guns. Presently the enemy's leading battleships came under the fire of Evan-Thomas's squadron, which besides firing on Hipper brought some of its heavier guns to bear at long range on the head of the "High Seas Fleet."

At this stage of the battle—between 5 and 6 P.M.—Admiral Scheer did not yet know that the Grand Fleet was out and would soon be in action. He was thinking only of helping Hipper and turning the scale against Beatty. It was only when he saw the flashes of heavy guns far off to the northwards that he rightly judged that Jellicoe was coming.

On both sides the main fleets were now joining up with their advanced forces of battle cruisers, and the general engagement of the united fleets was about to begin. We can best "set the board" for this tremendous fight by noting what was the general situation about 5:20 P.M. This will make it easier to follow in broad outline what happened later.

The situation may be thus summed up: Admiral Scheer, still with no idea a general engagement was near at hand, was in touch with Hipper, and his leading division had come into action to help him against Beatty and Evan-Thomas's battleships.

When he turned south to join Beatty, Jellicoe, still, it seems, unaware that the enemy's main force was at sea, had detached Hood's squadron of battle cruisers to the eastward to steam southward parallel to the Jutland coast and bar any attempt of Hipper to escape into the Skagerrak. Hood was now about 16 miles away from the enemy, on a course that would bring him into action between Hipper and the land. Jellicoe's battleships were some 30 miles away, with a covering force of cruisers, 10 miles in advance strung out on a broad front. Even the nearest of Jellicoe's ships were not yet in sight or hearing of Beatty's and Hipper's squadrons. By this time and for the rest of the evening visibility was often limited by weather conditions, and sometimes nothing could be clearly made out beyond some three miles.

At 5:30 the light cruiser *Chester*, attached to Hood's force, saw the flashes of Hipper's guns, and Hood turned to engage the enemy, the *Chester* being the first ship in action with Hipper's light cruisers ten minutes later. Events now developed rapidly, and soon the main battle was beginning in what for a while, till the British battle fleet came into action, was a fierce fight between British advanced squadrons and the German van. It seemed almost on the point of becoming a confused melee.

Battle plans of a colossal conflict like this give a misleading impression, unless one bears in mind the fact that they represent afterknowledge of what happened and tell more than even the chief commanders themselves could realize while the fighting was in progress. The battle plan of an action extending over hundreds of square miles of sea, with every squadron and unit in rapid move-ment, conveys a false impression unless one remembers how limited was the field of vision of each and all of the combatants. Even in clear air and the brightest sunlight no individual, however well placed, could watch anything but a small part of the tremendous totality. On this occasion, too, the fleets were coming into contact under difficult conditions of visibility, with the haze of the summer evening, and the drifting trails of funnel and cannon smoke blotting the view. At Jutland there was the further handicap that the wireless messages between the advanced squadrons and the British battle fleet gave defective information. As for the frequent limit to visibility it may be noted that in this stage of the battle Beatty had for a while no enemy in sight.

The critical half hour before Jellicoe's battleships came into the fight was the 15 minutes before and after 6 P.M. From Admiral Scheer's memoirs it appears that he still counted on having, for some time to come, a local superiority of force and did not realize that the British main battle fleet was so near at hand. His leading battleships were helping Hipper to reply to the fire of Evan-Thomas's squadron. For a while Beatty had ceased firing as he lost sight of the enemy battle cruisers. He changed his course to the eastward to regain contact. Hipper's light cruisers had been pushed out to engage the British light cruiser *Chester*, and she was soon suffering serious loss and damage in a fight of four against one. Hood was hurrying to her aid with his three big battle cruisers, sending on his escort of destroyers in advance, and the enemy squadron was driven off with its flagship, the *Wiesbaden*, ablaze and lamed by a well-placed British torpedo. Hood then engaged Hipper's battle cruisers at long range, and presently Beatty regained touch with his old opponent. The German cruisers had a trying time. Hipper's flagship, the *Lützow*, was seen to be down by the head, with much damage to her upper works and several guns out of action. But Scheer was now bringing division after division of his battleships into action, holding on to the northwest with his fleet in line ahead.

The first reinforcement for the squadrons that were engaged with him was supplied by the individual initiative of Arbuthnot. His four big armored cruisers had been steaming on a wide front to the west of Jellicoe. He was concentrating his squadron and pushing on towards the fight. His flag flew in the *Defence*, the *Warrior* was close up with him, and the *Black Prince* still far astern. With the *Warrior* and *Defence* he flung himself into the battle, firing on Hipper's battle cruisers as he came, and passing close ahead of Beatty's squadron. His two ships came under a storm of fire from the leading enemy battleships. At 6:16 the *Defence* blew up, "disappearing in a cloud of fire and smoke." Her consort the *Warrior* narrowly escaped the same fate. Badly holed near the waterline, and with engine rooms partly flooded, and upper works wrecked and on fire, she drifted out of the fight. When the *Black Prince* came into action she was soon crippled like the *Warrior*, fell away astern of the British advance, and was unseen for hours.

At 6:14 Jellicoe with the battle fleet was close enough up to make out the situation in his front and gave the order to his six divisions to form line of battle. The course had been so far nearly southeast. Following the leading ship each division swung around into line at right angles to this course, forming a single line ahead nearly northeastward—a line of giant Dreadnought battleships some seven miles long. Beatty's battle cruisers had been crossing Jellicoe's line of advance, and now took position nearly two miles in front of the leading battleship, with Hood's battle cruisers immediately in front of them, engaging Hipper's squadron at a range of eight miles. Evan-Thomas's battleship squadron took its station at the rear of the battle line. His ships bore the marks of their hard fight with the enemy's van, and one of them, the *Warspite*, had had a narrow escape from destruction about the time when the *Defence* was blown up. The *Warspite* was seen suddenly leaving the line, and heading direct for the enemy with a forest of shell geysers around her. She was flying the signal, "out of control." Her steering gear had jammed. But the mishap was dealt with and swinging around in a wide circle she rejoined her consorts.

As Jellicoe's battleships completed their deployment into line their course was altered to a little east of southeast, a direction that would bring them to landward of the enemy and menace his line of retreat. Fire was opened first by the rearmost ships and then all along the line. Scheer's account of how he first sighted the British battle line shows how soon he realized the terrible odds against him. He tells how, out ahead, he could see the array of great ships, miles in length, each end of the line disappearing in the mist. As they opened fire the whole north horizon seemed ablaze with the gun flashes. He altered his course to engage his enemy, line against line.

Soon after the deployment was completed Hood's flagship, leading the battle-cruiser line, was destroyed by an explosion. Of her hundreds of officers and men, only six escaped. As the other battle cruisers swept by they were seen on a life raft, cheering the passing ships. A destroyer picked them up.

For more than a quarter of an hour not a single German shell made a hit on the British battleships, but Scheer's van divisions were suffering seriously from the converging fire of the British line curving around their line of advance. The German commander-in-chief now realized that his best hope lay in an attempt to extricate his fleet from the unequal conflict. At 6:35 he sent some of his torpedo craft forward with a double mission—to mask his movements behind a huge smokescreen, and to make a long-range attack on the British line. The attack was little more than a feint. The few torpedoes discharged showed their approaching track plainly and were easily avoided. There was only one hit, on the *Marlborough*, but she was not seriously damaged. The German destroyers retired through the smokescreen, and as it drifted away, not one German ship was visible from the British side. Scheer's ships had turned simultaneously under cover of the smokescreen and were steaming away at full speed to the westward. For nearly half an hour the battle ceased.

It was a strange situation. The sky was heavily clouded, sunset was near and the light was bad. Over the gray sea, now broken with a ruffled swell, the mist hung heavily in many directions, with openings of clearer air between, but dulling all distant views. The enemy had vanished.

But he must be somewhere to the west, and Jellicoe held on steadily southwards, knowing that every mile brought his fleet more fairly between the Germans and channels through the minefields of the Heligoland Bight that were the way to their fortified bases. About 7 P.M. one of his flanking cruisers saw shadowy forms coming through the mist and radioed that the enemy was closing in again.

Scheer had decided to make a sudden attack, which he hoped would "throw the British line into confusion." His battleships came rushing out of the mist to attack the British center and rear while the battle cruisers kept the van occupied. There was a brief fierce cannonade, in which the concentrated fire of the British line told heavily on the enemy. Few British ships were hit. Fires were seen here and there ablaze in the enemy line. Once more Scheer broke off the fight, flinging his destroyers forward to make a torpedo attack and raise a smoke screen, while his battleships turned away. Again the torpedoes were easily evaded.

As the destroyers retired through their screen, Jellicoe ordered the course to be altered slightly west of south, hoping to gain touch again as the smoke cleared. Beatty with the battle cruisers was well forward leading the line. At 7:40, ten minutes after the enemy disappeared, he signalled that he had sighted them to the northwest, ten miles away. Jellicoe gave the order to follow his battle cruisers. The sun was setting, darkness would come soon, and the main battle was practically over.

The two fleets were now steaming on practically parallel lines, and between 8 and 9 P.M. there were a few brief exchanges of fire as hostile squadrons sighted each other. Beatty, as he had fired the first shots of the day, fired the last near 9 P.M. Under the cloudy sky it was now nearly dark. Both fleets were well out to sea northwest of the Horns Reef. Jellicoe sent off his mine-layer, the *Abdiel*, to block the channels south of the reefs along the Danish coast, and ordered his fleet to take up cruising order for the night. The battle fleet closed up in three columns line ahead, the battle cruisers about 12 miles away to the west, his light craft, cruisers, and destroyer flotillas forming a wide screen five miles astern. He had decided not to risk the confusion of a battle in the darkness. Dawn would come early on this summer night, and he counted on bringing the enemy again to action at the first light of day. He knew they were away to the westward, and considered that it was most probable that they would try to reach the western channels leading to their bases. He calculated that they could not get so far before dawn. Beatty radioed to his squadron that though losses had been heavy the enemy had suffered still more and would be dealt with next morning.

Until 9 P.M. the two fleets had been steaming on nearly parallel lines a little west of south. The course of the British fleet was then changed to south. Scheer can have only conjectured what its relative position to his own force was at any given time. He had reduced speed after dark, and might well expect that Jellicoe, who was maneuvering to cut off his retreat along the German coast to Wilhelmshaven, would be soon further to the southward than the High Sea Fleet would be. Counting on this he made a bold stroke to escape by attempting to cut across the wake of his enemy, and about 10 P.M. turned to the eastward.

He had got from a German wireless station one of the British orders intercepted during the battle, and only part of this, but a significant message. It gave him Jellicoe's order to his light craft to follow the fleet some miles astern. When about 10:30 P.M. there was a burst of firing to the eastward as some of his light cruisers met at close quarters in the dark some British light craft. In the brief fight the cruiser *Frauenlob* was sunk, but the encounter told Scheer that though fighting his way through the British light squadrons might bring the Grand Fleet back to attack him, he had a fair chance of making good his retreat by steering southeast to the neighborhood of the Horns Reef, whence there would be a clear run southward to the Jade and Wilhelmshaven.

From 11:30 till after 1 A.M. on June 1 the German fleet was making its way through the screens of light craft in rear of the British fleet. There was a series of desperate fights at close quarters when the British destroyers suddenly found themselves in conflict with enemies that suddenly loomed up in the darkness. It would need a volume to tell the story of this night fighting. It is impossible to exaggerate the reckless courage and self-sacrifice with which British destroyers, with gun and torpedo, met their opponents, among which were not only small craft of their own class, but light and heavy cruisers and battleships. Amongst their successes were the sinking of the light cruiser *Rostock* and the battleship *Pommern*. Another battleship, the *Nassau*, tried to run down the little *Spitfire*. The destroyer evaded the direct blow and met her enemy with a glancing shock bow to bow, and then, badly crippled, was kept afloat and struggled home to port, bringing as a trophy of her adventure several feet of plating from the *Nassau's* bow. Several British destroyers were sunk, and during this night fighting there came one of the tragedies of the battle. The crippled cruiser *Black Prince*, which had been drifting for hours far astern of the British fleet, came under the close fire of several heavy German ships. Two British destroyers saw her rush past them, with all her upper works on fire, and a few minutes later saw the huge flash of the explosion that blew her up.

The flashes of the night battle were seen from the rear of the main fleet, but Jellicoe never received the information that enemy battleships and cruisers were passing astern of his course. He had expected attacks by German destroyers in this direction, and there was nothing to tell him that any heavier craft were in action. So he held on his course. Soon after 2 A.M. the dawn was coming. The fighting astern had ended. As the light increased anxious eyes scanned the sea to the westward, but there was no sign of the enemy.

Scheer had by this time passed well to the northeastward of the British fleet, and as he steamed for the Horns Reef lightship he was getting his fleet into order again after the confusion of the night fighting. The light cruiser *Elbing* had been sunk in collision with the battleship *Posen*. The *Lützow* had been sunk by a German torpedo after her crew had been taken off by her escort of destroyers. At 3 A.M. the Horns Reef lightship was abeam and the course was set southwards. By a wonderful chance Scheer's fleet passed safely through a gap in the minefield laid by the *Abdiel*. By noon it was safe in its base ports, and Berlin was sending out by wireless its claim to a victory.

The British fleet had held on its southerly course till 2:45. Then all hope of finding the enemy in this direction was abandoned and the fleet turned north, making a wide sweep, partly with a lingering hope that the enemy might still be found, partly to make sure that there were no crippled ships to be succored. About 3:30, a Zeppelin appeared flying high and hovering over the fleet. It was fired at but was out of reach. Scheer, 40 miles away, received from it the news that his enemy was departing. It was not till 11 A.M. that the British fleet ended its search of the North Sea and began its homeward voyage.

The fleet had returned to its bases by the early hours of June 2, and at 9:45 that evening Jellicoe was able to report to the Admiralty that it had fuelled, and replaced expended ammunition, and was ready to go to sea again at four-hours' notice.

All but one of the badly damaged ships had reached port. The seaplane carrier *Engadine* had brought in the crew of the *Warrior*. She had taken the big cruiser in tow in the night after the battle, but had to abandon her before morning when she was in a sinking condition.

Until June 3 the British public was not allowed to know even that there had been a great battle in the North Sea. Rumors circulated that something serious had happened, but the censors of the Press Bureau were making the worst of their blunders by depriving the people of all information. Officers and men, who had taken part in the battle, were warned that for the time being they were not even to mention it. A veil of silence hung over the naval ports. Ships were arriving which had obviously been in action, but all inquiries were barred. By June 2 here and there in England and Scotland men were saying that there must have been a battle, and the government was keeping back bad news. Through Holland, the German official story had reached London. Those to whom it came hoped against hope that it was mere enemy "propaganda." At last, late on the second, the Admiralty sent out a press communiqué which appeared in next morning's papers. It was an ill-judged and misleading production. It told how there had been a "naval engagement" off the Jutland coast; the brunt of the fighting had fallen on the British cruiser fleet, which had heavy losses; when the British battle fleet appeared the enemy had avoided prolonged action, and aided by low visibility returned to port, after suffering severe damage. British losses of large ships were then enumerated, and it was suggested the enemy's losses must have been heavier. There was no hint that the greatest of naval battles had been fought; that the British fleet had more than held its own; and the enemy had escaped under cover of the night. On June 4, a longer communiqué was issued which to many seemed a lame attempt to explain away a failure.

It was only when fuller news was released by the authorities that England realized that there had been victory in the North Sea. Granted that, like many other great battles, the battle of Jutland had not been fought out to a finish with immediately decisive results. But it was the enemy who, by a daring maneuver and more than one favorable chance, had broken off the fight and avoided renewing it on the following day. The ultimate result was that the German admirals practically abandoned all hope of successfully challenging another trial of strength between their High Seas Fleet and the Grand Fleet of Britain.

The British losses had been heavy, but the enemy also had suffered serious loss, and the British fleet had such a margin of strength that its superiority remained unaffected. It must be added that mere reckoning up of sunken ships does not give a real estimate of loss. Many of the most powerful German ships received such severe injuries that they were out of action for months while under repair in the dockyards. After the war Captain Persius, recognized as one of the ablest of German naval experts, wrote: "Our losses were severe, and on June 1, 1916, it was clear to every thinking person that this battle must, and would be, the last one. Authoritative quarters said so openly." Soon after the battle Admiral Scheer wrote to the Kaiser that henceforth the only hope of success on the sea depended on the submarine warfare against commerce.

One thing is beyond all doubt or controversy. On both sides officers and men showed a magnificent courage and unfailing devotion to their country's cause in the face of terrors and trials unknown to all earlier naval wars. Furthermore, this tremendous sea fight proved to be the last of purely naval battles, decided by the skill and courage of the seaman and the fighting efficiency of the warship. A new element came into naval war. The seaplane that reconnoitered the German cruisers on the afternoon of May 31 and the airship that hovered over the British fleet at dawn next day were heralds of a new development that would become decisive in sea fights of the future.

CHAPTER 9

Jutland: Destroyer Work

Rudyard Kipling

I n the preceding chapter, John Richard Hale remarks that it would take "a volume" to do justice to the actions of British destroyers fighting at Jutland on the night of May 31, 1916. Evidently, he was not aware that Rudyard Kipling, long fascinated by the bantams of naval combat, had done the job much more briefly.

In the following report, which one can imagine Kipling writing with a grim yet cocky grin, he concentrates on the action "on one minute section of one wing" of the great battle.

Since this report, like the other Kipling selection in this book, was originally published during the First World War when the censor was looking over the author's shoulder, the reader must be warned not to take everything literally. Gehenna, Shaitan, Goblin, and Eblis are obviously invented names. Gehenna may in fact be Tipperary, one of the only two British destroyers present with both port and starboard torpedo tubes, *which came to grief in a similar manner. The real name of* Eblis *is obviously* Spitfire, *and she rammed not a cruiser but the German battleship* Nassau.

But whatever the real names, and whatever the precise actions in which these ships participated, Kipling shows himself here at his best. What could be more engaging than his picture of two badly damaged destroyers helping each other to limp home through a rain of heavy shell "as sociable as a couple of lame hounds"?

There was much destroyer work in the Battle of Jutland. The actual battlefield may not have been more than 20,000 square miles, but the incidental patrols, from first to last, must have covered many times that area. Doubtless the next generation will comb out every detail of it. All we need remember is there were many squadrons of battleships and cruisers engaged over the face of the North Sea, and that they were accompanied in their dread comings and goings by multitudes of destroyers, who attacked the enemy both by day and by night from the afternoon of May 31 to the morning of June 1, 1916. We are too close to the gigantic canvas to take in the meaning of the picture; our children stepping backward through the years may get the true perspective and proportions.

To recapitulate what everyone knows:

The German fleet came out of its North Sea ports, scouting ships ahead; then destroyers, cruisers, battle cruisers, and, last, the main battle fleet in the rear. It moved north, parallel with the coast of stolen Schleswig-Holstein and Jutland. Our fleets were already out; the main battle fleet (Admiral Jellicoe) sweeping down from the north, and our battle-cruiser fleet (Admiral Beatty) feeling for the enemy. Our scouts came in contact with the enemy on the afternoon of May 31 about 100 miles off the Jutland coast, steering northwest. They satisfied themselves he was in strength, and reported accordingly to the British battle-cruiser fleet, which engaged the enemy's battle cruisers at about 3:30. The enemy steered southeast to rejoin their own fleet, which was coming up from that quarter. We fought him on a parallel course as he ran for more than an hour.

Then his battle fleet came in sight, and Beatty's fleet went about and steered northwest in order to retire on our battle fleet, which was hurrying down from the north. We returned fighting very much over the same waters as we had used in our slant south. The enemy up till now had lain to the eastward of us, whereby he had the advantage in that thick weather of seeing our hulls clear against the afternoon light, while he himself worked in the mists. We then steered a little to the northwest bearing him off towards the east till at six o'clock Beatty had headed the enemy's leading ships and our main battle fleet came in sight from the north. The enemy broke back in a loop, first eastward, then south, then southwest as our fleet edged them off from the land, and our main battle fleet, coming up behind them, followed in their wake. Thus for a while we had the enemy to westward of us, where he made a better mark; but the day was closing and the weather thickened, and the enemy wanted to get away. At a quarter past eight the enemy, still heading south-west, was covered by his destroyers in a great screen of gray smoke, and he got away.

As darkness fell, our fleets lay between the enemy and his home ports. During the night our heavy ships, keeping well clear of possible minefields, swept down south to south and west of the Horns Reef, so that they might pick him up in the morning. When morning came our main fleet could find no trace of the enemy to the southward, but our destroyer flotillas farther north had been very busy with enemy ships, apparently running for the Horns Reef Channel. It looks, then, as if when we lost sight of the enemy in the smokescreen and the darkness he had changed course and broken for home astern our main fleets. And whether that was a sound maneuver or otherwise, he and the still flows of the North Sea alone can tell.

But how is a layman to give any coherent account of an affair where a whole country's coastline was background to battle covering geographical degrees? The records give an impression of illimitable gray waters, nicked on their uncertain horizons with the smudge and blur of ships sparkling with fury against ships hidden under the curve of the world. One sees these distances maddeningly obscured by walking mists and weak fogs, or wiped out by layers of funnel and gun smoke, and realizes how, at the pace the ships were going, anything might be stumbled upon in the haze or charge out of it when it lifted. One comprehends, too, how the far-off glare of a great vessel afire might be reported as a local fire on a nearby enemy, or vice versa; how a silhouette caught, for an instant, in a shaft of pale light let down from the low sky might be fatally difficult to identify till too late. But add to all these inevitable confusions and misreckonings of time, shape, and distance, charges at every angle of squadrons through and across other squadrons; sudden shifts of the centers of the fights, and even swifter restorations; wheelings, sweepings, and regroupments such as accompany the passage across space of colliding universes. Then blanket the whole inferno with the darkness of night at full speed, and—see what you can make of it.

A little time after the action began to heat up between our battle cruisers and the enemy's, eight or ten of our destroyers opened the ball for their branch of the service by breaking up the attack of an enemy light cruiser and fifteen destroyers. Of these they accounted for at least two destroyers—some think more—and drove the others back on their battle cruisers. This scattered that fight a good deal over the sea. Three of our destroyers held on for the enemy's battle fleet, who came down on them at ranges which eventually grew less than 3,000 yards. Our people ought to have been lifted off the seas bodily, but they managed to fire a couple of torpedoes apiece while the range was diminishing. They had no illusions. Says one of the three, speaking of her second shot, which she loosed at fairly close range, "This torpedo was fired because it was considered very unlikely that the ship would escape disablement before another opportunity offered." But still they lived—three destroyers against all a battle-cruiser fleet's quick-firers, as well as the fire of a batch of enemy destroyers at 600 yards. And they were thankful for small mercies. "The position being favorable," a third torpedo was fired from each while they yet floated.

At 2,500 yards, one destroyer was hit somewhere in the vitals and swerved badly across her next astern, who "was obliged to alter course to avoid a collision, thereby failing to fire a fourth torpedo." Then that next astern "observed signal for destroyers' recall," and went back to report to her flotilla captain—alone. Of her two companions, one was "badly hit and remained stopped between the lines." The other "remained stopped, but was afloat when last seen." Ships that "remain stopped" are liable to be rammed or sunk by methodical gunfire. That was, perhaps, 50 minutes' work put in before there was any really vicious "edge" to the action, and it did not steady the nerves of the enemy battle cruisers any more than another attack made by another detachment of ours.

"What does one do when one passes a ship that 'remains stopped'?" I asked of a youth who had had experience.

"Nothing special. They cheer, and you cheer back. One doesn't think about it till afterwards. You see, it may be your luck in another minute."

There were many other torpedo attacks in all parts of the battle that misty afternoon, including a quaint episode of an enemy light cruiser who "looked as if she were trying" to torpedo one of our battle cruisers while the latter was particularly engaged. A destroyer of ours, returning from a special job which required delicacy, was picking her way back at 30 knots through batches of enemy battle cruisers and light cruisers with the idea of attaching herself to the nearest destroyer flotilla and making herself useful. It occurred to her that as she "was in a most advantageous position for repelling enemy's destroyers endeavoring to attack, she could not do better than to remain on the 'engaged bow' of our battle-cruiser." So she remained and considered things.

There was an enemy battle-cruiser squadron in the offing; with several enemy light cruisers ahead of that squadron, and the weather was thickish and deceptive. She sighted the enemy light cruiser, "class uncertain," only a few thousand yards away, and "decided to attack her in order to frustrate her firing torpedoes at our battle fleet." (This in case the authorities should think that light cruiser wished to buy rubber.) So she fell upon the light cruiser with every gun she had, at between two and four thousand yards, and secured a number of hits, just the same as at target practice. While thus occupied she sighted out of the mist a squadron of enemy battle cruisers that had worried her earlier in the afternoon. Leaving the light cruiser, she closed to what she considered a reasonable distance of the newcomers, and let them have, as she thought, both her torpedoes. She possessed an active acting sub-lieutenant, who, though officers of that rank think otherwise, is not very far removed from an ordinary midshipman of the type one sees in tow of relatives at the Army and Navy Stores. He sat astride one of the tubes to make quite sure things were in order, and fired when the sights came on.

But, at that very moment, a big shell hit the destroyer on the side and there was a tremendous escape of steam. Believing—since she had seen one torpedo leave the tube before the smash came—believing that both her tubes had been fired, the destroyer turned away "at greatly reduced speed" (the shell reduced it), and passed, quite reasonably close, the light cruiser whom she had been hammering so faithfully till the larger game appeared. Meantime, the sub-lieutenant was exploring what damage had been done by the big shell. He discovered that only *one* of the two torpedoes had left the tubes, and "observing enemy light cruiser beam on and apparently temporarily stopped," he fired the providential remainder at her, and it hit her below the conning tower and well and truly exploded, as was witnessed by the sub-lieutenant himself, the commander, a leading signalman, and several other seamen. Luck continued to hold! The acting sub-lieutenant further reported that "we still had three torpedoes left and at the same time drew my attention to enemy's line of battleships." They rather looked as if they were coming down with intent to assault. So the sub-lieutenant fired the rest of the torpedoes, which at least started off correctly from the shell-shaken tubes, and must have crossed the enemy's line. When torpedoes turn up among a squadron, they upset the steering and distract the attention of all concerned. Then the destroyer judged it time to take stock of her injuries. Among other minor defects she could neither steam, steer, nor signal.

Mark how virtue is rewarded! Another of our destroyers an hour or so previously had been knocked clean out of action, before she had done anything, by a big shell which gutted a boiler room and started an oil fire. (That is the drawback to oil.) She crawled out between the battleships till she "reached an area of comparative calm" and repaired damage. She says: "The fire having been dealt with, it was found a mat kept the stokehold dry. My only trouble now being lack of speed, I looked around for useful employment, and saw a destroyer in great difficulties, so closed her." That destroyer was our paralytic friend of the intermittent torpedo tubes, and a grateful ship she was when her crippled sister (but still good for a few knots) offered her a tow, "under very trying conditions with large enemy ships approaching." So the two set off together, Cripple and Paralytic, with heavy shells falling around them, as sociable as a couple of lame hounds. Cripple worked up to 12 knots, and the weather grew vile, and the tow parted. Paralytic, by this time, had raised steam in a boiler or two, and made shift to get along slowly on her own, Cripple hirpling beside her, till Paralytic could not make any more headway in that rising sea, and Cripple had to tow her once more. Once more the tow parted. So they tied Paralytic up rudely and effectively with a cable round her after bollards and gun (presumably because of strained forward bulkheads) and hauled her stern-first, through heavy seas, at continually reduced speeds, doubtful of their position, unable to sound because of the seas, and much pestered by a wind which backed without warning, till, at last, they made land, and turned into the hospital appointed for brave wounded ships. Everybody speaks well of Cripple. Her name crops up in several reports, with such compliments as the men of the sea use when they see good work. She herself speaks well of her lieutenant, who, as executive officer, "took charge of the fire and towing arrangements in a very creditable manner," and also of Tom Battye and Thomas Kerr, engine-room artificer and stoker petty officer, who "were in the stokehold at the time of the shell striking, and performed cool and prompt decisive action, although both suffering from shock and slight injuries."

Have you ever noticed that men who do Homeric deeds often describe them in Homeric language? The sentence "I looked around for useful employment" is worthy of Ulysses when "there was an evil sound at the ships of men who perished and of the ships themselves broken at the same time."

Roughly, very roughly, speaking, our destroyers enjoyed three phases of "prompt decisive action"—the first, a period of day-light attacks (from 4 to 6 P.M.) such as the one I have just described, while the battle was young and the light fairly good on the afternoon of May 31; the second, towards dark, when the light had lessened and the enemy were more uneasy, and, I think, in more scattered formation; the third, when darkness had fallen, and the destroyers had been strung out astern with orders to help the enemy home, which they did all night as opportunity offered. One cannot say whether the day or the night work was the more desperate. From private advices, the young gentlemen concerned seem to have functioned with efficiency either way. As one of them said: "After a bit, you see, we were all pretty much on our own, and you could really find out what your ship could do."

I will tell you now of a piece of night work not without merit.

When the German fleet ran for home, on the night of May 31, it seems to have scattered—"starred," I believe, is the word for the evolution—in a general *sauve qui peut*, while the Devil, livelily represented by our destroyers, took the hindmost. Our flotillas were strung out far and wide on this job. One man compared it to hounds hunting half a hundred separate foxes.

I take the adventures of several couples of destroyers who, on the night of May 31, were nosing along somewhere towards the Schleswig-Holstein coast, ready to chop any Hun-stuff coming back to earth by that particular road. The leader of one line was *Gehenna*, and the next two ships astern of her were *Eblis* and *Shaitan*, in the order given. There were others, of course, but with the exception of one *Goblin* they don't come violently into this tale. There had been a good deal of promiscuous firing that evening, and actions were going on all around. Towards midnight our destroyers were overtaken by several three- and four-funnel German ships (cruisers, they thought) hurrying home. At this stage of the game anybody might have been anybody—pursuer or pursued. The Germans took no chances, but switched on their searchlights and opened fire on *Gehenna*. Her acting sub-lieutenant reports: "A salvo hit us forward. I opened fire with the after guns. A shell then struck us in a steam-pipe, and I could see nothing but steam. But both starboard torpedo tubes were fired."

Eblis, Gehenna's next astern, at once fired a torpedo at the second ship in the German line, a four-funnelled cruiser, and hit her between the second funnel and the mainmast, when "she appeared to catch fire fore and aft simultaneously, heeled right over to starboard, and undoubtedly sank." *Eblis* loosed off a second torpedo and turned aside to reload, firing at the same time to distract the enemy's attention from *Gehenna*, who was now ablaze fore and aft. *Gehenna*'s acting sub-lieutenant (the only executive officer who survived) says that by the time the steam from the broken pipe cleared he found *Gehenna* stopped, nearly everybody amidships killed or wounded, the cartridge boxes around the guns exploding one after the other as the fires took hold, and the enemy not to be seen. Three minutes or less did all that damage. *Eblis* had nearly finished reloading when a shot struck the davit that was swinging her last torpedo into the tube and wounded all hands concerned. Thereupon she dropped torpedo work, fired at an enemy searchlight which winked and went out, and was closing in to help *Gehenna* when she found herself under the noses of a couple of enemy cruisers. "The nearer one," he says, "altered course to ram me, apparently." The Senior Service writes in curiously lawyer-like fashion, but there is no denying that they act quite directly. "I therefore put my helm hard aport and the two ships met and rammed each other, port bow to port bow." There could have been no time to think and, for *Eblis*'s commander on the bridge, none to gather information. But he had observant subordinates, and he writes—and I would humbly suggest that the words be made the ship's motto for evermore—he writes, "Those aft noted" that the enemy cruiser had certain marks on her funnel and certain arrangements of derricks on each side which, quite apart from the evidence she left behind her, betrayed her class. *Eblis* and she met. Says *Eblis:* "I consider I must have considerably damaged this cruiser, as 20 feet of her side plating was left in my foc'sle." Twenty feet of ragged rivet-slinging steel, razoring and reaping about in the dark on a foc'sle that had collapsed like a concertina! It was very fair plating too. There were side-scuttle holes in it—what we passengers would call portholes. But it might have been better, for *Eblis* reports sorrowfully, "by the thickness of the coats of paint (duly given in thirty-seconds of the inch) she would not appear to have been a very new ship."

New or old, the enemy had done her best. She had completely demolished *Eblis*'s bridge and searchlight platform, brought down the mast and the fore funnel, ruined the whaler and the dinghy, split the foc'sle open above water from the stem to the galley which is abaft the bridge, and below water had opened it up from the stem to the second bulkhead. She had further ripped off *Eblis*'s skin-plating for an amazing number of yards on one side of her, and had fired a couple of large-caliber shells into *Eblis* at point-blank range, narrowly missing her vitals. Even so, *Eblis* is as impartial as a prize court. She reports that the second shot, a trifle of eight inches, "may have been fired at a different time or just after colliding." But the night was yet young, and "just after getting clear of this cruiser an enemy battle cruiser grazed past our stern at high speed" and again the judgmatic mind—"I think she must have intended to ram us." She was a large three-funnelled thing, her center funnel shot away and "lights were flickering under her foc'sle as if she was on fire forward." Fancy the vision of her, hurtling out of the dark, red-lighted from within, and fleeing on like a man with his throat cut!

(As an interlude, all enemy cruisers that night were not keen on ramming. They wanted to get home. A man I know who was on another part of the drive saw a covey bolt through our destroyers; and had just settled himself for a shot at one of them when the night threw up a second bird coming down full speed on his other beam. He had bare time to jink between the two as they whizzed past. One switched on her searchlight and fired a whole salvo at him point blank. The heavy stuff went between his funnels. She must have sighted along her own beam of light, which was about a thousand yards.

"How did you feel?" I asked.

"I was rather sick. It was my best chance all that night, and I had to miss it or be cut in two."

"What happened to the cruisers?"

"Oh, they went on, and I heard 'em being attended to by some of our fellows. They didn't know what they were doing, or they couldn't have missed me sitting, the way they did.")

After all that *Eblis* picked herself up, and discovered that she was still alive, with a dog's chance of getting to port. But she did not bank on it. That grand slam had wrecked the bridge, pinning the commander under the wreckage. By the time he had extricated himself he "considered it advisable to throw overboard the steel chest and dispatch-box of confidential and secret books." These are never allowed to fall into strange hands, and their proper disposal is the last step but one in the ritual of the burial service of His Majesty's ships at sea. *Gehenna,* afire and sinking, out somewhere in the dark, was going through it on her own account. This is her acting sub-lieutenant's report: "The confidential books were got up. The first lieutenant gave the order: 'Every man aft,' and the confidential books were thrown overboard. The ship soon afterwards heeled over to starboard and the bow went under. The first lieutenant gave the order: 'Everybody for themselves.' The ship sank in about a minute, the stern going straight up into the air."

But it was not written in the Book of Fate that stripped and battered *Eblis* should die that night as *Gehenna* died. After the burial of the books it was found that the several fires on her were manageable, that she "was not making water aft of the damage," which meant two-thirds of her were, more or less, in commission, and, best of all, that three boilers were usable in spite of the cruiser's shells. So she "shaped course and speed to make the least water and the most progress towards land." On the way back the wind shifted eight points without warning—it was this shift, if you remember, that so embarrassed Cripple and Paralytic on their homeward crawl—and, what with one thing and another, *Eblis* was unable to make port till the scandalously late hour of noon on June 2, "the mutual ramming having occurred about 11:40 P.M. on May 31." She says, this time without any legal reservation whatever, "I cannot speak too highly of the courage, discipline, and devotion of the officers and ship's company."

Her recommendations are a Compendium of Godly Deeds for the Use of Mariners. They cover pretty much all that man may be expected to do. There was, as there always is, a first lieutenant who, while his commander was being extricated from the bridge wreckage, took charge of affairs and steered the ship first from the engine room, or what remained of it, and later from aft, and otherwise maneuvered as requisite, among doubtful bulkheads. In his leisure he "improvised means of signalling," and if there be not one joyous story behind that smooth sentence, I am a Hun!

They all improvised like the masters of craft they were. The chief engine-room artificer, after he had helped to put out fires, improvised stops to the gaps which were left by the carrying away of the forward funnel and mast. He got and kept up steam "to a much higher point than would have appeared at all possible," and when the sea rose, as it always does if you are in trouble, he "improvised pumping and drainage arrangements, thus allowing the ship to steam at a good speed on the whole." There could not have been more than 40 feet of hole.

The surgeon—an intern—performed an amputation single-handed in the wreckage by the bridge, and by his "wonderful skill, resource, and unceasing care and devotion undoubtedly saved the lives of the many seriously wounded men." That no horror might be lacking, there was "a short circuit among the bridge wreckage for a considerable time." The searchlight and wireless were tangled up together, and the electricity leaked into everything.

There were also three wise men who saved the ship whose names must not be forgotten. They were Chief Engine-room Artificer Lee, Stoker Petty Officer Gardiner, and Stoker Elvins. When the funnel carried away it was touch-and-go whether the foremost boiler would not explode. These three "put on respirators and kept the fans going till all fumes, etc., were cleared away." To each man, you will observe, his own particular Hell which he entered of his own particular initiative.

Lastly, there were the two remaining quartermasters—mutinous dogs, both of 'em—one wounded in the right hand and the other in the left, who took the wheel between them all the way home, thus improvising one complete Navy-pattern quartermaster, and "refused to be relieved during the whole thirty-six hours before the ship returned to port." So *Eblis* passes out of the picture with "never a moan or complaint from a single wounded man, and in spite of the rough weather of June 1 they all remained cheery." They had one Hun cruiser, torpedoed, to their credit, and strong evidence abroad that they had knocked the end out of another.

But *Gehenna* went down, and those of her crew who remained hung on to the rafts that destroyers carry till they were picked up about the dawn by *Shaitan*, third in the line, who, at that hour, was in no shape to give much help. Here is *Shaitan's* tale. She saw the unknown cruisers overtake the flotilla, saw their leader switch on searchlights and open fire as she drew abreast of *Gehenna*, and at once fired a torpedo at the third German ship. *Shaitan* could not see *Eblis*, her next ahead, for, as we know, *Eblis* after firing her torpedoes had hauled off to reload. When the enemy switched his searchlights off *Shaitan* hauled out too. It is not wholesome for destroyers to keep on the same course within a thousand yards of big enemy cruisers.

She picked up a destroyer of another division, *Goblin*, who for the moment had not been caught by the enemy's searchlights and had profited by this decent obscurity to fire a torpedo at the hindmost of the cruisers. Almost as *Shaitan* took station behind *Goblin* the latter was lighted up by a large ship and heavily fired at. The enemy fled, but she left *Goblin* out of control, with a grisly list of casualties, and her helm jammed. *Goblin* swerved, returned, and swerved again; *Shaitan* astern tried to clear her, and the two fell aboard each other, *Goblin*'s bow deep in *Shaitan*'s fore bridge. While they hung thus, locked, an unknown destroyer rammed *Shaitan* aft, cutting off several feet of her stern and leaving her rudder jammed hard over. As complete a mess as the personal Devil himself could have devised, and all due to the merest accident of a few panicky salvoes. Presently the two ships worked clear in a smother of steam and oil, and went their several ways. Quite a while after she had parted from *Shaitan, Goblin* discovered several of *Shaitan*'s people, some of them wounded, on her own foc'sle, where they had been pitched by the collision. *Goblin,* working her way homeward on such boilers as remained, carried on a one-gun fight at a few cables' distance with some enemy destroyers, who, not knowing what state she was in, sheered off after a few rounds. *Shaitan,* holed forward and opened up aft, came across the survivors from *Gehenna* clinging to their raft, and took them aboard. Then some of our destroyers—they were thick on the sea that night—tried to tow her stern-first, for *Goblin* had cut her up badly forward. But, since *Shaitan* lacked any stern, and her rudder was jammed hard across where the stern should have been, the hawsers parted, and, after leave asked of lawful authority, across all that waste of waters, they sank *Shaitan* by gunfire, having first taken all the proper steps about the confidential books. Yet *Shaitan* had had her little crumb of comfort ere the end. While she lay crippled she saw quite close to her a German cruiser that was trailing homeward in the dawn gradually heel over and sink.

This completes my version of the various accounts of the four destroyers directly concerned for a few hours, on one minute section of one wing of our battle. Other ships witnessed other aspects of the agony and duly noted them as they went about their business. One of our battleships, for instance, made out by the glare of burning *Gehenna* that the supposed cruiser that *Eblis* torpedoed was a German battleship of a certain class. So *Gehenna* did not die in vain, and we may take it that the discovery did not unduly depress *Eblis*'s wounded in hospital.

The rest of the flotilla that the four destroyers belong to had their own adventures later. One of them, chasing or being chased, saw *Goblin* out of control just before *Goblin* and *Shaitan* locked, and narrowly escaped adding herself to that triple collision. Another loosed a couple of torpedoes at the enemy ships who were attacking *Gehenna,* which, perhaps, accounts for the anxiety of the enemy to break away from that hornets' nest as soon as possible. Half a dozen or so of them ran into four German battleships, which they set about torpedoing at ranges varying from half a mile to a mile and a half. It was asking for trouble and they got it; but they got in return at least one big ship, and the same observant battleship of ours who identified *Eblis*'s bird reported *three* satisfactory explosions in half an hour, followed by a glare that lit up all the sky. One of the flotilla, closing on what she thought was the smoke of a sister in difficulties, found herself well in among the four battleships. "It was too late to get away," she says, so she attacked, fired her torpedo, was caught up in the glare of a couple of searchlights, and pounded to pieces in five minutes, not even her rafts being left. She went down with her colors flying, having fought to the last available gun.

Another destroyer who had borne a hand in *Gehenna*'s trouble had her try at the four battleships and got in a torpedo at 800 yards. She saw it explode and the ship take a heavy list. "Then I was chased," which is not surprising. She picked up a friend who could only do 20 knots. They sighted several Hun destroyers who fled from them; then dropped on to four Hun destroyers all together, who made great parade of commencing action, but soon afterwards "thought better of it, and turned away." So you see, in that flotilla alone there was every variety of fight, from the ordered attacks of squadrons under control, to single ship affairs, every turn of which depended on the second's decision of the men concerned; endurance to the hopeless end; bluff and cunning; reckless advance and red-hot flight; clear vision and as much of blank bewilderment as the Senior Service permits its children to indulge in. That is not much. When a destroyer who has been dodging enemy torpedoes and gunfire in the dark realizes about midnight that she is "following a strange British flotilla, having lost sight of my own," she "decides to remain with them," and shares their fortunes and whatever language is going.

If lost hounds could speak when they cast up next day, after an unchecked night among the wild life of the dark, they would talk much as our destroyers do.

Jutland: Blowing Up the *Queen Mary*

Commander Georg von Hase

T he greatest horror of the Battle of Jutland was the blowing up of three British battle cruisers—the Indefatigable, the Invincible, and the Queen Mary—with more than a thousand lives snuffed out in each case.

No one can be certain of the cause since what evidence there is lies at the bottom of the sea. However, experts tend to attribute the disasters to a combination of superior German armor-piercing shells and the inadequate sealing-off of the magazines in the British ships.

The most articulate observer of the fate of one of the British battle cruisers, the Queen Mary, was Commander Georg von Hase, the first gunnery officer of the German battle cruiser Derfflinger. It was the Derfflinger—the largest, most powerfully armed and fastest warship in the German Navy—that was firing at the Queen Mary when fate turned against her.

A professional German naval officer for 22 years, von Hase was proud of his role at Jutland. "I had the good fortune to be in the thick of the fight and played a decisive part in the destruction of two English battle cruisers, Queen Mary *and* Invincible," *he wrote after the war. His description of what happened has been taken as authoritative by both British and German historians.*

When I reached the bridge I learned that the *Frankfurt* had reported sighting detached enemy forces in a westerly direction. The battle cruisers were already steaming in line ahead and at full speed towards the position indicated. We saw the light cruisers and their destroyers belching forth clouds of smoke as they hurried on ahead. Our own main body was no longer in sight. The destroyers that were screening us could scarcely keep pace with the battle cruisers, as they lost a great deal of speed owing to the heavy swell. Otherwise the sea was fairly smooth; there was a light breeze from the N.W.—force of wind 3 (*Windstärke* 3). I ascended to the forward Gunnery Control Tower. It was really rather a climb to get through the armored door to the platform where the gunnery periscopes stood. Reports were already coming in, such as: "Secondary battery cleared away" "Communications correct" "Foretop after Gunnery Control Tower, main-top, all cleared away" and so on. At length all positions had reported, and I then notified the captain, "All guns cleared away."

We officers adjusted our head telephones and were ready for the dance to begin.

All our periscopes and glasses were now endeavoring to pick up the enemy, but visibility was interfered with by the smoke from our light cruisers. Toward 5 P.M. we heard the first shots, and soon saw that the *Elbing* was under fire, which she was briskly returning. My chronicler in the Transmitting Station booked the following first orders which I gave to the guns: "5:05 P.M. Our light cruisers report four enemy light cruisers. Not yet in sight from 'Derfflinger'." "5:30 P.M. Our light cruisers have opened fire. Train on second light cruiser from right. Load with shell and half cock. Point of aim, right edge water-line, 180 Hundred. Engage opposite numbers from the right. Deflection 20 left, 170 Hundred." It was already growing warm in the Gunnery Control Tower, so I took off my cloak and had it hung in the chart-house abaft the Gunnery Control Tower. I never saw it again!

Up to this time none of us had really believed that we were

about to engage an enemy of equal strength, but now the Captain sent me a message that hostile battle cruisers had been reported, and I passed this news on to the gunnery personnel. We now realized that in a short time we should be fighting fiercely for our lives. For a moment we in the tower were rather more silent. But this only lasted a few minutes, cheerfulness soon regained the upper hand, and everything necessary was done with perfect order and coolness. I caused the guns to be trained in the approximate direction of the enemy. I had adjusted my periscope to the highest power (15), as being the best for such clear weather. But still there was nothing to be seen of the enemy. Ahead, however, the situation had changed; the light cruisers and destroyers had turned about and were seeking cover astern of us battle cruisers. We were therefore leading the line, the horizon in front of us was less obscured by smoke, and we could now make out some British light cruisers which also had turned about. And, suddenly, I saw through my periscope large ships: dark *Colossi,* six tall, high-sided mastodons, steaming in two columns. Although still far away they showed up clearly against the horizon, and even at that great distance they gave an impression of might and power. We held on our northerly course for a short time only, at 5:33 our Flagship *Lützow,* astern of which we were steaming as second in the line, altered course to the south. The enemy turned also on a southerly, converging course, and so the two lines steamed at highest speed to the southward, gradually closing one another. Admiral Hipper's purpose was manifest: he wished to fight a running action to entice the enemy towards our battle fleet.

At this time my recorder booked the following orders from me: "5:35. Ship turning to starboard. Change over switches for action on starboard side in normal positions. 170 Hundred. 165 Hundred. Heavy guns, armor-piercing shell. Train on second armored cruiser from left, 102°. Speed of ship 26 knots, course E.S.E. 170 Hundred. Our enemy has two masts and two funnels, with a third thin funnel close to foremast. Deflection 10 left. Rate 100 closing, 164 Hundred." Still no permission came from the Flagship to open fire. It was becoming more and more evident that both sides wished to fight a decisive action at medium range. Meanwhile I examined the enemy more closely. The six *Colossi* awakened memories of the day on which I had gone out to welcome the British Admiral and his squadron to Kiel Bay. Once more I saw a proud British Squadron approaching, but this time its welcome would be of quite another kind. How much larger and more formidable these six ships—which I seen identified as the enemy's latest battle cruisers—now appeared, 15 times magnified. Six battle cruisers against our five: the action would be fought between practically equal sides. It was a nerve-trying, majestic spectacle as these dark-grey *Colossi* drew steadily nearer, as remorseless as Fate. The six ships, which at first had been steaming in two columns, had now formed into line ahead. Like a herd of prehistoric mastodons they drove along, grey shadows one behind the other, their movements deliberate and irresistible. But I had more important matters to attend to than indulgence in such thoughts. The range steadily closed. When it was down to 165 hectometres, I ordered: "Armor-piercing shell." That was the projectile for close action, and everyone in the ship now knew that we were in for it hammer-and-tongs, for I had often enough explained how the two types of projectiles were to be used. I passed the ranges continuously to the guns as they reached me from the Range Officer. Immediately after altering course at 5:35 P.M. the Flagship hoisted the signal, "Fire distribution from the left." This meant that each German ship was to engage a British ship, counting from the left wing. Accordingly, we five German battle cruisers were to open fire on the first five British ships, and the *Derfflinger's* target was therefore the second ship, which I identified as a unit of the *Queen Mary* class. It was really the *Princess Royal*, a sister-ship of the *Queen Mary*. Everything was ready to open fire, the tension increased second by second; but still I dared not give the word until the Flagship had signalled, "Open fire." The enemy also held his fire, drawing gradually nearer and nearer to us.

I was giving my next order, "150 Hundred (16,400 yards)," when there came a dull thud, and peering ahead I saw the *Lützow* let go her opening salvo, simultaneously hoisting the signal "Open fire." In the very same second I called out "Salvo fire" and our first salvo thundered forth. The ships astern joined in at once, and we saw tongues of fire and clouds of smoke break out along the enemy's line.

The action had begun! At 5:48 P.M. my recorder in the Transmitting Station wrote down: "5:48. Ship turning to starboard. Rate 200 closing, 150 Hundred, salvo, fire!" Nearly 30 seconds went by before our splash clocks (*Aufschlagmeldeuhren*) sounded their "bleat," this time all three in unison. The new parts I had caused to be inserted had restored them to working order. The shots pitched well together, but over—that is to say—beyond the target and to the right. "Deflection two more left, down four-hundred, again." Those were my orders for the next salvo. "Down four-hundred," meant that the Midshipman working the Range Transmitter should put the telegraph pointer 400 meters lower; and "again" signified that as soon as he had made this correction he himself should give the order, "Salvo fire!" from the Transmitting Station. This arrangement not only relieved the Control Officer, but ruled out the possibility of the order to fire being given before the new correction had been made on the gun sights. By means of a special electrical Repeat Receiver the Midshipman in the Transmitting Station could check the sight-setting of each gun. The Range Transmitter in the Transmitting Station was worked by Midshipman Stachow, a youth aged 17, who also operated the range clock, passing my orders to the turrets and regulating the transmission of orders to fire. He was in communication with me by telephone headpiece, and I was thus able to check all his orders. To the end of the action this young Midshipman performed his duty of regulating the fire discipline of the main and secondary batteries with perfect coolness and skill; only at the outset did he make a mistake.

The second salvo crashed out. Again it was over. "Down four-hundred," I ordered. The third and fourth salvos were also over, notwithstanding that after the third I had ordered "down eight-hundred." "Himmeldonnerwetter, Midshipman Stachow," I swore; "that was a stupid mistake. Down eight-hundred again." The gunnery records showed later that the first "down eight-hundred" had not, perhaps, been understood by the Midshipman; in any case it had not been put on. Now, however, "down eight-hundred" was duly set, and the sixth salvo, fired at 5:52 P.M., straddled the target, three shots falling over and one short. Meanwhile we had closed the range to 119 hectometers, as the range clock was running at first with 2, then with 3 hectometer change of range per minute, and I had already come down 16 hectometers. Up to then we had been about four minutes in action, and had only just obtained our first straddle. That was not a very inspiring result. At first the target had been greatly overranged, owing to faulty range-taking and delay in transmitting the initial figures. For this large error I suggest the following explanation: The Range-takers were startled at the first sight of the hostile *Colossi*. Through his instrument each saw the enemy ship 23 times enlarged. Their thoughts were concentrated on the enemy's appearance, and they worried themselves trying to identify him. When, therefore, the order to open fire was suddenly given, they had not quite determined the range. This initial failure cannot have been due to any lack of skill, since the Range-takers measured perfectly for the rest of the action;

nor to any defect in the instruments—Zeiss stereoscopic range-finders—which, on the contrary, behaved superbly all through the action. The Range Officer informed me later that the results given by all the instruments, even at extreme ranges, seldom differed by more than 3 hectometers.

Precious minutes had been lost, but I was now well on the target, and at 5:52 P.M. my recorder booked my order, "Good, rapid; Hitting." "Good, rapid," meant that Midshipman Stachow in the Transmitting Station was to give the order: "Salvo, fire!" to the turrets every 20 seconds; and "Hitting" signified that the secondary armament should fire two salvos in succession immediately after each salvo from the turrets, and from now on continue to join in with the turret guns. An ear-splitting, deafening turmoil now began. Including the secondary armament, we were now firing mighty salvos at an average interval of seven seconds. Only those who have attended a practice shoot with full charges on board a Dreadnought can form any idea of what that meant. Whilst the salvos were being fired no verbal communication was possible. Dense clouds of smoke repeatedly formed at the gun muzzles, developing into tall clouds which for seconds at a time stood before us like an impenetrable wall, and were then dispersed over the ship by the wind and our own speed. It often happened, therefore, that we lost sight of the enemy for several seconds, as our Gunnery Control Tower was shrouded in dense smoke. Of course this rapid fire from both calibers could not be kept up for long. It demanded almost superhuman exertions from the gunners and ammunition parties; and, moreover, it finally became very difficult to distinguish between the splashes of heavy and light projectiles. Consequently I ordered the secondary armament to "Cease fire!" and for a time continued the action with the heavy guns alone. As a rule the target was soon over—or under—range, owing to the enemy's variations of course, in which case fire had again to be slackened. Each salvo was then separately controlled until the next straddle was obtained, whereupon the "Good, rapid" inferno broke out afresh, the heavy guns firing every 20 seconds and the secondary armament in the intervals. Unfortunately at that date the secondary armament could not shoot beyond a range of 130 hectometers.

I was astonished that we ourselves apparently had not yet been hit. Only very rarely did a projectile fall near us. I examined the gun turrets of our opposite number more closely, and found that this ship was not firing at us. She was firing at our Flagship. I looked for an instant at the third enemy ship; she was firing at our next astern. There was no doubt about it; through some error we had been overlooked. I chuckled grimly, and henceforth controlled our fire with ever-increasing accuracy, and as calmly as if it were a practice shoot. All thoughts of death or sinking were blown away. The pure sporting joy of gunnery awoke in me; I was filled with a wild lust of combat, and my thoughts were concentrated on the single idea of registering rapid and telling hits on our arrogant foe, and hurting him in every possible way. It would not be easy for him to prevent me from returning to my domestic hearth! I had half-whispered the words, "We are overlooked," but everyone in the Gunnery Control Tower caught the message and was filled with uncontrollable joy. Besides us two Gunnery Officers the only people who could see anything of the enemy were the two P.O.s at the training pointers and the Range-taker. True, we had left the look-out slips open—from a not entirely prudent curiosity—but with the naked eye little, of course, could be seen. The men in the Gunnery Control Tower therefore listened eagerly to what we said.

And now the action continued. Our salvos threw up water-spouts 80 to 100 meters in height, twice the height of the enemy's mastheads. Our satisfaction at being overlooked was short-lived. The enemy had discovered his omission, and from now on we were frequently straddled. I could see plainly how the turrets of our opposite number were trained exactly on our ship. Suddenly I discovered something that filled me with astonishment. At every salvo fired by the enemy I distinctly saw four or five projectiles approaching through the air. They looked like elongated black spots, gradually becoming larger and larger, until, in a moment, they were here. On striking the water or the ship they detonated with a terrific crash. I was soon able to determine whether the oncoming projectiles would fall over or short, or whether they would personally honor us with a visit. Hits in the water threw up enormous geysers, some of which appeared for half their height to be of a poisonous greenish-yellow color—obviously caused by lyddite. These spouts hung in the air for five to ten seconds before subsiding. They were gigantic columns of water, compared with which the celebrated Versailles fountains were mere toys. Later on in the action, when the enemy had our range more accurately, it frequently happened that these spouts broke over the ship, flooding everything and incidentally putting out all fires. The first hit in the ship that came under my notice penetrated above the casemate, first passing through a door fitted with a glass scuttle, behind which an efficient Boatswain's Mate, Lorenzen, had stationed himself to watch the action. Being in reserve he had no right to be in that place; but he paid dearly for his curiosity as the shell neatly decapitated him.

We had closed the enemy to 113 hectometers. At 5:55 P.M., however, I was again shooting with a range of 115 hectometers, and thereafter the range opened very rapidly. At 5:57 P.M. I put a rate of "plus 6" (600 opening) on the range clock. At 6 P.M. the range had opened to 152 hectometres and at 6:05 P.M. to 180 hectometres, and after that the enemy was no longer within range, because, at the date of Jutland, 180 hectometers (19,674 yards) represented the extreme range of our guns. It was possible to lengthen it a trifle by instructing the gunlayers to lay, not on the enemy's water-line, but on the upper edge of his funnels, the tops, and, finally, the mastheads. But even so the increase was limited to a few hundred metres. After Jutland our extreme range was lengthened by all manner of improvements. Now, however, we stood powerless before the enemy, unable to return his fire. This state of affairs endured till 6:17 P.M. At 6:10 our flagship altered course several points to starboard; apparently the enemy turned in also, and so the two lines closed each other again fairly quickly. At 6:19 the range had already closed to 160 hectometres. Sixteen kilometres is certainly a respectable distance, but with the weather so clear and the fall of our salvos so visible the shooting range was really moderate. The Zeiss lenses in our periscopes were splendid. Even when the range was greatest I could distinguish through my periscope every detail of the hostile ships, every movement of the turrets and of individual guns, which after each round were laid almost horizontally for reloading. Before the war no-one in our Navy had thought it possible to engage with effect at ranges beyond 150 hectometres. I well remember various war games played at the Officers' Club in Kiel a year or two before the war, under the direction of Admiral von Ingenohl, when no results were allowed for any firing above 100 hectometres.

How was the enemy faring all this while? At 6 P.M. his rear ship, the *Indefatigable*, had blown up. I did not see it, as my attention was fully occupied in controlling our fire on the second ship; and naturally it was impossible to hear even a big explosion amidst the inferno of noise in our own ship and the crash of shells bursting near at hand; though, whenever our guns were silent, we could hear the dull thudding of the enemy's salvos. But in the after Gunnery Control Tower the explosion in the *Indefatigable* was observed and logged. She had been under fire from our rear ship, *Von der Tann*, and was put out of action as the result of a magnificently controlled shoot. The successful Chief Gunnery Officer of the *Von der Tann* was Commander Mahrholz.

The N.W. wind had the effect of blowing the smoke of his own guns parallel with the enemy's ships, thus obscuring his vision and making it difficult for him to range us. Moreover, as the visibility towards the east was not so good as towards the west, the British battle cruisers had taken up a very unfavorable tactical position. We were but little troubled by the enemy's smoke, for with our stereoscopic range-finder it was enough if we could see only a small portion of masthead.

At 6:17 P.M. I again shifted on to the second battle cruiser from the left. I thought this was the same ship that I had previously been engaging, viz., *Princess Royal*, whereas it was in fact, the *Queen Mary*, third ship in the enemy's line. The truth was that at this time, while I was selecting my target, Admiral Beatty's flagship, *Lion*, had had to leave the line and in consequence of the enemy's smoke she was invisible to us. From subsequent reports in the English papers it transpired that Beatty had shifted his flag from the *Lion*, whose conning tower was no longer tenable, to the *Princess Royal*; just as, later on in the action, our Admiral Hipper was compelled to change his flagship. The flagship *Lützow* had opened a heavy and effective fire on the *Lion* with high explosive shell, and in order to avoid the disadvantageous ballistical results of a change of projectile, the Gunnery Officer of *Lützow* preferred to go on using this type of shell. The tremendous explosive and incendiary effects of these high explosive shell had forced the *Lion* to leave the line for a considerable period, in order to extinguish her fires. The consequence was that from 6:17 P.M. onward I was engaging the *Queen Mary*. The work of control now became somewhat troublesome owing to the lenses of the periscopes above the roof of the Gunnery Control Tower getting covered with soot from the guns and funnels, which made it difficult to see anything. At such times I had to depend entirely on the reports of the Spotting Officer in the foretop, Lieutenant von Stosch. This efficient officer observed and reported the fall of our salvos with amazing sang-froid and coolness, and his wonderfully accurate spotting reports—upon which I implicitly relied—contributed very substantially to the success of our arms. While we, therefore, could see nothing, Lieutenant von Stosch, in his eyrie, 35 meters (115 feet) above the waterline, kept his foretop periscope steadily trained upon the enemy. A receiver close to my periscope indicated the movements of this foretop instrument; my direction P.O. kept his pointer in step; and thus we were enabled to keep all guns trained on the enemy without seeing him ourselves. This was, of course, only an emergency measure. Midshipman Bartels, who stood next to me in the Gunnery Control Tower, and who assisted me in the action by calling out the ranges, working the rate instrument, and watching the enemy through the look-out slits, always endeavored promptly to clean the lenses by using the special wiper which could be worked from inside the tower. Later on in the action, when the spray from falling salvos had broken over the ship and the soot consequently adhered tenaciously to the wet glass, Bartels had to clean the lenses after nearly every salvo. Finally the "wiper" itself became covered with soot, and I was therefore compelled, with great reluctance, to station a man on the roof of the tower to clean the glasses by hand, a position in which, of course, he was exposed to enemy shell and splinters. This work was mainly performed by my messenger, Armorer's Mate Meyer, who throughout the action stood on the forward bridge next to the Gunnery Control Tower, until eventually fate overtook him in the form of a splinter, which shattered the lower part of one leg.

As mentioned above, from 6:10 P.M. both lines had been proceeding on a strongly converging, southerly course. At 6:15 P.M. we noticed the enemy was forming up his destroyers for attack. A little later our own destroyers and the light cruiser *Regensburg* broke through our line on their way to attack, and a miniature naval action now developed between the contending lines of battle cruisers. Here some 25 British destroyers and nearly as many German boats fought a stubborn artillery action, and mutually prevented one another from using their torpedoes against the battle cruisers. Towards 6:30 P.M. both sides fired torpedoes against the lines, but no hits were registered. From our point of view this destroyer fight was a magnificent spectacle.

During these destroyer combats the two lines had drawn nearer, and now followed the most interesting action of the whole day from the gunnery point of view. I discovered that the *Queen Mary* had selected the *Derfflinger* as her target. She fired more slowly than we; on the other hand, each of her salvos was generally a full broadside. As she had an armament of eight 13.5-inch guns this meant that eight of these tremendous "portmanteaux"—as the Russians named the heaviest projectiles in the Russo-Japanese War—were hurled at us simultaneously. I saw the projectiles coming, and must say that the enemy shot splendidly. As a rule all eight shots pitched well together; but almost invariably either over or short—only twice was the *Derfflinger* straddled, and on each occasion only one shell actually hit us. We were firing as if at a practice shoot. The headpiece telephones worked beautifully, and every order I gave was correctly understood. Lieutenant von Stosch was reporting with unerring precision the exact fall of the salvos. "Straddled, two hits!" "Straddle, the whole salvo in the ship." I was at pains to try and fire two salvos to the enemy's one, but I did not always succeed, as the enemy was firing full salvos with fabulous rapidity. The Gunnery Officer of the *Queen Mary* was, I found, personally firing his guns with the celebrated "Percy Scott Director"; for all the guns were discharged absolutely at the same instant, and the projectiles also arrived simultaneously. The British Gunnery Officer was probably sitting in the foretop, whence he was able to see well above the cordite smoke, and from this position he fired the guns electrically. This gave the British ships a great advantage. We, unfortunately, did not appreciate the possibilities of indirect firing from the foretop until after our experience in this battle. I myself was able, at a later date, to contribute materially to the introduction of Director Firing into our Navy and personally controlled the first German indirect shoot, from the *Derfflinger*, by means of a system I invented. Later on this system was generally introduced, and was known as the "Derfflinger System."

The *Queen Mary* and *Derfflinger* were now engaged in a regular artillery duel over the heads of the destroyers which fought between us. But the poor *Queen Mary* had bad luck. Beside the *Derfflinger*, the *Seydlitz* also was concentrating on her. And the Gunnery Officer of the *Seydlitz*, Commander Foerster, was one of our most skilful artillerists, who in every previous action had shown himself experienced, cool, and resolute. The *Seydlitz* mounted only 11-inch guns, and these weapons could not pierce the *Queen Mary*'s thickest armor. But in every ship there are thinly-armored places, where the penetration of 11-inch shell can cause very great damage.

Thanks to the good functioning of our "time of flight" or "splash clocks" (*Aufschlagmeldeuhren*), Lieutenant von Stosch or I were always able to distinguish our salvos from the 11-inch salvos of the *Seydlitz*. As the range continued to be above 130 hectometers, neither ship could use its 5.9-inch guns in the action with the *Queen Mary*. Moreover, it was possible for two ships to concentrate on a single target only if each used its heavy guns to the exclusion of the secondary armament. Had the 5.9-inch batteries also joined in, no one could possibly have differentiated between the fall of heavy and medium shot.

The surprising feature of this shooting record is the evidence it furnishes that the bearing of the turrets remained almost stationary, and that during these minutes of supreme importance for the guns the ship steered a wonderfully steady course.

The historic moment at which the *Queen Mary*, the proudest vessel of the British Fleet, met her fate was about 6:26 P.M. From 6:24 onward each of our salvos had landed in the ship. The salvo discharged at 6:26 fell when violent explosions in the interior of the *Queen Mary* had already begun. At first a dazzling red flame leaped up from the forward part of the ship. Then an explosion occurred in the same place, followed by one of much greater violence amidships; black debris shot into the air, and immediately afterwards the entire ship was riven by one tremendous explosion. A gigantic cloud of smoke formed, the masts collapsed towards the center of the ship, and the smoke, rising ever higher, blotted everything from view. Finally, in place of the battle cruiser, there remained nothing but this black curtain of smoke. Narrow at the base, it broadened out above until it took the outline of an immense fir cone. In my estimation this pillar of smoke reached a height of 300 to 400 meters (981 to 1,311 feet).

In the London *Times* of June 9, 1916, a gunlayer of the *Tiger*, which ship was next astern of the *Queen Mary* in the action, gave the following description of the *Queen Mary*'s loss:—"As the German squadron again approached us they concentrated all their guns on the *Queen Mary*. For some minutes they vainly tried to get the correct range. All at once, however, a very remarkable thing happened—every shell fired by the Germans suddenly seemed to be hitting the battle cruiser. It was like a hurricane smiting a forest. The *Queen Mary* seemed to roll slowly to starboard; her mast and funnels went and in her side there gaped a huge hole. She heeled far over, the hole disappeared below the surface, and the water which now poured into the ship caused her to capsize completely. A minute and a half later all that could be seen of the *Queen Mary* was her keel, and finally that vanished too."

In the further course of the action our destroyers picked up two survivors of the *Queen Mary*, a midshipman and a seaman, and brought them as prisoners to Wilhelmshaven. According to their statements, there were upwards of 1,400 men on board the *Queen Mary*, including a Japanese Prince, who was said to have been Naval Attaché in London. The Commanding Officer of the *Queen Mary* was Captain C. J. Prowse. In publishing the officers' casualty list the British Admiralty stated, *apropos* the *Queen Mary*, that "with the exception of four Midshipmen, all the officers on board were lost."

Zeebrugge: Twisting the Dragon's Tail

Sir Roger Keyes

For sheer audacity, no operation in modern naval history can surpass the British raid on German submarine pens at Bruges in Occupied Belgium on St. George's Day, 1918. In this case, St. George may not have slain the dragon, but, as one of the participants wryly observed, the dragon's tail was given a "damned good twist."

The cost was not small. Vice Admiral Roger Keyes counted more than five hundred casualties after he succeeded in blocking the entrance to the inland harbor at Bruges by sinking three old cruisers filled with concrete in the channel mouth at Zeebrugge (see photograph). A similar effort a few miles away at Ostend failed. Three weeks later, the Germans had dredged a new channel around the blockships and the pens at Bruges were operational once again.

But this was more than just a short-lived victory. Aside from giving a giant boost to the morale of the Allies, sagging after a series of defeats *earlier in the year, the raid planted the seeds for the bold, behind-enemy-lines Commando and Ranger assaults of World War II. One such raid in December 1941, aimed at killing German Field Marshal Erwin Rommel, was led by Lieutenant Colonel Geoffrey C. T. Keyes, the son of then Sir Roger Keyes. He was killed and Rommel escaped. Other such operations, however, achieved their purpose, although often at heavy cost in lives.*

Even more importantly, Zeebrugge nullified the Gallipoli disaster. It showed that an amphibious attack against a fortified coast need not suffer the same fate as at Gallipoli in 1915, but could, if led by men with an iron will, force its way ashore into the teeth of enemy resistance. The visionaries of the United States Navy who planned the daring American island-hopping campaign across the Marshall, Caroline, and Philippine Islands took courage from Zeebrugge.

My wife walked down to the pier with me to see me off, apparently quite unperturbed. She alone knew what a hell of a time I had been going through [when the mission was twice cancelled due to weather conditions]. Her last words were, that the next day was St. George's Day (which I had not realized), and that it was sure to be the best day for our enterprise, as St. George would bring good fortune to England, and she begged me to use "St. George for England" as our battle cry.

When I became director of plans and took a hand in the anti-submarine campaign in October 1917, it seemed to me vitally important, not only to make the passage of the Dover Straits dangerous to enemy submarines, but to strike at the root of the evil, by attempting to block the sea exits from Bruges, which the Germans had developed into a most formidable and well-equipped base for destroyers and submarines.

Zeebrugge harbor was connected by a ship canal with the inland docks at Bruges, which communicated again by means of smaller canals with Ostend harbor. The whole formed a triangle with two sea entrances. The eastern side, which was eight miles long, was the ship canal from Zeebrugge to Bruges; the southern side, which was eleven miles long, consisted of the smaller canals from Bruges to Ostend; the base, running northeast, was the twelve miles of heavily fortified coastline between Ostend and Zeebrugge.

This formidable system had been installed since the German occupation in 1914, and it was believed that Bruges provided a base for at least 35 enemy torpedo craft and about 30 submarines. By reason of its position and comparative security, it constituted a continual and ever-increasing menace to the sea communications of our Army, and to the seaborne trade and food supplies of the United Kingdom.

The main objects of the enterprise, therefore, were to block the Bruges ship canal at its entrance into the harbor at Zeebrugge [see photograph]; to block the entrance to Ostend harbor from the sea; and to inflict as much damage as possible upon the ports of Zeebrugge and Ostend.

When the operations were undertaken, it was believed that although the blocking of the Zeebrugge entrance was the most important of all objects, it would be necessary also to block the entrance to Ostend harbor, in order to seal up the Bruges ship canal and docks, for unless this was done the lighter craft would still be able to pass to and fro, more or less freely, through the smaller canals.

In accordance with the timetable for April 22–23, 1918, the whole force formed up punctually in their cruising order by 5 P.M., when the expedition set out for the Belgian coast.

The force immediately under my flag that night consisted of 76 vessels organised in 26 units, each distinguished by a letter and each of which had definite instructions for its conduct.

Before night fell, remembering my wife's last words, I made a general signal by semaphore, "St. George for England," and Carpenter [captain of the *Vindictive*] signalled back: "May we give the dragon's tail a damned good twist," which was very apt and to the point, but did not fit in with my mood at the moment.

After the twilight had faded, the full moon made it almost as bright as day—at least so it seemed to me, for I was very alive to the risks I had added by attempting the enterprise with a full moon, and the visibility appeared to be at least eight to ten miles. When I remarked on this, Tomkinson said dryly: "Well, even if the enemy expect us, they will never think we are such damned fools as to try and do it in bright moonlight." Soon after this it became misty; later it commenced to drizzle and the visibility was reduced to less than a mile.

On arriving at D buoy, the whole force stopped to enable all but the essential crews of the three blockships to be disembarked; some of them could not be found; in fact these men stowed away in the *Iphigenia*, determined not to be deprived of the honor of being present when their ship was sunk in the enemy canal. An admirable spirit, but it added to the difficulties of the rescue work.

We got under way again, with the *Iris, Daffodil,* and submarines still in tow, in time to pass G buoy at 10:30 P.M., precisely the program time.

The *Brilliant, Sirius,* two destroyers, and two small motor boats then parted company, bound for Ostend, while we continued on our way to Zeebrugge.

There was no sign of the air attack, which should have commenced an hour earlier, and we concluded that it had been held up by the rain.

After passing G buoy, the *Warwick,* followed by the *Phœbe* and *North Star* (L Unit), the *Whirlwind* and *Myngs* (F Unit) on her port beam, drew out a mile ahead of the main force to drive off any enemy vessels that might be out on patrol. L Unit was charged with the duty of protecting the boarding ships, and the approach of the blockships, from possible destroyer attacks. I decided to remain with them in my ship, the *Warwick,* because it seemed almost incredible that the enemy's destroyers—several of which were known normally to lie alongside the Mole [the fortified breakwater guarding the entrance to the Zeebrugge canal]—would not come out to seek action and at least attempt to torpedo the *Vindictive* after she arrived alongside the Mole; this was the only way she could be attacked, since all her vitals would then be protected from gunfire by the Mole itself, if she berthed anywhere near her proper position.

The bombardment by the *Erebus* and *Terror* should have commenced at forty minutes after X [the point of departure] but was also delayed; we learned later that it was on account of the low visibility, but fortunately they were able to pick up the Oost gas light and whistle buoy marking the limit of the Dutch territorial waters, which we knew to be accurately charted, and they commenced firing 15 minutes later than the program time. Captain Wills of the *Erebus,* who was in command of that unit, had orders to continue the bombardment at intervals throughout the operation, until ordered by wireless to cease fire; but in any case he was to get out of range of Knocke Battery by daylight.

Three small motor boats (Units A and B) went ahead at full speed at forty minutes after X to lay a smokescreen across our front, behind which the whole force was to advance. Another small motor boat (Unit C) also went off ten minutes later to lay a smoke float off Blankenberghe and renew it every 20 minutes. This she did very effectively, but owing to engine trouble was a little behind her timetable; anyhow, no enemy fast motor boats appear to have emerged.

Fifty minutes after passing X, one small motor boat (Unit D) proceeded towards the Mole at high speed to lay smoke floats in the western section, for screening in a northeasterly wind. She was then to patrol this line, making smoke, until relieved by eight motor launches (Unit G).

Another small motor boat (Unit E) proceeded at the same time to lay smoke floats and patrol the eastern section until relieved by eight motor launches (Unit I).

Two small motor boats (Unit H) proceeded at full speed, to fire their torpedoes at the enemy destroyers secured to the inner side of the Mole, and then run to the eastward making smoke, about a mile from the shore, to blank off the heavy batteries to the eastward of the canal entrance.

Two small motor boats (Unit V), 70 minutes after X, proceeded at full speed direct for the end of the Mole, to lay their smoke floats under the seaward side of the lighthouse extension, within 50 yards of the Mole if possible; the object being to mask the guns on the lighthouse extension during the near approach of the boarding vessels. These floats had their battle plates removed, so that the flame emanating from them would indicate the approximate position of the Mole end.

The smokescreens appeared to be excellent, and they were entirely responsible for enabling the whole force to close unseen. It was not until about 11:50 P.M.—about ten minutes before the *Vindictive* was due alongside the Mole—that the enemy appear to have heard the small motor boats, and then the star shells burst in the sky, making it as light as day, some well to seaward of us; one actually fell on the deck of the *Myngs*, three miles from the Mole. As they descended the lights were blanked out by the pall of smoke, which at that time rose to a good height above the sea level. Shortly after this, just before midnight, the enemy appeared to be thoroughly alarmed and with a roar like express trains, great shells passed over our heads, and a heavy barrage from the coast batteries was put down two or three miles outside us. It was an intense relief to me to know that the battle was now joined and there could be no more turning back.

I had been deploring the absence of our aircraft's flare parachutes, but the enemy's star shells provided all the illumination we required throughout the action.

The *Warwick* must have passed very close to the end of the Mole, but we were hidden in the smoke. The *Vindictive* was not so fortunate. She was steered from the conning tower, in which

Lieutenant Commander Rosoman was stationed. Captain Carpenter was conning the ship from the port *flammenwerfer* [flamethrower] hut, which had been specially protected against machine-gun bullets and splinters, and which gave an excellent view from the starboard bow to nearly right astern. Carpenter states that:

> . . . when the *Vindictive* emerged from the smoke and the lighthouse extension on the Mole was seen to loom out of the semidarkness, about 300 yards distant on the port bow, speed was immediately increased to full speed.

At one minute past midnight the ship bumped the Mole, taking the blow on the two specially prepared fenders, and the starboard anchor was let go.

It was very unfortunate that, during the brief moments that the *Vindictive* was within the arc of fire of the Mole battery, the smoke should have failed, as her upper works and personnel suffered heavily. Colonel Elliot, Major Cordner and Captain Halahan were killed—as in their ardor to lead, they were all in exposed positions.

The increase to full speed was also very unfortunate, as it carried the *Vindictive* far beyond the position I was so anxious for her to take up; she eventually brought up 340 yards beyond it, out of reach of her primary objective—the guns which commanded the approach of the blockships—and she was exposed to the direct fire of the shore batteries to the westward of the Mole, which did much damage to the ship while she was lying alongside.

The *Vindictive* went through a very trying time before she was berthed; the Mole anchors failed to grapple the parapet, owing to the derricks being too short, and it was not until the *Daffodil* arrived, three minutes later, and pushed the *Vindictive* bodily against the Mole, that the gangplanks could be dropped on the parapet and the disembarkation started. Unfortunately only two of these could be used at first—though two more were brought into use later—the others having suffered from the Mole end shell fire, and from crashing against the Mole before the ship was berthed.

A vessel drawing nineteen feet, proceeding at high speed in shoal water, of course, carries a considerable surge with her, and for some minutes there was a good deal of movement caused by this and the backwash when the *Vindictive* first went alongside; and it was not an easy matter for men carrying machine guns, ammunition, and portable flame-throwers, etc., to make their way along the gangplanks, which were sawing considerably on the Mole parapet.

The fixed flame-throwers were intended to keep the enemy at a distance, while the *Vindictive* was being berthed and the disembarkation was taking place. Brock, who had taken charge of the after flame-thrower, was very confident of being able to drive off the Germans manning the guns on the Mole, until a sufficient force had landed to rush them. Both flame-throwers, however, were put out of action by the oil-pipe connections being cut by gunfire during the approach, but in any case they would have been of no use in the *Vindictive*'s position, as no enemy came within their reach.

The command of the bluejacket assaulting force devolved upon Lieutenant Commander B. Adams, Halahan's second-in-command—Lieutenant Commander Harrison—having been knocked unconscious with a broken jaw before the *Vindictive* reached the Mole. Adams, followed by his men, was the first to land, and he reported that no enemy was in sight on the Mole. After fruitless efforts to help Rosoman place the Mole anchor in position over the parapet, he led the bluejackets along the footpath in the direction of the guns, and found a concrete lookout station about forty yards to the eastward of the *Vindictive*'s stern, with "what looked like a range-finder mounted behind it but higher up." This (according to German accounts) was the control station of the Goeben battery of four naval eight-inch guns. Nearly half of Adams's company were casualties in the *Vindictive*, and he had not many troops with him, but Brock and one of his party were among them, and he told Adams that he intended to go inside the lookout station and find out how the rangefinder worked, evidently thinking that this was what he was looking for. A bomb was thrown in and the place was found to be deserted. Brock went in, and Adams never saw him again.

There was an iron ladder abreast of the control station, from the pathway to the Mole, and Adams sent a few men down it to attack some Germans, who were endeavoring to run from the shelters abreast of the pathway to the shore side of the Mole. While under cover of the control station, Adams took stock of the situation. He reported that: "The whole Mole was lighted by German starshells and was well lighted all the time, our rockets fired from aft towards the three-gun battery assisting." He noted that two destroyers, lying alongside the Mole abreast of the *Vindictive*, were inactive; on the other hand the enemy seemed to be firing at the *Vindictive* from the shoreward end of the Mole. He said he could see clearly the three guns on the Mole end, and was certain that they never fired during the whole time that he was on shore. Adams also noted that barbed wire ran from Number 3 shed up to the end of the Mole, with at least one gap in it, and about 100 yards from the control station he could see what he took to be a trench, with stones heaped up in front of it. He then collected his men and led them with a rush along the pathway towards the guns, whereupon a machine gun from behind the trench opened fire on his party, and some Germans, who were evidently advancing to meet him, fired a volley and then retired. His small party suffered a good many casualties, and having no one in support, he fell back upon the control station and placed his men behind it. He then went back to get reinforcements and finding a few men of B Company—which had suffered severely in the *Vindictive* and had lost their officers, Lieutenant Chamberlain killed and Lieutenant Walker badly wounded—he took them back with him and led another rush along the parapet, but was again stopped by machine-gun fire, which caused several more casualties. He again took shelter behind the control station, but it was now under the fire of a machine gun from one of the destroyers, which added to his losses.

Harrison, meantime, had recovered consciousness, and though terribly wounded in the jaw, now appeared and took command; he sent Adams back to ask for Marine reinforcements. Adams found Major Weller, who had succeeded to the command of the battalion, and asked him to send help. Major Weller ordered a platoon to support the bluejackets; but the siren had already sounded the recall and all Adams could do was to rejoin his men at the control station, where he learned that Harrison had collected every man who could stand, and had led another rush along the pathway, until he and all his party were killed or wounded. Only one or two managed to crawl back to the shelter of the control station. They reported that Able Seaman Eaves had endeavored to carry Harrison's body back, but had himself been killed while doing do. Adams then recalled the men who had descended on to the Mole by the iron ladder, who had accounted for a few Germans in the shelters, and sent his party carrying their wounded back to the ship in obedience to the recall signal. While this was being done he went along the pathway again to try and find Harrison, and make certain that no wounded were being left behind, but the pathway was swept by machine-gun fire as soon as he appeared and he was lucky to escape.

After the *Vindictive* was berthed, Osborne left the foretop to lay the howitzers on to their target, having turned the top over to Lieutenant C. Rigby with instructions to cover the landing party as

The majestic bow of Dewey's flagship *Olympia*. (*National Archives*)

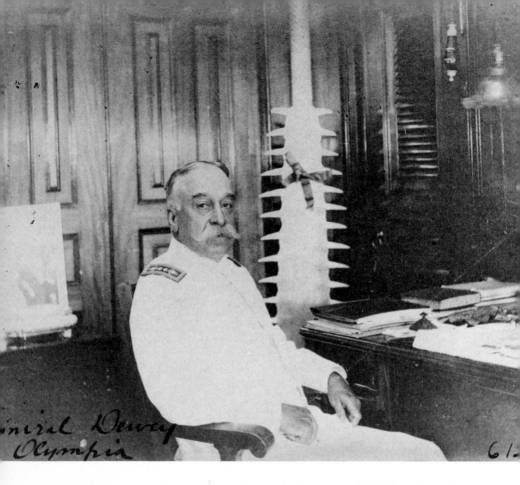

Above, Dewey decorated his cabin with a huge sawfish bill. Below, the charred hulk of the Spanish cruiser *Vizcaya* after the Battle of Santiago in 1898.

C. C. Mitchell, *Olympia's* bugler who sounded "General Quarters" at the Battle of Manila Bay in 1898.

A Japanese sailor guards the damaged Russian battleship *Orel* after her capture at the Battle of Tsushima in 1905.

Lieutenant Rizzo, above, receives a medal for sinking the Austrian battleship
Wien .... like the one below. His greatest tri-
umph was yet to come. *(National Archives)*

Above, concrete-filled blockships plug the harbor at Zeebrugge after the British raid in 1918. (*Imperial War Museum*) Below, U. S. Navy aircraft playfully buzz the fleet in the mid-1930s.

Above, Japanese carrier pilots bound for Pearl Harbor clown as they listen to a radio broadcast from unsuspecting Honolulu. (*Life Picture Service and Movietonews, Inc.*) Below, the gruesomely charred corpse of a Japanese pilot is hauled from the bottom of Pearl Harbor.

Above, adversaries in Leyte Gulf, Kurita, and Kinkaid. Below, strategists
Yamamoto and Nimitz. (*National Archives*)

Above, the *Bismarck* fights for her life shortly before her destruction in May 1941. Center, a kamikaze (barely visible at top) sweeps into the *Missouri*. (*National Archives*) Below, the *Lexington* is virtually lifted from the water by the force of an explosion at the Battle of Coral Sea in 1942. (*National Archives*)

An American carrier task force of the type that overwhelmed Japanese forces in World War II. (*National Archives*)

Above, proficiency in amphibious warfare helped defeat Japan. Center, the crew of the stricken carrier *Zuikaku* salute the lowering of their ensign. (*National Archives*) Below, at the height of the Cold War two U. S. Navy Phantoms escort a Badger as the Soviet aircraft overflies the *Kitty Hawk*.

Navy pilot Frank Elkins, reported missing in action in Vietnam in 1966.
(*Marilyn Elkins*)

far as possible—no easy task, for no enemy were in sight and it was difficult to locate the guns, which were hitting the *Vindictive* every few seconds, chiefly the funnels and upper works, splinters from which were causing many casualties. However, Rigby and his Marine artillerymen did yeoman service, and were probably responsible for preventing any hostile action in the enemy's destroyers, which were inactive for a long time. Unfortunately two shells—probably from the antiaircraft guns nearby on the Mole—wrecked the top, killed Rigby and killed or wounded every one else in it. Sergeant N. Finch, who was himself severely wounded, kept a Lewis gun in action until another direct hit completed the destruction of the whole armament of the top.

Meanwhile, Osborne, having ascertained where the *Vindictive* was actually berthed, and data having been previously worked out for every few yards, directed the howitzers to open fire on their selected targets. The 11-inch howitzer on the quarterdeck maintained a steady rate of fire on Goeben and the other batteries protecting the canal entrance, throughout the *Vindictive*'s stay alongside the Mole, under the direction of Captain R. Dallas Brooks. The 7.5-inch on the false deck was to fire at the outer lock gate until the blockships arrived, in the hope that it would be run back into its shelter and thus let the *Thetis* in. It was afterwards to fire at the batteries; unfortunately the gun was damaged by a shell which caused several casualties, and it was out of action until shortly before the *Vindictive* left the Mole.

The 7.5-inch howitzer on the forecastle, which was to shell the seaplane sheds, never opened fire; the original crew, who were ordered to keep under shelter until the *Vindictive* was berthed, were killed or wounded before she arrived alongside the Mole; a relief gun's crew was provided from the six-inch battery, but were wiped out almost at once by a shell which must have come from the batteries to the westward of the Mole. Most of the casualties on board the *Vindictive* after she ran clear of the Mole battery were due to splinters caused by shells bursting against the upperworks and funnels.

As originally planned, A, B, and D Companies of bluejackets were to attack the batteries on the Mole end and extension before the blockships passed; but as they were 340 yards further from their objective than was intended, with the intervening ground fully exposed to machine-gun fire from three directions, it was physically impossible for them to achieve their object, and so ended the gallant effort of the survivors of A and B Company to capture the guns on the Mole extension, which had inflicted such heavy loss on their comrades and had played such a decisive part in the action. During the whole of the engagement the bluejackets were never able to come to grips with the enemy, but were defeated by machine-gun and rifle fire from a distance, as I had feared might happen, unless they could be landed right on top of the guns.

At about 12:50, the blockships having been seen to pass into the harbor, Carpenter had ordered the *Daffodil* to sound the recall, as all the searchlights and sirens in the *Vindictive* had been destroyed. After waiting about 20 minutes, as no further men were returning, he requested *Daffodil* to tow *Vindictive*'s bow away from the Mole. The hawser parted almost at once, but the ship's head was already well clear of the Mole and, thanks to her smokescreen, she was not hit again on her way out.

On board the *Vindictive*, Carpenter, Osborne, Brooks, Ferguson, Rosoman, and Bramble and a number of men seem to have borne charmed lives as they went about their work. The two latter, though painfully wounded in the legs (Rosoman twice), crawled and hopped about, stuck to their work and refused to stay below; as did Hilton Young. Walker, too, was splendid, cheering and waving on the few survivors of his company after he had been hit by a shell which took off his hand.

When Halahan was killed, Edwards, who was standing alongside him, fell shot through both legs; finding that he could not move, he ordered two men who passed to carry him on to the Mole, as things did not seem to be going too well. However, in spite of his protests, they carried him below and thus probably saved his life.

Hilton Young—who received a wound early in the action which subsequently necessitated the amputation of his right arm—in a vivid account of his experiences, says that after he had had his wound dressed: "I went up one of the gangplanks on to the Mole in order to see how they were resting. The swell, which had been very bad at first, was diminishing and such of the gangplanks as survived, seemed to be resting comfortably enough." This was fortunate, otherwise the embarkation of the wounded, which was carried out with devoted bravery, up the scaling ladders from the Mole and across the gangplanks would have been well nigh impossible. Some lost their lives while so occupied, including Captain Tuckey of the Royal Marines.

Peshall the Padre, in addition to helping many gallant souls to pass, saved many lives. Like Harrison he had played rugby for

England, and exerting his great strength, he went backwards and forwards to the Mole carrying the wounded back on his shoulders until the ship left.

A shell hit a pile of boxes containing fused Stokes bombs and started a fire in the *Vindictive* which was difficult to extinguish. Petty Officer Youlton stamped on the burning material, without the smallest regard for his own safety, while shouting to others to take cover.

The *Daffodil* had passed the Mole battery without being hit. It was originally intended that after the *Vindictive* was secured the *Daffodil* should lie alongside her to disembark her men, but as the *Vindictive* was unable to secure herself the *Daffodil* continued to push her against the Mole throughout the action. The seamanship displayed by Lieutenant Harold Campbell, who during the greater part of the time was suffering from a wound in the head, which temporarily deprived him of the sight of one eye, was admirable, and the devotion of the engineers and stokers, who maintained a pressure of steam far higher, I was told, than had ever been attained previously, enabled the *Daffodil* to keep the *Vindictive* pinned to the wall in the strong tideway for 55 minutes. During this time, a shell entered the engine room and two compartments were filled, and the escape of the *Daffodil* was little short of a miracle, as she was a target for the guns to the west of the Mole, whenever the smoke blew clear. Campbell's skill and devotion undoubtedly saved the *Vindictive*'s assault from being an utter failure; but for the *Daffodil*, very few of the *Vindictive*'s storming party could have been landed, and hardly any could have been reembarked.

Meanwhile the *Iris* had been going through a very difficult time. Unfortunately her tow had parted at 11:11 P.M. and being unable to keep up, she reached the Mole ten minutes after the *Vindictive*. Like the *Daffodil* she passed the Mole extension battery without being hit, and went alongside the Mole and dropped her starboard anchor. Owing to the wave action she bumped heavily and great difficulty was experienced in placing the parapet anchors. An attempt was made to land by the scaling ladders before the ship was secured; Lieutenant Claud Hawkings managed to get one ladder in position and actually reached the parapet, the ladder being crashed to pieces just as he stepped off it. This very gallant young officer was last seen defending himself with his revolver, and was killed on the parapet.

Lieut. Commander Bradford then climbed up the derrick

rigged out over the port side, which carried a large parapet anchor. During this climb the ship was surging up and down and the derrick was crashing against the wall. Awaiting his opportunity, he jumped with the parapet anchor onto the Mole and placed it in position. Immediately after hooking the anchor on the parapet, Bradford was riddled with machine-gun bullets, and fell into the sea between the Mole and the ship. Most gallant efforts were made to recover his body, and Petty Officer Hallihan lost his life trying to do so. Unfortunately the anchor tore away when the strain came on it. Commander Gibbs, realizing the impossibility of securing the ship in this position, slipped his starboard anchor and, going around the *Daffodil*'s stern, secured alongside *Vindictive*'s starboard quarter, and commenced to disembark D Company of bluejackets and the Marines; but by this time the recall was sounded and very few got across the *Vindictive*.

While all this was going on, the explosives-laden submarines had been approaching their objective [the viaduct connecting the Mole to the shore. Their plan was to crash into this structure and blow it to pieces, thus cutting off reinforcements from the batteries at the seaward end of the Mole.] At 11:26 P.M., Submarine *C3* slipped her tow. Sandford, finding *C1* and the picket-boat were not in company, nevertheless proceeded on the prearranged courses, and duly sighted the viaduct right ahead, at a distance of about one and a half miles. *C3* being illuminated by the star shells, came under the fire of some four-inch guns to the westward of the Mole, but this was not long maintained. When the viaduct was approximately half a mile off, a flare on the far side silhouetted the Mole and the viaduct. Two searchlights were then switched on to *C3* and off again after a minute or two. Sandford turned on his smoke, but found that it drifted to seaward and was useless.

By this time the viaduct was clearly visible 100 yards away, and course was altered to insure striking the viaduct exactly at right angles. Sandford was now well placed to abandon ship and make use of the gyro steering gear, but decided not to risk failure by doing so, but to ram the viaduct with the crew on board. Indeed, I do not believe that he, or his brother, ever intended to make use of the gyro gear, and they only installed it to save me from a subsequent charge of having condemned six men to practically certain death.

As the submarine approached, men could be seen on the viaduct and could be heard laughing and talking, and there can be little doubt that the enemy were amused at the thought of catching a

British submarine alive in the network of their viaduct. Probably this was also the reason why the searchlights switched off, after they had picked up *C3* in the beam.

C3 struck the viaduct exactly between two rows of piers, at a speed of nine and a half knots, riding up on to the horizontal girders of the viaduct, which raised the hull bodily about two feet; she penetrated up to the conning tower. The crew, having mustered on deck before the collision, lowered and manned the skiff. The fuses were then ignited and the submarine abandoned. It was now found that the propeller of the skiff had been damaged, and the crew had to get out their oars and row as hard as they could to the westward, against the current, to prevent their skiff being swept under the viaduct. As soon as the skiff left the submarine, the two searchlights were switched on and fire was opened by machine guns, rifles, and pom-poms, the viaduct being lined by riflemen firing under the windscreen. The boat was holed many times, but was kept afloat by the special pumps which had been fitted. Sandford and two of his crew were severely wounded, but Lieutenant Howell Price and the other two men succeeded in getting about 200 yards away, before the submarine blew up with a tremendous explosion, hurling one hundred feet of the viaduct and all upon it into the air. Debris fell all around the boat, both searchlights were extinguished, and after that there was very little firing.

When the *Thetis*—the leader of the three blockships which were to play the principal part in our enterprise—rounded the light house at the end of the Mole she increased to full speed, and signalled to her consorts to do likewise. The *Thetis* tore through the net defense between the two outer buoys, carrying it with her. By this time the guns on the Mole extension were hitting her with salvo after salvo. The *Thetis* fired back at the Mole extension guns, and at a barge mounting a gun, which she sank. The piers of the canal entrance were in sight, when both engines were reported to have stopped and she grounded. The *Thetis* had cleared the net obstruction away, enough to enable the ships following to pass to starboard of her, and she signalled to them to do so. The sinking charges were fired; they detonated well and the ship sank quickly. The whole ship's company manned the one remaining cutter and rowed to motor launch *526*, which was standing nearby.

Next came the *Intrepid*, under heavy shrapnel and light flares ("flaming onions"); the latter being useless to the enemy on account of the smokescreen. After passing around the lighthouse she proceeded to the canal entrance, directed by the *Thetis*, which was aground on her port side. Very few guns fired at her and she suffered no damage. There was now nothing to prevent her from ramming the lock gates, or if open, running into the lock. However, in obedience to his orders, on reaching the narrow part of the canal entrance, Lieutenant Bonham Carter put the *Intrepid*'s helm hard-a-starboard, and went full speed ahead starboard, and full speed astern port. He then waited for the crew to get into their boats, but finding that the ship had stern way, and fearing that she would swing into the channel, instead of lying across it, he blew his charges without waiting for the engine room to be cleared.

Owing to the presence of the surplus crews, the boats were overcrowded. Engineer Sub-Lieutenant Meikle took charge of a cutter load and rowed into the harbor, where they were picked up by motor launch *526*. Another cutter rowed right out to sea and was picked up by the *Whirlwind*, and a skiff load was picked up by motor launch *282*.

Bonham Carter, Lieutenant A. Cory Wright, Sub-Lieutenant Dudley Babb, and four petty officers were the last to leave in a Carley float, and they paddled down the canal until picked up by motor launch *282*. The Carley float had a calcium flare, which they had great difficulty in detaching, and until they did so, it attracted the fire of the machine guns on shore, which they avoided as much as possible by dropping overboard and keeping as low as they could.

Incredible as it may seem, of the *Intrepid*'s crew of eighty-seven officers and men, the only casualty was one petty officer, killed by machine-gun fire while on board motor launch *282*.

The following account of the *Iphigenia*'s proceedings is the report made the next day by Lieutenant Billyard Leake:

> On rounding the Mole I proceeded at full speed. Shortly after turning, the harbor was lit by star shell, which showed the *Intrepid* heading for the canal and *Thetis* aground. On approaching the *Thetis* a green light was shown on her starboard side, which enabled me to find the entrance to the canal.
>
> The ship was hit twice on the starboard side, one shell cutting the steam pipes, and enveloping the fore part of the ship in steam. On approaching the canal entrance it became obscured with smoke, and I found I was heading for the western pier. I went full speed astern and brought the ship in between a dredger and barge, severing the barge from the dredger. I then went ahead starboard, and drove the barge up the canal. As soon as I was clear of the barge, I went ahead

both engines, and sighted the *Intrepid* aground on the western bank, with a gap between her bow and the eastern bank. I endeavored to close this gap, but collided with the port bow of *Intrepid* while turning. I then rang my alarm gong. Finding I was not completely blocking the channel, I rang down astern which got through to the engine room. As soon as I was clear, I sent Lieutenant Vaux to the engine room with an order to go ahead, which was promptly obeyed. The entire entrance was then covered in smoke.

As soon as I considered the ship had headway, I went astern port, ahead starboard, helm hard-a-starboard, and grounded on the eastern bank. I then abandoned ship and fired my charges, which all exploded. The ship's company left the ship in one cutter, as the other one was badly damaged. While in the cutter we came under more shrapnel and machine-gun fire, which caused some casualties. While endeavoring to pull clear, I sighted the bow of motor launch *282* across the stem of the ship and rowed up to her. The majority of the crew managed to get into the motor launch, which then went astern. The remainder in the cutter rowed around the stern and the motor launch picked them up.

The cutter was then made fast to the stem of the motor launch, which proceeded out of the harbor at full speed astern.

This modest tale is a very inadequate record of this cool-headed young officer's remarkable display of judgment, initiative, and good seamanship.

We were relying on the stems of the two blockships to penetrate the silt and ground hard and fast against the bottom on either side of the canal bank. Billyard Leake having expected to find the *Intrepid*'s bow run up on the eastern bank, in accordance with her orders, was intended to ram the western bank and swing the *Iphigenia*'s stern across the channel until it grounded on the eastern bank.

Having navigated his ship into a position in which he could easily have carried out his orders, he found that the *Intrepid* had been sunk with her bow well clear of the eastern bank, though her stern appeared to be very close to the western bank. It must have been a temptation to him to obey his orders, which he was in a position to do with absolute certainty of success. To have risked personal success, by going astern in that narrow channel, under shell and machine-gun fire, with the possibility of losing his bearings in the smoke and escaping steam, in order to try and retrieve the *Intrepid*'s failure, was an altogether admirable decision.

When he eventually had maneuverd the *Iphigenia* into a position in which he could swing her bow across the gap left by the *Intrepid*, and did so, he was still not content, but continued to work his ship around, with her propellers going ahead and astern, until both ends of his ship were firmly embedded in the silt.

Lieutenant P. T. Dean, whose motor launch was exposed to machine-gun fire at very close range, and impatiently waiting for the *Iphigenia* to sink, told me he thought: "The damned fellow would never stop juggling with his engines."

Immense credit is due to Ralph Sneyd, the cool, collected captain of the *Thetis*, whose ship had borne the whole brunt of the enemy's fire, which reduced her to a sinking condition, and killed or wounded 20 percent of his crew; nevertheless, having cleared the way for his consorts, he continued to direct them until they reached their goal.

But if it had not been for Billyard Leake's gallant initiative, the efforts of his two colleagues might well have been in vain.

It is astounding that the *Intrepid* and *Iphigenia* should have suffered so little from the guns on the extension and the destroyers alongside the Mole. I am of the opinion (based on a subsequent close examination of the extension battery and the arrangements for the supply of ammunition), that the guns were directed towards the shore, pounding the *Thetis* in the harbor, while the other ships, hidden in the smoke, slipped by from seaward; and that the supply of ready ammunition on the pathway had run out by the time they entered the harbor.

Goeben Battery and other shore guns also seem to have concentrated on the *Thetis*, after the Mole extension battery had reduced her to a sinking condition, with the result that the *Intrepid* and *Iphigenia* were able to enter the canal almost undamaged. The destroyers' failure to fire torpedoes is accounted for by the fact (disclosed in German accounts), that the men were nearly all ashore in dugouts, where some of them were found and killed by our men. Their machine guns, which took such heavy toll of the storming parties on the Mole, were being manned by officers, who happened to be having a party on board.

Owing to the breakdown of motor launch *128*, and the sinking of motor launch *110*, Dean was left with the task of bringing out all the rest of the blockships' crews, about double the number he anticipated. His skill and heroic determination were simply incredible. Under deadly machine- and heavy gunfire, he embarked over 100 officers and men in his frail craft. Hearing that an officer had been left behind in the water, he returned into the canal and picked him up. Having no room to turn, he went out full speed astern, towing a cutter from his stem, handling his ship with his engines, his steering gear having been damaged. When about to pass the Mole end battery, he ran in under the Mole and rounded the extension so close that the guns could not be depressed to fire on him, and he kept them in line while he went to seaward.

Throughout the escape, the motor launch was under constant machine-gun fire; Dean's second in command and three of his four deckhands were shot down beside him, and a great many of his passengers were killed and wounded.

After the withdrawal of the boarding vessels, the *Warwick* stood in again towards Zeebrugge to look for stragglers, and fortunately met motor launch *282* coming out. She was crowded, simply packed with men, who stood up and cheered wildly when they saw the *Warwick*. I hailed Dean and asked him how many people he had picked up, he replied about 70, and it seemed too good to be true. He said he had a great many wounded and I told him to come alongside. As the motor launch's helm was put hard over to do so, she took the ugly list of a top-heavy, overladen vessel. I don't suppose a motor launch would be licensed to carry more than 50 people in the quiet waters of the Thames; but 101 were counted out, including a good many killed and 20 odd wounded.

Dean's passengers were the survivors of the *Intrepid* and *Iphigenia*, including their captains, who came up on to the bridge at once to report to me. Billyard Leake might have stepped straight out of a military tailor's shop, equipped for the trenches, leather coat, shrapnel helmet all complete, very erect and absolutely unperturbed. He saluted and reported that he had sunk the *Iphigenia* with her bow hard aground on the eastern, and her stern on the western bank, in the narrow part of the canal.

Bonham Carter, bareheaded and dressed in a dirty wet vest and trousers—as he had been swimming in the canal in water covered with oil from the sunken blockships—made a good contrast. He said that he had sunk the *Intrepid* across the canal and thought that she filled the fairway.

Among the dangerously wounded on board were Sub-Lieutenants Lloyd (of the *Iphigenia*) and Keith Wright (Dean's second in command). They were both shot through the middle and the doctor declared that they could not survive. Lloyd had the *Iphigenia*'s white ensign wrapped round his waist, and it was saturated with his blood. I think he knew that his number was up, but was perfectly happy and fearfully proud of having been able to bring away the ensign, which I told him he should keep.

Keith Wright was suffering severely; I told him how splendidly his motor launch had done, and how distressed I was that he should have been so badly wounded. He said that he would not have missed it for anything, and that was the spirit of all that gallant throng.

U.S. Submarines:
A Comedy of
Errors

Lieutenant Harley F. Cope

The German U-boats of World War I gained a well-deserved reputation for their heartless efficiency in sending to the bottom unarmed freighters and passenger liners like the Lusitania. They also took an impressive toll of Allied warships.

In contrast, the boats of the fledgling American submarine service were like characters in a Marx Brothers comedy. Not one of our boats in the war zone ever sank an enemy ship. Nevertheless, they had their share of excitement—enduring underwater collisions, firing torpedoes that whirled back at them like boomerangs, getting stuck in the mud and, in one case, dodging the determined fire from an American destroyer skippered by the sub captain's Annapolis roommate.

That sub survived the encounter only to be attacked an hour later by a second American destroyer which fired six shots. This time the now

battle-hardened sub captain saved his boat by grimly radioing to his assailant a message that became legend:
"Three over, three short, deflection fine!"

America's entry into the First World War on April 6, 1917, found the United States quite unprepared to carry on submarine warfare in the enemy's waters. This was largely because the boats in commission at the time were not capable of taking the long trip across the Atlantic under their own power and of still being in condition to carry on war operations. However, the United States recognized no obstacles as insurmountable and great efforts were made to send a number of submarines overseas as quickly as possible. The first submarines scheduled to make the attempt was a division of K-boats, the *K-1* to *K-8* inclusive.

At that time the Diesel engine was very much in its infancy so far as our submarines were concerned, and it was feared that our undersea craft would be unable to make the transatlantic trip unless towed part of the way by the submarine tenders, as the submarines' engines were continually in a state of disrepair and the fuel capacity of the boats was small. The K-boat division was put through an intensive repair period, including meticulous overhaul of the engines and renewal of the storage batteries.

Of the eight K-boats that had been overhauled for duty in the war zone, only four, the *K-1*, *K-2*, *K-5* and *K-6*, managed to get as far as the Azores.

The *K-1* and the *K-2* left Brooklyn Navy Yard and put to sea for the war zone on the towline of the U.S.S. *Chicago*, while the *K-5* and the *K-6* started their ocean voyage on the towline of the tender, the U.S.S. *Bushnell*, during the latter part of September 1917.

The small submarines were uncomfortable to travel on even in the smoothest of weather, and when a storm came up and the towing vessels were forced to cast off their tows and let them shift for themselves, the little boats suffered so much that when they finally managed to limp into the port of Ponta Delgada, Azores, on October 27, 1917, they were unable to proceed any farther and carried on what war patrols they could in that vicinity.

The trip over had been such a strenuous one that a number of officers and men had to be transferred and given absolute rest for some time. The second officer of the *K-1*, Ensign Homer L. Ingram, tried to stick it out as long as possible and would only relinquish his duties when physically unable to stand on his feet any longer. He was sent home on sick leave, a mere shadow of the former 200-pound captain of a Navy crew and a football end who had sailed over seas just a few months before. Soon after his return he breathed his last.

None of the K-boats had any actual contacts with the enemy, although they had the usual number of scares. The end of the war found them still in the Azores, able only to carry on a war patrol in that neighborhood.

The next division of American submarines to arrive in the war zone consisted of seven L-boats. Although they had their full share of adventures with the enemy and also our own men-of-war, none of them managed to bag a German submarine, although they had a number of opportunities and only failed due to the worst breaks of luck.

On the trip across the Atlantic all the L-boats started on the end of a towline but such heavy storms were encountered that they soon had to shift for themselves. They all managed to arrive safely at the base at Berehaven, Bantry Bay, Ireland.

After receiving the latest submarine approach information from the experienced English submarine officers, all of our boats put out on their weekly war patrols in succession.

When they were not busy trying to run down U-boats, they were endeavoring to get off a recognition signal to some American destroyer that preferred to fire and ask questions afterwards. It would have been easily possible for some of our boats to have been sunk by our destroyers but all managed to come through without harm.

The *L-1* had an excellent opportunity at an enemy ship. While on patrol on May 22, 1918, in sight of Pendeed Watch House Light and Long Ship Light, this vessel had her first encounter with a German submarine.

On this eventful morning the *L-1* had dived at daybreak, as was customary. About noon a German submarine was sighted on the surface at a distance of about 8,000 yards. The American captain immediately maneuvered his submarine to place it in a good position for firing a torpedo. Estimating the course to be steered to gain that advantage, he went down to sixty feet and slowly stalked his victim, knowing that a slow speed was necessary, for the German boats were well equipped with listening devices.

At 2:35 P.M. the *L-1* again came up to periscope depth, about twenty feet, after having carefully located the target's position with the listening device. The U-boat was now seen to be at a distance of 2,000 yards, and was apparently of the U-110 class.

At 2:52 P.M. the *L-1* had reduced the intervening range to 800 yards and at 2:55 two torpedoes were fired, one at the conning tower and the other at the bow of the German. The sudden removal of almost two tons of weight from the forward part of the American submarine caused the bow to broach, and the German immediately maneuvered to avoid the onrushing torpedoes, which he succeeded in doing. Before diving he fired four shots from the deck gun at the American, all shots falling clear of the target, although the men in the engine-room said that they had heard the fall of shots near their compartment.

The *L-1* immediately attempted to ram. Failing to make contact, she came to the surface and went ahead on the engines, broadcasting the location of the U-boat.

On July 27 at 10:40 A.M. a U-boat was sighted just as it surfaced. Before an attack could be made the enemy had disappeared; apparently it had come to the surface only to enable the navigator to take a sun sight in order to fix his position on the chart. The German could be heard plainly but the American was unable to close in. An ocillator message was intercepted from the enemy, probably sent to the submarine working with him.

The *L-2* also had contact with a German submarine, but in a most peculiar way. It was only by the merest luck that the American submarine was not blown out of the water.

On July 10, 1918, the *L-2* was en route to Bantry Bay on the surface. About 6:30 in the evening the lookout reported seeing something on the starboard bow which resembled a buoy and the *L-2* proceeded to investigate. A little later the submarine was suddenly shaken by a terrific explosion, lifting the stern almost out of the water; the lights in the boats were dashed out, the circuit breakers tripped, the engine room floor plates were moved around and the ventilation motors were thrown out of alignment. At the same time a large geyser of water was observed about 60 yards away on the starboard quarter. As the boiling water receded, about six feet of the periscope of an enemy submarine was observed, which soon disappeared. A periscope was then noticed on the other side of the *L-2*. The American submarine immediately dived and tried to ram the other U-boat but was unable to make contact, although the high-speed propellers could be plainly heard in the listening device. The second U-boat sent out oscillator messages, trying to get an answer from the first, but no answer was received. The *L-2* tried to decoy the German by sending out an oscillator message with a high pitch but received no response.

Apparently, one German submarine had fired at the American boat and the torpedo had missed the target, had continued on its track, and had intercepted the other German, who was also about in position to sink the *L-2*.

The *L-4*, commanded by Lieutenant Lewis Hancock, later lost in the dirigible *Shenandoah*, certainly had more than her share of experiences.

On March 20, 1918, about 4 P.M., while on patrol, something was sighted on the starboard bow which, at first, was thought to be Fastnet Light. It was then made out to be a ship, which almost immediately turned away at high speed. The ship now resembled a submarine and the *L-4* headed for it at full speed. At 4:45 P.M. about two feet of brown periscope was sighted three hundred yards on the starboard bow. The rudder of the *L-4* was put hard over and the boat passed over the spot where the periscope had been seen.

The *L-4* then dived and the periscope was kept training about the horizon. Nothing was seen, although the propeller sounds could be heard very distinctly, showing that the German was only a short distance away.

The first loud propeller sounds were heard astern of the *L-4* and course was changed to bring the sound abeam. After this was done, course was again changed to bring it dead ahead. The sounds of the German propellers could be plainly heard in the American submarine without the use of the listening device. Just as the *L-4* swung around to place the German ahead of it a distinct jar was felt throughout the boat. An officer in the torpedo room reported that the shock was plainly felt in that compartment and it is only reasonable to suppose that the two had made slight contact while submerged. The German possessed more speed than the American and finally drew away and out of hearing distance.

On April 12, 1918, at 8 A.M., propeller noises were detected and at 9:20 a large German submarine was seen on the surface at a distance of one thousand yards. The enemy had apparently just come up, as his bow was well up and his stern still awash. As there was a considerable bow wave ahead of the U-boat, the *L-4*'s commander judged that it was making its best speed and gave credit to his belief when the torpedo was fired. Hardly had the torpedo left the tube when the U-boat started down. The torpedo made a straight, fast run and was seen to pass just ahead of where the U-boat had been, the shot missing the target due to overestimating the enemy's speed. The U-boat's conning tower was seen a little later and an effort was made to ram it, but the *L-4* could not get close enough. The American then trailed the German for two and a half hours by means of the listening device, and then abandoned the chase.

On April 24, about 5 A.M., in bright moonlight, a vessel was made out on the surface on the port bow of the *L-4*. The boat was seen to be a submarine and, as it was heading directly for them, the range rapidly closed, the distance soon being 1,000 yards. A moment later the German changed course, exposing his full left side, but at the same time he commenced to dive, evidently sighting the American. The *L-4* fired a torpedo at a range of 200 yards and watched the steel missile of destruction as it leaped toward its target. The torpedo made a perfect run and a trail of bubbles was seen just forward of the conning tower. Nothing happened, however, and it was never known whether the torpedo passed under the German or hit without exploding.

On April 26, a little after midnight, a vessel, thought to be a submarine, was sighted. The *L-4* fired two torpedoes at it; the first passed under the target, while the second ran around in circles, almost hitting the *L-4* during its erratic run. The target was then seen to be a friendly surface vessel.

On May 18, 1918, the *L-4* was almost lost with all hands on board and, incidentally, set a record for deep submergence of a submarine that held for many years after the war.

About 8:40 A.M. the submarine was on a submerged patrol, traveling at a depth of 25 feet, at a very slow speed, on the "half switch," to use submarine phraseology. After being submerged for some time, water began to creep into the boat through the sea valves and it was desired to lessen the weight in the vessel by taking water out of one of the variable tanks.

For this purpose the submarine had a small tank in the center of the ship, then called "adjusting" tank, with a capacity of about 1,000 pounds of sea water. The variable tank adjacent to it was called the "auxiliary" tank and had a capacity of about 18 tons of water.

The junior officer then on watch in the central operating compartment, desiring to rid the tank of water by sending compressed air into it, gave the order:

"Blow the adjusting tank!"

The man on the air manifold, not as experienced as he might have been, mistook the order and thought that the word had been:

"Open the auxiliary tank."

And thereupon he proceeded to do it.

In the meantime, the officer in command had stopped the motors and ordered the storage batteries to be hooked up in "series," as he would then be able to get more speed by this means. He then looked at the adjusting tank gauge to note the exit of the water from that tank. His attention was called by the man on the diving planes by "She is settling fast, sir!"

The officer then noticed that his order had been misunderstood and made every effort to rectify the mistake, but so much weight had been added to the boat, and the boat was going so slow, as the motors had been stopped, that she dropped like a rock and hit the bottom at 294 feet. The boat had only been designed and tested for 200 feet.

The chart showed that there was a depth of water in that vicinity of fifty fathoms, or 300 feet, and that the bottom was soft mud.

The submarine was now too far down to attempt blowing the water out of the ballast tanks by means of air, as the added pressure would undoubtedly carry away the already strained hull.

First, the motors went ahead at one-third their maximum speed and an attempt was made to plane the boat up. But it refused to leave the mud. Next, two-thirds speed was tried with the same results.

The ballast pumps were designed to pump water out of the boat at depths up to 300 feet. The high-pressure ballast pump was next placed on the forward ballast tank, all valves outboard on the tank being closed first. The pump could not take a suction as the circuit breakers tripped at the set amperage. The amperage on the breakers was doubled but still they refused to hold. They were then set for the maximum possible under any condition. For a few minutes the pump functioned and then the breakers tripped. The pressure in the tank had, however, been reduced from 127 pounds, the sea pressure at that depth, to 90 pounds. The pumping was discontinued as the motor was extremely hot, and the flanges on the pump discharge overboard valve were leaking badly, as was also the pump.

Backing the main motors was next resorted to, in the hope of breaking the suction of the soft bottom, but without success.

The small adjusting pump was then tried on the adjusting tank but after 700 pounds had been pumped out the fuses on the power line blew out as fast as they were put in.

The adjusting tank had been designed to withstand great pressure, so this tank was filled with water three times from the auxiliary tank and blown empty with high-pressure air. The bad feature of this method was that after each blowing the tank had to be vented into the boat before it could be refilled. A great pressure was soon built up within, so much that the needle on the barometer, used in a submarine to record the pressure, was bent up hard against the top of the instrument.

There are two ways of reducing the air pressure in a submarine while the boat is submerged. First, by pumping bilges until the water is out after which the pump takes the excess air through it. This method is not advisable in time of war because the air bubbles and oil slicks can be detected by surface craft and the position of the submarine disclosed. However, the pumps on the *L-4* were not functioning, so this method could not be used. The next method is to turn over the air compressors, which are connected to the main propeller shafts, and supply compressed air for the torpedoes and for blowing water from the ballast tanks. When air is compressed, heat is generated, and for that reason cooling coils surround the compression chambers. Before the compressor could be started the cooler shell would have to be opened to the sea so that the circulating water might enter the coils. The commanding officer realized that the shell would be subjected to a great pressure but decided to take the chance. The port compressor was started but had to be stopped almost immediately as the shell burst.

The stern tube glands on the propeller shafts began to leak badly, although the crew set up on them as much as possible. Soon, the water began to fill the bilges in the engine- and motor-room and was mounting to the main motors. Different valves in the engine-room began to leak and soon little trickles of water were in evidence throughout the compartment.

As the water level was rapidly approaching the main motors the commanding officer knew that something had to be done before they were permanently disabled, or they would remain on the bottom forever. He had every man except those on the necessary diving stations go as far aft in the boat as possible, with the idea of lightening the bow. Pressure was then put in the forward ballast tank until the safety valve on the air line blew; it was then reset at 15 pounds above the sea pressure, or at 140 pounds considerably above what it had been designed for. The main motors were then sent ahead at two-thirds speed, the chief electrician on the submarine coolly holding the circuit breakers closed, despite the fact that his arms would probably be burned badly.

The bow rose to the three-degree angle but held fast in the mud. Slowly it tilted to six degrees, then suddenly broke loose. The *L-4* headed for the surface at a very steep angle—approximately fifty degrees. At one hundred feet the middle main ballast tank was blown and a moment later the boat was on the surface, having been on the bottom for one hour and ten minutes. The after main ballast tank was left filled in order to keep the water in the bilges from coming over the flow plates and wetting the main motors, as the water was only three inches from them before leaving the bottom.

In a report on the accident, the commanding officer said:

> I cannot too highly praise the behavior of the personnel, both officers and men. Although every one realized that the situation was extremely serious, there was not the slightest evidence of panic or excitement. Every man stood in his station in as calm and efficient a way as if an ordinary drill was being conducted.

As the result of this accident the name of the adjusting tank was changed to regulator tank and the lever handle operating the auxiliary tank was painted a different color from the others and was kept locked or pinned down.

There were any number of instances when, while out on listening patrols, the L-boats heard a depth charge from a distance and soon afterwards heard the U-boat hurrying away. On every occasion effort was made to intercept the enemy but without success.

On the same day that the *L-2* had her unusual experience with the two German submarines, the destroyer *Allen* opened fire on her despite the fact that the *L-2* was making recognition signals and waving flags. The *Allen* only ceased firing when a range of two thousand yards had been attained. Some of the shots fell alongside the *L-2* but, fortunately, none hit her.

The *L-10*, commanded by Lieutenant Commander James C. Van de Carr, was almost destroyed by depth charges by one of our own destroyers. On March 25, 1918, about 5:50 P.M., a destroyer was seen approaching through the periscope of the *L-10*, and it was recognized as being the U.S.S. *Sterett*, commanded by Lieutenant Commander Simpson, the Naval Academy roommate of the *L-10*'s commanding officer. As it was not desired to surface at the time, the *L-10* planed down to 60 feet, with the idea of letting the *Sterett* go by. The propeller sounds could be heard getting closer and closer, and suddenly the submarine was shaken violently from stem to stern, throwing the lights out in the boat and jarring many things loose. The *Sterett* then threw over a buoy and proceeded to lay a barrage of depth charges around her proposed victim. The *L-10* was being shaken badly and threatened to burst after each explosion. As the *Sterett* reached the outer ring of the barrage circle, the *L-10* was quickly surfaced and the recognition signal got off before the destroyer could open fire with the deck guns.

The *Sterett* then came close aboard and held a conversation with the submarine commander:

"Your oil tanks are evidently leaking as I spotted you by the oil slicks. You are lucky I misjudged your position. Are you all right now?"

Van de Carr shouted back:

"All right now, Buck, old boy, but almost scared to death."

The destroyer commander then shouted over a parting admonition:

"The *Trippe* will be up here in about an hour. You had better remain on the surface until she gets here. So long."

An hour later another destroyer, presumably the *Trippe*, appeared over the horizon, and although the American flag was being waved on the submarine and the recognition signal was being made periodically, the destroyer fired six shots, three going over, three falling short.

Commander Van de Carr then radioed his famous message to the *Trippe*:

"Three over, three short, deflection fine!"

The *L-11*, commanded by Lieutenant A. C. Bennett, came very close to scoring our only hit of the war so far as our submarines operating in the war zone were concerned.

On May 11, 1918, while on a submerged listening patrol, a U-boat was sighted on the surface at a distance of about 6,000 yards, bearing on the *L-11*'s port quarter. The American slowly swung around to a firing position and reduced the firing range to nine hundred yards. Two torpedoes were fired at an interval of five seconds. The first one broached. A terrific explosion was seen to take place about 200 yards from the enemy submarine as the torpedoes exploded, and it seems only probable that one torpedo overtook the other and caused the premature explosion. The U-boat dived and was not seen again.

Torpedo Boats: David *vs*. Goliath

Hector C. Bywater

*N*aval fighting has always depended greatly on teamwork. There are, however, cases in which individual daring and initiative have achieved spectacular results.

No better example of this phenomenon could be found than in the following exploits of an amazingly intrepid member of the Italian Navy.

Previous to Italy's entry into the First World War on the side of the Allies, she had reinforced her navy with a number of "mosquito craft," considered to be well suited to the exigencies of campaigning in the relatively narrow waters of the Adriatic. Among them were the so-called "M.A.S." boats (an abbreviation of "Motobarche Anti-Sommergibili," literally anti-submarine motor-boats, or sub chasers.) Hundreds of these tiny craft were built, ranging from 15 to 30 tons. Speeds up to 40 knots were attained, but in the earlier boats the speed at sea in normal conditions did not often rise above 20 knots. But although so tiny, they were armed with a sting in the form of two torpedoes, and a few depth charges were carried for use against enemy submarines. An officer and half-a-dozen men formed the crew.

It was with one of these M.A.S. boats that Lieutenant Luigi Rizzo made history. An officer of the Italian merchant marine and of the naval reserve, he spent most of his war service in patrolling the Adriatic. But he chafed under the monotony of routine, and more than once incurred a reprimand for leaving his regulation "beat" in search of adventure. He importuned his superiors with schemes for breaking into the Austrian harbors and torpedoing ships at anchor, but as these bases were supposed to be impregnable it was long before his proposals were taken seriously.

But at length his chance came. In November 1917 the Italian army suffered the reverse of Caporetto and was forced to retreat. Its flank was covered by British monitors and Italian floating batteries, but these in their turn were annoyed by the long-range cannonade of two old Austrian battleships, *Wien* and *Budapest*, which came out of Trieste to support the advance. They retired every evening to an anchorage near Trieste which was strongly defended by shore batteries and minefields. If they could be put out of action it would be a distinct relief to the hard-pressed Italian troops, and once more, therefore, Rizzo begged for permission to conduct a lone-hand raid. This time he obtained it.

On the evening of December 9 he set out with the motor boats Numbers 9 and 13, and reached the approaches to the anchorage after night had fallen. With her engines just ticking over, Number 9, with Rizzo conning the vessel in the bow, crept forward foot by foot until she was brought up by some obstruction. This proved to be a number of cables which the Austrians had stretched across the entrance. Rizzo was not perturbed. He had expected something of the kind, and had come provided with the necessary tools. Working silently the Italian seamen soon cut through the cables, and as the severed ends sank to the bottom the two little boats glided through. A few minutes later Rizzo made out the dim shapes of battleships right ahead. He stopped his engines, waited until his consort had crept alongside, and then gave his final instructions in a whisper.

He then put his helm over and steered for a point on the port quarter of the leading battleship. In spite of the utmost care the throb of the engines must have been audible at a considerable distance on such a still night, but the enemy's lookouts were evidently dozing, for they made no sign. When barely 150 yards away Rizzo snapped his fingers as a signal for both torpedoes to be slipped from the launching cradles. Ten seconds later, with engines racing, the deadly "tin fish" were shooting through the water towards the unsuspecting foe. At the same instant Number 13 discharged her torpedoes at the second battleship.

Rizzo's target was the *Wien*, and so steady had been his aim that both torpedoes took her right amidships. Alarmed by the explosion, other ships in harbor switched on their searchlights, and both they and the shore batteries fired wildly in the supposed direction of the assailants. The *Wien*, with a great hole in her side, was obviously sinking, but the *Budapest* had been missed by the torpedoes from *M.A.S. 13*, though they had been fired at point-blank range.

Meanwhile Rizzo had turned his boat and was making for the gap in the boom at full speed, closely followed by Number 13. It seemed impossible that the daring intruders could escape, for they were clearly seen in the beams of the searchlights, and every gun ashore and afloat that would bear was firing at them. But the nerves of the Austrian gunners must have been badly shaken, since they failed to score a hit on either boat. Although the surrounding water was lashed into foam by the hail of shell, Rizzo and his consort cleared the harbor entrance and escaped to sea without a scratch, leaving behind them the sinking battleship, which foundered with the loss of many lives.

The moral effect of this audacious raid was very pronounced. No Austrian ship ventured outside Trieste for several days afterwards, and at night the entrance was patrolled by guard boats. At a later date another Italian motor boat, fitted with a caterpillar device for enabling it to climb over obstructions, attempted to penetrate the Austrian defenses at Pola—the most heavily fortified base on the Adriatic—but was detected and put out of action by gunfire before it could get within torpedo range.

It was in June 1918 that Rizzo performed the exploit which gained him worldwide renown. By this time the Otranto mine barrage, guarded by destroyers and drifters, had become a serious embarrassment to the German and Austrian U-boats which were operating in the Mediterranean from their bases on the Dalmatian coast. Admiral Horthy, the Austrian commander-in-chief, therefore decided to deliver a smashing attack on the barrage and its guardians in order to clear the way for his submarines. For this purpose he began to assemble a powerful fleet at Cattaro, from which base the blow was to be struck.

The four Austrian Dreadnoughts, hitherto kept out of harm's way at Pola, were ordered to sail for Cattaro, the *Viribus Unitis* and *Prinz Eugen* on June 8, the *Szent Istvan* and *Tegetthoff* on the day following. Three smaller battleships, four light cruisers, eight destroyers, and twelve submarines were also to take part in the attack on the barrage.

Had this plan been carried out the consequences to the Allies must have been serious. Choosing his own time, the enemy could have struck with stunning force. In the vicinity of the barrage there was nothing capable of opposing him. It is doubtful whether any of the drifters on the barrage or the light craft covering them would have escaped destruction. Many weeks, perhaps even months, must have elapsed before the barrage could be reestablished, and all this time hostile U-boats would have been passing up and down the Straits of Otranto without hindrance. It was due entirely to the heroism of one man, Luigi Rizzo, that the Allies were spared this grave setback at sea.

Rizzo had been promoted to the rank of commander for his sinking of the battleship *Wien*. On the night of June 9–10 he was patrolling the Upper Adriatic in *M.A.S. 15*, accompanied by *M.A.S. 21*. No sortie by the enemy was anticipated, for earlier in the evening Italian airplanes had flown over the harbor of Pola and noticed all the four Austrian Dreadnoughts at their usual moorings. But the airmen were, in fact, deceived by a simple ruse. The *Viribus Unitis* and the *Prinz Eugen* had sailed the previous night, their places at the mooring buoys having been taken by dummy ships camouflaged to represent the absent Dreadnoughts. Thanks to this stratagem the first pair of battleships got to sea unobserved. But the second pair were to be less fortunate.

At 3:15 A.M. on June 10 Rizzo and his consort were cruising off Premuda. On board *M.A.S. 15*, in which were Commander Rizzo and five men, there had been an engine breakdown which had forced them to anchor for half an hour while the damage was repaired. But for this delay the two boats would have been further to the southward and would probably have missed the unique opportunity that was about to be presented to them. There was brilliant moonlight, and visibility, considering the hour, was remarkably good. What followed may be told in the terse phrases of Rizzo's own report:

At about 3:15 A.M., when I was six and a half miles from Lutostrak, I sighted a cloud of smoke on the starboard quarter and well astern. Having reason to believe that I had been noticed during my patrol by sentinels on Gruiza Island, I inferred that the smoke was that of destroyers sent out from Lussin to overhaul and sink me. As dawn was already approaching, I judged it was unsafe to try to escape, as my best speed was twenty knots. Consequently, I decided to take a chance in the still uncertain light and attack.

With this purpose in mind I turned towards the enemy and proceeded at low speed in order not to make a foaming bow wave, which would have betrayed my presence. On coming nearer I found that my first judgment was wrong. The smoke was coming from two large battleships, screened by a flotilla of eight or ten torpedo boats. Having made up my mind to discharge my torpedoes at the shortest range possible, I crept straight in between the first two torpedo boats in the line on the starboard side of the battleships. In order to clear the second boat I had to increase speed from nine to twelve knots.

I therefore unexpectedly succeeded in penetrating 100 meters inside the protecting line, and was able to fire my torpedoes at a distance of approximately 300 meters. Both struck the *Szent Istvan*, one directly amidships between the funnels, the other halfway between the after funnel and the stern. The ship did not maneuver to avoid the torpedoes. As these detonated huge pillars of smoke and water rose out of the sea.

The enemy torpedo boat on my port quarter, realizing what had happened, turned to cut me off, but succeeded only in crossing my wake at about 150 meters distance. She opened fire, but the aim was too high and all the shells exploded ahead of me. Noticing that she was keeping directly in my wake I released a depth charge, which failed to detonate. I then dropped a second one, which exploded just under the bow of the pursuing boat. She at once swung eight points to starboard, and I turned sharply to port, so that I quickly outdistanced her and soon lost sight of her.

In this bald narrative there is little to indicate the superlative courage and resolution with which the attack was conducted. Rizzo in his cockleshell had steered right into the midst of the Austrian destroyers, any one of which could have blown him out of the water, selected his target, and calmly waited until the range was so short that his torpedoes could scarcely miss. He and his companions must have believed themselves to be going to certain death, for escape seemed to be out of the question. But their only thought was to make sure of driving the torpedoes home. That they did contrive to get away unscathed is at once a tribute to Rizzo's coolness and resource and striking proof of the confusion, not to say panic, into which the enemy had been thrown.

Although the *Szent Istvan* remained afloat for three hours after the attack, enabling most of her company to be rescued, over a hundred lives were lost when she took the last plunge. Rizzo's consort, *M.A.S. 21*, had also fired two torpedoes at the *Tegetthoff*, but they failed to run true and missed the mark. But the loss of the *Szent Istvan*, one of their finest Dreadnoughts, was quite enough for the Austrian naval command. Believing that their scheme for raiding the Otranto barrage had been betrayed, and that the torpedo attack on the Dreadnought division was part of a prearranged plan of counter-action, they decided to abandon the whole enterprise. Thus a most serious menace to the Allied defenses in the lower Adriatic was averted.

Nor was this all. The destruction of a mighty battleship on the open sea by a diminutive Italian torpedo boat must inevitably have caused widespread depression in Austria and contributed to the growing spirit of defeatism which was already sapping the national morale. It may, indeed, be doubted if any other single-handed action during the war had as great an effect on the ultimate issue as Rizzo's exploit off Premuda.

An unusual circumstance has helped to preserve a graphic record of this historic event. Confident in the success of his well-planned assault on the Otranto barrage, the Austrian commander-in-chief had installed motion-picture cameras and skilled operators in two of the destroyers which accompanied the fleet. It was his hope that films would be taken of the actual destruction of enemy ships by the victorious fleet, and that their exhibition would not only stimulate popular enthusiasm at home but exalt the national prestige beyond the confines of Austria–Hungary itself.

He cannot have foreseen the use to which these cameras were destined to be put. What they did was to record the death throes of the stricken Dreadnought—a fateful portent for the Hungarian kingdom, the name of whose patron saint was borne by the great battleship. Each stage of the disaster is shown in the film: first, the vessel listing slightly to starboard soon after the torpedo explosions;

then the decks aslant as the list increases, with the twelve big turret guns trained out on the port beam as a counterweight; then the moment of capsizal, with the ship on her beam ends, half the deck submerged, and men sliding overboard or already fighting for life in the water. After the war this unique film was secured by the Italians, who have employed it, quite legitimately and with wonderful effect, in the cause of naval propaganda.

Heroic drama, with more than a spice of mystery, is provided by yet another Italian naval venture. For reasons which will presently appear, this episode, which involved the sinking of a second Austrian Dreadnought, is unique in the annals of the sea. And not the least intriguing feature of the affair is that it has never been fully explained. The heroes were two naval officers—Major R. Rossetti, of the Corps of Constructors, and Surgeon Lieutenant R. Paolucci. Neither, it will be observed, belonged to the combatant branch of the service.

Major Rossetti was the inventor of a buoyant, self-propelling infernal machine, something between a torpedo and a mine. No description of the contrivance has ever been published, and to this day it remains an Italian naval secret. But judging by the effects it must have been a most formidable weapon. Rossetti conceived the idea of turning his ingenious instrument against the Austrian battle fleet, which was too well entrenched behind the batteries and minefields of Pola to be attacked by ordinary methods. He and his friend Dr. Paolucci were exceptionally fine swimmers, and both had performed many a long-distance swim. In consultation with the poet Sem Benelli, they worked out a plan for floating Rossetti's infernal machine into the man-of-war anchorage at Pola and blowing up the Austro–Hungarian flagship, *Viribus Unitis.*

Various circumstances delayed the execution of this daredevil project, but on October 31, 1918, all was ready, and at 1 P.M. the expedition left Venice on board a torpedo boat. Seven hours later they were off Brioni Island. Here the machine was lowered into the water, and the two adventurers boarded an electric launch which conveyed them silently to within a mile of the outer defenses of Pola, the machine being towed astern. Rossetti and his comrade then slipped over the side and the machine was cast loose.

"That was exactly ten o'clock," wrote Paolucci in his subsequent report. "We shook hands and embraced one another in silence, let go the ropes to which we were clinging, and were soon well away from the launch, which speedily disappeared. I was holding on at the bow of the machine, while Rossetti was at the stern. We proceeded rather slowly, as the phosphorescence of the water was uncommonly brilliant. Around and above us were night and the unknown, both dark and silent. It seemed as though everything in that immensity of somber mystery were dead save for two opposing animate objects, the searchlights of the enemy and our beating hearts.

"As Colonel Rossetti, who was controlling the machine, quickened the speed, a wave broke over me. It was colder than the water of the Venetian lagoon, in which I had been swimming every night for nearly a month past; though perhaps it only seemed colder to me because I was warm and my heart was beating very fast as a result of the injections of camphor which we had been given before entering the water. Out of the darkness began to take form the mass of Cape Compare, which we had been warned to keep on our right hand in order to pass through the outer obstructions. At 10:30 we reached these and found them to consist of a line of empty metal cylinders, from which depended heavy steel cables."

This was but the first of seven separate barriers of cables, nets, or timber baulks which guarded the inner anchorage, all of which the intrepid pair overcame with infinite labor. More than once it was necessary to manhandle the explosive machine over a solid barricade. So much time had been consumed in this work that it was 3 A.M. before they came in sight of their objective, and both now realized that unless they abandoned their purpose forthwith and turned back to the open sea they could not possibly hope to make good their escape. Nevertheless, they determined to go on.

Twice they floated past the very bow of a guard boat, and saw the armed sentries on board, but the swimmers' heads were camouflaged as Chianti flasks, and when in view of the sentries they were careful to bob their heads in imitation of the movements of floating bottles. Evidently the ruse succeeded, for they were not challenged. They had just reached the battleship anchorage when they suddenly perceived the machine to be sinking. "In the mingled rain and hail which now came beating down upon us I drew near to Rossetti and saw he was desperate, with water up to his mouth as he struggled to keep the machine afloat. Hastily I made sure that the immersion valve in the prow was closed, while Rossetti reached down to examine the one in the stern, which we found had in some way been opened. He shut it and opened the emersion valve, so that we at length saw the machine rising to the surface. Of all the trying moments we had spent this was undeniably the most painful."

They were able to identify the *Viribus Unitis* at the head of the line, as the great Dreadnought was brilliantly lighted up. Several attempts to float the infernal machine under the bow of the vessel and secure it there were defeated by the strong current, but eventually this was done. Almost at the same moment a searchlight beam swept the water and came to rest squarely on the two swimmers. They were discovered.

"A boat which we had seen moored alongside the *Viribus Unitis* came towards us. '*Wer da?*' '*Italienische Offiziere*,' I answered. They pulled us on board. A moment later I was mounting to the deck of the Dreadnought, a few yards below which there was a charge of the most powerful explosive, which would send the ship to the bottom in a very short time. It was just five minutes to six. They awoke the captain of the ship, von Voukovic, and brought us before him. Having decided to warn him, Rossetti asked for a word in private and then said:

" 'Your ship is in serious and imminent danger. I urge you to abandon it and save your men.' When the captain asked for information as to the source of the danger, Rossetti replied:

" 'I cannot tell you, but I warn you that she will go down in a very short time.' "

"Von Voukovic then shouted in German:

" '*Viribus Unitis*, let all who can save themselves. The Italians have put bombs in the ship!'

"We heard doors opened and shut in a hurry, we saw half-naked men running about as if demented and going up the gangways to the open deck. Then we heard the noise of bodies splashing as they threw themselves into the sea."

As Captain von Voukovic chivalrously gave the two Italians permission to save themselves, they, too, jumped overboard, but they had not swum far when a boat overtook them and they were ordered to return to the ship. Evidently the Austrians, having recovered from their panic, now believed the affair to be a hoax. For the second time, therefore, Rossetti and his companion were compelled to mount to the deck of the ship which they knew to be doomed. Threatened, and even roughly handled, by the exasperated Austrian sailors, they kept their eyes on the ship's clock, for the infernal machine was timed to explode at 6:30.

"Twenty-eight minutes past, twenty-nine—then the explosion came! A dull boom, a deep roaring, not loud or terrible but rather muffled, was followed by a column of water that shot high into the air. I felt the deck vibrate and tremble. I turned around and found I was practically alone. Every one had been seized with the single thought of saving himself. Captain von Voukovic was there, putting on a lifebelt. Rossetti was near, undressing, at the same time eating a piece of chocolate which had fallen out of one of his pockets. He turned to the commanding officer and reminded him that the laws of war permitted us to attempt to save ourselves. Von Voukovic then shook hands with both of us, and, pointing to a rope by which we might descend, indicated a passing lifeboat into which we could climb."

The two officers were picked up, and from the boat they gazed upon the results of their handiwork:

"The dawn had broken, and in this colorless light the great mass of the *Viribus Unitis* settled in her grave. As we looked, the word *Unitis* was already under water, and only *Viribus* could still be seen. What irony in that *Viribus*, which was now but a sinking corpse.

"The battleship listed more and more, and as soon as her rail was under she turned completely over. The big turret guns broke away from their moorings like toys, but it was only for an instant one saw them, for they quickly disappeared into the depths, leaving behind them nothing but the upturned keel, tinged with a greenish hue. After that the great hull slowly sank.

"Before it went entirely under I saw a man crawling along to the keel, where he stood upright. As he rose, I recognised Captain von Voukovic. A few minutes later he was killed by a beam which struck him on the head as he was swimming away from the suction of the whirlpool, from which he had just managed to extricate himself."

Such were the consequences of this astounding feat. By their own unaided efforts the two Italian officers had totally destroyed a Dreadnought of 21,400 tons, armed with twelve twelve-inch guns, and manned by a crew of over a thousand. As previously noted, the technical means they employed are still a mystery. In the course of his report Dr. Paolucci mentions two machines, one of which was sunk just before the other was attached to the side of the Austrian battleship. They cannot, therefore, have been very ponderous contrivances, yet it is difficult to imagine how an explosive charge of sufficient power to destroy a great battleship so quickly could be contained in the species of small mine which appears to have been used. Obviously the explosive itself must have been far more destructive than T.N.T. or the other compounds in general use.

Whatever it was, it appears to have been buoyed up by a small, boat-shaped raft, driven by an electric motor and fitted with a device for fastening it firmly to the hull of a ship. The charge was detonated by a clockwork time fuse. When the *Viribus Unitis* was examined by divers they found below the waterline a cavity considerably larger than could have been produced by an ordinary torpedo, or even a mine. Plating, beams, and bulkheads in the vicinity of the explosion were torn and twisted by the terrific force of the blast.

The enthusiasm which this marvellous exploit aroused in Italy was somewhat damped by the discovery that just before her destruction the *Viribus Unitis* had ceased to belong to Austria–Hungary. On the previous day, in consequence of the disruption of the Habsburg Empire, the whole fleet had been handed over to the Yugoslavs, and was therefore no longer a menace to the Allies. Nevertheless, this circumstance, of which the Italian government had necessarily remained in ignorance, in no way dimmed the glory of the laurels which Rossetti and Paolucci, like their gallant comrade in arms Luigi Rizzo, had earned by their heroism and their almost superhuman endurance.

WORLD
WAR II

An aircraft is blasted from the deck of the U.S.
carrier *Lexington* in the Battle of
the Coral Sea in 1942.
(U.S. Navy Photo)

Oran: When the British Navy Turned Against an Ally

Winston Churchill

At least once in modern naval history, the decision to fight was even more dramatic than the combat that followed. So it was in July 1940 when Winston Churchill, then prime minister of Great Britain, ordered a Royal Navy battle squadron to "use whatever force may be necessary" to prevent the French fleet at Oran, Morocco, from being surrendered intact to Nazi Germany.

The situation was this: In September 1939, Britain and France had entered the Second World War together against Germany; ten months later, France—overrun by the German Wehrmacht—capitulated.

By then, Britain, too, seemed close to defeat because of the relentlessly effective German attacks against the seaborne supplies upon which she depended. Furthermore, it seemed as if a German invasion of the British

Isles was imminent. The United States, mired in isolationism, showed no inclination to come to the rescue of Britain.

Suddenly, Britain was faced with yet another threat. In negotiating surrender, the French government, then based at Bordeaux, agreed to deliver its battle fleet to Germany.

Churchill and his cabinet were horrified and wrestled with the question of what to do. Finally, on July 3, 1940, they reached a historic decision "with aching heart but with clear vision," as Churchill put it. The next day, he addressed a spellbound House of Commons and revealed to the world the tragic action that had been undertaken. Here is his electrifying speech.

It is with sincere sorrow that I must now announce to the House the measures which we have felt bound to take in order to prevent the French Fleet from falling into German hands. When two nations are fighting together under long and solemn alliance against a common foe, one of them may be stricken down and overwhelmed, and may be forced to ask its ally to release it from its obligations. But the least that could be expected was that the French government, in abandoning the conflict and leaving its whole weight to fall upon Great Britain and the British Empire, would have been careful not to inflict needless injury upon their faithful comrade, in whose final victory the sole chance of French freedom lay, and lies.

As the House will remember, we offered to give full release to the French from their treaty obligations, although these were designed for precisely the case which arose, on one condition, namely, that the French Fleet should be sailed for British harbors before the separate armistice negotiations with the enemy were completed. This was not done, but on the contrary, in spite of every kind of private and personal promise and assurance given by Admiral Darlan to the First Lord and to his Naval colleague, the First Sea Lord of the British Admiralty, an armistice was signed which was bound to place the French Fleet as effectively in the power of Germany and its Italian following as that portion of the French Fleet was placed in our power when many of them, being unable to reach African ports, came into the harbors of Portsmouth and Plymouth about ten days ago. Thus I must place on record that what might have been a mortal injury was done to us by the Bordeaux government [the seat of the French Government after the fall of Paris] with full knowledge of the consequences of our dangers, and after rejecting all our appeals at the moment when they were abandoning the Alliance, and breaking the engagements which fortified it.

There was another example of this callous and perhaps even malevolent treatment which we received, not indeed from the French nation, who have never been and apparently never are to be consulted upon these transactions, but from the Bordeaux government. This is the instance: There were over 400 German air pilots who were prisoners in France, many of them, perhaps most of them, shot down by the Royal Air Force. I obtained from Monsieur Paul Reynaud [the French prime minister] a personal promise that these pilots should be sent for safekeeping to England, and orders were given by him to that effect; but when Monsieur Reynaud fell, these pilots were delivered over to Germany, in order, no doubt, to win favor for the Bordeaux government with their German masters, and to win it without regard to the injury done to us. The German Air Force already feels acutely the shortage of high-grade pilots, and it seemed to me particularly odious, if I may use the word, that these 400 skilled men should be handed over with the sure knowledge that they would be used to bomb this country, and thus force our airmen to shoot them down for the second time over. Such wrongful deeds I am sure will not be condoned by history, and I firmly believe that a generation of Frenchmen will arise who will clear their national honor from all countenance of them.

I said last week that we must now look with particular attention to our own salvation. I have never in my experience seen discussed in a Cabinet so grim and somber a question as what we were to do about the French Fleet. It shows how strong were the reasons for the course which we thought it our duty to take, that every member of the Cabinet had the same conviction about what should be done and there was not the slightest hesitation or divergence among them, and that the three service ministers, as well as men like the minister of information, and the secretary of state for the colonies, particularly noted for their long friendship with France, when they were consulted were equally convinced that no other decision than that which we took was possible. We took that decision, and it was a decision to which, with aching hearts but with clear vision, we unitedly came. Accordingly, early yesterday morning, July third, after all preparations had been made, we took the greater part of the French Fleet under our control, or else called upon them, with adequate force, to comply with our requirements. Two battleships, two light cruisers, some submarines, including a very large one, the *Surcouf*, eight destroyers and approximately 200 smaller but extremely useful mine-sweeping and antisubmarine craft which lay for the most part at Portsmouth and Plymouth, though there were some at Sheerness, were boarded by superior forces, after brief notice had been given wherever possible to their captains.

This operation was successfully carried out without resistance or bloodshed except in one instance. A scuffle arose through a misunderstanding in the submarine *Surcouf*, in which one British leading seaman was killed and two British officers and one rating [enlisted man] wounded, and one French officer killed and one wounded. For the rest, the French sailors in the main cheerfully accepted the end of a period of uncertainty. A considerable number, 800 to 900, have expressed an ardent desire to continue the war, and some have asked for British nationality. This we are ready to grant without prejudice to the other Frenchmen, numbered by thousands, who prefer to fight on with us as Frenchmen. All the rest of those crews will be immediately repatriated to French ports, if the French government are able to make arrangements for their reception by permission of their German rulers. We are also repatriating all French troops who were in this country, excepting those who, of their own free will, have volunteered to follow General [Charles] de Gaulle in the French Forces of Liberation, of whom he is chief. Several French submarines have also joined us independently, and we have accepted their services.

Now I turn to the Mediterranean. At Alexandria, where a strong British battle fleet is lying, there are, besides a French battleship, four French cruisers, three of them modern 8-inch gun vessels, and a number of smaller ships. These have been informed that they cannot be permitted to leave harbor and thus fall within the power of the German conquerors of France. Negotiations and discussions, with the details of which I need not trouble the House, have necessarily been taking place, and measures have now been taken to ensure that those ships, which are commanded by a very gallant admiral, shall be sunk or otherwise made to comply with our wishes. The anguish which this process has, naturally, caused to the British and French naval officers concerned may be readily imagined, when I tell the House that only this morning, in the air raid upon Alexandria by Italian aircraft, some of the French ships fired heavily and effectively with us against the common enemy. We shall, of course, offer the fullest facilities to all French officers and men at Alexandria who wish to continue the war, and will provide for them and maintain them during the conflict. We have also promised to repatriate all the rest, and every care in our power will be taken, if they allow it, for their safety and their comfort. So much for Alexandria.

But the most serious part of the story remains. Two of the finest vessels of the French Fleet, the *Dunkerque* and the *Strasbourg*, modern battle cruisers much superior to *Scharnhorst* and *Gneisenau*—and built for the purpose of being superior to them—lay with two battleships, several light cruisers, and a number of destroyers and submarines and other vessels at Oran and at its adjacent military port of Mers-El-Kebir on the northern African shore of Morocco. Yesterday morning, a carefully chosen British officer, Captain Holland, late naval attaché in Paris, was sent on in a destroyer and waited upon the French Admiral Gensoul. After being refused an interview, he presented the following document, which I will read to the House. The first two paragraphs of the document deal with the general question of the Armistice, which I have already explained in my own words. The fourth paragraph begins as follows—this is the operative paragraph:

> It is impossible for us, your comrades up to now, to allow your fine ships to fall into the power of the German or Italian enemy. We are determined to fight on to the end, and if we win, as we think we shall, we shall never forget that France was our ally, that our interests are the same as hers, and that our common enemy is Germany. Should we conquer, we solemnly declare that we shall restore the greatness and territory of France. For this purpose, we must make sure that the best ships of the French Navy are not used against us by the common foe. In these circumstances, His Majesty's Government have instructed me [that is, the British Admiral] to demand that the French Fleet now at Mers-El-Kebir and Oran shall act in accordance with one of the following alternatives:
>
> (*a*) Sail with us and continue to fight for victory against the Germans and Italians.
>
> (*b*) Sail with reduced crews under our control to a British port. The reduced crews will be repatriated at the earliest moment.
>
> If either of these courses is adopted by you, we will restore your ships to France at the conclusion of the war or pay full compensation, if they are damaged meanwhile.
>
> (*c*) Alternatively, if you feel bound to stipulate that your ships should not be used against the Germans or Italians unless

these break the Armistice, then sail them with us, with reduced crews, to some French port in the West Indies—Martinique, for instance—where they can be demilitarized to our satisfaction or be perhaps entrusted to the United States and remain safe until the end of the war, the crews being repatriated. If you refuse these fair offers, I must, with profound regret, require you to sink your ships within six hours.

Finally, failing the above, I have the orders of His Majesty's Government to use whatever force may be necessary to prevent your ships from falling into German or Italian hands.

We had hoped that one or other of the alternatives which we presented would have been accepted, without the necessity of using the terrible force of a British battle squadron. Such a squadron arrived before Oran two hours after Captain Holland and his destroyer. This battle squadron was commanded by Vice-Admiral Somerville, an officer who distinguished himself lately in the bringing off of over 100,000 Frenchmen during the evacuation from Dunkirk. Admiral Somerville was further provided, besides his battleships, with a cruiser force and strong flotillas. All day the parleys continued, and we hoped until the afternoon that our terms would be accepted without bloodshed. However, no doubt in obedience to the orders dictated by the Germans from Wiesbaden, where the Franco–German Armistice Commission is in session, Admiral Gensoul refused to comply and announced his intention of fighting. Admiral Somerville was, therefore, ordered to complete his mission before darkness fell and at 5:53 P.M. he opened fire upon this powerful French Fleet, which was also protected by its shore batteries. At 6 P.M. he reported that he was heavily engaged. The action lasted for some ten minutes and was followed by heavy attacks from our naval aircraft, carried in the *Ark Royal*. At 7:20 P.M. Admiral Somerville forwarded a further report, which stated that a battle cruiser of the *Strasbourg* class was damaged and ashore; that a battleship of the *Bretagne* class had been sunk, that another of the same class had been heavily damaged, and that two French destroyers and a seaplane carrier, *Commandant Teste*, were also sunk or burned.

While this melancholy action was being fought, either the battle cruiser *Strasbourg* or the *Dunkerque*, one or the other, managed to slip out of harbor in a gallant effort to reach Toulon or a North African port and place herself under German control, in accordance with the Armistice terms of the Bordeaux government—though all this her crew and captain may not have realized. She was pursued by aircraft of the Fleet Air Arm and hit by at least one torpedo. She may have been joined by other French vessels from Algiers, which were well placed to do so and to reach Toulon before we would overtake them. She will, at any rate, be out of action for many months to come.

I need hardly say that the French ships were fought, albeit in this unnatural cause, with the characteristic courage of the French Navy, and every allowance must be made for Admiral Gensoul and his officers, who felt themselves obliged to obey the orders they received from their government and could not look behind that government to see the German dictation. I fear the loss of life among the French and in the harbor must have been very heavy, as we were compelled to use a severe measure of force and several immense explosions were heard. None of the British ships taking part in the action was in any way affected in gun power or mobility by the heavy fire directed upon them. I have not yet received any reports of our casualties, but Admiral Somerville's fleet is, in all military respects, intact and ready for further action. The Italian Navy, for whose reception we had also made arrangements and which is, of course, considerably stronger numerically than the Fleet we used at Oran, kept prudently out of the way. However, we trust that their turn will come during the operations which we shall pursue to secure the effectual command of the Mediterranean.

A large proportion of the French Fleet has, therefore, passed into our hands or has been put out of action or otherwise withheld from Germany by yesterday's events. The House will not expect me to say anything about other French ships which are at large except that it is our inflexible resolve to do everything that is possible in order to prevent them falling into the German grip. I leave the judgment of our action, with confidence, to Parliament. I leave it to the nation, and I leave it to the United States. I leave it to the world and history.

Now I turn to the immediate future. We must, of course, expect to be attacked, or even invaded, if that proves to be possible—it has not been proved yet—in our own island before very long. We are making every preparation in our power to repel the assaults of the enemy, whether they be directed upon Great Britain, or upon Ireland, which all Irishmen, without distinction of creed or party, should realize is in imminent danger. These again are matters upon which we have clear views. These preparations are constantly occupying our toil from morn till night, and far into the night. But, although we have clear views, it would not, I think, be profitable for us to discuss them in public, or even, so far as the government are concerned, except under very considerable reserve in a private session. I call upon all subjects of His Majesty, and upon our Allies, and well-wishers—and they are not a few—all over the world, on both sides of the Atlantic, to give us their utmost aid. In the fullest harmony with our dominions, we are moving through a period of extreme danger and of splendid hope, when every virtue of our race will be tested, and all that we have and are will be freely staked. This is no time for doubt or weakness. It is the supreme hour to which we have been called.

I will venture to read to the House a message which I have caused to be sent to all who are serving in positions of importance under the Crown, and if the House should view it with sympathy, I should be very glad to send a copy of it to every member for his own use—not that such exhortations are needed. This is the message:

> On what may be the eve of an attempted invasion or battle for our active land, the Prime Minister desires to impress upon all persons holding responsible positions in the government, in the fighting services, or in the civil departments, their duty to maintain a spirit of alert and confident energy. While every precaution must be taken that time and means afford, there are no grounds for supposing that more German troops can be landed in this country, either from the air or across the sea, than can be destroyed or captured by the strong forces at present under arms. The Royal Air Force is in excellent order and at the highest strength it has yet attained. The German Navy was never so weak, nor the British Army at home so strong as now. The Prime Minister expects all His Majesty's servants in high places to set an example of steadiness and resolution. They should check and rebuke expressions of loose and ill-digested opinion in their circle, or by their subordinates. They should not hesitate to report, or if necessary remove, any officers or officials who are found to be consciously exercising a disturbing or depressing influence, and whose talk is calculated to spread alarm and despondency. Thus alone will they be worthy of the fighting men, who, in the air, on the sea, and on land, have already met the enemy without any sense of being outmatched in martial qualities.

In conclusion, I feel that we are entitled to the confidence of the House and that we shall not fail in our duty, however painful.

The action we have already taken should be, in itself, sufficient to dispose once and for all of the lies and rumors which have been so industriously spread by German propaganda and through Fifth Column activities that we have the slightest intention of entering into negotiations in any form and through any channel with the German and Italian governments. We shall, on the contrary, prosecute the war with the utmost vigor by all the means that are open to us until the righteous purposes for which we entered upon it have been fulfilled.

Merchant War: Freighters That Fought Back

Sir Archibald Hurd

D uring the first months of World War II, German submarines and surface-going commerce raiders began a series of attacks against British shipping which came close to strangling the empire. Britain then began arming her freighters. It was more a gesture of defiance than an adequate defense since mounting a gun on vessels designed to carry cargo could not possibly make them the equal of high-speed, armored, and heavily armed warships.

Nevertheless, the resulting contests were not always as one-sided as might be expected. And no reporter wrote about these battles with more skill and stirring passion than Archibald Hurd—one of the rare naval journalists who knew and cared as much about the merchant fleet as about the warships they were pitted against.

Hurd was Britain's best-known naval journalist during the first three decades of the twentieth century, but he did not become Sir Archi-

bald for writing about the Royal Navy. He was knighted in 1928 after the publication of the second volume of his monumental three-volume work, The Merchant Navy, *an account of Britain's merchant fleet during World War I. This work was recognized as nationally important by a country whose survival depended on the uninterrupted comings and goings of sea traders from around the world.*

The Second World War was not a day old—barely nine hours had elapsed since its opening—when British merchant seamen experienced the lawless methods of the Germans. Many of these seamen entered the struggle with memories still fresh of the events of the years from 1914–18. But one and all were undismayed.

The *Athenia*, a Donaldson liner of 13,600 tons, was on her way to the United States with 1,418 men, women, and children on board, more than one-fourth of them returning Americans, when the ship was attacked. She was unarmed; she carried no explosives or munitions of war; she was manned by her customary merchant crew; her passengers were protected by the laws of God and man. Without warning, a submarine sent a torpedo into the side of the ship at 7:45 P.M. on the fateful date of September 3, 1939. The ship at once listed to port under the force of the explosion. Lights went out. There was no panic. Passengers were directed in orderly fashion to their boat stations, and in less than an hour 26 lifeboats had been lowered and the passengers embarked. The U-boat came to the surface, moved around the sinking liner, fired a shell which exploded on the C deck, and then the German captain, satisfied that he had done his worst, left the helpless men, women, and children to their fate—200 miles off the Irish coast.

The *Athenia*'s dead numbered 112. Of these, 93 were passengers and 19 members of the crew. The others were picked up during the night by rescuing vessels which answered the *Athenia*'s radio call. It was characteristic that German propaganda forthwith denied that a German submarine was involved, and claimed that Prime Minister Churchill had ordered the ship sunk in order to embroil Germany with the United States in war. It was the most ridiculous misrepresentation of which even German propagandists were capable.

There was nothing new in the "sink at sight" policy. The Germans were pledged not to resort to it again, but in the critical days when war seemed inevitable the Admiralty, doubting their sincerity, had fortunately made some preparations. The system of sailing ships in convoys escorted by warships, so long delayed before being put to trial in the First World War, was adopted at the outset. Merchant ships were also defensively armed as quickly as guns could be put on board. There were, however, new methods of attack, the effectiveness of which both the Royal Navy and the merchantmen could learn only by experience. The bombing airplane had little part in the sea warfare of 1914–18. Planes could now be fitted to carry bombs or to drop torpedoes on the ocean surface. The mine at sea had been made more deadly, but the British Admiralty at least was fully informed on the subject of the magnetic mine.

It was soon realized that the U-boat and the mine would be powerfully reinforced by the bombing airplane. The destruction of the liner *Empress of Britain*, the pride of the Canadian people and as a cruising vessel well known in all the chief ports of the world, was the first conspicuous victim of this new form of attack. This flagship of the Canadian Pacific Company's fleet had brought home the King and Queen of Great Britain from their tour in Canada. A vessel of 42,348 tons, she was on an Atlantic voyage in October 1940, with 643 people on board when, 150 miles off Ireland, bombers swept down on her out of the morning sky. Women and children were at once shepherded below. The gun crews fought the enemy till all were killed or disabled by the machine-gun fire which raked the decks, and the guns were silenced. Then the German pilots circled to closer attack, and sweeping over the ship dropped high explosive bombs. One made a direct hit. Incendiary bombs followed, and soon the *Empress of Britain* was ablaze amidships. Some of her boats, taking fire, burned fiercely as they swung on the davits. Captain Charles Howard Sapworth, faced with an emergency unique in the annals of war, displayed marked coolness, standing on the bridge while it burned beneath him; he remained on the ship's forepart till the very end. The liner was eventually sunk by a torpedo from a German submarine while in tow in an effort to save her. The submarine was, incidentally, herself sunk later, and her commander captured.

Against the additional dangers now to be faced and overcome by our merchant seamen sailing on their lawful occasions were to be ranged certain important factors. Britain had a Royal Air Force. Coastal Command, its strength rapidly built up, also guarded the overseas convoys from the time they came into the island approaches. A Fleet Air Arm had also been organized to play its part in the protection of the ships, and there were seagoing long-range aircraft moving at a pace of three hundred miles an hour, in place of the slow old gas-filled "blimp" of the last war. But the enemy had the initial advantage. Germany had seized the initiative, knowing that most of the merchant ships, widely distributed over the trade routes, had no defense and that some time would elapse before they could be placed in convoy.

Everything depended on the seamen themselves. Their skill and spirit and bravery alone could decide whether the measures undertaken should turn out a success—or a failure. Without the fighting tradition of the Royal Navy, or the bluejackets' training for war, their lives spent in a hazardous but peaceful calling, they were suddenly thrown into the vortex of war at sea. A large proportion of the merchant seamen were above the age at which men are called up for military service. They could have stayed safely ashore. They did not do so, nor did they seek an easier task. They decided to "carry on"—come what might. The record of the war is full of inspiring examples of men who, after passing through the gravest perils and experiencing hardships which called for the sternest endurance, returned again and again to take their part; in some cases facing the perils of the new piracy again even after eight ships had been sunk under them.

For the most part their feats of heroism, their skill and their endurance, have passed unrecorded. Only now and again is anything learned of an adventurous voyage, of daring acts performed by seamen at the risk of life.

The first straight fight of the war between a defensively armed British merchantman and a German U-boat was that of the *Stonepool*, a slow vessel of 4,803 tons, owned at West Hartlepool. She put up a very gallant resistance with her 4-inch gun mounted in the stern. Outward bound from the Bristol Channel with coal and machinery, the *Stonepool* at 6 A.M. sighted a U-boat on the surface about three miles distant. It opened fire almost at once. Captain Albert White swung his ship away, sent out wireless calls, and in two minutes had his gun in action. A shell from the submarine holed the merchantman above the waterline, and other shells fell around her as she zigzagged at full speed. The port lifeboat was smashed. Still the gun crew fought on—a veteran crew, for the gunlayer, John Hayter, was a retired Navy man, John Shipman, a steward, was 62 years old; and the third was Mr. Corney, the third mate. They returned shot for shot, the submarine having every advantage in that she presented a small and difficult target. The U-boat, possessing superior speed over the damaged *Stonepool*, drew ahead. She submerged and then a torpedo raced towards the merchant ship, breaking surface for a moment—and missed.

The fight on the surface was resumed. The merchantman seemed at her adversary's mercy with her port lifeboat riddled and other damage. The U-boat, zigzagging at speed astern of the steamer, kept up her fire. The *Stonepool* replied; but when she had fired her fifteenth shot in the unequal contest the submarine suddenly submerged. Five minutes later the enemy reappeared. Through his glasses Captain White saw her gun lying over on its side. He had scored a good hit. Obviously, too, there was hull injury, for the vessel rose high out of the water.

The submarine hastened off, leaving the crew of the badly leaking *Stonepool* to staunch her wounds and steer her towards port. Her wireless calls had been picked up by a British destroyer. Tearing along, this vessel came upon the U-boat on the surface, unable to submerge or to fight. As the destroyer approached, the Germans began hurried preparations to scuttle their ship. Her officers and men were made prisoners of war before she sank. "Good work!" the destroyer signalled to the battered and victorious *Stonepool*. Decorations were given. "By his resolute and skilful action," said the award, "the master saved his ship. The discipline was excellent, and the gunlayer and the gun's crew did very well." As in so many cases, the fight had been maintained by ordinary merchant seamen, only John Hayter, the gunlayer, having been trained for the violence of war.

A sister ship of the same company, the *Rockpool*, its Captain William Harland, later had a similar duel in the North Atlantic, after circumstances had compelled her to fall away from her convoy. She had a running fight with a U-boat for over ten miles, and got ahead and escaped, to learn subsequently that her wireless signals had called up a British warship which destroyed the German.

British pluck combined with readiness for instant action has never been better illustrated than by the narrative of the coastal steamer *Highlander*, weighing 1,220 tons. Incidentally, it set two records, one of which is likely to stand unchallenged, for her master, bringing his vessel safely into port, brought with him all that remained of a German aircraft which was still lying where it fell on the ship's stern. Captain William Gifford was the particular hero of the exploit. The *Highlander* was passing along the East Coast, about three and a half miles from land, just before midnight, when the sound of a plane flying low was heard. This might have been British, as at first was thought, but the master was taking no chances. The ship's two light guns were manned and speed increased. In a few minutes the plane disclosed its nationality. Machine-gun bullets swept the steamer's superstructure, riddling the funnel and deck fittings and piercing the side. There were no casualties. The plane passed astern, circled, and then returned for a second attack, at still closer range. The *Highlander* opened fire on the attacker as he came on, and probably a shot reached the pilot, for the plane collided with the ship's port lifeboat, twisted around after the contact, and crashed over her stern. A couple of cranes were demolished, a light gun smashed flat onto the deck, and the two seamen who manned it knocked out—neither, it happened, was seriously hurt. Shedding its port wing, most of which remained on the ship's deck, the rest of the plane went on for one hundred yards or so, then at great speed hit the water and disappeared.

It was a good night's work, but unfinished. The *Highlander* had started zigzagging. Within ten minutes there came a second plane, burning her side lights and flying low. Again the *Highlander* was the target for machine-gun fire, which she returned with interest with her remaining gun. Her bullets were seen to hit the plane. A few moments later it dived into the North Sea with a great splash, a little distance astern. The bag was two enemy planes in ten minutes, a great feat for a small, lightly-armed coasting vessel. The *Highlander*, battered and scarred, duly landed her trophy.

Many gallant deeds performed in merchant ships illuminate the record of the war at sea. The epic story of the *Jervis Bay* is one of the finest ever told. A turbine steamer weighing 14,164 tons, owned by the Aberdeen–Commonwealth Line and converted into an armed cruiser, she was sailing as escort ship of an Atlantic convoy of thirty-eight vessels. Royal Navy Captain Fogarty Fegan was in command, himself the son of Rear Admiral F. F. Fegan, and one of three brothers serving in the Royal Navy. This was in November 1940. As the winter nights had lengthened, the possibility that German warships would attempt to slip out into the Atlantic was realized. A stronger escort would have been desirable. But the surrender of France and the entry of Italy into the war had increased the responsibilities of the Royal Navy in guarding Britain's commerce in many seas. The Admiralty could do no more than provide as large a measure of safety as the circumstances permitted. The convoy, when just over halfway between Nova Scotia and Ireland, on November 5 sighted a warship to the northward, upon her port beam. It was a sunny evening, little more than an hour before dusk. The stranger was about seven or eight miles distant when she opened fire at long range. The first shells—they came more quickly as the distance was closed—were directed at the New Zealand liner *Rangitiki*, 16,698 tons, the largest ship in the convoy. No doubt the raider took her for the escort vessel, and was attempting to get rid of her first. The gunfire was accurate and very heavy. The *Rangitiki* was hit but managed to escape, and in her crippled condition reached a British port.

The *Jervis Bay*, in the words of the skipper of one of the convoyed ships, "went right out to meet the German challenge—a perfect target. Every man knew what her fate would be." Her crew, facing almost certain death, maintained the highest traditions of British seamen. A proportion were of the merchant service. The ships of the convoy under their commodore, Rear Admiral Maltby, in the *Cornish City*, turned to starboard away from the enemy and dropped smoke floats, which in the light breeze made an effective screen. They scattered into the night. Those on the port wing column, nearest the raider, fired their defensive guns when able to bear at the turn away, but ineffectually owing to the distance; indeed, it is doubtful if the *Jervis Bay*'s own six-inch guns ever got within range.

As the *Jervis Bay* steamed to the encounter she was hit, some said, by the German's third salvo. Soon she was disabled, her steering gear being out of action, but her guns continued to fire. The vessel was holed below the waterline; she was ablaze; she took a list; and then began to sink. Still she fought on. The flag was shot away and a seaman ran up the rigging with a new ensign and nailed it to the mast. The flag was still flying when the *Jervis Bay* took her last plunge and disappeared.

Captain Fegan's gallant action saved the convoy by keeping the raider busy. He died a hero's death, going down with his blazing ship, of which he remained in command to the end. Many of the escaping merchantmen witnessed the fight for some time, and as they steamed away in the gathering darkness could still see the flash of the guns on the far horizon. A posthumous Victoria Cross was awarded to Captain Fegan, and never has the coveted decoration been more worthily bestowed. In the words of the Admiralty communique: "The vessels owe their escape to the armed merchant cruiser *Jervis Bay*, which was escorting the convoy and which fought the raider for two hours, though heavily outclassed in guns, and sacrificed herself so that the ships of the convoy might have time to elude the German warship."

There was a heartening sequel to this story of supreme sacrifice. Sixty-five survivors of the fight were brought home to Britain. Their lives were saved by the heroic action of Captain Sven Olander, the master of a Swedish freighter sailing with the convoy. "It was glorious," he said simply, when he came ashore. "I shall never forget the gallantry of the British captain, sailing forward to meet the enemy. They did so well for us that I did not like to leave them." And so, with the hearty approval of all his men, Captain Olander had turned his ship back to the scene of the struggle, daring attack and destruction by the raider, to pick up such as were left of the *Jervis Bay*'s officers and crew. The Germans promptly announced that they had sent to the bottom the whole of the convoy. Actually, of the 38 ships, all except 4 reached British ports.

The salvage of the *San Demetrio* gave occasion for acts of heroism which cannot be read without a thrill. She was one of the convoy escorted by the *Jervis Bay*, a motor tanker weighing 8,073 gross tons, with a full cargo of oil. She scattered with the others, but the pursuing raider concentrated his gunfire upon her, damaging her severely and starting fires on board. At the captain's order, the ship was abandoned, and a few minutes later she was struck by another salvo and burst into flames. The crew had left in three boats, and so they lost touch. In the night shells passed over them as the raider continued the chase and the bombardment of the merchant ships, but they escaped harm.

During the whole of the first day, a boat commanded by the *San Demetrio*'s second officer, Mr. Arthur Godfrey Hawkins, with fifteen other members of the crew, was kept head on to heavy seas. After two days they again sighted the tanker, still burning, with oil floating on the water. The weather made close approach impossible, and the boat lay off all that night. With dawn the weather moderated, a sail was hoisted, and by noon a perilous attempt at boarding succeeded. Fires raged fore and aft, and the tanker was glowing like a furnace amidships. Seamen of less courage and resource might have considered the position hopeless. The bridge had been destroyed, with all the surrounding structure, compasses, steering gear, charts, and wireless had gone; the one alternative method of control, the steering gear aft, was partially destroyed, and the wheel had only four spokes. Holes made in the collision bulkhead resisted all efforts to plug them. The deck over the aft tanks was pierced in many places by shells and splinters, and with every roll of the ship spurts of oil were shot into the air and washed over the decks, threatening further to extend the fires. Yet the ship was brought safely into port.

All through the night of November 7–8 the boat's crew fought the fires, having, after about six hours' work, raised sufficient power to put the hose into action. Before midday the fires were mastered, and gradually they were extinguished. That afternoon the main engines were started. The problem of steering was solved by the construction of a temporary steering platform. With only four men on board competent to steer, exposure of lights prohibited, and the danger present of explosion from oil or gas, which made the use of oil lamps impossible, the vessel ploughed along at a speed rising to nine knots. The crew had no sextant, and kept to an easterly course by the North Star, with a check by the moon and the sun. It was deemed too dangerous to light the galley fire, and they lived mainly on monotonous meals of cold vegetables, "but occasionally buckets of boiled onions and boiled potatoes came up, cooked on the main drain," Mr. Hawkins afterwards stated.

There was heroic work in the engine room. Normally its complement was fourteen men. Only four were available. These four carried on, overcoming every difficulty. One of them, John Boyle, a greaser, who did not live to see the vessel into port, had received grave injuries when getting into the boat as the *San Demetrio* was abandoned, but took his part in the engine room for three days until strength failed him. His comrades moved him to one of the few cabins which had not been burned out. The next morning they found him dead.

The stricken ship, with a linen cloth as a distress signal, made a landfall on November 13. A party of naval officers and enlisted men were put on board, and assisted to bring the *San Demetrio* into the Clyde on November 16—with sixteen feet of water in her forehold, after a 700 miles' voyage from the point where she was boarded, and with 10,000 tons of her precious cargo of oil still remaining in her. No wonder that Justice Langton and the Elder Brethren of Trinity House sitting with him to adjudicate the salvage claim congratulated Mr. Hawkins and all his comrades on the magnificent services they had given.

The record of the merchant fleet is crowded with inspiring stories. There was the *Sussex*, a P. and O. Liner weighing 13,647 tons. She had a cargo mainly of wheat and wool, but also carried some forty tons of explosives packed in steel cylinders, for which a large wooden locker had been built between decks. The long voyage from New Zealand via the Cape was almost over, and she was off the Irish coast, when at daybreak one morning a high-flying airplane was seen. It dived, to be greeted with heavy antiaircraft gunfire, and then it dropped two bombs. Both unluckily took effect. One exploded on the funnel, which crashed on deck and did serious damage. The second burst on a hatch, starting flames in the cargo of wool. Firing furiously, the ship's gunners three times drove off the raider as he sought to attack, and he gave up the attempt. By this time the fire amid the wool was serious, and engaged all hands in an effort to prevent its spreading. The men knew well what defeat would involve. The locker of explosives was just above, and flames kept leaping about it. Hoses were directed at the steel containers to keep them cool, but despite everything one exploded—happily only one. A boy, Frederick Trundley, climbed to the top of the explosives, and from that perilous seat played his hose wherever the fire threatened most, joking while at work. The long struggle ended, but not until the afternoon was the fire out. The gallant crew had saved the ship from being blown to pieces, and their own lives from gravest peril. Now new dangers had to be faced. Compasses, chronometers, wireless, everything on the bridge and in the chart room had been smashed, but the engines still worked. Amid rough seas, Captain Clarke steered a course by the sun, being aided by a small boat's compass. In fog, the crippled *Sussex* was rammed by a trawler, but fortunately not holed; the fog was in fact friendly, for it hid the shower of sparks that poured from the hole where the funnel had stood. A destroyer put the ship on its true course, and port was safely reached.

The end of the *Western Prince,* weighing 10,926 tons, torpedoed in the Atlantic in mid-December, will have a lasting place in the annals of the sea owing to the master's devotion to duty. A lonely figure, Captain John Reid was seen standing on the bridge waving good-bye to the passengers and crew whom he had got safely into the lifeboats. He had refused a place in the last boat, because he thought her to be already loaded to capacity. A moment before the ship took the final plunge, Captain Reid sounded three blasts on her siren in token of farewell. Among the passengers sailing in the *Western Prince* was Mr. C. D. Howe, Canadian minister of munitions and supplies, who said it was due to the magnificent seamanship shown by the captain in getting the lifeboats away in dangerous seas that the survivors owed their lives.

The offensive spirit was gallantly displayed by the *Clan Macbean,* weighing 5,000 tons, which at dusk was the target of a torpedo which went wide. A little later a U-boat broke surface nearby to continue the attack with her gun. Captain Ernest Coultas kept his course, steering straight into the gunfire; three shells whistled by, but scored no hit. After this, the German dived at full speed, leaving his gun's crew in the water. A rescue boat lowered by the *Clan Macbean* made them prisoners, while the ship itself got away in the darkness. The Germans did not know that the *Clan Macbean* was *unarmed*.

CHAPTER 16

Bismarck: The Witches' Sabbath

C. S. Forester

I n May 1941, after World War II had been in progress for a year and a half, the new 45,000-ton German battleship Bismarck sortied into the North Atlantic. Admiral Gunther Lutjens and Captain Ernst Lindemann, both embarked on the Bismarck, planned to hunt and destroy British merchant convoys.

Well aware of the danger, the Royal Navy dispatched no fewer than 46 warships in hot pursuit. On first contact, shells from the Bismarck damaged the British battleship Prince of Wales and had a catastrophic effect on the battle cruiser Hood. The Bismarck's fourth salvo was seen to snap the Hood "like a bath tub toy." From a crew of 1,419 there were only three survivors. And then the German warship vanished into the Atlantic.

On May 26, the Bismarck was spotted by aircraft from the carrier

Ark Royal *and damaged by their torpedoes. The next morning, the British battle fleet closed in to avenge the* Hood.

C. S. Forester, *author of the world-famous Captain Horatio Hornblower novels, as well as works on naval history, brought together his talents as a novelist and historian in telling of the death of the* Bismarck. *The dialogue that follows is invented, he cautioned his readers, although no doubt similar conversations took place.*

"Good morning, admiral," said Lindemann.

"Good morning, captain," said Lutjens.

"Destroyers out of range on the starboard bow, sir," said Lindemann. "And there's a cruiser somewhere to the northward of us. I'm sure she's the *Suffolk*."

"That was the ship that sighted us in Denmark Strait," said Lutjens. "Still with us, is she?"

One of the lookouts blinked himself awake and stared forward through his binoculars. "Ship right ahead! Two ships right ahead!"

Lutjens and Lindemann trained their glasses forward.

"Battleships?" asked Lutjens.

"I think so, sir. Battleships."

The lookout in *King George V* was staring through his glasses. "Ship right ahead!"

The lookout in [the British battleship] *Rodney* reported. "Ship bearing green five!"

"That's *Bismarck*!" said an officer on the bridge of *Rodney*.

Down the voice pipe over the head of the quartermaster at the wheel of the *Rodney* came a quiet order.

"Port ten."

"Port ten, sir," repeated the quartermaster, turning his wheel.

Up in the gunnery control tower the captain's voice made itself heard in the gunnery officer's earphones.

"We are turning to port. Open fire when your guns bear."

The gunnery officer looked down at the "gun ready" lights. He looked through his glasses with the pointer fixed upon the silhouette of the *Bismarck*.

"Fire!" he said.

Out on the wing of the bridge stood an American observer and a British lieutenant, glasses to their eyes. Below them, just as on the evening before, the 16-inch guns were training round and reaching upwards towards extreme elevation. Then came the incredible roar and concussion of the salvo. The brown cordite smoke spurted out from the muzzles to be borne rapidly away by the wind as the shells took their unseen way on their mission of death.

"Short but close. Damned close," said the Englishman; the last words were drowned by the din of the second salvo, and he did not speak again during the brief time of flight. But when he spoke it was in a voice high-pitched with excitement. "A hit! At the second salvo! I told you the old *Rodney*—"

Again his words were drowned by the roar of the guns and he forced himself to keep his glasses steady on the target. Next it was the American who spoke.

"Another hit," he said. "She doesn't stand a chance now."

Down in the radar room of the *Bismarck* the same disciplined team was still at work.

"Range seventeen thousand meters," said the rating [seaman] at the screen.

There was a roar like thunder then, all about them, as the first salvo hit the *Bismarck*. The lights went out and came on, went out and came on, and the yellow-green eye of the radar screen abruptly went lifeless. The rating there reached for other switches, clicked them on and off; he tried another combination.

"Radar not functioning, sir," he announced.

"You've tried the after aerial?" asked the officer.

"Yes, sir. No result."

"No connection with gunnery control, sir," announced another rating.

"No connection with—" began another rating, but another rolling peal of thunder cut off his words, and again the lights flickered. "No connection with the bridge, sir."

"Very well."

"No connection with the chart house, sir."

"Very well."

The first wisps of smoke had begun to enter the radar room through the ventilating system. Wisp after wisp it came, seeping in thicker and thicker, swirling in, while the lights burned duller and duller. And peal after peal of thunder shook the whole structure, the shock waves causing the wreaths of smoke to eddy abruptly with each impact, and a section of panelling fell from the bulkhead with a sudden clatter. It was as if the witches' Sabbath in which they had been engaged had now roused the infernal forces for their own destruction. Throughout the doomed ship the lights were burning low and smoke was creeping in thicker and thicker.

In the [British] War Room the young officer was repeating the messages heard on the telephone.

"Most immediate from *Suffolk*. *Rodney* has opened fire. *King George V* has opened fire. *Bismarck* is returning the fire. *Bismarck* hit. *Bismarck* is hit again."

It was almost possible for the men listening to him in the War Room to visualize what was actually going on. As the *Bismarck* trained her guns around she was surrounded by a forest of splashes from *Rodney*'s salvo, and before she could fire the splashes from *King George V*'s salvo surrounded her. Hardly had her guns spoken before a shell hit the second turret from forward and burst with a roar and a billow of smoke. The blast and the fragments swept everywhere about the bridge. The fabric was left a twisted litter of stanchions, and lying huddled and contorted in it were a number of corpses, among them those of Lindemann—conspicuous by its Knight's Cross with diamonds—and of Lutjens. The voice of the officer at the telephone went on describing what was going on. "*Bismarck* on fire aft. *Bismarck* hit. *Bismarck* hit. *Bismarck*'s fore turret out of action."

Another officer broke in.

"*Ark Royal* signalling, sir. 'All planes away.' "

"*Ark Royal*? I can't believe her planes will find anything to do. But quite right to send them in."

On the flight deck of the *Ark Royal* the sound of the gunfire was plainly to be heard, loudly, in the intervals of the Swordfish torpedo bombers revving up their engines and taking off. Conditions were as bad as ever as the ship heaved and plunged in the rough sea under a lowering gray sky, yet somehow the lumbering aircraft managed to get away, and circle, and get into formation, and head northwards, low over the heaving sea and close under the dripping clouds. It was only a few seconds before the leader saw what he was looking for. There was a long bank of black smoke lying on the surface of the water, spreading and expanding from the denser and narrower nucleus to the northward, and it was towards that nucleus that he headed his plane.

"My God!" said the leader.

The smoke was pouring from the battered, almost shapeless hull of the *Bismarck*, stripped of her upper works, mast, funnels, bridge and all. Yet under the smoke, plainly in the dull gray light, he could see a forest—a small grove, rather—of tall red flames roaring upward from within the hull. But it was not the smoke nor the flames that held the eye, strangely enough, but the ceaseless dance of tall jets of water all about her. Two battleships were flinging shells at her both from their main and from their secondary armaments; and from the cruisers, twenty 8-inch guns were joining in. There was never a moment when she was not ringed in by the splashes of the near misses, but when the leader forced his eye to ignore the distraction of this wild water dance he saw something else; from bow to stern along the tortured hull he could see a continual coming and going of shell bursts, volcanoes of flame and smoke. From that low height as the Swordfish closed in he could see everything. He could see the two fore turrets useless, one of them with the roof blown clean off and the guns pointing over the side at extreme elevation, the other with the guns fore and aft drooping at extreme depression. Yet the aftermost turret was still in action; even as he watched he saw one of the guns in it fling out a jet of smoke towards the shadowy form of the *King George V*; down there in the steel turret nestling among the flames some heroes were still contriving to load and train and fire. And he saw something else at the last moment of his approach. There were a few tiny foreshortened figures visible here and there scrambling over the wreckage incredibly alive amid the flames and the explosions, leaping down from the fiery hull into the boiling sea.

He swung the Swordfish away from the horrible sight, to lead the way back to the *Ark Royal*. While that bombardment was going on there was no chance of a frail plane delivering a successful torpedo attack. He had seen the climax of the manifestation of sea power, the lone challenger overwhelmed by a colossal concentration of force. He was not aware of the narrowness of the margin of time and space, of how in the British battleships the last few tons of oil fuel were being pumped towards the furnaces, of German U-boats hastening just too late from all points in the North Atlantic to try to intervene in the struggle, of German air power chafing at the bit unable to take part in a battle only a few miles beyond their maximum range.

While he was leading his squadron back to the *Ark Royal* the officer at the telephone in the War Room was continuing to announce the signals coming through.

"*Bismarck* hit again. She is only a wreck now. *King George V* and *Rodney* turning away."

In the War Room people looked sharply at each other at that piece of news. The admiral looked at the clock.

"That's the last minute they could stay. They'll only just have enough oil fuel to get them home. Not five minutes to spare."

"Here's a signal from the flag, sir," interposed another young officer. " 'Ships with torpedoes go in and sink her.' "

"And here's *Suffolk* again," said the first young officer. "*Dorsetshire* going in."

Bismarck lay, a shattered, burning, sinking hulk, as *Dorsetshire* approached. At two miles *Dorsetshire* fired two torpedoes which burst on *Bismarck*'s starboard side. At a mile and a half she fired another which burst on the port side of the wreck. She rolled over and sank, leaving the surface covered with debris and struggling men.

"*Bismarck* sunk," said the young officer in the War Room. "*Bismarck* sunk."

Those words of the young officer were spoken in a hushed voice, and yet their echoes were heard all over the world. In a hundred countries radio announcers hastened to repeat those words to their audiences. In a hundred languages newspaper headlines proclaimed "*Bismarck* Sunk" to a thousand million readers. Frivolous women heard those words unhearing; unlettered peasants heard them uncomprehending, even though the destinies of all of them were changed in that moment. Stock-exchange speculators revised their plans. Prime ministers and chiefs of state took grim note of those words. The admirals of a score of navies prepared to compose memoranda advising their governments regarding the political and technical conclusions to be drawn from them. And there were wives and mothers and children who heard those words as well, just as Nobby's [a British seaman's] mother had heard about the loss of the *Hood*.

CHAPTER 17

Pearl Harbor: Hurling Monkey Wrenches in Exasperation

Samuel Eliot Morison

Pearl Harbor may have been the greatest single event of the twentieth century. It was, after all, the event that drew the United
States into World War II, eventually into the nuclear age, and on to a
commanding position on the world stage—a position from which America
has not retreated.

It was also one of those terrible shocks, like the assassinations of
Abraham Lincoln, John F. Kennedy, and Martin Luther King, that
define what it is to be an American. It burned its way into the national
psyche.

And who better to portray this pivotal event than Samuel Eliot
Morison, the dean of naval historians from the outbreak of World War
II until his death in 1976. He taught history at Harvard from 1915 to
1955, and won Pulitzer Prizes for his biographies of Christopher Co-
lombus and John Paul Jones. Appointed official historian of naval opera-

tions during World War II, Morison covered much of the fighting first hand. The result was his 15-volume The History of the United States Naval Operations in World War II.

Shortly after 0700 the sun, rising over the Tantalus Mountains, cast its first rays on Pearl Harbor, heightening the green of the canefields that stretch up the slopes above Aiea and deepening the blue of the lochs, as the arms of this harbor are called. Even for Oahu, favored by nature, this was an uncommonly bright and peaceful Sabbath morning. On board ships the forenoon watch was piped to breakfast while the men it would relieve at 0800 concluded their various duties, such as cleaning brass and wiping dew off the machine guns and the 5-inch dual-purpose guns. Of these, only about one in four was fully manned. The main batteries were not manned, nor were the plotting rooms, directors, and ammunition supply; ready ammunition was in locked boxes whose keys were in the hands of the officer of the deck. All ships had at least one boiler lighted, but few had enough steam up to get under way in a hurry. Among the 70 combatant ships and 24 auxiliaries in the harbor, only one, a destroyer, was under way.

At about 0740 the first Japanese attack wave, 40 torpedo bombers, 49 high-level bombers, 51 dive-bombers and 51 fighters sighted the Oahu coastline. They then deployed—the fighters to destroy parked planes at Wheeler Field and Kaneohe, the high-level bombers for Hickam Field, the torpedo planes and dive-bombers for "Battleship Row." By 0750 they were ready to strike, and Captain Fuchida, the strike commander, gave the word.

The sound of church bells at Honolulu, ringing for mass at 0800, came over the harbor, whose calm surface was only lightly rippled by the breeze. Many officers were at breakfast, others were just rising; seamen were lounging on deck talking, reading, or writing letters home. As the hour for morning colors approached, sailors in white uniforms removed the jack and ensign from their lockers, a bluejacket on the signal bridge hoisted the Blue Peter, and boatswains were set to pipe the preparatory signal at 0755.

A few seconds before or after that hour—nobody could remember which—the air suddenly seemed filled with strange planes, hovering, darting, diving. A brisk dive-bomber got in the first lick, on Ford Island naval air headquarters, where Commander Ramsey, the operations officer, who had been discussing the midget submarine sinkings over the telephone, thought it was accidental, from an overzealous Army plane. Hardly anyone, for seconds or even minutes, even after seeing the red "meat ball" on the fuselages, recognized the planes as Japanese. Some thought they were United States Army planes camouflaged as Japanese to give the Navy a scare. Others assumed that this was an air drill and thought it too realistic. Across the harbor, Rear Admiral William R. Furlong, in the minelayer *Oglala*, who had studied Japanese plane types, recognized the torpedo-bombers when they zoomed up the main channel between him and Ford Island; and as he happened to be senior officer present afloat, he ordered the signal hoisted, "All Ships in Harbor Sortie." Almost simultaneously, someone in the signal tower ashore made the same observation and telephoned to Cincpac headquarters, "Enemy air raid—not drill." The Navy air arm on Ford Island took a little longer to realize the truth, so it was not until 0758 that Admiral Bellinger broadcast a message which shook the United States as nothing had since the firing on Fort Sumter:

AIR RAID, PEARL HARBOR—THIS IS NO DRILL.

Now, to quote John Milton, "All hell broke loose." The Sabbath calm was shattered by bomb explosions, internal explosions, and machine-gun fire, with the hoarse signal of General Quarters as obbligato. At least two battleships were already doomed and hundreds of American seamen dead by 0758.

Let us now concentrate on the first phase of the attack, from 0755 to 0825, during which about 90 percent of the damage was done.

Battleship Row was located along the southeast shore of Ford Island, a few hundred yards across the main channel from the Navy Yard. The battlewagons were moored, some singly and others in pairs, to massive quays a short distance off the island shore. *Nevada* occupied the northeasterly berth, with an ammunition lighter outboard. Next came *Arizona*, with tender *Vestal* outboard. Southwest of them were *Tennessee* and *West Virginia* side by side, and the next pair was *Maryland* and *Oklahoma*. *California* alone had the southernmost berth. *Pennsylvania* was in drydock across the harbor, where five cruisers were also berthed. Twenty-six destroyers and minecraft were moored in groups in various parts of the harbor.

The Japanese aviators knew exactly where to find the battleships, completely unprotected from torpedo attack, and made first for *Arizona* and the two pairs. The major attack was made by twelve "Kate" torpedo-bombers launching torpedoes from low altitudes— 40 to 100 feet above the water. Four more Kates followed. Almost simultaneously, "Val" dive-bombers began combing Battleship

Row fore and aft, dropping not only conventional bombs but converted 16-inch armor-piercing shells which penetrated the decks and exploded below. Then five more planes attacked cruiser *Raleigh* and three other ships moored on the northwest side of Ford Island. Most of these planes, after they had dropped bombs or topedoes, flew back over their targets, strafing viciously in order to kill as many sailors as possible.

Imagine the consternation that this sudden onslaught created among the officers and men on board! A surprise attack in war is bad enough to cope with, but this was a surprise attack in time of peace when, so far as anyone in Hawaii knew, diplomatic negotiations at Washington were continuing. What made defense even more difficult was the absence on weekend leave of many senior officers and chief petty officers to whom juniors were accustomed to look for orders and guidance. Yet the junior officers' and bluejackets' reaction, against fearful odds, was superb. Between explosions one could hear sailors knocking off the padlocks from ready ammunition chests with axes and mauls. Dive-bombers swooped so near that sailors could see the Japanese pilots' toothy grins, and in exasperation hurled monkey wrenches at them. At what moment return gunfire was opened is still uncertain. Some said within a minute, others within five; but photos taken by the Japanese as late as 0805, when *California* was torpedoed, show not a single black burst of ack-ack [antiaircraft fire] in the sky, and all but one or two of the first wave of torpedo-bombers got away unscathed. The Navy's machine guns at that time were not very effective—the 3-inch was not rapid-fire enough, and the 1.1-inch was liable to heat and jam after a few rounds; it was not until next year that the 20-millimeter Oerlikon and 40-millimeter Bofors were installed.

Oklahoma, outboard of the southernmost pair of battlewagons, one of our 1916 Dreadnoughts, never had a chance to fight back. While the crew were running to battle stations, a few moments after the first bomb exploded on Ford Island, three torpedoes blasted huge holes in her and she promptly listed 30 degrees. There was no time to set Condition Zed (complete watertight integrity), or to counterflood, or to bring machine guns to bear. Before 0800 the senior officer on board ordered Abandon Ship. Men crawled over the starboard side as she rolled over, and two more torpedo hits completed her doom. Fifteen minutes later, parts of her bottom were facing the sky. Many survivors climbed on board *Maryland* alongside, to help her fight. She, protected by *Oklahoma* from the torpedoes, got off with only two bomb hits, and became the first of the stricken Battle Fleet to return to active service. *Oklahoma* lost 415 officers and men killed out of 1,354 on board.

Tennessee and *West Virginia* made the next couple on Battleship Row. The latter, outboard, took six or seven torpedoes, the first before 0756, and two bombs. An exceptionally well-trained crew, who loved their "Wee Vee," as they called the ship, saved her from the fate of *Oklahoma*. Ensign Brooks, officer of the deck, saw the first bomb hit Ford Island and immediately ordered "Away Fire and Rescue Party!" This brought everyone topside on the double, and saved hundreds of lives. *West Virginia* listed so rapidly that the guns on the starboard side, which opened fire promptly, could be served only by organizing a double row of ammunition handlers—one to pass and the other to hold the passer upright. Lieutenant Ricketts ordered counterflooding on his own initiative, and, ably assisted by Boatswain's Mate Billingsley, corrected a 28-degree list to 15 degrees; this allowed her to settle on the bottom almost upright. Captain Bennion, disemboweled by fragments from a bomb that exploded on *Tennessee* alongside, was *in extremis*; his only thoughts were for his ship and crew until his life flickered out a few minutes later; but his fighting spirit lived on. All hands fought fires, although frequently dive-bombed and strafed. "Their spirit was marvelous," reported the surviving executive officer. "Words fail in attempting to describe the magnificent display of courage, discipline, and devotion to duty of all." *West Virginia* lost 105 killed out of about 1,500 on board.

Tennessee, moored inboard, naturally suffered less. She received two bombs early in the action, but most of her damage came from fires started by flaming debris from *Arizona*, exploding 75 feet astern. Fire-fighting continued all the rest of that day and the following night, and she did not sink. Her losses were only 5 killed; and within three weeks she, in company with *Maryland* and *Pennsylvania*, sailed to the West Coast for a complete overhaul.

Arizona was moored inboard of a short repair ship which afforded her slight protection. Within one minute of the opening attack the battleship was literally torn apart by torpedo and bomb explosions. A bomb exploded in the forward magazine before it could be flooded, wrecking half the ship, killing Captain Van Valkenburgh and Rear Admiral Kidd, who were on the bridge, and causing the ship to settle so fast that hundreds of sailors were trapped below. Even so, the machine guns topside opened fire on the enemy planes, and she was not abandoned until 1032. Owing to lack of warning and to the magazine explosion, *Arizona*'s casualties were over half those suffered by the entire Fleet at Pearl Harbor—1,103 officers and men killed out of some 1,400 on board. Her remains, and most of theirs, are still there today; she has never been formally decommissioned, and every day a color guard faithfully raises and lowers the ensign on a mast built on a platform over the wreck.

Battleship Row tapered off to a lone battlewagon at each end. Southernmost was *California*, flagship of Admiral Pye and, at the age of twenty, youngest of the Battle Fleet. At 0805 she was the last to be hit, but in the worst condition to take it—completely "unbuttoned" in preparation for an admiral's inspection—so that the two torpedoes that hit her, together with one bomb that exploded below and set off a magazine, were enough to cause her to settle into the mud. Prompt counterflooding, directed by Reserve Ensign Fair, prevented her from capsizing, which would have meant a far greater loss of life than the 98 officers and men actually killed. *California* was also restored to the Fleet and performed excellent service in the latter half of the war.

Nevada, at the northern end, oldest battleship present—well past her twenty-fifth birthday—had a little more grace than her immediate neighbors; color guard began making morning colors and the band struck up "The Star-spangled Banner" before anything lethal came her way. A Kate that had torpedoed *Arizona* skimmed across her stern during the ceremony and the rear gunner tried to strafe the sailors at attention, but managed only to rip the ensign. A second strafer came in, but the band finished the national anthem without a pause; nobody broke ranks. Ensign Taussig, officer of the deck, then ordered "Battle Stations," set Condition Zed, and *Nevada* went into action with her machine guns and port 5-inch battery. One and possibly two torpedo-bombers were hit, and the rest gave *Nevada* a wide berth; but one torpedo tore a hole in her side, 45 by 30 feet. Prompt counterflooding corrected the list, and as her power plant was intact, Lieutenant Commander Francis J. Thomas, senior officer present, eighth in the chain of command, made the wise decision to get under way. In the meantime *Nevada* had taken two bomb hits amidships, causing many casualties and great damage. Ordinarily, four tugs were required to get a battleship under way from the mooring quays, but *Nevada* did it unaided; Chief Boatswain E. J. Hill jumped onto the quay, cast off the lines under strafing fire, and swam back to the ship. Down the ship channel she stood, fighting off dive-bombers of the second Japanese attack wave who concentrated on her, and at one time surrounded by a curtain of smoke and spray so dense that spectators thought her gone; but most of the bombs were near-misses. A proud and gallant sight she made, with her tattered ensign streaming from the fantail. She could easily have gone to sea, but in the confusion Admiral Bloch or Kimmel, fearing lest she sink and block the channel, sent her an urgent signal not to leave the harbor. Commander Thomas then decided to anchor off Hospital Point. Just as she was about to drop the hook, dive-bombers attacked and made three hits, one of which "opened the forecastle like a sardine can" and killed the entire anchoring detail, including Boatswain Hill. *Nevada* then slid gently aground. The captain now came on board and ordered her towed across the harbor to Waipio Point where, despite strenuous effort at damage control, she flooded and settled. Fifty officers and men had been killed, and the old battlewagon was thoroughly wrecked topside. Floated in February, she steamed to Puget Sound under her own power and, after modernization, rejoined the Fleet in 1943.

Pennsylvania, flagship of the Pacific Fleet, was happily in dry dock at the Navy Yard and so could not be reached by torpedo-bombers. She threw up powerful antiaircraft fire, took but one severe bomb hit, and lost only 18 men. But several bombs meant for her hit destroyers *Cassin* and *Downes* in the same dry dock, and pretty well demolished them.

Thus, in half an hour the Japanese bombers accomplished their most important objective, wrecking the Battle Line of the Pacific Fleet beyond any possibility of offensive action within a year.

Too much praise cannot be given to the officers and bluejackets in these and other ships. Once they had recovered from the initial surprise they served their vessels nobly, and the damage-control parties were especially effective. There was no flinching, no attempt to escape. On the contrary, from the moment of the first alarm, officers and men on leave in Honolulu and elsewhere began hastening to their stations. Dozens of barges, gigs, launches, and small yard craft took men out to their own ships, evacuated the wounded from the stricken vessels, and helped fight fires, with complete disregard for their own safety. Chief Jansen, commanding *YG-17*, one of the yard's garbage lighters, received high praise for closing *West Virginia* to fight her fires until they were quenched, when he moved over to another post of danger, alongside *Arizona*. Ensign Sears of *West Virginia* was taken to the wrong ship but jumped overboard and swam to his own to bear a hand. Chief Boatswain Hill of *Nevada*, and every one of his detail, and the exposed gunners of the 5-inchers, fought as one man, and that man a hero; and almost every one of them lost his life. So, while we deplore the surprise, let us never forget the heroic reaction. "That strife was not inglorious, though the event was dire."

During the initial phase of the attack, between 0755 and 0825, the enemy inflicted severe punishment on military aircraft in Oahu. A flight of dive-bombers worked over Ford Island and in a few minutes Patrol Wing Two lost 33 planes, almost half its number. At Ewa, the Marine Corps air base, halfway between West Loch and the ocean, some 50 planes were based. Captain Ashwell, officer of the day, was having breakfast when he heard aircraft, stepped out, sighted the first flight of torpedo-bombers making for Battle-ship Row, immediately recognized them; and, as he ran to the guardhouse to sound an alarm, saw 21 "Zeke" fighter planes roaring in over the Waianae mountains. They struck Ewa before sprinting Ashwell reached his goal. Swooping low, they attacked with short bursts of gunfire the planes parked wing to wing, and destroyed over thirty in a couple of minutes. By the time a second attack came in the Marines had organized defense, dragging one undamaged plane to a good position to use as a machine-gun mount, breaking out spare machine guns from ordnance rooms and wrenching them off damaged planes to set up elsewhere. These were able to keep the would-be strafers at a healthy distance, and threw back a third attack by 15 Zekes. Only four men were killed in these attacks, but the Marine air arm on Oahu was almost completely destroyed.

Yamamoto had also marked for destruction Kaneohe, a Navy patrol wing station on the windward side of Oahu. A squadron of Vals made for the Catalinas parked there at 0755. Almost everyone was asleep; the duty officer thought they were Army planes gone berserk, and telephoned to Pearl Harbor for help. Another strike came in at 0820, blasted a hangar and destroyed three Catalinas inside; an hour later, a third strike mopped up. As a result, twenty-seven of the 36 PBY "flying boats" at Kaneohe were destroyed, and six more damaged; the three saved were out on patrol when the attack came in.

Three principal Army airfields on Oahu caught it badly. At Hickam, adjoining Pearl Harbor Navy Yard, a dozen A-20s, thirty-three B-18s and six B-17s were lined up in the open, wing to wing. A few seconds after 0755, bombers earmarked to destroy them barreled in. One bomb crashed through the roof of the mess hall and exploded in the midst of the breakfast tables, killing 35 men. Others destroyed the parked planes. It was even more difficult to fight back ashore than on board ship, since many antiaircraft guns spotted around Hickam and in the Navy Yard, all operated by the Army, were not manned, and none had ready ammunition. Soldiers had to run to the depots and break down doors to get bullets; others wrenched machine guns off planes and blazed away. At Wheeler Field, in the central valley of Oahu, sixty-two P-40s and other planes too were parked as close as possible, in lines only 20 feet apart. Most of these were destroyed by twenty-five dive-bombers which attacked at 0802. Two small squadrons of P-40s at Bellows Field near Lanikai were also pretty much wiped out. Army Air Force had 231 aircraft on Oahu when the attack came in, but at close of day had only 166 units left, half of them damaged. Navy and Marine Corps had only 54 left out of about 250.

From 0825 to 0840 there was a lull, broken only by a few laggards from the first wave. Then the second wave struck. It consisted of 50 Kates equipped for high-level bombing, 80 Val dive-bombers, and 40 fighter planes. These came in around Diamond Head, concentrating largely on Hickam, on *Nevada*, and on other ships already hit. But this second wave of Japanese attackers was met by a lethal barrage of antiaircraft fire and did comparatively little damage. The destroyers, which were moored in groups of three to five in East Loch, the cruisers tied up at docks in Southeast Loch, and the minecraft moored off the Naval Hospital in Middle Loch were under way by this time, and escaped serious damage.

At 0945 all Japanese planes over Oahu returned to their carriers. All but 29 got back, though some 70 were shot full of holes. One plane crash-landed on the island of Niihau, where the pilot, with the aid of a local Japanese, managed to terrorize the unarmed native populace for a week. At the end of that time a burly Hawaiian grappled with the pilot and, although shot by him in diverse places, managed to kill him with bare hands and a stone.

By the end of two morning hours on December 7, the Navy had lost over 2,000 officers and men killed and 710 wounded, about thrice as many as in the two wars of 1898 and 1917–1918. The Army and Marine Corps together lost 327 killed and 433 wounded. In addition, some 70 civilians were killed—mostly men who happened to be on one of the airfields, but some in Honolulu where a few naval antiaircraft shells, whose fuses in the confusion had not been cut, exploded on city streets.

The rest of this terrible day was passed in expectation of worse to come. Japanese ships were reported to be on every side of Oahu, preparing to land troops. In the Hawaiian Islands were 160,000 people of Japanese blood; surely from among them Black Dragon bands had been recruited, to assassinate Americans? Japanese maids and butlers, it was said, told their employers to "scram," as their house had been assigned to a Japanese general. Every one of these rumors was later found to be false, and not one disloyal act was committed by the local Nipponese. General Short, for whom that day marked the end of a distinguished Army career, promptly executed his plans for deployment in the event of enemy attack. At about 1000, Army contingents in trucks or afoot began to move toward the supposed danger spots, now that the danger had passed.

Sunset over the Pacific inaugurated a hideous night for all hands. Fire-fighting continued on many of the stricken ships. Surgeons and nurses in the overcrowded hospitals were up all night attending the wounded and dying; hundreds of women and children whose husbands' quarters had been bombed huddled miserably in the university auditorium, or in a storage tunnel at Red Hill. Trigger-happy sentries and machine-gunners fired at everything that moved, supposing it to be a Japanese invader. Saddest of all accidents was the shooting down at night of four dive-bombers from the carrier *Enterprise*. These had landed at Ford Island during the morning lull and were then sent out to search for the enemy. When they returned after nightfall with running lights on, an antiaircraft gunner, who failed to get the word because the airbase communications had been ruptured, opened fire and started a panic of shooting all around the harbor.

Daybreak December 8 revealed a "dismal situation waste and wild"—half the aircraft on the island destroyed, seven battleships sunk or badly damaged, three destroyers reduced to junk. And the atmosphere was one of tormenting uncertainty. Nobody knew where the Japanese task force was; the one radar fix on it was interpreted 180 degrees wrong, so many a ship and most of the flyable planes were sent scurrying southward.

But, as the days elapsed, one saw that the situation might well have been worse. Our three aircraft carriers were safe; the repair shops, which did an amazingly quick job on damaged ships, were almost untouched, as was the fuel-oil tank farm, filled to capacity, whose loss would have tied up the Fleet for months.

Nevertheless, the armed forces and the nation had been struck a treacherous, devastating, and humiliating blow. When someone in Washington proposed that a medal be issued to Pearl Harbor combatants, one of the survivors replied, "Better make the ribbon of black crepe."

Pearl Harbor: When the *Arizona* Went Down

Paul Stillwell

T he massive hulk of the battleship Arizona—and the fragile white
memorial that seems to hover over her like a guardian angel—
have frozen in time one of the unforgettable moments of American history.
But the immolation of the Dreadnought itself could never be captured in
a snapshot; it was a complex chain of calamities both large and small in
which 1,177 individuals perished and only a relative handful escaped.

As director of oral history for the United States Naval Institute,
Paul Stillwell has been seeking to recapture the details of the tragedy for
years. The result of his intensive and far-flung research and interviewing
was the publication of Battleship Arizona:An Illustrated History, from
which the following excerpt is taken.

On staff at the Naval Institute since 1974, Stillwell is also editor-
in-chief of Naval History. He is the author of two previous books published

by the Naval Institute Press: Air Raid: Pearl Harbor! Recollections of a Day of Infamy *and* Battleship *New Jersey*: An Illustrated History.

At 7:30 that Sunday morning the *Arizona*'s duty department head, Lieutenant Commander Sam Fuqua, arrived in the wardroom for breakfast and joined the ship's doctor, chaplain, and the just-relieved head of the marine detachment. The latter, Major Alan Shapley, told his table companions that he had been ordered back to the United States, so he would soon be on his way home. At about 7:50 the officer who had just been relieved of the quarterdeck watch came to the wardroom to eat. When the ship's air-raid siren sounded five minutes later, Fuqua asked the recent officer of the deck whether this was a drill and whether the antiaircraft battery was manned. The OOD replied, "I think so" to both questions. Fuqua then tried to call the new officer of the deck, Ensign Henry Davison, to make sure the antiaircraft guns were manned for the customary tracking drill.

Since Fuqua couldn't get Davison on the telephone, he decided to go topside and talk to him directly. He emerged onto the quarter-deck from a hatch on the port side and noticed that the color detail was on deck, preparing to raise the American flag at the stern at 8:00. Just then a plane passed over quite low, guns blazing. Fuqua looked up, saw a red ball on the underside of a wing, and realized it was Japanese. Surmising that it was an isolated aircraft from a Japanese submarine, he felt that the American guns would soon make short work of it. He then double-timed around the after end of turret four to get to the station of the officer of the deck so that he could order the crew to general quarters. As he did so, he looked up and saw a formation of high-level bombers flying down the line of battleships. He also saw, as he described later, "what appeared to be bowling balls, and had the terrible realization we were under attack."

Fuqua's next conscious memory was of picking himself up from alongside a crater on the deck near the after gangway and finding fires all around him. A Japanese bomb had penetrated the wood-topped steel deck near him and exploded on the deck below. The bomb's concussion had knocked him unconscious for a time. By then, burning, dying men were pouring onto the quarterdeck from the boat-deck area. With help from the crews of turrets three and four, Fuqua organized teams of fire-fighters to try to keep the flames away from the quarterdeck area where wounded men were lying.

At that point, Fuqua remembered, "the forward magazine blew up and the whole ship erupted like a volcano." The explosion of the powder magazines for the two forward 14-inch turrets took place right around 8:10 A.M. It was the single most dramatic event that day at Pearl Harbor, turning the battleship *Arizona* into a roaring inferno.

After that, fighting the fires was a futile effort because there was no water pressure in the fire mains. When the valves were opened, the only thing that poured out was smoke. Hand-held fire extinguishers were useful to a degree; they were able to extinguish the flames on men who were burning when they ran from the boat deck to the quarterdeck. Communication was difficult throughout the *Arizona* because the ship's service telephone system was no longer operating. Fuel oil escaped from the stricken *Arizona* and caught fire when it reached the surface of the water.

Because of the overwhelming nature of the damage and the futility of trying to fight fires without water, Lieutenant Commander Fuqua directed the men to abandon their ship. Members of the crew went over the side and swam to the *Arizona*'s boats that were tied up to quays and booms. These boats became rescue vessels, and so did a motor launch that arrived from the hospital ship *Solace* to take away stretcher cases. Men cut down cork life rafts from their stowage places on board ship and threw them into the water, but the rafts were unwieldy and difficult to paddle. Most of the men leaving the ship did so either by swimming or catching a ride in a motor launch.

As Gunner's Mate Second Class Earl Pecotte was leaving the *Arizona*, someone gave him a boost from behind to help him get over the lifelines. He couldn't see but was sure that it was Fuqua. As he reported soon afterward of his view from the water, "The last thing I saw was Mr. Fuqua alone on the quarterdeck and the ship was ablaze from turret three forward."

Ensign Davison, the in-port officer of the deck, was a busy man as the attack planes flew far above the *Arizona* and began pummeling her. He had to sound alarms and notify key people, including the skipper and duty officer, about what was happening. When Fuqua appeared on the quarterdeck, he directed Davison to call the center engine room and order pressure on the fire mains. Davison had just stepped into the officer-of-the-deck booth to make the telephone call when a bomb hit nearby and started a roaring fire. The flames that trapped both him and the boatswain's mate of the watch in the booth had, he recalled, "a sweetish, sickening smell." The two men decided to run through the fire to the quarter-deck but couldn't, so they went over the starboard lifeline into the water. The ensign's first impulse was to return to the ship, but one look at her told him that would be futile because she appeared broken in two. He was pulled from the water into a motor launch and began helping the boat officer, Ensign William Bush from the *Arizona*, rescue as many men as they could.

Even though he had been officially detached, Major Shapley was hanging around so he could play first base that day in a baseball game against the team from the carrier *Enterprise*. He went to his stateroom to change into his baseball uniform when he heard messages passed over the ship's general announcing system. The first order was to get below the armored deck (which was the second deck); then came an order to report to battle stations. Second Lieutenant Carleton Simensen, one of the junior officers in the marine detachment, succeeded in getting a number of sailors turned around, and then he headed up the tripod mainmast to his station in the maintop. On the way, he was badly wounded in the chest, either by shrapnel, machine-gun bullets, or both. Right behind him was Major Shapley, who was almost blown off the ladder by the same bomb blast. He boosted the mortally wounded lieutenant onto the searchlight platform and continued on up to man the secondary battery director.

When the major arrived, only a few marines were there ahead of him. There wasn't much they could do because their job was to direct the five-inch broadside guns against surface targets. Japanese surface ships weren't the problem that day. When he looked down from his lofty perch, as Shapley said later, "I thought we were all going to get cooked to death because I couldn't see anything but fire down below after a while." He climbed back down the tripod, talked briefly with Fuqua on the quarterdeck, and then went over to the *Arizona*'s mooring quay to starboard. An explosion blew him off the quay into the water. Whatever hit him was intense because when he arrived on Ford Island, after swimming there, he was wearing nothing but his khaki trousers, and he was dazed.

Another marine whose battle station was in secondary aft was Private Russ McCurdy, Admiral Isaac Kidd's orderly. McCurdy had been relieved of duty at 7:30 that morning and was waiting to go ashore for a visit with the family of a man who worked in the Pearl Harbor Navy Yard. A number of civilians regularly took sailors and marines home for meals and recreation, in part for the company they provided and in part to keep them away from some of the less wholesome liberty activities available in downtown Honolulu. On this particular morning McCurdy was in the forward part of the *Arizona* when the attack started, so he headed aft and began climbing a leg of the mainmast to get to his battle station in the maintop, the place where he and others had earlier played word games during boring "general quarters" drills. This was no drill, and it certainly wasn't boring. On his way up the mainmast, the private noted the red circles on the wings of the Japanese planes flying close by Battleship Row.

It was a perilous climb because some Japanese planes were strafing while others were bombing. Machine-gun bullets bounced off the legs of the tripod or splintered the deck. McCurdy managed not to be hit. As he looked down from the ladder on the mast, he saw a bomb go through the deck, then explode. The tripod leg shielded him, but Second Lieutenant Simensen didn't have that protection and was badly wounded. McCurdy recalled of the pieces of wood and steel that hurtled past him that morning, "That was my indoctrination. I think at that moment I became a veteran right then. From then on, it seemed the worse it got, the calmer I got."

Once on station, McCurdy tried to set up communications, but there wasn't much else to do because there was no role for the broadside guns. Thus he became a witness to history; high above Pearl Harbor he had a panoramic view of one catastrophe after another. In the distance were Hickam Field, an Army Air Forces base, and closer by was Ford Island, a naval air station; both were under heavy Japanese attack. Torpedo planes bored in with canopies open so McCurdy could see the faces of the Japanese pilots. They launched their deadly missiles toward the port sides of the moored battleships. The *Oklahoma* and *West Virginia* were especially hard hit. McCurdy saw the former capsize slowly to port, exposing the bottom of her hull; she looked like a beached whale.

When the *Arizona*'s forward magazines exploded, McCurdy observed a great upward thrust. He thought that the forward part of the ship came out of the water. The force was so strong that he couldn't keep his knees stiff enough to remain standing. The entire maintop quivered back and forth noticeably, and the vibration threw him and his shipmates off balance. "We ended up in a human ball up there, really," he remembered, but no one was hurt. McCurdy jumped up and looked forward and down, and what he saw looked like a white-hot furnace. Debris had already flown past the maintop. Shapley then said that the communications were out, the ship was burning, and the situation looked bad. There was no point in their remaining in the maintop. He told the men to meet at the quarter-deck and stand by for further orders.

The wind was in favor of the maintop crew because it was blowing from the port quarter to the forward part of the ship, giving the marines and sailors up there a path to come down. There were no exits other than the ladders they had used to climb up, which were on the two forward legs of the tripod, the slanting ones. The men burned their hands coming down because the rungs were so hot. They stopped part way down as Shapley waited for more wind. After they got down the ladder, the marines stayed on deck for only five or six minutes before they abandoned ship. They were on the boat deck initially, and they saw charred bodies lying all over. Down on the galley deck McCurdy saw more bodies. Passageways looked like furnaces with blackened men coming out wearing no clothes. The only contrast to the blackness came from the whites of eyes and teeth.

Commander Fuqua was calmly directing things on the quarter-deck, and McCurdy said he did a wonderful job of helping men and trying to get boats lined up for people. On the quarterdeck were people whom McCurdy knew, but he could recognize them only by their voices because they were so badly burned. McCurdy and the rest of the marines swam ashore to Ford Island. By then the ship had sunk somewhat, so the level of the water was not far below the level of the quarterdeck.

The men there essentially stepped off into the water and began swimming through a layer of oil. There were also debris and splinters in the water. Above flew high-level Japanese bombers. "Every bomb, when you looked up, looked like it was pointed right at you," recalled McCurdy. So he and the others swam under the surface of the water as much as they could. Major Shapley was shouting words of encouragement to them as they swam, telling them how good they were on the drill field, the race-boat team, and so forth. McCurdy wasn't a strong swimmer, so he was convinced that Shapley's encouragement helped considerably. When bombs went off in the water, the vibration was so great that it moved the flesh of his legs; he felt as if it was going to pull away from the bones.

At last the private completed the oil-soaked swim to Ford Island, greatly helped by a rest stop on the way at a pipeline. Once he got onto the island, McCurdy went through the gate of some naval officer's quarters. He knocked on the door of a house. No one answered, probably because the occupants had gone to an air-raid shelter. McCurdy went in and walked through the house. He saw oatmeal cooking on the range in the kitchen, so he took the oatmeal off and turned the range off. It is curious what people will do in the face of completely unexpected circumstances.

Private McCurdy was on Ford Island throughout much of December 7. He spent part of the day with a navy group in an armory, taking weapons out of the Cosmoline grease in which they had been stored and assembling them. From time to time men came around to muster the survivors, and he dutifully gave them his name and service number. Despite his responding to several such requests, the information never got to the right place, and his parents were notified that he had been killed. It was about two weeks later before they learned otherwise from the Marine Corps.

Boatswain's Mate Second Class Tom White was one of many sailors of the *Arizona* who displayed coolness and presence of mind as the events of Sunday morning unfolded. When general quarters sounded, he went from the quarterdeck to his battle station in the gun pits of turret three. Soon after he heard a big explosion up above, he got orders from the turret booth behind the pits to go out and help fight fires topside. Like so many others, he was frustrated when the fire hoses failed to produce water. He was then ordered to go to an engine room and help the men who were trying to get pressure in the fire mains, but he couldn't get there because a wall of fire in the marines' berthing compartment blocked his way.

When White got back to the quarterdeck, he noticed that the awning there had begun to burn, so he cut it down with a shipmate's knife to prevent it from falling on anyone. Then he went down the admiral's hatch to see if he could find any fire extinguishers below. He couldn't breathe when he got to the second deck and so returned topside. But he discovered that his division officer, Ensign Jim Dick Miller, who had accompanied him down, didn't return with him, so White went below once more. He found Miller searching in the captain's cabin to see whether Captain Van Valkenburgh might be there unconscious. The skipper had already gone to the bridge by then, so White and Miller returned once more to the quarterdeck.

When orders came to abandon ship soon after that, White manned the captain's gig, which had been in the water overnight. The ship had settled so much that the starboard boat boom nearly pinned the gig down. White and some of his shipmates managed to get the boat free and began making rescue runs to Ford Island. During one of the runs the boat's propeller fouled on a piece of canvas in the water. White dived under the water to try to free the screw. Unsuccessful in that, he swam to an empty motor whaleboat from the *Nevada* and began operating it. He picked up a number of men trying to swim through the oily water to Ford Island and carried them to safety.

Once he was on the island, he glanced back at the *Arizona* and realized that because of the chaos, no one had raised the American flag on the battleship's fantail. So he returned once more to his ship and raised a flag on the staff at the stern. He escaped being strafed as he made still more boat runs and finally reported in at the dispensary at the submarine base. To remove the coat of oil he had picked up while trying to unfoul the screw of the *Arizona*'s gig, he had to take baths in gasoline, glycerin, and hot, soapy water.

Seaman Second Class Oree Weller could not keep from following ingrained habits. His battle station was up in the maintop with the marines whose experiences have been described already. When it came time to descend from the aerial perch, Weller first took off his sound-powered telephone headset, unplugged the cord from the jack, coiled it up, and stowed the cord and headset in their proper place. Then he set out to save his life. As he went down he noticed the remains of the smokestack. Part of the stack had been included in his regular cleaning station, and his first thought when he looked at the stack was, "My God, we're going to have to scrape and paint it."

He scrambled down to the flaming boat deck and saw that the ladder to the quarterdeck was gone, as were the other ladders on the starboard side of the superstructure. So he had to jump down to the quarterdeck. There he took cover under the overhang of turret three for a time to get protection from strafing. He saw many bodies on the deck but was able to recognize only one. Lying there with his eyes burned, able neither to see nor to speak, was 17-year-old Charles Brittan. Weller recognized him only by a small tattooed bird on his right shoulder. Weller and Brittan had gone to boot camp together and had ridden from San Pedro to Pearl Harbor in the oiler *Neosho* to report in mid-July for duty on board the *Arizona*. Now his friend was burned so severely that he didn't live long enough to be put aboard a motor launch that had come alongside from the hospital ship *Solace*. Charles Brittan would remain forever 17 years old.

After helping for a while with the wounded, Weller obeyed when the order came to abandon ship. As he had done with the phones, the seaman took care to be neat. He took off his shoes and socks and put them together on the deck with his white hat neatly atop them. Then he went over the starboard side of the *Arizona* into the water. As did many others that day, Weller struggled with the heavy coat of oil on the water. The flames advanced closer and closer as he swam toward the officers' landing on Ford Island. Then he looked to his right and saw salvation. Another motor launch from the *Solace* came by, and a member of the crew extended a boat hook. Weller hung on while eager hands hauled him aboard. The coxswain offered a white jumper sleeve so Weller could wipe his mouth, and a pharmacist's mate gave him a wad of gauze to clean his eyes. The young seaman was simultaneously scared, relieved, numb, covered with oil, and breathing heavily from his exertions in the water. But he was safe.

Back in November, Seaman Carl Christiansen had reported to the *Arizona*, having requested to serve on the same ship as his older brother Ed. The ship's operating schedule since then had offered them only a couple of opportunities to go ashore together. On the morning of the seventh they were going to Honolulu to find a photo studio where they could have their picture taken together, their first time as Navy men; they would send the portrait home to their parents in Kansas. Carl got to the quarterdeck first and was waiting there for his brother to come down from the galley deck. When Ed arrived, he said he wanted to get something else to take with him. He went away, and Carl never saw him again.

Carl's first awareness of trouble came when water from a bomb or machine-gun strafing splashed Coxswain Ken Edmondson. Edmondson had his head out a port, so he started ordering those around him to close the portholes as a damage-control precaution. At the time, Christiansen thought the coxswain was bossy, but he later realized that it was good that someone was willing to take charge. The ship was hit about that time, and then sounded the call to general quarters.

A member of the fourth division, Christiansen headed down to his battle station in a handling room, near the 14-inch powder magazines for turret four. Before long the electricity failed and the lights went out. The dark was disquieting to those down in the nether regions of the ship, especially when gas began to fill the area. It was not smoke but had a decided odor, so perhaps it was chlorine gas released by spillage from the lead-acid storage batteries. The batteries were located in the electric deck of each turret as a backup in case the ship's electrical power to operate the turret was cut off.

One member of the group—his name now forgotten—did most of the talking, and his leadership had a calming effect on the men in the handling room. He seemed to know the ship better than most and said that he would lead them to safety. In the darkness the men followed him, each keeping a hand on the shoulder of the man in front. Unable to find their way out, they returned to the handling room. The men were frightened but not panicky, though they seemed to have forgotten some of their normal training. One of them suggested lighting a match to help them see. The others, mindful of the gunpowder all around them and the growing presence of gas, quickly stifled his suggestion.

Then they decided to try another route. They went into a passageway connecting the handling rooms for the two aft turrets and finally managed to get into the handling room for turret three. There the gas was not so unpleasant, although it did increase with time. Then they climbed up the series of ladders from the lower decks to the turret itself—again in darkness. When the sailors got to the top, they felt comforted to a degree by the presence of a small amount of light coming in. At the direction of Ensign Guy Flanagan, one of the officers in third division, the men in the turret took off their shirts and stuffed them into the telescope slots for the pointer and trainer to keep the smoke out. Finally, they went out the hatch at the rear of the turret and climbed down the ladder on the side of the barbette of turret three and onto the quarterdeck.

At last, Seaman Christiansen was out in the open, able to see again and to breathe air that wasn't quite so stifling as down below. On the other hand, he was now exposed to new hazards, including the machine guns of the Japanese planes. He and others took shelter for a bit under the overhang of turret three. There they took off their shoes and lined them up before jumping into the water to swim ashore. Christiansen didn't get far because of the heavy oil. He made his way back and climbed aboard. After a while a boat came along and began taking men off the *Arizona* at the stern, near where the American flag was still flying. Among that group, Carl Christiansen didn't have far to descend to get into the boat. The main deck, which normally had a freeboard of a little more than 17 feet, was by then only a few feet above the level of the water. The *Arizona* was settling into the harbor.

Coral Sea: "Scratch One Flat-Top!"

Stanley Johnston

About five months after Japan's devastating attack on Pearl Harbor, the U.S. Pacific Fleet engaged a segment of the Imperial Japanese Navy on almost equal terms in the Coral Sea. A huge and far-flung naval battle raged for five days. In the end, a planned Japanese invasion of Port Moresby, the Papuan capital of New Guinea, had been thwarted, and both sides had suffered the loss of an aircraft carrier—the Japanese Shoho and the American Lexington.

After the smoke had cleared, naval experts realized that for the first time in history the decisive blows in a major fleet action had been struck by naval aircraft while the opposing warships never even came within sight of each other—a phenomenon to be repeated throughout the course of the Pacific war.

Stanley Johnston, an American war correspondent for the Chicago Tribune, was the only reporter with the American forces during the

Battle of the Coral Sea. Embarked on the Lexington, *he made his notes both before and after the ship was blown up under him (see photograph). Like other survivors, Johnston slithered 50 feet down a rope into the sea, dragged himself into a lifeboat, and was rescued by an American destroyer.*

As with many eyewitnesses caught up in the heat of battle, and given only limited perspective, Johnston's estimates of the number of ships sunk and planes splashed are not reliable. What is more important, however, he immediately grasped how this "engagement between aircraft carriers" was something new in the annals of naval warfare, revealing "how completely the carrier had displaced the battleship in modern war."

Johnston also had the journalist's knack for recognizing a memorable line when he heard one. He did not fail to report the voice of one of the Lexington's *dive-bomber pilots that came crackling over the radio after attacking the Japanese carrier* Shoho: *"Scratch one flat-top!"*

From the deck of an aircraft carrier that was bombed, machine-gunned, and torpedoed I witnessed the Battle of the Coral Sea. For five full, never-to-be-forgotten days I lived with the American heroes—airmen and seamen alike—who there won a magnificent victory.

Now, five weeks after the battle, its story, replete with the dramatic details of deeds of valor as thrilling as any in American history, can be told. The veil of official silence can be lifted. The vivid pictures of this action etched in my memory and hurriedly scratched in disjointed exclamations in my notes in the midst of battle shocks can be reported fully.

It was a battle that naval authorities believe may prove to have been the turning point in the Pacific phases of World War II. It was the first great naval defeat ever dealt Japanese fleets, and, ironically enough, it was fought entirely in the air. It was a battle of aircraft carriers.

The naval developments of these five days were scattered over four hundred thousand square miles of tropical seas. The surface fleets that fought the battle never saw each other and during most of the fighting were 80 to 180 miles apart.

First of all this was an engagement between aircraft carriers—two American against three Japanese. It was disclosed how completely the carrier had displaced the battleship in modern war. It was a battle of dive-bombers, torpedo-bombers, and fighter pilots. It also was a battle of antiaircraft gunners. When it was finished two of the Japanese carriers had been sunk and another was out of action.

I stood on the bridge of the gallant old *Lexington* and watched her crew fight the Japanese, defend her, and make desperate efforts to save her. I saw them beaten by internal fires started by explosions which rocked the ship hours after her Japanese assailants had been beaten off. With her officers and men I slid 50 feet down hemp lines into the sea.

I was picked up by lifeboats of other United States vessels that rescued everyone who survived the air combats, exploding bombs, and torpedoes. And, finally, I saw her sunk by an American destroyer.

"She never wavered; she kept her head up and went down like the lady she always was," one of her executive officers said to me as we watched her flaming hull, still upright, go to the bottom at dusk on May 8.

Our airmen and ship gunners shot more than 140 Japanese airplanes out of the skies, 120 of these falling to our pilots. We lost 25 airplanes in air duels, and perhaps 60 more went down on the *Lexington*'s decks. We have no way of knowing how many Japanese planes were lost with their carriers.

For me the commencement of the Coral Sea epic was a notification last April 16. It came from the Navy and reached me at Wakiki. It told me to report for sea duty. I was to be at Pearl Harbor at 7 A.M. the next day, bag, typewriter, and toothbrush.

I reported on time and to my delight was led aboard the *Lexington*, then barren of aircraft and strangely empty. I could not understand as we threaded our way out of the harbor's tortuous channel why we were leaving without planes.

"Are we going without our planes?" I asked the ship's executive officer.

"They'll pick us up at sea," he grinned.

And they did, hours later, when we were hitting a fast clip southward. They came out of the sky in practice-bombing dives, aiming light smoke bombs at a target sled towed 1,000 feet back on our foaming wake. Then a scout bomber appeared towing a sleeve target at which all the ship's gunners fired live shells.

It was my first look at the high-speed automatic cannon with which this ship bristled. The pound and roar of the guns shake your very teeth. When this was over the ship's fighters came along, dived on the now shattered sleeve, and finished by shredding it with their .50-caliber gun batteries.

"Looks like we're sharpening our teeth," I said.

"Sure, for Japs," a senior officer said.

Later I learned what we were getting into. It seems that in order to take Port Moresby the Japanese had established land-based aircraft on New Guinea, at Salamaua and Lae; New Britain, at Gasmata and Rabaul; on Deboyne Island, eastern end of the Louisade Archipelago, and in the Solomon Islands.

To control the Coral Sea they had sent two powerful naval striking forces. One force moved south from the big Japanese base on the Isle of Truk, 720 nautical miles north of Rabaul. It was to control the Jomard Passage, the only channel from north and south through the coral reefs at the southeastern tips of New Guinea. The second moved southeast of Truk and took the long open sea passage around the Solomon Islands to the east into the Coral Sea.

These two fleets were intended to be a pair of pincers, nipping any American naval forces that might be in this area. Finally the pincers were to be assisted by occupation forces, cruisers, destroyers, and troop and supply ships concentrated at Deboyne Islands and in Tulagi Harbor.

We didn't know all this at the time. But that was the situation when our task force arrived in the Coral Sea area on May 1. I tell this now so that the various aspects of the Coral Sea fight may be best understood.

Our force from Pearl Harbor had consisted of the *Lexington* and a retinue of cruisers and destroyers. On May 1 we made a rendezvous with a similar United States force, raising our strength considerably.

Throughout our two weeks' voyage we had our air scouts ranging the seas for 200 miles or more on all sides of us. On the afternoon of May 3 an aviation ensign spied 15 enemy craft, warships and transports, in Tulagi Harbor.

Rear Admiral Frank J. Fletcher, who had assumed command of the entire force, laid his plans as darkness descended that night. We turned northward, steaming hard, and at dawn lay south of Guadal Canal Island, 100 miles due south of Tulagi. This position was taken to screen us from possible enemy scouts.

We were up before dawn, airplane motors turning on the flight deck of the carrier. Scout planes were off in the predawn dark. Soon they were reporting the enemy still unsuspicious of our presence. Immediately dive-bombers and torpedo planes took the air, and in less than thirty minutes were roaring down on the Japanese ships.

Surprise was complete. The first antiaircraft fire came only with the second wave of bombers. Our boys unloaded; came home, loaded bombs again, and flew off.

A few fighters accompanied the second wave and liquidated the minor Japanese opposition (five seaplane fighters). The bombers came back for their last missiles.

Fourteen of the fifteen Japanese ships were sunk or beached and burning. This occupation threat had been removed.

Photographers' and pilots' reports indicated enemy loss of life here must have been terrific, particularly on the crowded troopships that were blasted from above and below.

On the afternoon of May 6 our scout planes had exciting news. They had located north of the Isle of Mizima a Japanese carrier and cruiser force. We didn't know it then, but this was the enemy spearhead bound for Jomard Passage.

Admiral Fletcher ordered our force northeast this time. At dawn on the morning of May 7, we were standing eastward of the Island of Tagula and about 180 miles southeast of the second Japanese force. Again we caught them by surprise, our dawn scouts reporting their planes still all aboard their carrier.

When our striking force of torpedo planes and dive-bombers arrived the Japanese had nine fighters in the air, but obviously they did not expect attack. Their carrier, believed to be of the biggest and newest type, turned into the wind to launch planes as our dive-bombers started down. This was a fatal move, for it kept the Japanese carrier on a steady course, presenting a perfect target.

Back on our carrier, anxiously awaiting the outcome, I crowded into the wardroom with officers off duty. Loudspeakers there were connected with the *Lexington*'s receivers tuned to the communication circuits of the planes in the air. There was a jumble of orders and meaningless calls between the planes until suddenly Lieutenant Commander Robert Dixon, skipper of the scout bomber squadron, identified himself to the carrier.

"Scratch one top-flat—scratch one flat-top," he said, and abruptly signed off.

The ship's loudspeaker system carried the message to the entire crew and the craft rocked with cheers. The men knew that Commander Dixon was reporting the total destruction of the Japanese carrier. Our own losses (it seemed even more of a miracle then than it does in writing it now) were only two scout dive-bombers.

Our fliers shot down 23 enemy planes in widely scattered engagements, and later in the day learned that a heavy cruiser was sunk at the same time. Our luck, it seemed, was extraordinary.

As if it was to continue forever we had even more extraordinary luck that evening. At dusk as our last patrols were gliding out of the rain squalls and curtains of low clouds, nine planes certainly not from our carrier approached us. We were at battle stations with every gun manned for a raid, when to our amazement all nine flashed on landing lights.

Later one officer, describing the situation, said:

"They slowed down and strung out into landing position like tired birds come home to roost."

The men at the guns on our carrier first recognized them as enemy planes even though the leader of the planes was flashing a landing signal with his lights. Our gunners opened up and the destroyers around us took up the barrage.

Almost with a disdainful air the Japanese doused their lights and flew off in line astern. We learned by following them that a Japanese fleet similar to our own was only thirty miles away, hidden from our sight in the darkness and rain storms. The Japanese pilots had mistaken our carrier for their own!

The information was electrifying. We expected a night action but in the darkness the fleets never met. Nevertheless, this incident opened the final twenty-four hours of the *Lexington*'s career, forecasting, if we had known it, her doom.

All night we maneuvered so as to be in the vicinity of the enemy for an early-morning attack. Again off before dawn, our scout planes found the enemy. It was 8:10 A.M. The fliers radioed that the Japanese fleet consisted of two carriers, some heavy cruisers, and many destroyers.

Later the scouts reported three battleships. This force was the second Japanese pincer. The Japanese fleet was 180 miles northeast of our warships.

It had been one of those still, perfect tropical dawns. The black night faded swiftly into gleaming, torrid day. Our force swished along, the gray ships spaced around us sliding quietly about their ominous business. Aboard the *Lexington* we went about our business, the air crews warmed up their planes, breaking the silence with the engine roars. Business on the huge boat went on as usual.

But all of us were tense inside. The pilots were jumpy as they gathered in the ready room, like athletes before a big contest. Even the stewards who handed around steaming mugs of coffee showed the strain. All of us knew that fateful hours were ahead.

Midway: I Dive-Bombed a Jap Carrier

Captain Tom Moore, as told to Frank Gervasi

I f the Battle of the Coral Sea first announced to the world that naval battles of the future would not be decided by the great guns of capital ships, Midway provided a thunderous affirmation.

At this tremendous clash of forces in June 1942, once again the rival surface fleets never came within sight of each other. Nevertheless, American dive-bombers destroyed no fewer than four Japanese aircraft carriers. This staggering loss of ships, planes, and highly-trained men was something Japan could not possibly replace in the course of the next few years, given her industrial and manpower capabilities.

As a result, the Battle of Midway is seen today as a critical turning point in the war. Captain Tom Moore, a Marine Air Corps dive-bomber pilot based on Midway, was in the thick of it.

The night before, the Navy had thrown a torpedo attack at the Japs. Big PBY "flying boats" attacked the enemy formation about three hundred miles somewhere west of Midway. The approaching enemy fleet was composed of troopships carrying occupational forces.

There was no doubt what the Jap intended doing. His mission was to take and occupy Midway. The Jap desperately needed it as a land base to smash Pearl Harbor. The Jap had been so careful in bombing Midway. He'd kept his bombs off the runways he'd hoped to use.

Dawn would bring the Japanese fleet within range of the fighters and dive bombers of the Marine Air Corps. We'd been waiting for this for a long time.

We looked forward to the prospect of action with mingled emotions. But when we saw those B-17s in the air—Army ships— morale went up 100 per cent. The Navy got first crack at the Jap fleet. The PBYs went for the troopships.

It was our turn now. We were to get their aircraft carriers, to knock out their air force. After us, the Army would go to work on the battleships and cruisers.

We were up at three in the morning. It was dark and cool and clear. We swallowed some hot coffee and downed some buttered toast and went to our planes. It was bright daylight before I got off. I made one long run, but my plugs fouled up, and I couldn't get the plane off. It was a Douglas SBD, and its heavy gas load and single 500-pound bomb kept it earthbound when the engine failed to develop maximum power.

I thought for a moment that I'd just go back and turn the ship over to the mechanics. But I saw the others get away. I always feel safer in the air than I do on the ground anyhow, so I decided to give it another try. This time I got away. I had only about seventy knots at the end of the runway, so I had practically to pull the plane into the air.

I headed the ship to the rendezvous point. I wasn't in the air two minutes when a voice said in my earphones, "Island now under heavy attack . . . Island now under heavy attack. . . ."

I looked back. I could see the bombs falling. High-level bombers and dive-bombers were giving Midway hell. I saw smoke columns and a few fires. It didn't seem real, and yet I had had a premonition that this would happen. That was why I was so anxious to get away on this mission. I kept on my course, wide open.

Within a few minutes, our squadron assembled. The radio-phone instructed us to attack an enemy carrier. It gave the bearing and the distance, course, and speed of the Jap ship. From the course the Japanese had taken, it was obvious that they were moving right down on Midway, and I for one determined in that moment that the Jap wasn't going to reach his objective if I could help it. We couldn't use our radios. We were close enough together, however, to see one another's expressions. I could tell from the looks on the faces of the others that they were thinking thoughts identical with mine.

About a thousand yards away, I spotted Joe's ship. "Joe" was Major Lofton Henderson. You may have heard of Major Henderson. They named a field for him at Guadalcanal. We called him Joe among ourselves. He didn't like the Lofton much. It was Henderson who flew his dive-bomber into the smokestack of a Jap carrier and blew the thing apart when his plane was hit, and he knew his number was up anyhow but wanted it to pay off.

On this day, Joe was doing a sort of roving patrol ahead of the squadron and off to one side, acting as our eyes.

We had about 8,000 feet and had been in the air about 70 minutes. I think it was Henderson—I can't be sure—but somebody calmly said, "Attack two enemy carriers on port bow. . . ." I glanced quickly to my left and saw the carriers and I saw Zeros taking off from the flight decks. The voice had hardly faded away when the Zeros hit us. There are various estimates now as to how many. There were sixteen of us, of that I'm positive. But the enemy might have been a hundred or they might have been just twenty. Anyhow, we had our hands full.

I heard the guns open up. I heard the guns from my own plane and knew that Private Charles Huber, a short little kid, maybe about nineteen years old, with brown hair and a quick smile, was on the job. I heard twenty rounds from my gun and then silence. The Zeros were making fancy passes, doing slow rolls and acrobatics when it wasn't necessary. I saw two or three of the ships in my squadron go down in flames. I was just about to pick up my mike and ask Huber why he wasn't firing when his voice came through angrily to tell me his gun was jammed and that he couldn't fire.

I told him not to just sit there, but to aim his gun at them anyhow. I realized immediately what a difficult thing I'd asked him to do. I had asked him to point a dead gun at Japs who were throwing lead at him and I wished I hadn't given him such an order.

But it worked. I looked back several times, and there was this kid aiming his silent gun at the oncoming Japs. It kept them at a fairly respectful distance, which maybe proves something about Japs.

The carriers below us were throwing plenty of ack-ack, but it wasn't very effective. I circled the target once, while the boys peeled off one at a time, going down as along the spokes of a wheel. Finally it was my turn. I was number two in the last section. I came out of a cloud, and there was the carrier lying straight up and down in the sights. I learned later it was either the *Kaga* or the *Akagi*, or one of their class.

I saw the huge orange disk of the rising sun painted on the vessel's clean, yellow flight deck and I wondered why. It seemed as though they'd painted a bull's-eye there for me to aim at. And that's just what I did. I screamed down from several thousand feet, hypnotized by that big orange blob. I felt that I'd been in the dive for a long, long time. I snapped out of it for a glance at the altimeter, which showed I was close to the water.

I didn't waste any time grabbing the bomb release. I must have released my package at several hundred feet. I started to pull out, when my plane was thrown out of control by a severe concussion. I don't know yet whether the blast that shook me was from my bomb or from the bursting egg of the preceding bomber. All I knew was that I was fighting to recover. I regained no more than twenty-five feet off the water. The Zeros, by the way, were attacking all the way down.

I looked back when I'd pulled out of it to see where my bomb had hit and I stared right into the noses of three Zeros. I flew low on the water. This prevented the Japs from coming down on me from altitude, passing me, and pulling out from underneath. If they tried that, they'd go swimming, but they didn't bother about diving on me. They flew behind me at the same level and slightly above, and kept pumping lead at me. Huber was hit.

He phoned and said he was hit and that he couldn't aim his gun any longer. Lead had shattered the instrument panel and ripped up the ship. The hydraulic system was gone and the radio was shot away. I didn't like this much and decided to make for the clouds.

I began climbing when one of the Zeros made a pass and dumped a lot of lead into the cockpit. My engine quit. I nosed over to make a water landing, but meanwhile switched tanks with the fuel selector valve. Then I reached for the wobble pump to increase pressure in the fuel system in the hope of pumping new life into the dead motor.

But Huber had beat me to it. In his cockpit there was a duplicate pump and he'd got up considerable pressure although he was bleeding profusely from wounds in his left leg. The first stroke I took on the wobble pump almost broke my arm, as I was unprepared for the pressure. What a man, this Huber!

The engine was out from five to ten seconds, just long enough for the Jap pilots to see that I was a dead pigeon. Two of the three broke off the attack and headed back for their carrier in the hope of picking up another or two of our dive-bombers. One remained to see that I was through or to finish me off if necessary. I was nicked twice. One bullet tore my helmet open behind my right ear, removed some hair, and brought blood. Another grazed me across my left index finger but this didn't bother me much.

I figured I was dead. I wondered who was flying the plane. I touched that burning patch behind my right ear and brought my fingers before my eyes and saw they were red with blood—my blood. I knew I was through, but I knew also that there was a Zero behind me. Therefore, I reasoned, I wasn't altogether dead. I still had time to get that Zero. I rationalized it this way: I'm going and I'm going to take that Zero with me.

The engine came to life with a sneeze and a roar. Instantly I knew what had gone wrong. The last Jap burst had shot away the fuel connection to the tank which had been feeding the engine. The connections to the new tank were okay.

I knew he'd make a pass at me as I climbed. So I climbed. He dipped his right wing and I dipped my left, turning into him. Here, I figured, is where I find out just how brave and fatalistic and suicidal these Jap pilots are. Just as I got him into the sights of my forward guns and was about to squeeze the trigger, he scooted out of it.

This same operation recurred three or perhaps four times. I wondered why he didn't attack me from the rear, where Huber and his gun lay helpless. I was climbing all the time and eventually I made a cloud. As I nosed into the cloud I looked back and saw the Zero turn away. I knew then I was very much alive. I remember saying aloud, "I guess he's afraid to tail me on instruments. I wonder if he knows that I'm afraid too. I haven't any instruments." I did have a compass left.

I flew for several minutes, trying to pull myself and my thoughts together. I wondered how I'd find Midway. I hadn't any plotting board for navigation and had expected to rely on my radio—a radio which I no longer had. I looked around when I popped out of the clouds to see if I could find someone from my squadron to join up with and let him navigate me back to Midway. Also, I'd have the protection of concentrated fire if attacked en route to the base.

But there wasn't anybody in sight. I emerged from the clouds at three- and four-minute intervals looking for someone to tail back home, but each time there was nothing but sky—cold and friendless sky. I tried to raise the base on the radio. At times I screamed into the mike, although I knew, in my heart, that the thing was dead. I could see Huber was still conscious. There was blood on his life-jacket. We could faintly hear each other's voices over the roar of the motor but couldn't make out what the other said. The intercom was dead, too.

I knew where I'd gone and approximately how far I'd traveled, but I didn't know the most important thing of all: how much drift I'd had at the various altitudes or what the wind speeds had been. I was, in short, lost.

I figured that the safest bet for me would be to fly the reciprocal of the course I'd gone out on. I flew for about an hour (the time I calculated should bring me in sight of Midway) and saw nothing.

Five minutes later, I spotted a reef with two small islands within. I started to congratulate myself on my navigation and to make my recognition signal, so that our own guns below wouldn't fire on me. I made an easy approach and was well down when I realized with a stabbing, angry regret that this wasn't Midway at all. But I did know that the green splotch below was either Kure Island or Pearl and Hermes Reef.

I had a little black book in the knee pocket of my flying suit. I yanked it out. In it I had recorded the bearing and distances of these two points from Midway. My gas gauge told me I didn't have enough fuel to take me to Midway if this was the Pearl and Hermes Reef. This, I said to myself, simply *must* be Kure!

I laid my course accordingly and flew the time required to take me to Midway—55 miles away. The other point was 82 miles on an opposite bearing.

I flew the required time. There was nothing in sight. I guess I went off my rockers completely. I started making left-hand turns. I didn't know why. I was just waiting for the gas to run out, to set the ship down. I didn't have enough gas to get me back to Kure if it was Kure that I had sighted. I was sure now it hadn't been.

While I was in a left turn, Huber attracted my attention by kicking one of the rudder pedals. I looked back and he was pointing off to port. I saw what looked like a black cloud lying on the water.

I didn't know just what it was. I thought it might be a ship burning. I had nothing better to do. I turned down for a look. I saw two Flying Fortresses—and this Leatherneck was really glad to see the Army! I trailed in behind them, dipping my wings, so they could see the white stars.

A few minutes later, there was Midway, smoke pouring from the fires the Japs had started. The wheels went down of their own weight the moment I released them, but the flaps wouldn't go down. They required hydraulic pressure and that's one of the many things we were completely out of. I didn't know exactly how much gas I had left, as I came in for a landing and lost no time getting down.

I'd never landed without flaps before. I landed hot and fast and made a half ground loop. One of the tires either blew or had been punctured in the fight, and I almost cracked up. I managed to keep the plane steady, though, and taxied to a point near one of the sick bays where a few men hauled Huber out of his cockpit. He was still conscious. An indestructible Leatherneck, that Mr. Huber!

The doc looked at my head. It was just a graze, and an emergency bandage fixed it up okay. While an engineer checked over my ship, I went to the Command Post and reported.

After I'd made my preliminary report, I went over to the engineering shacks where they'd been checking my plane. The mechanics told me that the ship's motor went dead while they were checking it. It had run out of gas. I must have landed with only two or three minutes' supply of fuel remaining in the tanks. It was then that I knew fear.

I hadn't been really scared up there. But here, standing by my ship, I knew fear. I remembered the men who'd been shot down and the picture of Huber lying there behind me in bloody semiconsciousness. I remembered that first bullet that hit my ship. In that first momentary flashback, I remembered saying to myself, "Here comes a hunk of the Sixth Avenue El!" It had seemed a curious thought at the time.

As I walked away from the engineering shack, I ran into Lieutenant Jesse Rollow. He'd been on the flight with me. We tried to figure out who'd survived the flight and to estimate how much damage we'd done. We didn't check at all. We might as well have fought in separate battles. It's amazing how circumscribed is your knowledge of what happens in a fight. You see just your own immediate little piece of the show—like not seeing the chorus for the fascination of one particular pair of legs.

Then we walked about, looking over the damage the Japs had done. We wound up at the mess, where we managed to find a can of fruit juice. We shared it. Pineapple juice. Good. It was about ten-thirty—which meant we'd been in the air about four hours all told, four unforgettable hours. I knew I'd hit that Jap carrier, and this knowledge exhilarated me.

About a half hour later, our spotters picked up the sounds of approaching aircraft. The air-raid siren sounded. I didn't bother going to my plane. I knew it couldn't fly for a while. I saw a lone Marine fighter taking off, the only serviceable ship left on the island. I know now that he'd been ordered to remain on the ground, but as I watched him take off, I thought to myself: One man against God knows how many!

This was the same pilot, Marion Carl, who got the Navy Cross later for knocking off fourteen Jap planes in the Solomons. He bagged a couple in the Battle of Midway too.

It turned out, however, that the approaching aircraft were our own from one of our carriers nearby.

I tried to sleep that afternoon. We all tried to sleep with more or less indifferent success. Some of the boys went out on a night attack that evening after their ships had been patched up. Mine wasn't ready. I wasn't ordered out. Rollow was left behind too.

We were detailed to lighting the runway when our boys returned. We didn't expect them back until eleven or twelve that night, so we went into a dugout for a nap. The night before, five of us had slept there. Now there were just the two of us.

About nine o'clock, I heard a loud report and a whistling sound. I had never heard a shell before. I'd heard bombs, but never shells. I knew this sound belonged to a shell. Rollow was asleep. I yelled to him and yanked him out of his bunk. We flattened ourselves out on the floor of the dugout. We were certain the enemy was coming in this time, and this was the bombardment that would precede a landing. We decided we'd go out and watch the party.

We saw the searchlights of our shore batteries switch on and reach long fingers into the darkness. We opened up for a few minutes, and the noise was terrific. Then there was silence. It developed that this wasn't a major attack, but that a Jap submarine had surfaced and tossed a few shells into us. The batteries claimed they hit the sub. One of our destroyers went out the next morning to search for it.

On the sixth of June, I was assigned to a scouting mission to look for a Jap seaplane tender which might be assisting Jap seaplane bombers for an attack on Midway. Over Kure, I developed an oil leak, whipped the plane around, and just managed to make Midway.

When the Midway fight was definitely over and done with, we were all told we could get some sleep now. Well, we slept. . . .

For a few days, we resumed normal patrol activities, and on June 25 they piled us into B-17s—what was left of us—and headed for Pearl Harbor. Forty-eight hours' leave to the Royal Hawaiian Hotel and back to the base to form a new squadron.

A month later, we were on our way to the Solomons. I had meanwhile qualified as a carrier pilot. I didn't know it, but I was in for another and greater adventure on Guadalcanal. Huber, by the way, was made a sergeant and won the Purple Heart and the Distinguished Flying Cross. A great kid!

Leyte Gulf: Kinkaid *vs.* Kurita, Etc.

Hanson W. Baldwin

T he Imperial Japanese Navy was far from being licked in the fall *of 1944 when Vice Admiral Takeo Kurita lashed out against Admiral Thomas C. Kinkaid at Leyte Gulf in the Philippines. True enough, the Japanese had been staggered at the Battle of Midway, but their two monstrous 70,000-ton battleships—the biggest ever built by any nation—were cards yet to be played, and the terrors of the kamikaze campaign were still largely unknown.*

The result was an epic struggle—probably the last great sea battle of the twentieth century—testing the courage, tenacity, and military-industrial power of two great nations.

Hanson W. Baldwin, the chief military correspondent of The New York Times, *who died in November 1991, was specially qualified to tell the story of Leyte Gulf. An Annapolis graduate, he served on the battleship* Texas, *and the destroyer* Breck.

Baldwin joined the staff of the Times *in 1929, and soon became the best-known and most influential military journalist of his generation. When war broke out, his dispatches from Guadalcanal and the Western Pacific earned him a Pulitzer Prize in 1943. He wrote the following account, partly as a historian and partly as an eyewitness.*

In October 1944, the greatest sea fight in history—perhaps the world's last great fleet action—broke the naval power of Japan and spelled the beginning of the end of the war in the Pacific. The Battle for Leyte Gulf, fought off the Philippine Archipelago, sprawled across an area of almost 500,000 square miles, about twice the size of Texas. Unlike most of the actions of World War II, it included every element of naval power from submarines to planes. It was as decisive as Salamis. It dwarfed the Battle of Jutland in distances, tonnages, casualties. But, unlike Jutland, there was no dispute about the outcome. After Leyte Gulf, the Japanese Fleet was finished. Yet it was a battle of controversy. . . .

The Empire was dying, and there were some who faced the fact. The long retreat was over, the great spaces of the Pacific had been bridged by the countless ships of the American "barbarians," and the enemy was knocking upon the inner strongholds of the Samurai. For Japan it was now the desperate gamble, the all-out stroke—to conquer or to die.

And so, the *Shō* ("to conquer") plans were drawn; if the inner citadel—the Philippines, Formosa, the Ryukyus, the main islands— were penetrated by the U.S. Fleet, all the remaining Japanese naval power that could steam or fly would be mobilized for a desperate assault.

In October 1944, when U.S. troops in Europe were smashing into German Aachen street by street and the opposing armies faced a bitter winter of grudging gains, the time for *Shō* I—the defense of the Philippines—had almost come. Tarawa, with its bloody reef, was proud history; so, too, were the Gilberts, the Marshalls, the Marianas, New Guinea, Biak, Palau, and Morotai; B-29s were con- verging on the new fields in Guam, Saipan, and Tinian to bomb Japan; U.S. submarines were preying upon the enemy's commerce, and the U.S. flag flew above palm-fringed islands once remote strongholds of the Emperor's power.

From August 31 to September 24 the fast carriers supported by the battleships of Admiral William F. Halsey's Third Fleet had raked over Japanese bases from Mindanao to Luzon, and on the twenty-first, while Radio Manila was playing "Music for Your Morning Moods," naval pilots combed Manila Bay. The bag throughout the islands was large, the enemy opposition was surprisingly feeble, and Admiral Halsey reported to Admiral Chester W. Nimitz, commander-in-chief, Pacific:

" . . . no damage to our surface forces and nothing on the screen but Hedy Lamar."

The weak Japanese reaction led to a change in American strategy. The planned capture of Yap and step-by-step moves to Mindanao in the southern Philippines and then northward were eliminated; the amphibious assault upon the island of Leyte in the central Philippines was advanced by two months to October 20, 1944. . . .

It started, according to plan. A great armada of more than 700 U.S. ships steamed into Leyte Gulf at dawn on the twentieth; a lone Japanese plane braved the skies. Initial Japanese opposition was weak; the vast American armada—the greatest of the Pacific war, with some 151 LSTs, 58 transports, 221 LCTs, 79 LCIs, and hundreds of other vessels, may have overawed the defenders. By the end of A plus 2—October 21—103,000 American troops had been landed on Leyte with few casualties, and only three warships had been damaged.

Four hours after the first landing on Leyte, General Douglas MacArthur waded ashore; later Colonel Carlos Romulo, the little Filipino, who was with him, was to quip: "There was the tall MacArthur, with the waters reaching up to his knees, and behind him there was little Romulo, trying to keep his head above water."

In front of a Signal Corps microphone on the beach just won and beneath rain-dripping skies MacArthur recalled the bloody epic of Bataan: "This is the Voice of Freedom, General MacArthur speaking. People of the Philippines: I have returned. . . ."

But the Japanese had not been fooled. At 0809, October 17, just nine minutes after U.S. Rangers had made preliminary landings on one of the smaller islands in the mouth of Leyte Gulf, Japanese forces had been alerted to carry out the *Shō* I plan. Admiral Soemu Toyoda, commander-in-chief of the Japanese Combined Fleet and leader of what he knew was a forlorn hope, had his last chance to "destroy the enemy who enjoys the luxury of material resources." From his headquarters at the Naval War College just outside Tokyo, he sent the word "to Conquer" to his widely scattered units.

The *Shō* plan was daring and desperate—fitted to the last months of an empire strained beyond its capabilities. The Japanese

Fleet had not recovered from its cumulative losses, particularly from the heavy blow it had suffered four months earlier in the Battle of the Philippine Sea, when Admiral Raymond W. Spruance, covering our Marianas landings, had destroyed more than 400 Japanese planes, sunk three Japanese carriers, and broken the back of Japanese naval aviation. In mid-October, when Halsey—in a preliminary to the Leyte Gulf landing—struck heavily at Formosa, Toyoda had utilized his land-based planes and had also thrown his hastily trained carrier replacement pilots into the fight. The gamble failed. But the "pathology of fear" and the curious propensity of the Japanese for transforming defeats into victories in their official reports, magnified the normally highly inflated claims of enemy aviators; Tokyo declared the Third Fleet had "ceased to be an organized striking force."

An enemy plane dropped leaflets over recently captured Peleliu:

FOR RECKLESS YANKEE DOODLE:

Do you know about the naval battle done by the American 58th [sic] Fleet at the sea near Taiwan [Formosa] and Philippine? Japanese powerful Air Force had sunk their 19 aeroplane carriers, 4 battleships, 10 several cruisers and destroyers, along with sending 1,261 ship aeroplanes into the sea. . . .

Actually only two cruisers—*Canberra* and *Houston*—were damaged; less than 100 U.S. planes lost; the Japanese were to have a rude awakening as the great invasion armada neared Leyte Gulf.

But for Toyoda, the Battle of the Philippine Sea and his futile gamble in defense of Formosa had left the Japanese Fleet naked to air attack. Toyoda had carriers, but with few planes and half-trained pilots. *Shō* I, therefore, must be dependent upon stealth and cunning, night operations, and what air cover could be provided chiefly by land-based planes operating from Philippine bases and working in close conjunction with the fleet.

Toyoda also confronted another handicap—a fleet widely separated by distance. He exercised command—from his land headquarters—over a theoretically "Combined Fleet," but Vice-Admiral Jisaburo Ozawa, who flew his flag from the carrier *Zuikaku*, and who commanded the crippled carriers and some cruisers and destroyers, was still based in the Inland Sea in Japanese home waters. The bulk of the fleet's heavy units—Vice-Admiral Takeo Kurita's First Diversion Attack Force of battleships, cruisers, and destroyers—was based on Lingga Anchorage near Singapore, close to its fuel sources. The Japanese Fleet was divided in the face of a superior naval force; it could not be concentrated prior to battle.

These deficiencies, plus the geography of the Philippines, dictated the enemy plan, which was hastily modified at the last minute, partially because of the Japanese weaknesses in carrier aviation. Two principal straits—San Bernardino, north of the island of Samar; and Surigao, between Mindanao and Dinagat and Leyte and Panaon— lead from the South China Sea to Leyte Gulf, where the great armada of MacArthur was committed to the invasion. The Japanese ships based near Singapore—the so-called First Diversion Attack Force—were to steam north toward Leyte, with a stop at Brunei Bay, Borneo, to refuel. There the force would split; the Central Group, Vice Admiral Takeo Kurita, flying his flag in the heavy cruiser *Atago*, with a total of five battleships, ten heavy cruisers, two light cruisers, and fifteen destroyers, would transit San Bernardino Strait at night; the Southern Group, Vice Admiral Shōji Nishimura, with two battleships, one heavy cruiser, and four destroyers, was to be augmented at Surigao Strait by an ancillary force of three more cruisers and four destroyers under Vice Admiral Kiyohide Shima, which was to steam through Formosa Strait, with a stop in the Pescadores, all the way from its bases in the home islands. All these forces were to strike the great American armada in Leyte Gulf almost simultaneously at dawn of October 25 and wreak havoc among the thin-skinned amphibious ships like a hawk among chickens.

But the key to the operation was the emasculated Japanese carriers, operating under Vice-Admiral Jisaburo Ozawa from their bases in Japan's Inland Sea. These ships—one heavy carrier and three light carriers, with less than 100 planes aboard—"all that remained of the enemy's once-great carrier forces"—were to steam south toward Luzon and to act as deliberate decoys or lures for Admiral Halsey's great Third Fleet, which was covering the amphibious invasion of Leyte. The northern decoy force was to be accompanied by two hermaphrodites—battleship-carriers, the *Ise* and *Hyuga*, with the after turrets replaced by short flight decks, but with no planes, and by three cruisers and ten destroyers. Ozawa was to lure Halsey's Third Fleet to the north, away from Leyte, and open the way for Kurita and Nishimura to break into Leyte Gulf.

At the same time all three forces were to be aided—not with direct air cover, but by intensive attacks by Japanese land-based planes upon American carriers and shipping. As a last-minute "spur-of-the-moment" decision, the Japanese Special Attack Groups were activated, and the Kamikaze (Divine Wind) fliers commenced their suicidal attacks upon U.S. ships. As early as October 15, Rear Admiral Masabumi Arima, a subordinate naval air commander, flying from a Philippine field, had made a suicide dive and had "lit the fuse of the ardent wishes of his men." All of these far-flung forces were under the common command of Admiral Toyoda far away in Tokyo.

Such was the desperate *Shō* I—perhaps the greatest gamble, the most daring and unorthodox plan in the history of naval war.

It committed to action virtually all that was left of the operational forces—afloat and in the air—of Japan's Navy—four carriers, two battleship-carriers, seven battleships, nineteen cruisers, thirty-three destroyers, and perhaps 500 to 700 Japanese aircraft—mostly land-based.

But the opposing American forces were far more powerful. Like the Japanese forces which had no common commander closer than Tokyo, the U.S. Fleet operated under divided command. General MacArthur, as theater commander of the Southwest Pacific area, was in overall charge of the Leyte invasion, and through Admiral Thomas C. Kinkaid, he commanded the Seventh Fleet, which was in direct charge of the amphibious operation. But Admiral Halsey's powerful covering force of the Third Fleet—the strongest fleet in the world—was not under MacArthur's command; it was a part of Admiral Chester W. Nimitz's Pacific Command forces, and Nimitz had his headquarters in Hawaii. And above Nimitz and MacArthur, the only unified command was in Washington.

The gun power of Kinkaid's Seventh Fleet was provided by six old battleships—five of them raised from the mud of Pearl Harbor, but he had sixteen escort carriers—small, slow-speed vessels, converted from merchant hulls—eight cruisers and scores of destroyers and destroyer escorts, frigates, motor torpedo boats, and other types. Kinkaid's job was to provide shore bombardment and close air support for the Army and antisubmarine and air defense for the amphibious forces.

Halsey, with eight large attack carriers, eight light carriers, six fast new battleships, fifteen cruisers, and fifty-eight destroyers, was ordered to "cover and support forces of the Southwest Pacific [MacArthur's command] in order to assist in the seizure and occupation of objectives in the Central Philippines." He was to destroy enemy naval and air forces threatening the invasion. He was to remain responsible to Admiral Nimitz, but "necessary measures for detailed

coordination of operations between the . . . [Third Fleet] . . . and
. . . the [Seventh Fleet] will be arranged by their . . . commanders."

The combined Third and Seventh Fleets could muster 1,000 to
1,400 ship-based aircraft—32 carriers; 12 battleships; 23 cruisers;
more than 100 destroyers and destroyer escorts, and numerous
smaller types and hundreds of auxiliaries. The Seventh Fleet also
had a few tender-based PBY patrol planes (flying boats). But not
all of these forces participated in the far-flung air attacks and the
three widely separated major engagements which later came to be
called the Battle for Leyte Gulf.

Such was the stage, these the actors, and this the plot in the
most dramatic and far-flung naval battle in history.

It opened with first blood for the submarines. At dawn on
October 23 the U.S. submarines *Darter* and *Dace*, patrolling Pala-
wan Passage, intercepted Admiral Kurita, bound for his rendezvous
with destiny. The *Darter* put five torpedoes into Kurita's flagship,
the heavy cruiser *Atago*, at 1,000 yards range; damaged the cruiser
Takao. *Dace* hit the cruiser *Maya* with four torpedoes. The *Atago*
sank in nineteen minutes as Kurita shifted his flag to the destroyer
Kishinani and later to the battleship *Yamato*. The *Maya* blew up
and sank in four minutes; *Takao*—burning and low in the water—
was sent back to Brunei, escorted by two destroyers. Kurita steams
on, shaken but implacable, toward San Bernardino Strait.

October 24: Aboard the battleship *New Jersey*, flying "Bull"
Halsey's flag, the plans are ready for this day as the sun quickly
burns away the morning haze. In the carriers, bowing to the swell,
the bull horns sound on the flight decks—"Pilots, man your
planes."

At 0600 the Third Fleet launches search planes to sweep a wide
arc of sea covering the approaches to San Bernardino and Surigao
straits. Submarine reports from *Darter*, *Dace*, and *Guitarro* have
alerted the Americans—but not in time to halt the detachment of
the Third Fleet's largest task group—Task Group 38.1 commanded
by Vice Admiral John S. ("Slew") McCain, with orders to retire to
Ulithi for rest and supplies. The fleet's three other task groups are
spread out over 300 miles of ocean to the east of the Philippines
from central Luzon to southern Samar; one of them—to the
north—has been tracked doggedly all night by enemy "snoopers."
As the planes take off to search the reef-studded waters of the
Sibuyan and Sulu seas and the approaches to San Bernardino and

Surigao, Kinkaid's old battleships and little carriers off Leyte are supporting the G.I.s ashore.

At 0746, Lieutenant (j.g.) Max Adams, flying a Helldiver above the magnificent volcanic crags, the palm-grown islands, and startling blue sea of the archipelago, reports a radar contact, and a few minutes later Admiral Kurita's First Diversion Attack Force lies spread out like toy ships upon a painted sea—the pagoda masts unmistakable in the sunlight.

The tension of action grips flag plot in the *New Jersey* as the contact report comes in; the radio crackles "urgent" and "top secret" messages—to Washington, to Nimitz, to Kinkaid, to all task-group commanders. McCain, 600 miles to the eastward, enroute to Ulithi and rest, is recalled and Third Fleet is ordered to concentrate off San Bernardino to launch strikes against the enemy.

But at 0820 far to the south, the southern arm of the Japanese pincer is sighted for the first time; Vice-Admiral Nishimura—with battleships *Fuso* and *Yamashiro*, heavy cruiser *Mogami*, and four destroyers—steaming toward Surigao. *Enterprise* search-attack planes attack through heavy antiaircraft fire; *Fuso*'s catapult is hit, her planes destroyed, and a fire rages; a gun mount in destroyer *Shiguro* is knocked out—but Nishimura steams on to the east, his speed undiminished. And Halsey continues the concentration of his fleet near San Bernardino to strike the Japanese Central Force.

There has been no morning search to the north and northeast, and Ozawa's decoy carriers, steaming southward toward Luzon, are still undiscovered.

The *Shō* plan now moves toward its dramatic denouement. Japanese planes flying from Philippine bases commence the most furious assault since the landing upon the Seventh and Third Fleets. To the north off Luzon, carriers *Langley*, *Princeton*, *Essex*, and *Lexington* face the brunt of the winged fury. Seven Hellcats from the *Essex*, led by Commander David McCampbell, intercept sixty Japanese planes—half of them Zeke fighters—and after a melee of an hour and thirty-five minutes of combat the Americans knock down twenty-four Japanese with no losses. *Princeton* claims thirty-four enemy from another large raid; the *Lexington*'s and *Langley*'s "fly-boys" are also busy; over the air come the exultant "Tally-hos," and "Splash one Betty—Splash two Zekes" of the pilots.

But the Japanese draw blood. At about 0938, as Third Fleet starts converging toward San Bernardino and the carriers prepare to launch deckloads to strike the enemy's center force, a Japanese Judy dives unseen and unrecorded on the radar screen out of a low cloud. She drops a 550-pound bomb square on *Princeton*'s flight deck; the bomb penetrates to the hangar deck, ignites gasoline in six torpedo planes, and starts raging fires. The fight to save her starts, but at 1002 a series of terrific explosions split open the flight deck like the rind of a dropped melon, throw the after plane elevator high into the air, and by 1020 *Princeton*'s fire mains have failed and she is dead in the water, with a 1,000 foot pall of smoke above her and hundreds of her crew in the water. The task group steams on southward to the San Bernardino rendezvous, while cruisers *Birmingham* and *Reno* and destroyers *Gatling*, *Irwin*, and *Cassin Young* hover about wounded *Princeton* in a daylong fight to save her.

But as *Princeton* flames and staggers, Kurita's Central Force of five battleships, accompanied by cruisers and destroyers, is running the gantlet. Carrier strikes start coming in against Japan's First Diversion Attack Force about 1025, and the exultant U.S. pilots concentrate against targets none of them had ever seen before— the largest battleships in the world. *Yamato* and *Musashi*, long the mysterious focus of intelligence reports, lie beneath the wings of naval air power—their 69,500-ton bulk, 18-inch guns, 27.5-knot speed—dwarfing their sisters. *Musashi* is wounded early; oil smears trail on the blue water from her lacerated flank as a torpedo strikes home. But she is strong; her speed is undiminished. Not so *Myoko*'s. This heavy cruiser is badly hurt in the first attack; she drops to fifteen knots and is left astern to limp alone into port; Kurita has lost four out of the ten heavy cruisers that sortied so gallantly from Brunei.

But he has no respite. At three minutes past noon another strike comes out of the sun. The Japanese AA fire blossoms in pink and purple bursts; even the battleships' main batteries are firing. Several American planes are hit; one goes down flaming—but *Musashi* takes two bombs and two torpedoes; she loses speed and drops back slowly out of formation.

An hour and a half later *Yamato* takes two hits forward of her Number one turret, which start a fire—but her thick hide minimizes damages; the fire is extinguished. But *Musashi* is now sore-wounded; she takes four bomb hits in this attack and three more torpedoes; her upper works are a shambles, her bow almost under water, her speed down first to sixteen and then to twelve knots.

But Kurita's slow agony drags on during this long and sunlit day. He hopes in vain for air cover. *Yamato* is hit again in the fourth attack and the older battleship *Nagato* damaged.

At six bells in the afternoon watch (3 P.M.) Kurita orders the limping *Musashi* to withdraw from the fight. But not in time.

The final and largest attack of the day seeks her out as she turns heavily to find sanctuary. In fifteen minutes *Musashi* receives the coup de grâce—ten more bombs, four more torpedoes; she's down to six knots now, her bow is under water, and she lists steeply to port—a dying gladiator.

Kurita is shaken. He has had no air cover; he has been subjected to intense attack; his original strength of five battleships, twelve cruisers, and fifteen destroyers has been reduced to four battleships, eight cruisers, and eleven destroyers; all of his remaining battleships have been damaged; fleet speed is limited to twenty-two knots. There is no sign that Ozawa's northern decoy force is succeeding in luring the Third Fleet away from San Bernardino. At 1530 Kurita reverses course and steams away toward the west. And American pilots report the "retreat" to Admiral Halsey aboard *New Jersey*. . . .

To Admiral Halsey there is "one piece missing in the puzzle—the [Japanese] carriers."

The northern task group of Third Fleet has been under attack by enemy carrier-type planes, which might have been land-based—but none of the sightings has reported enemy carriers. Where are they?

At 1405, as Kurita's central force is pounded in the Sibuyan Sea, *Lexington*'s planes take off to find out. They are under orders to search to the north and northeast in the open seas untouched by the morning search.

The search planes fly through a cloud-speckled sky and intermittent rain squalls, leaving behind them a task group harassed by fierce, though intermittent Japanese air attacks.

The flaming *Princeton*, billowing clouds of fire and smoke, is still afloat, with her covey of rescue ships around her. Despite intermittent explosions and singeing heat, cruisers *Birmingham* and *Reno*, the destroyers *Morrison*, *Irwin*, and *Cassin Young* have clustered alongside, pouring water from their pumps on the blazing carrier. Submarine contacts and enemy air attacks interrupt the fire fighting; the rescue ships pull off. At 1523, about the time Kurita, 300 miles away, reverses course and heads to the westward in the Sibuyan Sea, the cruiser *Birmingham* comes alongside *Princeton*'s blazing port side again. The cruiser's open decks are thick with men—fire-fighters, line handlers, antiaircraft gunners, medical personnel, fire and rescue squads, watch-standers. There is 50 feet of open water between blazing *Princeton* and her salvor, *Birmingham*; a spring line is out forward between carrier and cruiser.

Suddenly a "tremendous blast" rips off *Princeton*'s stern and flight deck; steel plates as big "as a house" fly through the air; jagged bits of steel, broken gun barrels, shrapnel, helmets, debris rake *Birmingham*'s bridge, upper works, and crowded decks like grape-shot; in a fraction of a second the cruiser is a charnel house, her decks literally flowing blood—229 dead, 420 mangled and wounded—the ship's superstructure sieved.

Aboard *Princeton* all the skeleton fire-fighting crew are wounded. Captain John M. Hoskins, who had been scheduled to take command of *Princeton* shortly and had remained aboard with the skipper he was relieving, puts a rope tourniquet around his leg, as his right foot hangs by a shred of flesh and tendon. The surviving medical officer cuts off the foot with a sheath knife, dusts the wound with sulfa powder, injects morphine. . . . Hoskins lives to become the Navy's first "peg-leg" admiral of modern times.

But still *Princeton* floats on even keel, flaming like a volcano, manned by a crew of bloody specters. . . .

At 1640 the search to the north pays off. U.S. planes sight Ozawa's decoy force of carriers. The contact reports electrify Third Fleet, but mislead it, too; Ozawa's northern group of ships, which were sighted about 130 miles east of the northern tip of Luzon, includes two hermaphrodite battleships, but our fliers mistakenly report four. Nor do our fliers know Ozawa's carriers are virtually without planes.

The contact reports decide *Princeton*'s fate; her weary crew of fire-fighters are removed, the day-long struggle is ended, and at 1649 *Reno* puts two torpedoes into the flaming hulk and the carrier blows up, breaks in two, and sinks. Mangled *Birmingham*, which lost far more men than the ship she was trying to save, steams with her dead and dying to Ulithi—out of the fight. . . .

Two hours later, near Sibuyan Island, the giant *Musashi*, pride of Kurita's Central Force, loses her long fight. Fatally wounded, she settles slowly deeper and deeper in the calm sea, and as the evening closes down, the greatest battleship in the world capsizes and takes with her to the depths half of her crew. But no American sees her passing. . . . And no American has seen Kurita, earlier in the afternoon, alter his course once more and at 1714 head once again with his battered but still powerful Central Force back toward San Bernardino Strait. . . .

At 1950, with the tropic dusk, "Bull" Halsey makes his decision and informs Kinkaid, commanding Seventh Fleet: "Central force heavily damaged according to strike reports. Am proceeding north with three groups to attack carrier force at dawn."

Third Fleet concentrates and steams hard to the north in what irreverent historians of the future are to call "Bull's Run." Night snoopers from *Independence* shadow the Japanese northern force, and orders go to the carriers to launch planes at sunrise. San Bernardino Strait is left uncovered—not even a submarine patrols its waters; Kinkaid and Seventh Fleet, protecting the Leyte invasion, believe it is barred by Halsey; Halsey, banking too heavily on exaggerated claims from his pilots, thinks Kurita's central force has been stopped by the day's air attacks and the battered Japanese survivors can be left safely to Kinkaid. On such misunderstandings rest the course of history and the fate of nations.

Surigao Strait is dark under the loom of the land. Since the morning there have been no sightings of the Japanese southern force; even its exact composition is not known. But Kinkaid and the Seventh Fleet have no doubts; the Japanese will try to break through this night. Kinkaid and Rear Admiral Jesse B. Oldendorf, his OTC (officer in tactical command) have made dispositions for a night surface battle. They have provided a suitable reception committee, including PT boats deep in the strait and covering its southern approaches, three destroyer squadrons near the center, and at the mouth—where the strait debouches into Leyte Gulf—six old battleships and eight cruisers.

Into this trap the Japanese southern force blunders in two divisions—each independent of the other. Nishimura, with battleships *Fuso* and *Yamashiro*, cruiser *Mogami*, and four destroyers, lead the way. Cruising twenty miles behind Nishimura is Vice Admiral Shima with three cruisers and four destroyers from Japanese home bases. The two Japanese forces attack piecemeal and uncoordinated; neither knows much of the other's plans. Shima and Nishimura were classmates at the Japanese Naval Academy; their careers have bred rivalry; Nishimura, formerly the senior, has been passed in the processes of promotion by Shima, who commands the smaller force but is now six months senior in rank to Nishimura. But Nishimura, a seagoing admiral, has seen more war. Neither seems anxious to serve with the other; there is no common command.

Radars on the PT boats pick up the enemy about 2300 as "sheet lightning dim[s] the hazy blur of the setting moon and thunder echoe[s] from the islands' hills."

Thirty-nine PT boats, motors muffled, head for Nishimura and attack in successive waves as the enemy advances. But the Japanese score first. Enemy destroyers illuminate the little boats with their searchlights long before the PTs reach good torpedo range; a hit starts a fire in *PT 152*; a near-miss with its spout of water extinguishes it; *PT 130* and *PT 132* are also hit. But Nishimura is identified; course, speed, and formation are radioed to Kinkaid's fleet and the harassing PT attacks continue.

Aboard destroyer *Remey*, flag of Destroyer Squadron 54, Commander R. P. Fiala turns on the loudspeaker to talk to the crew: "This is the captain speaking. Tonight our ship has been designated to make the first torpedo run on the Jap task force that is on its way to stop our landings in Leyte Gulf. It is our job to stop the Japs. May God be with us tonight."

The destroyers attack along both flanks of the narrow strait; their silhouettes merge with the land; the Japanese, in the middle, can scarcely distinguish dark shape of ship from dark loom of land; the radar fuzzes and the luminescent pips on the screen are lost in a vague blur.

It is deep in the mid-watch—0301 of October 25—when the first destroyer-launched torpedoes streak across the strait. In less than half an hour Nishimura is crippled. His slow and lumbering flagship, the battleship *Yamashiro*, is hit; destroyer *Yamagumo* is sunk; two other destroyers are out of control. Nishimura issues his last command: "We have received a torpedo attack. You are to proceed and attack all ships."

Battleship *Fuso*, cruiser *Mogami*, destroyer *Shigure* steam on toward Leyte Gulf.

But before 0400 a tremendous eruption of flames and pyrotechnics marks *Yamashiro*'s passing; another American torpedo has found her magazine, and the battleship breaks in two and sinks, with Nishimura's flag still flying.

Fuso does not long outlive her sister. Up from the mud of Pearl Harbor, the avengers wait—six old battleships patrol back and forth across the mouth of the strait. This is an admiral's dream. Like Togo at Tsushima and Jellicoe at Jutland, Kinkaid and Oldendorf have capped the T; the remaining Japanese ships are blundering head on in single column against a column of American ships at right angles to the Japanese course. The concentrated broadsides of six battleships can be focused against the leading Japanese, and only his forward turrets can bear against the Americans.

Climax of battle: As the last and heaviest destroyer attack goes home in answer to the command—"Get the big boys"—the battle line and the cruisers open up; the night is streaked with flare of crimson.

Fuso and *Mogami* flame and shudder as the rain of shells strikes home; *Fuso* soon drifts helplessly, racked by great explosions, wreathed in a fiery pall. She dies before the dawn, and *Mogami*, on fire, is finished later with the other cripples. Only destroyer *Shigure* escapes at thirty knots.

Into this mad melee, with the dying remnants of his classmate's fleet around him, steams Vice Admiral Shima—"fat, dumb, and happy." He knows nothing of what has gone before; he has no cogent plan of battle. *Abukuma*, Shima's only light cruiser, is struck by a PT torpedo even before he is deep in the strait; she is left behind, speed dwindling, as the two heavy cruisers and four destroyers steam onward toward the gun flashes on the horizon. About 0400 Shima encounters destroyer *Shigure*, sole survivor of Nishimura's fleet, retiring down the strait.

Shigure tells Shima nothing of the debacle; she simply signals: "I am the *Shigure*; I have rudder difficulties."

The rest is almost comic anticlimax. Shima pushes deeper into the strait, sees a group of dark shadows; fires torpedoes and manages an amazing collision between his flagship, the *Nachi*, and the burning stricken *Mogami*, which looms up flaming out of the dark waters of the strait like the Empire State Building. And that is all for futile Shima; discretion is the better part of valor; dying for the Emperor is forgotten and Shima reverses course and heads back into the Mindanao Sea and the obscurity of history.

The Battle of Surigao Strait ends with the dawn—debacle for the Japanese. One PT boat destroyed, one destroyer damaged for the Americans. The southern pincer toward Leyte Gulf is broken.

October 25: Dawn of the twenty-fifth of October finds Admiral Ozawa with his decoy force eastward of Cape Engano (fortuitous name: Engano is Spanish for "lure" or "hoax"), prepared to die for the Emperor. At 0712, when the first American planes appear from the southeast, Ozawa knows he has at last succeeded in his luring mission. The day before he has at times despaired; some seventy to eighty of his carrier planes—all he has, save for a small combat air patrol—have joined Japanese land-based planes in attacks upon Halsey's northern task group. But his planes have not come back; many have been lost, others have flown on to Philippine bases. This day twenty aircraft—token remnants of Japan's once great flying fleets—are all that Ozawa commands. A few are in the air—to die quickly beneath American guns, as the first heavy attacks from Halsey's carriers come in.

The American carrier pilots have a field day; the air is full of the jabberwock of the fliers.

"Pick one out, boys, and let 'em have it."

The Japanese formation throws up a beautiful carpet of antiaircraft fire; the colored bursts and tracers frame the sky-sea battle. The Japanese ships twist and turn, maneuver violently in eccentric patterns to avoid the bombs and torpedoes—but their time has come. Before 0830 with the day still young, some 150 U.S. carrier planes have wrought havoc. Carrier *Chiyoda* is hit; carrier *Chitose*, billowing clouds of smoke and fatally hurt, is stopped and listing heavily; the light cruiser *Tama*, torpedoed, is limping astern; destroyer *Akitsuki* has blown up; light carrier *Zuiho* is hit, and Ozawa's flagship, the *Zuikaku*, has taken a torpedo aft, which has wrecked the steering engine; she is steered by hand.

A second strike at 1000 cripples *Chiyoda*, which dies a slow death, to be finished off later by U.S. surface ships. In early afternoon a third strike sinks carrier *Zuikaku*, the last survivor of the Japanese attack upon Pearl Harbor. She rolls over slowly and sinks, "flying a battle flag of tremendous size." At 1527 carrier *Zuiho* "follows her down." The hermaphrodite battleships, with flight decks aft—*Hyuga* and *Ise*, "fattest of the remaining targets"—are bombed repeatedly, their bulges are perforated, their decks inundated with tons of water from near misses; *Ise*'s port catapult is hit—but they bear charmed lives. Admiral Ozawa, his flag transferred to cruiser *Oyodo*, his work of luring done, straggles northward with his cripples from the battle off Cape Engano. Throughout the day he is subject to incessant air attack, and in late afternoon and in the dark of the night of the twenty-fifth U.S. cruisers and destroyers, detached from the Third Fleet, finish off the cripples.

The price of success for Admiral Ozawa's decoy force is high; all four carriers, one of his three cruisers, and two of his eight destroyers are gone. But he has accomplished his mission; Halsey has been lured, San Bernardino Strait is unguarded, and the hawk Kurita is down among the chickens.

Off Samar that morning of the twenty-fifth, the sea is calm at sunup, the wind gentle, the sky overcast with spotted cumulus; occasional rain squalls dapple the surface. Aboard the sixteen escort carriers of the Seventh Fleet and their escorting "small boys" (destroyers and destroyer escorts) the dawn alert has ended. The early missions have taken off (though not the search planes for the northern sectors). Many of the carriers' planes are already over Leyte, supporting the ground troops—the combat air patrol and antisubmarine warfare patrols are launched, and on the bridge of carrier *Fanshaw Bay*, Rear Admiral C. A. F. Sprague is having a second cup of coffee.

The coming day will be busy; the little escort carriers have support missions to fly for the troops ashore on Leyte, air defense and antisubmarine patrols, and a large strike scheduled to mop up the cripples and fleeing remnants of the Japanese force defeated in the night surface battle of Surigao Strait. The escort-carrier groups are spread out off the east coast of the Philippines from Mindanao to Samar; Sprague's northern group of six escort carriers, three destroyers, and four destroyer escorts is steaming northward at fourteen knots fifty miles off Samar and halfway up the island's coast.

The escort carriers, designated CVEs in naval abbreviation, are tin-clads-unarmored, converted from merchant ship or tanker hulls, slow, carrying eighteen to thirty-six planes. They are known by many uncomplimentary descriptives—"baby flat-tops," "tomato cans," "jeep carriers," and new recruits "coming aboard for the first time were told by the old hands that CVE stood for Combustible, Vulnerable, Expendable!" Their maximum of eighteen knots speed (made all-out) is too slow to give them safety in flight; their thin skins and "pop-guns"—five-inchers and under—do not fit them for surface slugging; they are ships of limited utility—intended for air support of ground operations ashore, antisubmarine and air defense missions—never for fleet action.

Yet they are to fight this morning a battle of jeeps against giants.

Admiral Sprague has scarcely finished his coffee when a contact report comes over the squawk box. An ASW pilot reports enemy battleships, cruisers, and destroyers twenty miles away and closing fast. " . . . check that identification," the admiral says, thinking some green pilot has mistaken Halsey's fast battleships for the enemy.

The answer is sharp and brief, the tension obvious: "Identification confirmed," the pilot's voice comes strained through the static. "Ships have pagoda masts."

Almost simultaneously radiomen hear Japanese chatter over the air; the northern CVE group sees antiaircraft bursts blossoming in the air to the northwest; blips of unidentified ships appear on the radar screens, and before 0700 a signalman with a long glass has picked up the many-storied superstructures and the typical pagoda masts of Japanese ships.

Disbelief, amazement, and consternation struggle for supremacy; the escort carriers, Admiral Kinkaid himself—in fact, most of the Seventh Fleet—had been convinced the Japanese center force was still west of the Philippines and that, in any case, Halsey's fast battleships—now far away to the north with the carriers in the battle for Cape Engano—were guarding San Bernardino Strait. But Kurita has arrived. . . . And about all that stands between him and the transports, supply ships, and amphibious craft in Leyte Gulf and Army headquarters and supply dumps on the beach are the "baby flat-tops" and their accompanying "small boys."

There's no time for planning; within five minutes of visual sighting Japanese heavy stuff—18-inch shells from *Yamato,* sister ship of the foundered *Musashi*—are whistling overhead. Sprague, giving his orders over the voice radio, turns his ships to the east into the wind, steps up speed to maximum, orders all planes scrambled. By 0705 escort carrier *White Plains,* launching aircraft as fast as she can get them off, is straddled several times, with red, yellow, green, and blue spouts of water from the dye-marked shells foaming across her bridge, shaking the ship violently, damaging the starboard engine room, smashing electrical circuits, and throwing a fighter plane out of its chocks on the flight deck.

White Plains makes smoke and the Japanese shift fire to the *St. Lo,* which takes near misses and casualties from fragments. The "small boys" make smoke—and the carriers, their boiler casings panting from maximum effort—pour out viscous clouds of oily black smoke from their stacks, which veils the sea. . . . There is a moment of surcease; the planes are launched, most of them armed with small-size or antipersonnel or general-purpose bombs or depth charges—no good against armored ships. But there has been no time to rearm. . . .

The airwaves sound alarm. Sprague broadcasts danger in plain language; at 0724 Admiral Kinkaid, aboard his flagship *Wasatch* in Leyte Gulf, hears the worst has happened; the Japanese fleet is three hours' steaming from the beachhead; the little escort carriers may be wiped out. Just five minutes before, Kinkaid has learned that his assumption that a Third Fleet cork was in the bottle of San Bernardino Strait was incorrect; in answer to a radioed query sent at 0412 Halsey informs him that Task Force 34—modern fast battleships— is with Third Fleet's carriers off Cape Engano far to the north.

Kinkaid in "Urgent and Priority" messages asks for the fast battleships, for carrier strikes, for immediate action. . . .

Even Admiral Nimitz, in far-off Hawaii, sends a message to Halsey: "All the world wants to know where is Task Force 34 [the fast battleships]?"

But in Leyte Gulf and Surigao Strait the tocsin of alarm sounded via the radio waves puts the Seventh Fleet—red-eyed from days of shore bombardment and nights of battle—into frenetic action. Some of the old battleships and cruisers are recalled from Surigao Strait, formed into a task unit, and they prepare feverishly to ammunition and refuel. Seventh Fleet's heavy ships are in none too good shape for surface action; their ammunition is dangerously low from five days of shore bombardment, many of their armor-piercing projectiles were used in the night battle; destroyers are low on torpedoes, many ships short of fuel. . . .

And in the battle off Samar, Sprague is fighting for his life.

Within 20 minutes, as the baby carriers steam to the east, launching planes, the range to the enemy has decreased to 25,000 yards—easy shooting for the big guns of the Japanese far beyond the effective reach of the American five-inchers. . . .

Destroyer *Johnston*, Commander Ernest E. Evans, commanding, sees her duty and does it. Without orders she dashes in at 30 knots to launch a spread of 10 torpedoes against an enemy cruiser working up along a flank of the pounding carriers. She spouts smoke and fire as she charges—her five-inchers firing continuously as she closes the range. She escapes damage until she turns to retire; then a salvo of three 14-inchers, followed by three 6-inch shells, hole her, wound her captain, wreck the steering engine, the after fire room and engine room, knock out her after guns and gyro compass, maim many of her crew, and leave her limping at 16 knots.

Sprague and his carriers, veiled in part by smoke, find brief sanctuary in a heavy rain squall; the curtain of water saves temporarily wounded *Johnston*. But well before 0800 Kurita has sent some of his faster ships seaward to head off and flank the escort carriers; gradually Sprague turns southward, the enemy coming hard on both his flanks and astern. . . .

"Small boys, launch torpedo attack," Sprague orders over the TBS circuit (talk-between-ships voice radio).

Destroyers *Heermann* and *Hoel* and wounded *Johnston*, her torpedoes already expended but her guns speaking in support, answer the command—three destroyers in a daylight attack against the heaviest ships of the Japanese fleet, three tin-clads against four battleships, eight cruisers, and eleven destroyers.

"Buck," Commander Amos T. Hathaway, skipper of the *Heermann*, remarks coolly to his officer of the deck: "Buck, what we need is a bugler to sound the charge."

Hoel and *Heermann*, followed by limping *Johnston*, sally forth to their naval immortality.

In and out of rain squalls, wreathed in the black and oily smoke from the stacks and the white chemical smoke from the smoke generators on the fantails, the destroyers charge, backing violently to avoid collisions, closing the range. They hear the express-train roar of the 14-inchers going over; they fire spreads at a heavy cruiser, rake the superstructure of a battleship with their five-inchers, launch their last torpedoes at 4,400 yards range. Then Hathaway of the *Heermann* walks calmly into his pilothouse, calls Admiral Sprague on the TBS, and reports: "Exercise completed."

But the destroyers are finished. *Hoel* has lost her port engine; she is steered manually; her decks are a holocaust of blood and wreckage; fire control and power are off; Number 3 gun, wreathed in white-hot steam venting from the burst steam pipes, is inoperable; Number 5 is frozen in train by a near miss; half the barrel of Number 4 is blown off—but Numbers 1 and 2 guns continue to fire.

By 0830 power is lost on the starboard engine; all engineering spaces are flooding; the ship slows to dead in the water and, burning furiously, is raked by enemy guns. At 0840, with a twenty-degree list, the order is given to "Abandon Ship." Fifteen minutes later she rolls on her port side and sinks stern first—holed repeatedly by scores of major-caliber shells.

In *Heermann*, the crimson dye from enemy shell splashes mixes with the blood of men to daub bridge and superstructure reddish hues. A shell strikes a bean locker and spreads a brown paste across the decks. *Heermann* takes hits but, fishtailing and chasing salvos, she manages to live.

Not so, wounded *Johnston*. Spitting fire to the end, and virtually surrounded by the entire Japanese fleet, she is overwhelmed under an avalanche of shells, to sink about an hour after *Hoel*.

The four smaller and slower destroyer escorts make the second torpedo attack. *Raymond* and *John C. Butler* live to tell about it; *Dennis* has her guns knocked out, but *Samuel B. Roberts*, deep in the smoke and framed by shell splashes, comes to her end in a mad melee. She is hit by many heavy-caliber projectiles, her speed reduced, and by 0900 a salvo of 14-inch shells rips open her port side like a can opener, wrecks an engine room, starts raging fires. The *Roberts*, abaft her stack, looks like "an inert mass of battered metal"; she has no power; she is dead in the water.

But the crew of Number 2 gun load, ram, aim, and fire by hand. They know the chance they take; without compressed air to clear the bore of the burning bits of fragments from the previous charge, the silken powder bags may "cook off" and explode before the breach can be closed. But they fire six rounds, despite the risk. The seventh cooks off and kills instantly most of the gun crew; the breach is blown into a twisted inoperable mass of steel. But Gunner's Mate Third Class Paul Henry Carr, the gun captain—his body ripped open from neck to groin—still cradles the last 54-pound shell in his arms, and his last gasping words before he dies are pleas for aid to load the gun.

But smokescreens, rain squalls, and torpedo attacks have not saved the slow and lumbering baby flat-tops. Kurita has sent his cruisers curving seaward; slowly the fight swerves round from south to southwest; Sprague's carriers, strung out over miles of ocean, steam wounded toward Leyte Gulf, with the enemy destroyers coming hard on their landward flank, battleships astern and Japanese cruisers to seaward.

The flat-tops dodge in and out of the 150-foot waterspouts from the major-caliber Japanese shells; they chase salvos and fire their five-inchers defiantly. *Fanshaw Bay* takes six hits from eight-inch shells, which wreck the catapult, knock holes in the hull, start fires. *Kalinin Bay* takes fifteen hits; *White Plains* is racked from stem to stern by straddles. But their thin skins save them; most of the huge armor-piercing projectiles pass clean through the unarmored carriers without exploding. *Gambier Bay*, trailing and on an exposed windward flank where the smoke screens do not shield her, takes a hit on the flight deck, a near miss close alongside, loses an engine, drops to eleven knots, then loses all power—and is doomed. For an hour, far behind the chase, she dies in agony, hit about once a minute by enemy fire. She sinks about 0900, flaming brightly, gasoline exploding, a Japanese cruiser still riddling her from only 2,000 yards away.

Well before 0930 the chase which is drawing closer and closer to crowded Leyte Gulf, where frantic preparations are in progress, has enveloped the northern group of escort carriers; the central group is now under fire, and the 16 jeep flat-tops have lost 105 planes.

" . . . it seemed only a matter of time until the entire Northern Group would be wiped out and the Middle Group overtaken . . ."

Two destroyers, a destroyer escort, and a carrier are sunk or sinking; two carriers, a destroyer, and a destroyer escort are badly hurt.

Aboard *Kitkun Bay*, an officer quips: "It won't be long now, boys; we're sucking 'em into forty-millimeter range."

Suddenly at 0925, Vice Admiral Kurita, with victory in his grasp, breaks off the action, turns his ships to the north, and ends the surface phase of the battle off Samar.

"Damn it," a sailor says. "They got away."

Kurita's action, inexplicable at the time, has some, though incomplete, justification. The charge of the American "small boys"—one of the most stirring episodes in the long history of naval war—and the desperate gallantry of the uncoordinated and improvised air strikes by the pilots of the escort carriers have had their effect. During the early action off Samar, U.S. carrier pilots—from the little CVEs—have harassed Kurita constantly, have shot down more than 100 enemy planes, dropped 191 tons of bombs and 83 torpedoes. The enemy ships have turned and maneuvered violently to avoid torpedoes. Effective smokescreens have confused the Japanese. The air attacks have been mounting in intensity and effectiveness as planes have been launched from the center and southern group of escort carriers and have been diverted from ground-support missions on Leyte to the new emergency. Pilots have strafed the Japanese ships recklessly, have dropped depth charges and antipersonnel bombs, have zoomed above Japanese mastheads with no ammunition and no weapons to win time and to divert and to distract.

The torpedo attacks by surface ship and aircraft had damaged enemy ships, and Kurita's fleet—composed of units now capable of widely differing speeds—is strung out over miles of ocean. The cruiser *Kumano*, torpedoed, is down to sixteen knots; the cruisers *Chikuma* and *Chokai* are crippled; superstructures, charthouses, and communication equipment in other ships are damaged by five-inch shell fire and aircraft strafing; the Japanese are shaken. Kurita, who has lost close tactical control of his command, does not comprehend his closeness to victory; he thinks he has engaged some of the big, fast carriers of Third Fleet instead of merely the escort carriers of Seventh Fleet. Intercepted U.S. radio traffic convinces him—erroneously—that Leyte airstrips are operational. He believes the rest of Halsey's powerful forces are nearby; he knows that Nishimura's southern pincer has been defeated in Surigao Strait; he has never received messages from Ozawa, far to the north, reporting the success of his decoy mission. So Kurita recalls his ships and assembles his scattered forces—and his chance has gone.

Admiral Sprague notes his thankful bewilderment: ". . . the failure of the enemy . . . to completely wipe out all vessels of this Task Unit can be attributed to our successful smokescreen, our torpedo counterattack . . . and the definite partiality of Almighty God."

The rest was anticlimax.

Kurita's irresolution was reinforced by mounting American attacks. Only two hours from the soft-skinned amphibious shipping in Leyte Gulf—his original goal—Kurita wasted time assembling his scattered forces and aiding cripples, and his fleet milled around in much the same waters, steering varying courses. *Suzuya*, a cruiser, was fatally damaged by air attack, and at 1030, two to three hours' flying time to the eastward, Admiral "Slew" McCain's Task Group 38.1 (which had been sent to Ulithi for rest, hastily recalled, and was steaming hard to the rescue) launched a strike. The bell has tolled for Kurita, and Japan's rising sun has passed the zenith. And far to the north, "Bull" Halsey, striking at Ozawa's decoy force, was alarmed at length by Kinkaid's frantic appeals for help; his fleet reversed course when within 40 miles of decisive surface action, and Halsey detached some of his fast battleships to steam southward at high speed—but too late to intervene.

The rest of that day, the twenty-fifth, and all of the next—the twenty-sixth—was mop-up and fierce stab, as the Japanese survivors fled and Japanese land-based aircraft struck hard in angry futility. Japanese kamikaze planes, attacking after the crescendo of battle, hit the escort carriers—damaged three and broke the back of *St. Lo*, which had survived the 18-inch guns of *Yamato*. But Kurita, who reached so closely to the verge of fame, paid heavily for the luxury of indecision. Air attacks struck him again and again during the afternoon of the twenty-fifth. Three of his damaged cruisers, crippled and on fire, had to be sunk. *Tone*, one of his two remaining heavy cruisers, was hit aft and damaged, and during the night of the twenty-fifth, as Kurita took his battered survivors back through San Bernardino Strait, U.S. surface forces caught and sank destroyer *Nowake*. At midnight of the twenty-fifth only one of Kurita's ships, a destroyer, was wholly undamaged.

On the twenty-sixth there was more slow dying as Halsey's and Kinkaid's fliers, augmented by some Army Air Force land-based bombers, chivvied and attacked the retreating Japanese; and the First Diversion Attack Force, "which had already undergone more air attacks than any other force in naval history, once again braced itself for the final ordeal." Destroyer *Noshiro* was sunk; *Yamato*, with its gigantic but futile 18-inchers, was hit twice and its superstructure sieved with splinters, and other cripples of the battle off Samar and the Battle of Surigao Strait, including cruiser *Abukuma* and destroyer *Hayashimo*, were finished off. And there still remained the gantlet of U.S. submarines. . . .

At 2130, October 28, "what remained of the Japanese Battle Fleet reentered Brunei Bay."

The *Shō* plan—the great gamble—had failed completely. In the sprawling battle for Leyte Gulf, Japan had lost one large and three light aircraft carriers, three battleships, including one of the two largest warships in the world, six heavy cruisers, four light cruisers, and eleven destroyers; most of the rest of her engaged ships were damaged severely or lightly; hundreds of planes had been shot down, and between 7,475 and 10,000 Japanese seamen died. The Japanese Navy as a fighting fleet had ceased to exist; Leyte Gulf was a blow from which the enemy never recovered.

But for the United States it was, nevertheless, incomplete victory when we might have swept the boards. The penalty of divided command, of failure to fix definite areas of responsibility, and unwarranted assumptions by both Kinkaid and Halsey led to the surprise of our jeep carriers and to the escape of Kurita with his battered survivors, including four battleships, and of Ozawa with ten of his original seventeen vessels. Admiral Halsey ran to the north, leaving behind a force (the Seventh Fleet) inadequate in strength and speed to insure Kurita's destruction, and then just at the time when he was about to destroy all of Ozawa's force, he turned about and ran to the south in answer to Kinkaid's urgent calls for help. The Japanese lure worked, but the *Shō* plan, which depended fundamentally upon good communications, split-second coordination, and bold leadership, foundered in complete and fatal failure.

To the United States the cost of overwhelming victory was 2,803 lives, several hundred aircraft, one light carrier, two escort carriers, and the "small boys" who had helped turn the tide of battle—destroyers *Johnston* and *Hoel* and destroyer escort *Samuel B. Roberts*, fought by "well-trained crews in an inspired manner in accordance with the highest traditions of the Navy."

PART FIVE

VIETNAM

A launch officer on the *Kitty Hawk* signals for a
Phantom to be catapulted into the air.
(U.S. Navy Photo)

Yankee Station: Frantic Little Situations of Life and Death

Frank Harvey

B ecause most Vietnam war correspondents focused their attention on the ground fighting, few Americans had much understanding of the areo-naval action taking place during that war. Not until 1967, that is, when Frank Harvey published his startling book Air War–Vietnam, which described in vivid detail a wholly new type of warfare then being waged.

Harvey had journeyed to Vietnam on assignment for Flying Magazine in 1966, and, because of his background as a Navy veteran and an amateur stunt pilot, he was permitted to fly in virtually every type of aircraft then operating in the war zone. His magazine article was soon expanded into the book mentioned above, and with that such terms as "Jolly Green Giant," "cluster bombs," "the Huey Hog," "Bouncing Bettys," "miniguns" and "recon by fire" became part of the American vocabulary.

"I am leaving the political situation strictly alone," Harvey wrote. *"My assignment is to tell about the air war, not the reasons for it."* The result was that his book was praised by doves as well as hawks.

Like many American writers in the Erskine Caldwell mold, Harvey bummed his way around the United States and the world after serving a hitch in the Navy during World War II. Somewhere along the way, he qualified as a pilot and later became flying reporter for Argosy magazine. As a freelance writer, he published several novels and wrote for the Saturday Evening Post, Esquire, and True.

In the following excerpt from Air War–Vietnam, Harvey reports from Yankee Station, a position in the South China Sea where American aircraft carriers were cruising, launching, and recovering the aircraft then striking North Vietnam.

"I thought I saw a glimmer of light," Lieutenant Commander Glenn McGeorge radioed to his element leader, Commander Bud Ingley, as the two of them flew their tiny Skyhawk bombers on instruments through the inky darkness of North Vietnam. "Okay to drop a flare?"

"I didn't see anything," replied Commander Ingley, "but go ahead."

McGeorge toggled a magnesium flare and it settled under its parachute, lighting up the main north–south supply route, Highway One, and in the sun-bright glare there stood revealed a long convoy of trucks loaded with war supplies. Instantly the air around the jets lit up with tracer fire as the truck-guard gunners let loose. The two little Navy bombers broke hard, in formation, and rolled in on the lead truck of the convoy, 20 millimeter cannon winking. There was a sudden fierce glare of fire.

"Got him," Ingley said shortly. "That corks the front. Let's get Tail-End Charlie."

The two jets tilted steeply into the high darkness above the falling flare, racked over almost inverted and came smoking down on a reverse course. Again their cannon stammered in the heavy, leisurely manner of 20 millimeter cannons, and the last truck in the convoy shuddered, heeled over on its side, and burst into flame.

"Call the Blue Tails!" Ingley told his wingman. "We got those jokers locked in now."

McGeorge got on his radio to the carrier *Constellation*, 100 miles away, making her standard racetrack pattern in the throat of the Gulf of Tonkin, giving the coordinates of the truck target;

Commander Dave Leue, boss of the Blue Tail Fly Squadron, sitting in the ready room, got the message, and his guys headed for their Skyhawks on the run; and in the same spread of seconds, Bud Ingley was coming in very low, directly over the column of trapped trucks, walking his 20 millimeter bullets from one end of it to the other. The black gap between the two burning end trucks lit up with the fury of fire fed by gasoline and ammo, and even as Leue's bombers were flung off the steam cats of the *Constellation* the light from the burning target became visible on the bridge of the carrier across 100 miles of ocean.

"We clobbered them that night," Bud Ingley said. "What we didn't have the ammo for, the Blue Tails did. And after the fire really got going, its light showed us an entire second convoy that had pulled off the road; they were trying to hide under some trees. When we found them, we hit them—and they went up in flames. I'd say we destroyed about 36 trucks that night. Conservatively. It might have been more."

This incident illustrates what goes on with the jets that fly off Yankee Station and that hit North Vietnam with about half the total number of strikes the United States directs against that battered country. (The Air Force out of Thailand and, to a small extent, out of Danang, accounts for the other half of the strikes.)

Yankee Station has had little or no publicity. Few people in the United States would know what you were talking about if you mentioned it. Yankee Station is not a siding in Back Bay, nor a rock 'n' roll radio station playing Colonial music. It's a position in the South China Sea about 100 miles northeast of Danang, where American aircraft carriers cruise around in a methodical pattern and launch and recover fighter and bomber airplanes that are hitting North Vietnam. Yankee Station is really a patch of ocean. But the jets that come from this patch of ocean are uniquely bothersome and deadly to the North Vietnamese. The first reason is that they work so close to shore that they are always within a few minutes' flying time from a hurry call to hit a target (the Air Force planes in Thailand are hundreds of miles and many minutes away). For example, when Bud Ingley and Glenn McGeorge found that convoy of trucks, they were able to call in the Blue Tail Fly Squadron and destroy them all in just a few minutes.

These Navy carriers (there are usually at least two or three working on Yankee Station simultaneously) are right on the North Vietnam doorstep, day and night. They have airtight security, since spies cannot infiltrate them (as they sometimes do in a shore base).

There are no problems about sailors getting local belles in trouble or busting up bars, since there are 100 miles of deep water between the crew and such temptations.

The carrier on Yankee Station is a mobile, privileged sanctuary. It can be replenished from home with whatever it needs to fight. It can go anywhere in the world on short notice. It is immune from sneak missile attacks, since it is always moving. No capricious foreign government can order it closed (as can happen to a land base). The carrier can control its food, water, health, and recreation very tightly. There are no mosquitoes to give you malaria. And because the carrier is isolated and there is really no recreation but "work," the crews "amuse" themselves by working an average of 15 hours a day. They stay "on the line" for 30 to 35 days and then take 10 days or two weeks off for repairs and rest and relaxation.

The air war waged by the carriers on Yankee Station is one of the most efficiently fought operations in the Vietnam conflict, and what is particularly interesting is this: Just a few years ago, people were screaming, "Junk those obsolete, vulnerable, impotent carriers in favor of ICBMs and long-range B-52s!"

That song has left the Top Ten! Navy aircraft carriers have now proved their worth in this Vietnam war—and their potential for any wars of a similar type that might erupt sometime in the foreseeable future. I spent 23 days aboard the USS *Constellation* during the summer of 1966, and now I would like to take the readers aboard this mighty ship and show you, close up and at first hand, how it really is to fly off a carrier in a high-performance jet.

The *Connie* is a seagoing airfield that can move around at thirty-five knots; houses more than five thousand officers, men and tech reps; can hurl jets off her four steam cats like shooting beans; carries enough power to flatten targets just as flat as the Strategic Air Command's massive intercontinental bombers and missiles; can launch and recover day or night in very lousy weather; has a flight deck of 4½ acres; carries dozens of planes—fighters, bombers, photo-recon, radar picket, on-board delivery and planeguard helicopters.

In a nutshell, this carrier and others like her are the most complex, dangerous, glamorous, and exciting weapons in the world. The labyrinth of passages, ladders, rooms, shafts, vents, and ducts is so complex that it would take one man months to set foot in every space on board—if, indeed, he could find them all. Men spend their entire tour of duty on a big carrier like the *Connie* without being familiar with anything but the tiny fraction of her interior that they must frequent in their jobs. There was actually a large room on the *Kitty Hawk* that had no doors at all. It was a great, hollow, black void for months before somebody cut a hatch in it and started using it!

There are all kinds of crazy things going on aboard a carrier. Would you believe that "jet-fuel bugs" grow in the tanks of JP-5 and must be carefully eliminated before the fuel is put in the planes, lest they cause the engine to stop in midair? Would you believe that Russian long-range jet bombers pay a visit to all American carriers in mid-ocean between Hawaii and Japan, and when the call "Snooper X!" goes out over the ship's command public-address system, we zap Phantom jets up there to fly within spitting distance of the Russians and escort them while they are in the area? I had expected hackles would bristle at a time like this. Not necessarily. Our guys have taken to holding up the latest *Playboy* foldout Play-mate of the Month in their cockpits for the Russians to admire from their bombers through binoculars! Maybe this kind of thing, and not diplomats in striped pants, is the avenue that will lead us to world peace. We'll overcome them with Playboy bunnies!

I sat in the Silver Fox Ready Room (A-4 Skyhawks led by U.S. Navy Commander Jim Morin, on the *Connie*) and watched movies with them as we steamed toward our combat station. The film fare was, it must be admitted, a bit dated. Groans, sounds of wonder, and suggestions of a fairly earthy sort were frequently heard above the whirring of the projector and the soundtrack of the film. If a man was particularly moved, he might take off his baseball cap and hurl it at the screen. Carrier pilots do not take themselves seriously. "Stay loose" is a general slogan on a carrier. If a man tended to tighten up on Yankee Station, he'd strip his emotional threads and crack up in a short time.

Frantic little situations of a life-or-death nature happen daily to carrier pilots. Commander Jim Morin was leading a Skyhawk raid over the delta of North Vietnam looking for mobile missile sites to destroy, when one of the men in his group, Lieutenant Paul Moore, took a .37 millimeter shell through his wing that blew a gaping hole in the wing tank and set jet fuel streaming back in a hissing white froth. Luckily, it didn't catch fire! Then a second shell smacked Moore's Skyhawk in the belly and severed a main fuel line, and the fuel pump, upstream of the break, was merrily pumping the precious stuff overboard like a fire hose. To top off his difficulties, Lieutenant Moore had just finished strafing an enemy stronghold, was down to 800 feet, and his engine flamed out.

"My main idea was to get as far away from there as I could," Paul Moore told me. "It isn't considered desirable to make a crash landing in the vicinity of folks you have just been strafing. They tend to be antisocial."

Moore must have been a fairly cool head, for he managed to get his jet engine restarted in midair as he settled like the well-known rock toward the boondocks. But he found himself with certain handicaps. The throttle had been jammed at 83 percent rpm—just enough to keep the airplane flying at around 200 knots— and it was 150 miles back to the carrier.

"I headed for the ocean," Moore said. "If you can reach the water before you jump out, your chances of being picked up by a destroyer or a helicopter are good. If you jump out over North Vietnam, forget it. Those little buddies ring the church bells when they see a chute blossom and everybody and his brother grabs a hoe and takes off after the foreign devils!"

Flying close to Paul Moore, Commander Morin summoned a Navy tanker plane that was orbiting on station high above the carrier. It came screaming down from the heights and got in line in front of Moore's now nearly fuelless Skyhawk. The problem was unique. Moore had no throttle, no speed brakes. He could not gradually ease up and jab his probe into the basket. If a hookup was to be made, the tanker *had to back into Moore!*

A third pilot, the executive officer of the squadron, now slid in alongside the tanker and the stricken jet and "talked the tanker back, inch by inch, until the connection was made." But trouble came almost instantly. Moore, flying at a steady 200 knots, was now about five knots faster than the "backing" tanker. He started to overrun it, jamming the drogue up at a 35-degree angle and moving fearsomely in for a low-speed collision.

"Speed up!" Moore shouted frantically to the tanker pilot. *"Speed up, goddammit!"*

The tanker goosed throttle and pulled free. Things were almost hopeless, but Moore tried again; and this time, thanks to the help of the exec in the plane off to the side, he made a hookup and began taking fuel. This was a day, however, when he couldn't do anything right. The added fuel made him heavier. The added weight made him slower. He couldn't get a single additional rpm above 83 per-cent. His speed sagged to 190 knots. This was too slow for the tanker—heavy with fuel—and the tanker had to pull away. Even then, Moore was in deep trouble. He had enough fuel to fly home, but not enough power to carry it and maintain altitude. Twenty miles short of a search-and-rescue (SAR) destroyer and with seventy-five feet of altitude and sinking, Moore took the only course left: he punched out. He got a good chute just above the surface, hit with a giant geyser of seawater and got trussed up like a Christmas turkey in his shroud lines.

"We carry an emergency hunting knife in a shoulder holder," Moore told me. "I got mine out. I shudder to think what would have happened if it had slipped out of my hands before I cut myself free of those shrouds."

Jim Morin called out a gaggle of Skyraiders to fly a Rescap (rescue combat air patrol) over the downed flyer, because this was Indian country. An enemy junk could have hurried over and captured Moore, without protection from the sky. Some time later, Moore was taken aboard a destroyer and returned to his carrier. It was all in the day's work. He was out flying raids again the next day, good as new—except, perhaps, for a couple of gray hairs he hadn't had before.

Now, for a moment, let's look at the big picture of operations on Yankee Station. The three big attack carriers often work as a team, and the planes from all three ships—more than 200 of them— go off in coordinated waves in strikes against a single target, sometimes going back time after time, for days, until that particular target is simply battered to a pile of dust and rubble.

On June 15, 1966, three carriers on Yankee Station, the *FDR*, the *Constellation*, and the *Oriskany*, working together, attacked the industrial complex around Than Hoa—railway yards, a thermal powerplant, oil supplies, flak sites, a massive concentration of North Vietnamese power—in continuous waves. All the various planes were used. The Phantom jets, which are doublesonic, went in first at terrific speed, firing rockets to suppress the flak. Following them came a "gang bang" of little Skyhawks, which screamed in at treetop level, pulled up, sighted the target, rolled in and bombed. They did it in a screeching melee, from all angles, making it very hard for the defending gunners to concentrate on any one plane. Then the Grumman A-6 Intruders, which look like pregnant bumblebees, but have the most deadly and sophisticated electronics bombing system in the world, lugged in loads of bombs (these funny-looking birds can carry 15,000 pounds of bombs in one load!) and pinpointed the big structures. The smoke and flame from this massive, continuous, hour-after-hour, day-after-day destruction raid could be seen for 100 miles in all directions. When it was over, the Than Hoa complex was simply leveled, finished!

Raids like this are undertaken, from time to time, when it is decided to eliminate a target for good and all. They are devastating. Their destruction would have to be seen to be believed. Dry-bones communiques detailing numbers of items hit and numbers of sorties flown simply do not tell the story at all. Yankee Station happens to be one of the most important offensive bases of operations in this whole war, and nobody even knows the place exists, except a few experts who follow these matters closely.

Having lived on the *Constellation* for many days, I got a fairly good idea of how she works and why she is such a deadly fighting machine. Two innovations make the carrier the efficient weapon she is: 1) the canted deck and 2) the steam catapult. In the good old days of the straight deck, it was necessary to raise a high barrier of powerful steel cables amidships, directly in front of landing planes. If a plane overshot the low arresting-gear wires or came aboard in some kind of difficulties, it wound up in the barrier, often burning brightly. Now it's different. The planes land at a small angle to the fore-and-aft line of the ship, on a so-called "angle deck." This deck is open at the end. If you can't make it, or if you miss the arresting wires, you simply add power and go around for another try. Also, with the canted deck, you can work planes much faster. As soon as they are down, they unhook and jazz their engines, taxiing out of the way. They couldn't do this on a straight deck. The barrier had to be lowered. They then taxied over it. Then it had to be raised again. All of which took time. It is possible to bring jets aboard safely every 40 seconds with a canted deck and a smooth-working team.

The steam catapult is important because it makes possible a much more rapid launch. The principle is quite simple. Enormous reservoirs of steam are stored up by the boilers. This steam is then released suddenly, in powerful surges, to fling a jet down the groove and off into the sky. There is no delay while pressure is built up. You've got the pressure on tap, ready for use. If the *Constellation*, for example, got word from one of its Super Fudd radar picket planes that there was an incoming raid of Communist jets, there would still be time to launch a strike of nearly all flyable planes on the ship before the raiders arrived to attack. There are four steam cats. Sometimes, when things are going well, two planes can be in the air off the cats simultaneously—bow and waist. You can clear the whole deck in an incredibly short time. In fact, one of these red-rush launches is about the noisiest, fiercest exhibition of man and machinery in action known in war.

A carrier launch or recovery, however, is a very tight operation, time-wise. In the words of a carrier pilot, "We have no fuel to fool." If there is an emergency on the deck and the air around the ship is full of "low-state" jets, things can get desperate—I mean that word literally—in a few minutes. The jets come back to the ship from strikes with just enough fuel for a couple of extra passes. There are, of course, tanker planes standing by for guys who have to get a drink immediately or ditch. And there is always the land field at Danang as an alternative. But even so, planes can run out of fuel and go in the water.

Life aboard the *Connie*, except for Flight Quarters, was confining and often boring to me. I turned into a chow hound like everybody else. I went down to the ship's store and bought pogie bait (candy) by the carton and dropped in about six times a day at the Fighter Pilots' Mess on the galley deck up forward. This mess is a place where you can go in your flight coveralls, your hair matted with sweat and not be thrown out (as opposed to the Senior Officers' Mess below the hangar deck aft, where you have to be in uniform). The food was plentiful, fattening, and superb. It was served by a bunch of Filipino boys, one of whom wore a red ribbon around his ear for some personal reason (nothing to do with Benny Boys; these kids were he-men) and he could fry an egg any way you wanted it to a lovely, golden perfection. There was an urn full of hot chocolate in the lounge and beside it, there was a huge container of heavy, doughy buns with sweet icing and raisins which I would munch on at odd hours. I began looking like Colonel Blimp in no time at all.

The guys I kind of pity on an aircraft carrier are the tech reps. They are the ones, often middle-aged, who stay on board for the nine months of the cruise to fix the complex electronics and other gadgetry that modern planes are fitted with. They sit at the table eating; they look glum and lonely—at least some of them. They share an overcrowded cabin with perhaps a bunch of wild young CPOs or ensigns who play rock 'n' roll half the night. They spend their working time studying through manuals, examining dials and ailing connections, and if the cotton-picking black boxes don't do what they are supposed to do, everybody and his brother bitches and screams at the tech rep. If the black boxes *do* perform well, the pilot comes back and says, "Well, I sure was on the money today!" I would rather be a tech rep than an elevator operator, but that is about as far as I will go.

I was interested in the moral issues of the war, and I noticed that the pilots were too. The *Connie* has a large library stocked with the latest books on Vietnam, and the pilots of the Skyhawk squadrons (Silver Foxes and Blue Tail Flies), with whom I spent most of my time, were toting these books around and reading them in their spare time. I think it is safe to say that, almost without exception, the pilots I talked to were heartily in favor of the war, felt no compunctions at all about bombing things in North Vietnam, and held the standard GI opinion: "We have to stop communism here—or face it later, closer to home." Considering the really grave danger they were facing in bombing North Vietnam, it would not have been easy for them to go into that flak storm holding any other views.

I experienced tragedy too on the *Constellation*. Commander Chuck Peters, a huge man of six feet four or more, weighing over 200 pounds, was the executive officer of the Silver Fox Squadron (who wore green baseball caps and green scarves). Chuck was courteous, brave, likeable in every way, and it was not surprising that he was known to his squadron mates as "The Jolly Green Giant." He had survived a crash landing in the ocean at night, when his plane hit at 218 knots, in what seems close to miraculous. The plane was badly smashed up and Chuck Peters was in it, stunned. He realized he was sinking. His ankle was broken and he was badly shaken, but he did what anybody who has ever tried to get out of a torso harness dry, standing up in a lighted room, will tell you is almost superhuman. He got out of that tight webbing with those fiendish metal buckles while he was under water—and he fought his way out of the cockpit and swam up to the surface. All his survival gear was attached to the torso harness, so he lost it. Luckily for him, one of the wing tanks was empty. It ripped off when the plane hit the water and was floating nearby. Chuck grabbed hold of it and held on in the darkness. At one point, he told me, "Something came up behind me and nibbled on my ass. It felt like something big—but not hungry. And I guess it wasn't, because it went away." Six hours later, he was rescued by a destroyer.

Commander Jim Morin left the *Constellation* on June 30, 1966, and Commander Chuck Peters took over as CO of the squadron the next day, July 1. Coming back from a strike over North Vietnam, when he was nearly over the ocean, Peters took a heavy hit on his Skyhawk. The plane began to burn. He stayed with it, trying to get away from the shore guns. Then it began to go out of control.

"I'm ejecting!" Peters radioed.

He passed over a Communist-held island. The plane now began

to somersault, end over end, a mass of fire. He ejected and his parachute blossomed. As he drifted toward the water, his squadron mates screamed around him like angry hawks ready to gun down anybody who tried to fire at him. Then the parachute hit the sea—but Chuck did not fight free this time. He must either have been dead or unconscious. He sank from sight. His loss was a sad thing. He was one of the Navy's finest.

Before I close this piece, I would like to pay my respects to Captain Bill Houser, who was skipper of the *Connie* when I was aboard and who was my genial host. Bill Houser didn't look like the captain. He looked like the commander of the air group. He was tall, lean, fit-looking—the kind of a guy who'd beat your eyebrows off at handball any Tuesday. His pomposity quotient was zero. When he talked to the crew after a serious accident or important event, he held it to the facts, spoke in a businesslike but friendly way, and then shut up.

When we put in at Yokosuka, Japan, for fuel and repairs, before going into combat, Captain Houser turned the crew loose ashore with his blessing to whoop it up. Each division had its own party. Captain Houser was invited to them all. He went to them all. I went along to one of them and we arrived when the boys were on their seventeenth beer apiece. A big old chief hit me on the back in a friendly way and I thought he'd broken a vertebra. Then he shoved a beer in my hand and roared for me to drink it. Gasping slightly, I did.

Then they brought in the lovely Chinese strip-teaser. She wore high-heeled blue sandals, a kind of glittery medallion at a crucial point, and *nada mas*. A hurried and excited consultation was held with her, and she was seen to smile warmly and nod her assent. Then she came forward—rather demurely, I thought, for a stripper—grasped my old head firmly in her dainty little hands, thrust it between her naked breasts and shook them gently and warmly against my ears. The sound of approval was awesome in the room. Then she did the same to Captain Houser. A less sophisticated man might have stood on his dignity or ducked around coyly. The captain took it with smiling aplomb, and the cheers shook the whisky bottles behind the bar.

Then the captain was called upon to make a speech and what he said was classic. "Your beer is fine," he said. "Your hostess is even better." (Wild hoots of approval.) "I have only one thing to say to you. When we get out at sea in combat and any of you want to talk to me about anything—you know where my office is. I don't keep the door locked." This is exactly the way to talk to sailors with (or without) 17 beers.

A few days later, when I was standing in Primary Flight Control with the air boss and Captain Houser, we spied "Sweet Willie" Williams waving one of his large fists in a typical explanatory motion under the nose of one of the other Red Shirts. He was wearing the red cloth helmet with a radio transceiver in it, as the key men do on a flight deck.

Ken Enny, the air boss, picked up his mike, and said, "Hey, Willie. What's the trouble?"

Williams knew Ken's voice, of course, and he stared up at us with his hot, brown glare. "Nothing, Commander!" he said.

"I've got the captain here with me," Enny said. "I don't want you to screw up while he's watching."

Sweet Willie's burning stare shifted to the skipper and his voice boomed in over the wall speaker: "Tell that old rate-grabber we're onto him," he said. "We know he's eager as a bride on the wedding night—but give him my congratulations anyhow."

I was a junior-grade lieutenant in the Navy at one time and I would have never dreamed of calling my skipper a rate-grabber. I took a deep breath, wondering what Captain Houser would do.

He picked up Ken Enny's hand mike and said, "Thanks, Willie. I appreciate those good wishes."

I learned, then, what it was all about. Captain Houser had just been elevated to admiral by the powers in the Navy Department and would move onward and upward to take over duties as chief of strategic planning for the Navy in the months to come. That was what Willie meant by "rate grabber."

I had my first contact with the Navy's side of the out-country war in Yokosuka, Japan. This was when *Constellation* was on her way to Dixie Station from Pearl Harbor. We had put into Yokosuka for fuel and last-minute precombat maintenance. *Constellation's* sister carrier, *Kitty Hawk*, was also at Yokosuka. She had just come off the line at Yankee Station, where her air group had been hit very hard. The purpose of the conferences was to point out mistakes that had been made—and try to prevent them from happening again. There had been heavy losses of RA-5C Vigilantes, shot down on recon missions. The *Connie* Vigilante pilots, as a result of the talks, decided to fly a very cool profile—"Not risking those big seventeen-million-dollar birds for a twenty-five cent target," was the way one old pro phrased it. There are times when risks must be taken, but there are also times when it is better to skirt a place and leave it for a "gang bang" (a wild pounce by a bunch of free-firing, free-dropping Skyhawks).

"In any mission," Commander Charlie Smith, boss of *Constellation*'s Vigilantes, said to me, "you get out of it what you put into it. I know that's obvious. But people sometimes forget it. I mean this. If you study every scrap of information available on the target you are after, and check with the latest reports from guys who've been over there, and then you study the terrain and the deployment of the defenses as best you know them, you can plan a safer show. And you can bring back better pictures. In our business you don't flap a red scarf around your neck, rush down, kick the tire, and light the fire. Not if you want to come home with the good stuff."

At the time *Kitty Hawk* had been on Yankee Station, the Navy was still in the process of learning the deadly lessons of the SAMs (Russian made antiaircraft missiles). They were finding out that you were safer if you stayed under the SAM envelope (below 3,000 feet) but that when you did that, you opened yourself up to ground fire from automatic weapons. Hence you not only had to stay very low but ride behind the ridgelines too. Or else you had to jink, and the RA-5C jinks "majestically"—which is not the safest way to jink.

One of *Kitty Hawk*'s A-6 Intruder pilots, Lieutenant Bill Westerman, was shot down in a freakish manner. Westerman and his bomber-navigator (BN), Brian Westin, were out on a napalm run over North Vietnam. (Why was his sophisticated bird being used to drop napalm on hootch lines? I don't know, but I think it had something to do with the bomb shortage.) At any rate, a farmer standing in a field shot Bill Westerman in the left shoulder with a rifle. This was the only hit the plane sustained. "I instinctively pulled back on the stick," Lieutenant Westerman said. "Brian said I was getting too high, up in the SAM envelope. I was feeling nauseous. Things began to go dark. Brian took over by reaching across me (the pilot and BN sit side by side in an A-6) and turned us toward the sea. He flew it and at the same time he managed to get out a two-ounce bottle of brandy we carry for emergencies. I drank that and felt a little better."

But Westerman was bleeding, and shock was setting in. He was alternately losing and regaining consciousness, coming in and out of the dark. Accompanying the stricken plane was Commander R. J. Hayes, the third commanding officer the A-6 outfit had had in six months. About thirty miles offshore it became evident that Westerman would not be able to fly the plane aboard. Though Westin, the BN, could maintain level flight, he could not perform the complex task of making a carrier landing, which is tricky business even for a seasoned pilot. The decision was made for Westerman and Westin to bail out while Hayes circled overhead. It is normal practice for the pilot to bail out last, but Westin wasn't taking any chances on Westerman blacking out after he, Westin, had jumped. He insisted that Westerman go out first, which Westerman did.

Westin then punched out and was picked up, after firing a flare, by a rescue chopper. Westin directed the pilot to the spot where he thought his injured buddy might be floating, and they sighted him. He had become separated from his life raft. They settled low. Westerman looked up and smiled but he was obviously exhausted. The helo crew dropped the sling. But the violent turbulence of the whirling rotors washed so powerfully down on the wounded pilot that he could not help himself readily. Brian Westin grabbed an old-fashioned Mae West (he'd already taken off his own Mark 3 Charlie flotation gear and torso harness) and was lowered by the sling to help his buddy. Working under such conditions requires an unusual amount of effort due to the sea motion, the fact that the gear is soaked, and the general fury of the downwash whipping everything to a foam in front of your face. After some trouble, Westin got the pilot hooked up properly and saw him lifted safely to the rescue helicopter.

Meanwhile, the rescuer—Brian Westin—was in trouble. He'd put on the old Mae West improperly in his hurry. When it inflated, instead of holding his face out of the water as it was designed to do, it was forcing his face under the waves. "I tried to get into a makeshift sling they had lowered to me," Westin said. "For a few minutes I was suffocating and about to drown. I think I almost gave up. But finally I managed to blow up my anti-G suit—and with it and the Mae West to support me, I waved the helo off to take Bill to medical aid. The secondary sling was too small for me to fit into."

Westin wanted his buddy to get to medical aid before he lost too much blood. The helo dropped a smoke flare to mark the spot and took off. Five minutes later (the longest of his life, Westin felt) another helo arrived with the right kind of sling. They took him aboard. After they hauled him up, a crewman pointed to the water at something. He said it was a shark. Westin never saw it. For his part of the rescue of the wounded pilot, Westin received the Navy Cross.

The air war has, of course, been escalating. Rivers in the North have been mined by Navy P2V Neptune bombers so that traffic—

both war goods and civilian goods—will be hampered and the economy slowed down. Navy ships have been bombarding the shores of North Vietnam and 175 millimeter long-range cannon have been firing into North Vietnam across the Demilitarized Zone. The new steel mill north of Hanoi—the pride and joy of the North Vietnamese—has been heavily bombed. It was one of the most important industrial innovations since Ho Chi Minh came to power. There has been talk of mining or bombing Haiphong harbor, to deny this key port to Russian ships arriving with war supplies. But opponents of this idea have pointed out the danger of drawing Russia into the war on a massive scale if this is done—and they have stated too that the loss of the harbor might not stop the supplies anyhow. They could be offloaded onto beaches, using small craft, as has already been done by both sides successfully in the past.

The North Vietnamese have made every effort to counter our bombing by dispersal of their oil in 55-gallon drums spaced at intervals along back roads, and have also stored them in bomb craters. We have bombed and strafed these dispersed stores of oil with considerable success—particularly the drums stored in craters, which have been ignited by dive bombing and strafing with 20 millimeter cannon.

The North Vietnamese are reported to be trying very hard to get the Soviet Union to send them SA-3 Guideline missiles to replace the SA-2s now deployed there. If this should take place it could be extremely serious. The SA-2s are the SAMs that have been used without much effectiveness against our planes heretofore. They are not as sophisticated as the new super SAMs, so to speak, the SA-3s—which have longer range, more sophisticated guidance, and are much more difficult to avoid. There has been increasing pressure in Congress, by Senator Stewart Symington, for one, to bomb the airfields in North Vietnam—to knock out the MiG-21s that have been increasingly active lately—but our high command has been slow to do this. Perhaps on the theory that if we knock out the MiGs the Soviets may just decide to send those new super SAMs as a further escalation of the war.

Our B-52s are now flying bombing missions out of the recently completed superbase (11,500-foot runways) on the Gulf of Siam near Sattahip—just one hour from their targets, as compared with a 12-hour round-trip mission out of Guam. A program is under way to replace the F-105 fighter-bombers with twin-jet F-4s for the runs against North Vietnam targets. The F-105s have suffered heavily and are, in fact, going to be in short supply eventually—so the substitution of the faster F-4 Phantoms is really looking ahead; it's an attempt to make the replacement in an orderly fashion rather than on a crash basis.

American ingenuity has made an urgent attempt to outwit the attacks on our fighter bombers by North Vietnamese surface-to-air-missiles. Special planes fitted with countermeasure gear have been sent along with the fighter-bombers to "fake out" the ground guidance systems of the SAM sites. This little caper, known as "Wild Weasel," has been only partly effective. The North Vietnamese missile men have, in their turn, been playing games with the Wild Weasel planes, trying (and sometimes succeeding) in faking *them* out. Another electronic countermeasure (ECM) plane has been the Douglas RB-66, which has been used to pave the way for bombing planes by going in first and screwing up the acquisition radars of the ground missile sites.

In the meantime, the smaller Lockheed F-104 Starfighters—known as "the razorblade on a pregnant hatpin" because of its needlelike fuselage and tiny seven-foot wings (so sharp they cut like a dull butcher knife if you run your finger along the leading edge)—have been used to strike at Communist Pathet Lao activities in nearby Laos out of their Thailand base at Udon. The C-130 Hercules propjets—fitted with seven rapid-firing machine guns pointing out the side and also beefed up with armor plate—are also flying out of Udon-Thani against targets in Laos. This is known as the AC-130 and is a kind of Magic Dragon—faster than the old DC-3 Dragon Ship of the Mekong Delta, but not having the rotating Gatling guns.

For a long time we did not admit that we were using Thailand as a base from which to attack North Vietnam. Now the lid is off. We have openly stated that our planes are coming from Thailand and will continue to come from there. The tension is increasing almost daily. How far it will go is anybody's guess. President Johnson is under great pressure to bring the North Vietnamese to the conference table before reelection time comes around. The military people are strongly urging him to give them more and bigger targets "to smash them flat and get it over."

Vietnam: The Search for Lieutenant Elkins

Marilyn Elkins

T hose who do the fighting are not the only heroes in modern war. Bravery is also called upon from wives, mothers, and other kin.

A special test of endurance is reserved for the loved ones of the MIAs—those servicemen listed as "missing in action" whose fate is unknown.

In the United States, the numbers of MIAs has been fairly well documented. In World War I, there were 2,913; in World War II, nearly 79,000; in Korea, 8,200; and in Vietnam, 2,273.

None of their survivors can have demonstrated greater courage and persistence than Marilyn Elkins, now an assistant professor of English at California State University at Los Angeles. Lieutenant Elkins's diary The Heart of a Man, which Mrs. Elkins edited, was published by the Naval Institute Press in 1991.

Compared to the numbers of American MIAs from earlier wars, the 2,273 listed from Vietnam seem almost insignificant. The number in relation to the total killed—4 percent—also pales compared to the figures for some earlier wars: 5.5 percent in World War I; 27 percent in World War II; and 15.1 percent in Korea. It is an insignificant number of people, that is, unless you happen to be related to one of them.

Few of their wives or other family members were prepared for the length of time these servicemen would be listed as either POWs or MIAs; no American soldiers had ever officially been held for more than three and a half years. While the law provides that a person who has been missing for seven years can be presumed dead, this does not apply to MIAs during a time of war. Americans had never fought in such a long war, and no military policy had been established for such an event. A majority of the MIAs in Vietnam were pilots—America's best and brightest. Exceptional athletes, intellects, and aviators, they had seemed invulnerable. They had not been expected to fall prey to a small, Asian enemy.

Certainly I thought my husband, U.S. Navy Lieutenant Frank Callihan Elkins, was immune to MiGs and SAMs. Married for only nine months, he was twenty-seven and I was twenty-two when his A-4 Skyhawk disappeared during a flight from its vessel, the USS *Oriskany*. I still believed that death was for other people. When I received the notification on October 13, 1966, I had just returned from spending two weeks with Frank in the Philippines and Hong Kong. He had December orders to a test squadron in China Lake, California; I was residing with my parents while I waited out his Vietnam tour. When the casualty assistance officer arrived, I answered the doorbell in a blue floral housecoat, half-awake and half-smiling: I knew that this man would be embarrassed when he learned he had delivered his message to the wrong wife.

The officer told me that Frank had been killed. After making a telephone call to report that he had delivered his message, he returned to say that he had misunderstood the original communication: Frank was only missing. Eager to see this as portentous, I interpreted the whole episode as additional proof that Frank was invulnerable.

Because Frank's father had a serious heart condition, I immediately contacted my brother-in-law and asked him to break the news to his parents. I didn't want them to receive the same misinformation I had. I could not cry but was shiveringly cold, despite the numerous quilts my parents wrapped around me. I seemed to be watching myself participate in conversations, observing these events as though they were happening to someone else.

While official policy demanded that such news be delivered in person by an officer of equal or higher rank, practice—as in my case—sometimes fell short of the ideal. No matter how it bungled the delivery of such news, the Pentagon assumed that families of MIAs in the Vietnam War would maintain the official expected silence—the traditional stiff upper lip that guaranteed a husband's continued military success—as they had done in past wars.

The Korean War was the first one in which the behavior of POWs under stress had been blamed on the prisoners rather than on their captors. Suspected of conspiring with the enemy and succumbing to Communist brainwashing (this was during the McCarthy era), the Korean POW became a symbol of national dishonor, although the number of Americans who chose not to return—twenty-one—was small when compared to the 88,000 Chinese and North Korean prisoners who refused repatriation (more than half of those who fell into American hands).

Consequently, the U.S. military code of conduct used in the 1960s insisted that a captive conduct himself as a fighting man rather than as a powerless prisoner. The code was designed to produce soldiers who could resist torture, remain silent, and attempt escape against overwhelming odds and under brutal conditions. As part of this doctrine, pilots who were being prepared to fly over Vietnam were sent to a weeklong survival school in which they were beaten, forced to curl up in a tiny black box for hours, and verbally assaulted if they failed to escape from their "captors." When he returned from this week of "captivity" in March 1966, Frank had bruises on most of his body and slept for a full 24 hours from exhaustion. While many of the simulations were classified and therefore not subjects he could discuss, he confided that he had found the solitary confinement most difficult. To occupy his mind during these seemingly endless episodes, Frank had imagined happy scenes from his childhood and of his return home.

I soon found that equal stoicism was expected of military wives. The official policy was to give us as little information as possible so that we could not harm our husbands with any indiscretion. The government ensured our silence through effective manipulation of our concern for our husbands' safety. The Navy's telegrams and other communications insisted that because my husband might be "held by hostile force against his will," "for his safety" I should reply to inquiries from outside sources by revealing "only his name, rank, file number, and date of birth." These were exactly the orders given to Frank during his survival training.

Determined not to compromise him in any way, I began a period of intense, silent waiting. My own needs for comforting were subordinated to government policy which, for most of the period of 1966–68, insisted that secrecy was in the MIAs' best interest. Designed to protect national policy without considering their effect on family members, the government's instructions did not include tips on how to survive this silent vigil. No one suggested that I might find psychological counseling helpful. No one offered to explain what Frank's chances for survival might be. No one offered suggestions as to what I should do—except wait in silence. Treatment of MIA wives during the recent Persian Gulf War seems to indicate that this atavistic attitude toward the exigencies of military wives remains relatively unchanged—even though American soldiers now are instructed to give transparently false "confessions," rather than simply remain silent, if they are captured.

I was left in the hands of whatever emotional support I could find—primarily a group of navy wives who generously called me from their homes in California to extend what comfort they could spare from their concern about their own husbands. I now realize how emotionally costly this solace must have been; surely I must have reminded these women that their husbands could suffer Frank's fate at any moment. No wonder they sometimes presented me with unfounded rumors and speculations.

Except for my cousin Shirley, whose husband was also a pilot on the USS *Oriskany*, no one in my immediate family or community knew what to say or do. My parents live on a farm in rural Tennessee; the nearest town, Pikeville, has a population of about 1,000 people. I soon found that even though I had remained silent, most of these people knew about my husband's status and wanted to help. However, no one had provided any of us with a script for appropriate behavior. I couldn't understand why people kept arriving with casseroles, pies, and cakes—rural custom following a death. On the other hand, a friend of my father's who had been a POW in World War II returned home after everyone but his immediate family had given up hope; Clint's experiences, known by everyone in our community, became the repeated "evidence" they could offer that Frank would survive.

But I needed no assurance of that. Within a few weeks I insisted that my father install another telephone line so that I could be reached immediately when Frank came tap-dancing out of the jungle. I was certain that my teenage brothers' constant conversations were responsible for the delay in news about Frank.

On October 26, 1966, fire broke out on the USS *Oriskany*, and many of Frank's friends were killed. One friend, Bill Johnson, had already sent me Frank's diary, which I carefully stored away for Frank; he had kept it with the intention of writing a novel about his Vietnam experience. Bill was killed in the fire, before he could ship the rest of Frank's gear. When the Navy finally forwarded Frank's belongings, many items—including the typewriter I had given him and a surprise Christmas gift that I knew he had purchased for me in Hong Kong—were missing. The Navy was unhelpful in retrieving these items, which I had embroidered with sentimental significance.

By December I had become accustomed to the fact that my presence often made other people uncomfortable, I had lost twenty pounds, and had nearly perfected the role of zombie. I remained intent, however, on fooling myself: I was convinced that I was helping Frank by staring at my special phone, willing it to ring. Finally, my first bout with Crohn's disease, a chronic ailment that is exacerbated by stress, forced me to spend Christmas week in the hospital. My doctor convinced me that I might die if I continued to do nothing but wait. Even I knew my death wouldn't help Frank.

So I decided to get on with plans we had made prior to his disappearance. We both had wanted to become English professors, and I took my first step toward that goal by enrolling in graduate school. A large number of other MIA wives also earned degrees while they waited for their husbands' return. Initially we were not entitled to benefits mandated by the GI Bill because we weren't widows, and we were not allowed to collect our husbands' full salaries; the Defense Department required that a percentage be held in savings. Eventually, when the length of time men were listed as MIA continued beyond that of earlier wars, wives who persisted were given full benefits. But I did not apply because neither my casualty assistance officer nor my monthly updates from the Navy informed me that I was eligible. Instead I held part-time jobs to finance my studies.

I was still under government orders not to reveal my husband's status, and so when I was asked about the wedding ring I wore, I'd reply, "My husband's in Vietnam." I often didn't like the immediate response that statement received: an almost instantaneous look of pity, or, rarely, a diatribe about how reprehensible U.S. activities in Vietnam were.

Within a year of Frank's disappearance, the government negotiated with the North Vietnamese to allow wives to send letters
and, eventually, packages to their missing husbands. Soon, Navy
communiqués detailed what could be included in the monthly letters
(good news and cheer) and what could not (the war or any other
bad news). Last year the Navy returned one of my letters; it had
"been found" in materials that they received from the North Vietnamese. Speaking encouragingly about Frank's family and my continuing education, the letter closes with this:

> What else can I say? I love you and am here waiting. And
> will be. I do live chiefly by longing, cherishing our past, trusting
> in our future, but I endure. I keep a thousand experiences to
> share with you; buy records I know you'll want to hear, books
> you'll want to read, and clothes I think you'll like. You are the
> controlling force in my life. I hope you are able to have me
> with you as much as I have you here. Oh, Frank, I love you so
> much! I pray I can be worthy of such love.

Rereading these words today, I am embarrassed by how closely they
follow Navy guidelines. Had he received this letter, I suspect Frank
might have found it disconcerting. To anyone who knows my independent nature, it sounds as artificial as the deliberately staged
confessions of captured American fliers during the recent Persian
Gulf War. Coming from someone who, prior to her marriage, had
negotiated an agreement that she didn't have to be the kind of
military wife who held squadron teas and luncheons and would be
free to pursue a career, this letter sounds suspect. But it illustrates
just how fully I had adopted the official government role.

Whenever the government's rules changed, I followed the new
orders. Every two months I could send Frank a six-and-a-half-pound
package. Suggested contents included toothpaste, playing cards,
vitamins, socks, underwear, soap, canned meat, bouillon cubes, raisins, candy, cheeses, and photographs. I remember how apprehen-
sive I was the first time I also included cigars, an item not mentioned
on the list.

About once a month I received a letter that detailed any changes
of policy. With each letter, the government's insistence on silence
about MIAs grew increasingly irritating. Why couldn't I talk about
my husband? Why was I being treated as though Frank and I had
done something shameful? And although I had been asked to remain
silent, information about me was being used by politicians. Many
of them were not interested in Frank's fate or mine so much as in

furthering their careers. My local congressman, Bill Brock, told a story in his local campaign speeches about my asking him for help (which, following Navy guidelines, I had stressed should remain confidential); he colored both my request and the possibility of what he could do to appeal to local voters.

In 1969 I joined the National League of Families of American Prisoners and Missing in Southeast Asia—an organization founded by the families, but fundamentally upholding government policy and receiving government support and encouragement. The league's primary spokeswoman was Sybl Stockdale, the wife of Commander James Stockdale, who was a frequently photographed prisoner and had been the commander of the first air wing of the USS *Oriskany*. She supported the government's argument that we must win the war to free the prisoners. Angered by my congressman's actions, I had written to Allard Lowenstein, the congressman who started the dump-Johnson campaign and who had been a mentor of Frank's at the University of North Carolina, asking for his help and suggestions. I tried to arrange a meeting between Lowenstein and Stockdale, but she refused to cooperate because of his antiwar stance. I have always suspected that her actions were being dictated by government policy, but I have no way of knowing how much official advice she received or followed.

I often resented the rhetoric of war protesters as well. The *Saturday Review* published a letter from a writer who called the first prisoners released by the North Vietnamese in 1969 "obscene biological charades" who wear their uniforms like "the skin of a predator." I responded with a letter of my own, which the magazine also printed. Yet I continued to talk to people like Cora Weiss, cochair of the left-wing Committee of Liaison, whom I asked for help in establishing communications with the North Vietnamese.

From these disparate sources I tried to piece together a realistic picture, one that would allow me to act in Frank's interest. It became clear to me that the MIA/POW issue was being presented as an excuse to continue an otherwise unpopular war; the missing were being used to justify our increased bombing. Repeatedly calling attention to Hanoi's refusal to abide by the Geneva Convention, President Nixon's speeches included his promise to continue the U.S. presence in Southeast Asia "until the prisoners of war are freed."

Al Lowenstein suggested that my going public might actually help Frank, rather than harm him. He put me in touch with John Siegenthaler, the editor of the *Nashville Tennessean*. (By this time I had moved to Nashville and enrolled at Vanderbilt University in another master's degree program.) Siegenthaler sent Kathy Sawyer to interview me, and she wrote a story that the paper timed to appear on the third anniversary of Frank's disappearance.

The government did not object. For reasons never clearly stated, its policy had changed. After the release of the first three prisoners in 1969, the word went out through our monthly newsletters from the military, through our casualty assistance officers, and through the National League of Families that now we could take our suffering to the public. At league meetings we were asked to conduct letter-writing campaigns to show the Vietnamese what the people in the villages of America thought of their treatment of prisoners. Businessman H. Ross Perot spoke at these meetings, garnering support for his attempts to take food and supplies to the prisoners. The Pentagon encouraged us to woo the media to mobilize world opinion against the North Vietnamese. In an international contest for moral approval and goodwill, our government started calling attention to North Vietnam's refusal to follow the rules of the Geneva Convention.

Kathy's well-written, sensitive articles received a lot of attention, and many of my fellow graduate students seemed shocked to learn that my husband was an MIA. Generally, they were kind and supportive. But I received a number of phone calls from heavy breathers who offered to help me out with my sex life, and others who offered to find Frank for me using a variety of methods that ranged from witchcraft to prayer. When I was interviewed on local television and radio shows, I was surprised by the questions some interviewers and callers asked. They seemed more interested in knowing intimate details about my life than in learning about the MIA situation. Many people just wanted me to look pretty, vulnerable, and sad; they certainly didn't want me to have a political opinion. Privately, I had felt for some time that the war was wrong—both morally and practically—but I hesitated to express these sentiments because I feared such remarks might have serious repercussions for Frank, or might be used as propaganda tactics against other POWs. So I remained officially silent about my doubts.

In the spring of 1970, encouraged by both our government and the trips other wives had made, I went to Paris. Calling at the North Vietnamese Consulate at 2 rue le Verrier, the two translators I had found through the American Embassy and I were greeted civilly and allowed to enter. But a Vietnamese gentleman, who never told me his name, insisted that we should "ask President Nixon" about my husband's whereabouts, and he asked us to leave.

I was struck by the contrast between the elegance of the American Embassy and the shabbiness of the North Vietnamese Consulate. This was my first encounter with Vietnamese people, and I was also humbled by their small physical stature. By comparison, I felt Brobdingnagian, insensitive, and clumsy. The difference in our size seemed, somehow, a metaphor for the war in which America's superior numbers and strength were becoming liabilities.

When I returned to the States, I continued to criticize Hanoi's policy concerning prisoners. But often my speeches, and those of other wives of MIAs, were used for other political purposes. (In fact the number of MIAs itself was, from the beginning, a highly politicized question. A recent article in the *Atlantic Monthly* claims that of the 2,273 servicemen listed today, the Defense Department has recognized 1,101 as killed in action, since the time of their disappearance. This marks the first time in American military history that registered KIAs were added to the MIA figures.) At a Veterans of Foreign Wars meeting, when the local commander suggested that he and members of the audience should "go over to Arkansas and whip Fulbright's ass for this little lady and her husband," I announced that I was not present to support the continuance of the war in Vietnam or to attack those people who opposed it; I had come only to express my concern about the prisoners. My audience became quiet and unresponsive. No one spoke to me afterward.

The National League of Families meeting held in Washington in July 1970 crystallized my decision to pursue my own course and ignore the one our government was dictating. When Vice President Spiro Agnew made an appearance to address the members, I didn't stand; the rather stout woman beside me started tapping me on the shoulder with her handbag, increasing the force with each tap. At last I stood up, and left—both the meeting and the organization. I had had it with everyone's political agenda. I wanted no part of a group whose allegiance precluded questioning such leaders as Nixon and Agnew.

By this time President Nixon, Defense Secretary Melvin Laird, and other administration officials had escalated the frequency of their claims that we must remain in Southeast Asia to ensure the release of American POWs. The Navy was not happy with my public statements that the "identification, treatment, and release of prisoners should be handled as a separate issue."

In March 1971 I decided to move to Paris and make daily visits to the North Vietnamese Consulate, vowing to stay until they told me something about Frank's status. Before my departure the Navy sent an official to caution me about my action and about any statements that I might make: "The foreign press may misinterpret your remarks if you say anything critical about the war, and you don't want your husband to be hurt by your carelessness." He also advised me to watch out for suspicious people who might want to kidnap me.

So commenced a series of days in Paris that always began with a trip to the North Vietnamese Consulate. The French police guarding the consulate would often nudge each other and say, "C'est la femme. Encore, eh?" Usually, a Frenchwoman of about forty-five with blue-black hair and bright red lips, dressed in a white blouse and black skirt, would come to the door demanding in French, "Who's there? What do you want?" I would respond, "It's Madame Elkins. I would like to ask you about my husband." Her "We can't give you any information; go away!" would follow.

Over 200 relatives of MIA/POWs had already come knocking on this door, but I was the first to make it a daily activity. If I knew foreign visitors were likely to be present at the consulate, I would try to time my visit to coincide—making an effort to embarrass the North Vietnamese. Occasionally I would be given admittance and admonished to "go home and tell President Nixon to stop bombing our country. Then you'll get your answer." Sometimes members of the North Vietnamese delegation would yell at me and criticize American bombing; at other times they would apologize and look genuinely moved by my request.

Once I asked the secretary, directly, if Frank was dead. Lowering her eyes, she replied, "Oui." But she would provide me with no additional information. I explained that it would be to her advantage to give me all the information she had on all the men so that President Nixon would have fewer names to use as an excuse for keeping our troops in Vietnam, but she refused. Eventually she began greeting me with "Bonjour, Madame Elkins," but I never obtained the audience I requested with Delegate General Vo Van Sung.

Sometimes I tried to get the secretary to pass him copies of articles that Kathy Sawyer had written about me for the *Tennessean*, notes explaining my position and my plans to return every day, and cards with my address and phone number. Occasionally the secretary would give me pamphlets that restated her instructions to me in English. The details changed, but these conversations always ended with my standing in the shadows before a closed door and saying, "A demain."

Because I had great sympathy and respect for these people, this adversarial role was especially stressful for me. I certainly couldn't blame the North Vietnamese for shooting down Frank's plane when he had been bombing their country. Sometimes I would run into members of the delegation in shops. If I spoke, they usually refused to acknowledge me. I suspect they feared I was a little crazy. Perhaps I was.

Other wives of MIAs or POWs would arrive for short stays in Paris, and I would sometimes accompany them to make their requests. After almost three months, the North Vietnamese delegation must have realized that I was there to stay. They finally admitted me and told me that Frank was dead. But when I asked them to put the information in writing, they refused, saying that all the other wives would then come to Paris and harass them.

By March 1971 the North Vietnamese had begun returning letters addressed to men whose names were not included on the official POW list released to Senator Edward M. Kennedy in December 1970. Stamped "KUONG NGUOI NAHAN TRALAI" (this person unknown), my returned letters seemed more official than any information I had received from American sources about Frank. The Defense Department suggested that North Vietnam was reinforcing its contention that the list was complete and final, but insisted that our government would not accept letter or package returns as evidence of the fate of MIAs. Frank Sieverts, an assistant to the secretary of state, maintained that the men's status would not be changed without concrete proof.

My wait for news about Frank continued, and remaining in Paris was more comfortable than returning home. I was relieved to be anonymous, free from people who asked about my husband's status:

"Have you heard anything yet?"

"No."

"Guess you never will, huh? Bless your heart. It's such a pity."

Though well-intentioned, such remarks—sometimes coming from the mouths of complete strangers—always left me fighting back tears. I was also tired of the either–or stance that everyone seemed to insist upon when discussing the war. Simultaneously caring about my husband's return and wanting our troops to withdraw did not seem incongruous to me. I was amazed at how angry hawks could become when I refused to denounce the North Vietnamese, and at how upset doves became when I wouldn't criticize the men who were fighting.

But I had begun to realize that Frank might not return, and I began editing his diary for publication—an act I had not attempted earlier because I believed he would use it himself, as the basis for a novel. Publishing his diary now seemed my responsibility. Editing his writings during 1972, I thought I had finally achieved some catharsis. I hoped that writing its prologue had also provided me with closure. When the book was published in the fall of 1973, I returned to the United States to push its sales—and discovered that the public that had once seemed so eager to know about the war had become largely apathetic. They did not want to be reminded of our national defeat.

Almost a year after the return of the 591 POWs in early 1973, I left Paris for San Francisco. Feeling that I had done all I could to ascertain Frank's fate, I hoped the government would now assume its responsibility for finding him. After all, it had promised to bring him home when the war was over.

Once the war ended, however, public interest in the MIA issue also ended. After the prisoners returned, leadership of the National League of Families shifted from wives to other family members of MIAs. E. H. Mills, the father of Lieutenant Commander James Mills (shot down on September 21, 1966), became the director in 1973, and he was eventually succeeded by his daughter Ann Mills Griffiths. Her 14-year reign has produced various critics and at least one splinter group, directed by Dolores Alfond, who insists that Griffiths has responded less to the needs of the families than to those of the government. Many MIA family members now echo my earlier suspicions that the league is basically a government organization. (During the Nixon administration, its long-distance telephone bill was paid out of White House funds.) In February 1991, Colonel Millard Peck, a highly decorated veteran, quit his post as chief of the POW/MIA unit of the Defense Intelligence Agency, contending that the official government "mind-set to debunk" evidence of live MIAs is encouraged by Griffiths, whom he describes as "adamantly opposed to any initiative to actually get to the heart of the problem." He accused Griffiths of sabotaging POW/MIA investigations.

During the mid-1970s the league did little to slow down the speed with which the government began perfunctorily changing MIA status to "presumed finding of death" (PFOD). In December 1976 a House panel determined, later with President Carter's agreement, that no live MIAs remained in Southeast Asia. In March 1977 a presidential commission traveled to Hanoi; it subsequently agreed with a House select committee that the Vietnamese were acting in good faith to "repatriate" the remains of all American MIAs. The government provided wives and family members with no explanation for these decisions. Because they were made by our government, we were simply expected to assume they were trustworthy.

These announcements only confirmed my suspicions that Frank had been used as a pawn. I became convinced that our government would make no more real efforts to recover him—alive or dead. And I realized how powerless I remained.

The Navy changed Frank's status to PFOD on October 31, 1977; the telegram arrived at my door in Oakland along with a group of young trick-or-treaters. The following year Frank's family and I held a memorial service for him at the National Cemetery in Wilmington, North Carolina. By 1978 the Pentagon had declared all MIAs to be PFODs, except for Colonel Charles E. Shelton of the Air Force, who remains listed as a POW for symbolic reasons. His wife took her own life in October 1990. She left no explanation, but friends suggest that her suicide is a result of battling about POW/MIA issues for more than twenty years. To me, her action seems as symbolic as her husband's status.

In 1983 President Reagan announced that the MIAs were a high priority for his administration. He sent delegations to Vietnam, and 150 sets of remains were identified and returned. The military's Joint Casualty Resolution Center at Barbers Point in Hawaii, established in the 1970s, increased its efforts to recover remains and make identifications. In 1985 Vietnam turned over the remains of another five persons believed to be MIAs; in 1988 the first joint American–Vietnamese team uncovered two more sets of MIA remains.

But no one had asked me for additional information about Frank, and by the time another twelve, silent years had gone by I felt sure that I would never know his exact whereabouts. Consequently, I was unprepared for the telephone call I received from the Navy in December 1989 asking me if I "happened to have" a copy of my husband's dental X rays.

"No . . . . Why?"

"Well . . . uh . . . we have a piece of a jawbone and some teeth that we think may have belonged to him."

My anger at the unfeeling language obscured my initial shock.

How could this stranger choose his words so carelessly, ignoring their possible effect upon me? But his tone of voice indicated that he was not so unfeeling as his choice of words implied. He explained that Frank was only one of several men who were being considered as the possible source for a box of remains that the North Vietnamese had turned over to American authorities in June. I suggested that he contact my husband's family. Then, as I had during the previous twenty-three years, I tried to remain calm as I confronted this latest unexpected reminder of Frank and of my own, irretrievable loss.

On January 22, 1990, exactly twenty-four years from the day I married Frank, the Navy notified me that these remains had been positively identified as his. (The bones included those of the torso, legs, and a part of the lower jawbone that seemed to be broken. No bones were available from the rest of the face and head or the feet and hands.) If I regarded the pathologists' reports as "inconclusive," I would have the "option" to arrange for someone else to review the paperwork and remains to provide "quality assurance" of this decision.

A few days later, members of Frank's family and I met with military officials to review their evidence. They explained that the government research group reached their decision based upon a combination of evidence. First they looked for the names of all of the men who were listed as having disappeared in the area of Dien Chau District, Nghe Tinh Province—the area from which the bones had been recovered. Using a section of the pelvic bone to determine the age of the person at death, they were able to narrow the possibilities even more. By measuring the torso and leg bones, they were also able to estimate the person's height. Because of the prominent muscle insertion in the bones, the pathologists were certain that the person had had an unusually muscular build. Frank's medical records show that he had a 42-inch chest, 31-inch waist, and 22-inch thigh and could military-press 200 pounds; he had begun lifting weights when he was in high school, an activity that he continued. Using information from the computer data base of missing persons' dental records, they narrowed the possibilities to three men. And while they were able to obtain dental X rays on all of the men except Frank, none of their X rays fitted the dental work remaining on the lower jawbone. Although no X rays of Frank's teeth were available, the dental charts showing his fillings and earlier extractions matched those of the jawbone. So he filled the description in every possible way, as did no one else who had disappeared within a fifty-mile radius of the site.

With the recounting of each explanation, I was asked if I wanted to see photographs of the bones or medical records substantiating each claim. At first I could only respond, "I don't know yet. Wait a minute, and I'll let you know." Then I would tell myself that I had to look or continue to doubt their judgment. Each decision to look at the evidence became a little easier, and I managed to get through the afternoon without embarrassing any of us by becoming hysterical. Frank's family told me later that if I had not agreed to look at the photographs they would have done so; they also felt we needed to look to be able to know.

At first I did wonder if the remains were really Frank's. But because I had put no pressure on our government since the early 1970s, its decision to assign them to him, rather than to the husband of a more insistent wife, seems to serve no ulterior purpose. The government had nothing to gain by returning Frank's remains; this made its analysis more convincing to me. I can imagine no other motivation for this vicissitude. Frank and I were just lucky.

Frank appears to have died in the crash of his plane. The fragmentation of the bones and the broken jaw make this the likeliest explanation. The bones were encrusted with dirt since Vietnamese bury the dead directly in the ground without a coffin and then, approximately three years later, after the flesh has rotted away, dig up the bones and place them in a smaller grave. This process also partly accounts for the missing smaller bones. When this ritual was explained to me, it was described as something the Vietnamese do because of their "superstitions" about the dead. I couldn't help thinking that we characterize our own practices in such matters, really no more civilized, as "respect for the dead."

I was touched that the Vietnamese had gone to such trouble to bury someone who had been bombing their country. Their humane customs are partly responsible for my having Frank's remains for reburial. And I was beginning to discover how grateful I was.

Frank's was one of ten sets of MIA remains identified and returned to the U.S. mainland for interment in 1990. They were shipped to Travis Air Force Base and in late February brought home to North Carolina, where our families held a private, quiet interment in the National Cemetery in Wilmington. Knowing the whereabouts of Frank's remains has helped me begin a healing process I was helpless to effect earlier. Unconsciously, I had been unable to forgive myself for "deserting" him, for failing to negotiate the labyrinth of government policies and foreign terrains. My earlier insistence that his final whereabouts did not matter had been dishonest. I had been diminishing the importance of what I could not change. Now I can draw comfort from envisioning his grave site, from having a specific physical location that automatically comes to mind when I think of him. His flesh had already become part of Vietnam, but his bones no longer lie—like those of Thomas Hardy's Drummer Hodge—uncoffined and unmarked beneath "foreign constellations."

THE
COLD WAR

At the height of the Cold War two U.S. Navy
Phantoms escort a Badger as the Soviet
aircraft overflies the *Kitty Hawk*.
(U.S. Navy photo)

Mediterranean: Playing Chicken

William H. Honan

I f the fighting in Korea and Vietnam were the most visible outbreaks
of the Cold War, one of the least noticed yet potentially dangerous
was the advance of the Soviet Navy into the Mediterranean in 1966 to
challenge the supremacy of the United States Sixth Fleet.

This direct confrontation of the Soviet Union and the United States
led to a number of narrow scrapes as the two superpowers spied on each
other's fleets and frequently used their high-performance aircraft to test
their adversary's defensive tactics and capabilities. Wryly called "Chicken
of the Sea," this aggressive mutual surveillance high up—and sometimes
not so high—over the Mediterranean claimed a number of lives.

Here is a detailed, firsthand account of this frightening yet rarely
acknowledged engagement of the superpowers, reported by the author
when a young reporter for The New York Times. Partly as a result of
such public exposure, representatives of the United States and the Soviet

Union met in Moscow in 1971 and refined what they called "the rules of the road" in order to lessen the danger of precipitating nuclear war.

Aboard the U.S.S. *Saratoga*,
with the Sixth Fleet in the Mediterranean.
November, 1970

"I intercepted a couple of Russian Badgers at twenty-five thousand feet heading for the carrier. I got right in between the two of them just—oh, a few feet behind the leader. I guess he didn't like it. His tail gunner aimed his guns at me. I slid from side to side, but wherever I went he kept following me with those guns. So I decided there were better places to be and got out of there, but continued to escort in the wing position. There was, I guess you could say, apprehension."

The words are those of a boyish-looking pilot of one of this attack carrier's F-4 Phantom interceptors—the nation's fastest, most expensive and deadliest jet fighters, charged with the defense of the U.S. Sixth Fleet here in the Mediterranean. The pilot is describing one of an increasing number of encounters between United States and Russian airmen in a hair-raising game of confrontation, surveillance, and occasional brinkmanship that might wryly be called "Chicken of the Sea."

Although the intensity of the game slackened last fall during the Jordanian civil war when the Sixth Fleet conducted noisy, round-the-clock maneuvers south of Cyprus—a performance Soviet fliers respectfully shied away from—recently contacts have been on the rise again. This has been the case sporadically since 1966 when a Russian naval squadron, or *eskadra*, first sortied through the Dardanelles to challenge the Sixth Fleet and establish a Soviet presence in the Mediterranean.

Clearly, the *eskadra* is no war fleet—it was, and remains, smaller than the Italian Navy. And although cartoonists in Europe and the United States like to picture Premier Kosygin glowering from the deck of a Soviet aircraft carrier, the fact is that no such vessel exists in the Soviet Navy. What the Russians have, instead, are four cruiser-sized helicopter carriers designed for antisubmarine warfare but with flight decks too small to accommodate modern jets—surely no match for the two 75,000-ton American attack carriers regularly on station here, which are able to fling up a swarm of fighters that move two and a half times the speed of sound and, individually, pack more firepower (even without nuclear weapons) than the B-17 heavy bomber of World War II.

Since the *eskadra* has no naval aircraft, the Russians have tried to make up for this critical lack by outfitting their ships with surface-to-surface missiles, some of which have a range of more than four hundred miles. The Russian missiles cannot match American carrier-based jets in tactical radius or destructive capacity; and, in the unlikely event of all-out naval warfare here, the Russian missile ships would need additional help to seek out the Sixth Fleet from among the 3,000-odd vessels that ply the Mediterranean on an average day, and then get close enough to select the best targets and guide home the warheads. Such reconnaissance tasks are best performed by aircraft, since the submarine fleets here are pretty well stalemated, and since a breakthrough in electronic warfare that could defy all countermeasures is believed unlikely. And that is why "Chicken of the Sea" is being played these days not only on the surface of the Mediterranean, and beneath it, but most in earnest high up in this azure sky, at blinding speeds, in unearthly states of gravitational distortion and with electronic devices sophisticated enough to raise even Buck Rogers's eyebrow.

The air arm the Russians bring to bear in the Mediterranean is, of necessity, land-based—a squadron or so of long-range, twin-jet Tupolev TU-16 reconnaissance bombers known by their NATO code name as "Badgers" and based near Alexandria.

These planes are marked with United Arab Republic insignia, but the fact that their pilots have been monitored talking Russian over the radio betrays their true nationality.

The object of the game, from the Soviet point of view, is both military and political. Militarily, the Russians are testing to learn which tactics will get their aircraft to the Sixth Fleet soonest with the least risk of detection. "We know they're playing around trying to find the goodie," I was told by Jack Winkowski, the handsome, jaunty commander of Fighter Squadron 103. Politically, the point of the Soviet game is to keep tabs on the Sixth Fleet and send out the Badgers every once in a while to overfly American warships at low level—sometimes as low as 100 feet—as if to say, "We always know where you are, and if things ever got really serious we could annihilate your fleet just as quickly as the Japanese did at Pearl Harbor back in 1941."

This message is aimed not only at the United States. The Badgers commonly arrive in pairs so that one can film the other skimming the decks of an American carrier—making photographs the Russians proudly display at chancelleries around the Mediterranean.

The object of the game from the American point of view is also two-fold. Militarily, the United States admirals want to learn all they can about first-line Soviet planes and tactics, and accordingly they make so many hundreds of photographs, and record so many radar signatures of the Badgers whenever they approach the fleet, that it is likely that some of the older Russian pilots have appeared on more film and made more recordings than Bing Crosby.

Politically, the Americans are engaging in a form of nonverbal communication, too. The Phantoms are sent out to intercept the Badgers about a hundred miles before they reach the carriers and then escort them as long as they stay within that radius—as if to say, "We always know when you are coming. And if things ever got really serious we could swat you out of the sky before you could get close enough to guide or launch a missile, and then we could annihilate your unprotected *eskadra* just as quickly as the Japanese did at the Strait of Tsushima back in 1905."

Likewise, this message is directed not just to the Soviet Union. When a Phantom intercepts a Badger, it snuggles up alongside the Russian plane—with as little as twenty feet between their wingtips—so that any photograph one Badger may take of another skimming the decks of an American warship will show a dart-like Phantom poised at its side. The Russians could, of course, retouch their photographs to eliminate the Phantom, but U.S. Navy photographers try to snap these scenes, too, and their photographs, also, are said to emerge from attaché cases in diplomatic chambers around the Mediterranean.

Needless to say, air encounters such as these are likely to be, in the parlance of the pilots' ready rooms, pretty hairy. Not only are the Phantoms and the Badgers flying at enormous speeds when just a few feet apart, but they are heavily armed. The Badger is classified as a medium bomber approximately equal to the B-47, and although the model normally used to overfly American ships is a reconnaissance version not fitted out to carry nuclear bombs or long-range air-to-surface missiles, it does have three gun turrets, each of which mounts a brace of 23 millimeter cannons. The turrets are always manned and the cannons are doubtless loaded.

Consequently, when escorting Badgers, Phantom pilots keep a sharp lookout. If the Badger takes certain hostile actions, the Phantom pilot is under orders to whirl into an offensive position, flip an arming switch on the left side of his instrument panel and squeeze the trigger on the end of the stick to let fly with a Sparrow IIIB or Sidewinder air-to-air missile—a response that could, conceivably, start World War Three. The Navy's "rules of engagement," spelling out for Phantom pilots the precise circumstances in which they might be called upon to open fire, are classified because, according to the highest-ranking officer aboard this ship, "we don't want to let the Russians know how far they can go." This officer insists that a shoot-out in these skies is most unlikely, because the unwritten rules of aerial etiquette are being observed by both Russian and American fliers "in exquisite detail." For example, he points to the fact that when the Soviets fly out of northern Russia on reconnaissance missions over U.S. ships with their long-range strategic "Bear" bomber, the Bears, like tame lions, actually open their bomb bays when intercepted, permitting Phantom pilots to peer up into the bays to satisfy themselves that bombs are not being carried. The Phantom pilots, however, do not by any means unanimously agree with their senior officer about the impeccable manners of Russian aviators, and point instead to numerous incidents, such as the one in which the young pilot on this ship reported having been menaced by a Soviet tail gunner. They also tell of provocative actions of their own.

Officially, no gun or missile fire has ever been exchanged between the Phantoms and the Badgers. Nevertheless, a couple of years ago, a Badger crashed about five miles off the bow of the carrier *Essex* after having made four low passes over the ship. None of its crew of seven survived. Since parts of three bodies and pieces of uniforms were recovered by the *Essex*, the Soviet defense ministry made one of its rare acknowledgments of the loss of a military plane. For its part, the U.S. Navy conceded that planes from the *Essex* were in the air at the time of the crash but insisted that they did not "interfere with, hamper, or threaten" the Badger. The full Navy report on the incident remains classified.

Many Phantom pilots and their radar-intercept officers have been killed out here also; since the Badger crash in 1968 the death toll stands at Badgers 7, Phantoms 9. The *Saratoga* lost two of that number in a horrifying crash in full view of the ship just a few weeks ago. The Mediterranean had been calm and glassy that day—a dangerous condition for Navy fliers because the horizon tends to disappear and sky blends with sea—and the Phantom, on a low pass beside the ship, simply flew into the water at about 400 knots. All of these fatalities, of course, are listed as accidental, which they may well be, although it would not strain anyone's credulity out here to learn that Badgers and Phantoms have had midair collisions or even that aircraft have been shot down and the facts suppressed in order to avoid an international rumpus that could get out of hand.

The *Saratoga*, like her sister ships the *Independence* and the *John F. Kennedy* here, is remarkable not only for her leviathan immensity but also for the appalling racket she makes. The 25-ton jets that get flung off her deck by four catapults do not just whine or howl; they make an almost unbelievably loud roaring scream. When as many as five or six of them are revving up, with the lead two gunning their afterburners and shooting blasts of hot, kerosene-reeking air whooshing down the flight deck, it is a madhouse. The steampowered catapults, which could probably toss a Cadillac a mile or two, shake the ship from stem to stern when fired. Watching a launch, I would always find myself caught off guard by the next, so rapidly did they take place. I would feel the ship shudder first, and then would turn to see a jet screaming aloft. And then another. And another.

Only moments after the last launch, planes start landing every few seconds. This is even worse on the ears—"Mickey Mouse" earmuff noise-attenuators notwithstanding. The problem is that the Phantom, which is reputedly as graceful as a gull when traveling supersonically, is all but unmanageable when dribbling along at its landing speed of 150 miles an hour. Accordingly, the only way to bring it down on an aircraft carrier is to practically stand the plane on its tail and execute what the Navy calls a "controlled crash" which, if one were not watching, could be mistaken for a train wreck. And, of course, the pilot goes to full throttle at the moment of collision with the deck so that if his landing hook fails to snag one of the four arresting cables—which would produce an ear-splitting screech—he can bolt the plane into the air again with an equally ear-splitting roar. Alternately, the Phantom may come in too high and get waved off by the landing signal officer, in which case it treats the ship's crew to a full-power fly-over at perhaps 100 feet—something that has to be heard to be believed.

After watching one Phantom on this ship bolter (miss the arresting cables) twice, only to blast off again, next go screaming overhead after being waved off on another try, and finally "crash-land" in the prescribed thunderous and screeching manner, I retreated below to the ready room of one of the fighter squadrons. There, I found the pilots lounging about and talking, but all watching out of the corner of their eyes a small TV set showing the landing deck so that they could clap their hands over their ears just before each jet hammered down, occasionally knocking pictures off the wall. "It's not too bad today," one pilot told me as he put his hands to his ears with a wince, and then shouted: "YOU SHOULD HAVE BEEN HERE DURING THE JORDANIAN CRISIS!"

Even when the ship is not conducting flight operations, mechanics are almost continuously testing engines on the flight deck and on the hangar deck below. In this relative peace and calm, when the ship happens to be cruising east of Sicily and Malta where the prospect of Badger overflights is great, a sleek, droop-snouted Phantom is always parked on the Number 2 catapult. The plane's two-man crew—the pilot and his R.O., or radar-intercept officer— are seated in the cockpit ready and waiting. Whenever a suspicious flying object approaching the ship is detected—either by the ship's radar, by a Hawkeye radar picket plane cruising 100 miles or more from the task force, or perhaps by some intelligence source such as Israeli ground radar—the bullhorns on the flight deck sputter: "Launch the ready CAP," meaning scramble the Combat Air Patrol. Almost immediately, a squat yellow tractor beside the Phantom begins to emit a high scream as its compressor plunges a starting blast of air into the plane's two huge General Electric J-79 turbojets. A seaman dashes under the plane and hooks up a holdback device. Safety chains are released. In the cockpit, the pilot and the R.O. are popping on their helmets, cinching tight seat belts, shoulder straps, and leg restrainers.

"It's the most exciting moment in a fighter pilot's life," says Phil Crosland, a Phantom pilot who intercepted two Badgers while on duty with the *Kennedy*. "You know, of course, it isn't the beginning of the Third World War. But this is what you've been training for. You've been given lectures. You know the admiral is concerned about the overflights. And you know that in a very few minutes you may come face-to-face—literally face-to-face—with a Russian."

As soon as the engines crank up to the proper rpm, the pilot presses the igniter buttons and the engines fire. Then the pilot begins checking his instrument panel and chanting replies to the queries of the R.O. in a challenge-and-response dialogue programmed to make sure nothing is overlooked in readying the plane for flight—"Controls?" "Checked." "Wings?" "Locked and warning light out." "Trim?" "Set." "Flaps?" "Full down." "Hook?" "Up." "Harness?" "Locked." "Warning lights?" "Out." "Pins?" "Pulled." . . .

Unlike the pilots of commercial airliners who may sit parked on the runway dabbling with controls and instruments to their hearts' content, an interceptor pilot is expected to get airborne in two and a half minutes. In fact, the Phantom pilot is told his initial vector, or course, over the flight deck bullhorns because his plane will be in the air even before his radio is warmed up.

No matter how able or well-trained the pilot and the R.O. may be, they are invariably haunted at this moment with the fear that they are forgetting something. And the penalties for forgetfulness, of course, are lethal. If they forget to tighten a leg restrainer and have to eject in mid-flight, their legs are likely to be "rearranged" by the instrument panel as they shoot out of the cockpit. Any of a dozen other oversights might cause the plane to plunge into the sea moments after leaving the carrier's deck.

As the Phantom's jets begin to scream louder—to the point at which it seems impossible that one small airplane is generating so much noise—the flight director who has raced out on deck beckons and the ungainly looking plane taxis forward about ten feet. A seaman hooks on the catapult's husky wire hawser that looks like a giant slingshot. The pilot advances the throttles to full power and calls out a last few readings to the R.O.—rpm, exhaust gas temperature, and oil pressure. Then he says, "Here's burner!" and slaps the two throttles all the way up, opening the afterburner nozzles that spray raw fuel into the hot tail pipes, adding an almost explosive forward thrust to the plane's power. The Phantom now generating 16 tons of push, trembles and blares. When ready, the pilot salutes the catapult officer who, in turn, sweeps his arm in a circle and touches the deck—the signal for the plane to be slung off the deck accelerating to 180 knots, or 207 miles an hour, in 2.1 seconds.

"It's like being in a car wreck and making love at the same time," one of the young pilots told me, mixing his metaphors but capturing the strange combination of terror and exhilaration of the experience. To leave the ship, I took a "cat shot" myself. The wind is knocked out of you and you can't breathe. Vision is blurred, because, it was explained to me, the G-force momentarily flattens eyeballs. You have to remember to put your head firmly against the headrest so that the force of the stroke will not bang your head against it and knock you cold. The pilot must dig his right elbow into his rib cage so his arm will not fly back and yank the stick prematurely.

"To an older pilot," I was told by Gene Geronime, the trim, taut-faced commander of Fighter Squadron 31, "a good hard cat shot gives a feeling of relief. We live in fear of a cold cat shot— when the steam pressure in the cat is too low and you go off the deck at less than flying speed. That can be rather embarrassing. It can ruin your whole day."

A few seconds after launch, the Phantom reaches a speed of 400 knots (460 miles an hour), the pilot points the nose 30 to 40 degrees up and commences climbing at a rate of almost 10,000 feet per minute—an angle of attack so steep the Navy calls this interceptor, with not much exaggeration, "a reusable missile." (At a later point in the flight when its fuel tanks are lighter, the pilot can actually rear the Phantom on its tail and accelerate vertically, although the maneuver would rapidly exhaust his fuel supply.)

About one and a half million of the four-million-dollar cost of each Phantom goes into its radar system. As the plane rises on an intercept mission, the R.O. is busy manipulating this recently redesigned and now very hush-hush equipment in such a way as to pick up a target on his scope and compute a path to rendezvous that will place the Phantom—and not its adversary—in a favorable offensive position. The New Westinghouse A.W.G.-10 radar, according to one R.O. on the *Saratoga*, supplements the conventional pulse-emission and bounce-reception radar with apparatus "based on wholly new principles" that, while not without a few bugs, is especially good at picking up planes that fly low enough to go undetected by ordinary radar. Despite such sophistication, however, even when an R.O. locates the target the ship has assigned him to intercept and plots his course to it, he cannot tell the pilot for sure what sort of intruder they are about to tangle with.

"We get certain indications from the ship," says one R.O. "For example, if the target is emitting radar, the ship can usually tell you something from that—a combat radar signature is different from that of a weather radar. Still, you never know what you'll find. I've gone up and found a Greek or French fighter peacefully humming along at 30,000. Sometimes there's a British Vulcan bomber from Malta way up at 40,000."

Commander Geronime recalls closing with a group of planes at extremely high altitude and finding, to his amazement, a British Victor tanker "giving a drink" to a couple of Lightning fighters at the remarkable height of thirty thousand feet. Another young Phantom pilot says he recently intercepted a couple of Israeli Phantoms—they waggled their wings at each other.

Perhaps the strangest intercept of all was made by Lieutenant Commander Howard Young, a Vietnam veteran with more than 1,600 hours of flying time in Phantoms. After one launch, his on-board radar failed to pick up the assigned target, and so he was directed to an intercept point by the ship's radar control. When Young reported to the ship that he still could not see the target, the radar controller replied, "You've merged with it." "I rolled over," Young recalls, "and saw a flock of geese. I couldn't believe they'd been picked up by radar so I broke away from them and asked the radar controller to give me the bearing and distance again. He sent me right back to the geese."

Most frequently, the target turns out to be a Boeing 707 "taking somebody's mother to Tel Aviv," as one pilot expressed it. Ideally, of course, commercial airliners should be identified to the fleet by their transponders—electronic devices that respond automatically to an inquiring radar pulse from the ground or sea surface by "squawking" a code that identifies the plane. A good many European airliners, however, do not carry transponders. Some do, but have defective equipment. Many private planes do not carry them because of their considerable cost. And military planes, of course, carry transponders, but those on Soviet planes do not respond, or do not respond correctly, to electronic inquiries from U.S. ships and planes. Accordingly, whenever the radar scanning the skies above and around the Sixth Fleet picks up a confusing "squawk" from an approaching "blip," or a "blip" that does not "squawk" at all, up goes a Phantom to have a look.

"Personally, four or five times a week I go out after a target that turns out to be a commercial airliner," says one pilot. "When we suspect that's what it is, we try to approach from way below and behind so they can't see us, and then we float up and take a look at their national markings. We can usually see that from about a mile away. We approach from behind because we don't want the pilot to see us. That can cause trouble. Airline pilots are the most easily spooked guys in the world. You can understand that, because the most dreaded thing to them is a midair collision. We can always eject, but they have no way out. So when they see a jet fighter coming up real close they get pretty nervous. American pilots are not bad. If you intercept a T.W.A. or Pan Am flight you don't feel too worried about it because chances are those guys come from the military themselves and they understand. The Italian pilots are the worst. They'll call Rome Control and report your number and make a complaint against you almost as soon as they see you. We don't want that. It's highly political. There's so much air traffic over the Mediterranean and we don't want to interfere with it. So we try not to be seen."

Another pilot recalls an intercept that threatened to get him into trouble. "I was launched against what they thought was a Badger approaching the ship. We went out after it and all I could find was this twin-engine transport-type aircraft. I reported that, but the ship was worried because they'd seen it come out of the south from Egypt and it was coming right at them so they said go back again and get a positive identification. This time I went up very close to it and slowed way down and sat maybe 500 feet off its wing and identified it as this Russian-built transport used by an Egyptian airline. It was going from Cairo to Athens and just happened to be passing right over the fleet. Well, when I got back to the ship, they'd received a complaint from Air Athens, which is like our F.A.A., about an air violation. They said I came too close and created a dangerous situation. They had my numbers all wrong and they had described me as an A-6 [Intruder] instead of an F-4 [Phantom]. I was on another ship then, and of course the admiral denied the whole thing, and the State Department said 'no comment,' but we all got some lectures after that about the need to be extra careful not to get too close to airliners, especially Egyptian airliners."

Quite commonly, of course, the target turns out to be a Badger. About half of the pilots here have intercepted them. In one Phantom squadron on the *Kennedy,* 13 out of 15 pilots intercepted Badgers during one particularly eventful cruise. When the *Saratoga* was in the eastern Mediterranean a few weeks ago, Badger intercepts ran as high as two or three per week for a time.

Here is a Phantom pilot describing a typical Badger intercept: "On this occasion, we were in the eastern Mediterranean somewhere south of Crete. We were sent up to check something out and when we got up there we saw two blips together on the scope and we realized it's gotta be some type of military aircraft because commercial planes would never fly that close together. We were pretty excited. Well, I saw them at 1 o'clock flying at about 25,000 feet— big, sweptwing things. I was really excited. I said, 'Tally ho! A couple of Badgers at 1 o'clock!' The R.O. agreed with me. So we went for them. I was sure they were Badgers from the shape of the fuselage. You know, silhouettes are pounded into us. Every week for a half hour they flash these images at us for just a tenth of a second and we learn to identify very quickly. Usually, on a clear day you can see what you've gone up after anywhere from ten to fifteen miles away, but you have to get within about five miles before you can say for sure it's a Badger.

"Just about the time I saw the Badgers I also saw the other

Phantom who'd discovered them too. Since there were two blips, the ship sent up two Phantoms. As we joined with them, the two Badgers kind of split apart. The other F-4 took the one in front and I took the one behind. We made a beam approach—we approach these planes from the side so as not to make them think we're doing anything hostile. If we come in behind them, we'd be in a missile-launch situation and that would make them very nervous. It's a matter of etiquette. We're just joining on them—a peaceful type approach. Well, I got right in close. There was only about 20 feet between our wingtips. I wasn't worried about hitting him. Flying in formation is an everyday thing for a fighter pilot. The buddy on your wing is your life line. If you have a power failure and lose navigation aids, the guy on your wing can get you home. Bomber pilots, however, aren't accustomed to flying close to another plane, so some Badger pilots get worried and motion for us to keep away. But this pilot didn't hassle with me. I could see his big rosy cheeks and there wasn't any doubt in my mind that he was a Russian, not an Egyptian. I escorted him for about 40 minutes until he turned and headed back for Egypt. I waved good-by. He waved back."

Some Phantom pilots tell of friendly and jovial contacts with Soviet airmen. The latest *Playboy* Playmate of the Month is often displayed to Russians (from a Phantom cockpit). Last summer, one Phantom crew was caught by surprise when a Badger flier held up his *own* copy of *Playboy*. John McTigue, the *Saratoga* Phantom pilot who was killed here a few weeks ago, once made funny faces at a sobersided Badger tail gunner until the Russian broke up and laughed so hard, according to another pilot, "the whole tail end of the Badger almost bounced up and down."

Phil Crosland, another Phantom pilot, describes a very human series of contacts that occurred while escorting a Russian Bear as it overflew the *Kennedy*. (Unlike Badgers, the longer-range Bears usually take off from northern Russia, fly south between Iceland and Great Britain, and try to overfly relief aircraft carriers en route to the Mediterranean somewhere between Spain and the Azores.) "I found this big Bear—a four-engine turboprop job considerably bigger than a seven-oh-seven—flying at about 20,000 feet," Crosland recalls. "He must have been doing only 350 knots—really slow because he wanted to conserve fuel. This is about a 20-hour mission for those guys. They get refueled in the air on the way. I got right in close, reported his number, direction, flight speed, altitude and disposition—and then I had a chance to really look him over. Well, it was really good. We started waving at first. I got the feeling they were really glad to see me—they'd been on such a long mission and seeing me was, well, like a sailor who sights the first land bird.

"They were wearing leather helmets like in World War II. It all looked very old-fashioned. I'm in a standard Phantom pilot hardhat with all this sophisticated equipment. They were smiling at me. So I took off my oxygen mask and smiled at them. I wanted them to see my face so they wouldn't think I was Steve Canyon or something, but a real person."

"The Bear started descending," Crosland continues. "We went through some clouds together. He could have pulled a lot of maneuvers to try to shake me in the clouds. That would have been dangerous. He didn't. I guess he was just as worried about hitting me as I was about hitting him. He went down to three hundred feet above the water. I was pretty surprised. Then he drove right over the carrier. He was very polite. Everytime he'd go to make a turn for another pass over the carrier he'd point like in a car making a turn in traffic. He made one pass over the carrier at 100 feet. They were taking pictures of the carrier and pictures of me and I was taking pictures of them. Then this guy wanted a shot of my underside—the missiles and stuff. He motioned to me with both hands indicating he wanted me to lift up a few feet. I shook my head and didn't move. He motioned again. I shook my head again. Then he shot me a bird—flipped me the old one-fingered international salute. He was annoyed. But later, he produced a clear glass bottle and held it up as if it were vodka and he pretended to drink a toast. So we parted friends."

Other pilots tell of less chivalrous encounters with Soviet airmen. "Most of the time the Russians respect the fact that the ship is an airport," one pilot recalls with bitterness in his voice. "But I know of two occasions—once during the nighttime in September 1969—when a Badger cut right through the landing pattern when we were recovering planes. It disrupted the landings. One or two planes had to be diverted. We protested through the Egyptian Embassy and they didn't do it again."

Another pilot, Joe Deitch, who has intercepted as many as four Badgers, maintains that Soviet pilots have occasionally tried to force him into the water by flying as low as 75 feet and turning sharply, or by skimming over an American ship so low "they were obviously trying to brush me off against the mast."

For their part, the Phantom pilots are not always little angels either. American planes overfly Soviet ships, too—"at many orders of magnitude greater than the number of times they overfly us," acknowledges a senior officer. Most of the time, these reconnaissance missions are performed by A-7 Corsairs, but when Phantoms are on their way back to the carrier and have an opportunity to swoop low and buzz a Soviet warship, a good many pilots cannot resist the temptation. "Why not? It's fun," I was told by one high-spirited pilot.

Asked how close they had come to Soviet ships, a couple of Phantom pilots burst into laughter. Then one pilot said with a spreading grin, "We wouldn't do anything to endanger the personnel or property of the Union of Soviet Socialist Republics."

Another Phantom pilot recalls that once when flying with an R.O. who happened to speak Russian, they heard Russian voices suddenly burst in on their radio. The American R.O. barked a few Russian obscenities at the Soviet radiomen and the Russians replied with some equally indelicate remarks.

One young *Saratoga* pilot named Wieselberg has made a sign for his cockpit reading: "NOW SWEAT BUDDY IM JEWISH" But he has yet to summon the nerve to hold it up for a Russian to see.

By far the most dangerous encounters between Soviet and American planes are those that occur after dark. For safety's sake, both the Badgers and the Phantoms usually turn their navigation lights on at night (which, of course, they would never do in a combat situation), but sometimes the Russians come in blacked out, or shine searchlights in the eyes of the Phantom pilots—causing a temporary loss of night vision—or trickily switch their navigation lights on and off.

Here is a Phantom pilot describing one such incident which almost cost him his life: "It was about ten o'clock at night when we were launched. From the ship, I was told there were two of them together, so we were pretty sure they were Badgers. My R.O. set up a rendezvous, but we got sucked a little behind and so we tried to cut 'em off at the pass, so to speak. To catch up, you light the burners. Well, we caught up all right. We had about 200 knots overtake speed! I guess the Badger could see our closure rate on his radar so he snapped on his lights fast. But we almost had a midair. This huge, big airplane was suddenly right there—like about 15 feet above me. It scared the hell out of me, and my R.O.—he about passed out! We whipped by. If the Russian had had a missile, he could have shot us. He must have thought, 'Those crazy Americans!' Well, I really stuck my feet out—I did everything I could to slow down. I went up and to the left and then came in on his wing.

Maybe he was sore at me because he turned his lights off. Then he turned different ones on and off. Fortunately, I could see him all the time because once I got close my own navigation lights illuminated him and we weren't in any clouds. But that was hairy. That was the closest I ever came."

Is this madness? Are these young men toying dangerously with the peace and safety of the world? Who is winning the game of Chicken of the Sea, and *is* it worth playing at all? I put these and related questions to Rear Admiral James L. Holloway, a soft-spoken native of South Carolina who makes this carrier his flagship. We talked together seated on comfortable beige-colored sofas in his attractive quarters, and continued the discussion with members of his staff over dinner (where the silver wine goblets were filled with a Spartan draft of ice water). Since none of these officers wished to be quoted by name, I will attribute the answers to my questions to an "officer."

I started by saying that I understood from the pilots that the Badgers occasionally beat the Phantoms. The pilots told me that they are expected to intercept Badgers 100 miles from the carriers, but oftentimes the Badgers get much closer before being caught. The Soviet plane that disrupted the landings on the *Kennedy* back in 1969 did not have a Phantom on its wing until just moments before it passed over the ship, and only last summer another Badger zoomed over the *Saratoga* completely unchaperoned. What is the significance of that?

"I don't know about the cases of which you speak," the officer began a little cagily, "but if they happened tonight I would say it means we're lacking in proficiency. You might say it would be a Brownie point for them. We wish it hadn't happened. But an isolated case is not important."

I replied that if as many as two unescorted Badger flights had come up in my brief conversations with the pilots, such instances were probably not isolated. Furthermore, I was surprised to find the *Saratoga* conducting flight operations in cycles that always began punctually at 8 A.M., or noon, or some other round-numbered hour, and always lasted exactly an hour and a half—the very sort of foolish regularity that cost the Egyptians their air force in 1967.

"There are various levels of readiness," the officer replied unsmilingly. "What we have here today is a peacetime situation in which the two major powers are keeping an eye on each other. But do you think we would behave in this way in a Cuban-missile-crisis situation? During the Jordanian crisis we had two carriers south of Cyprus and they were flying pretty much around the clock and at irregular intervals in a status of increased alert."

Still, I persisted, couldn't the Sixth Fleet be caught off guard at a time like the present? "Any military force," the officer said, "is susceptible to surprise attack. But if you say that that is the only way the Russians could successfully attack the Sixth Fleet, then maybe the best possible purpose the fleet could serve would be to provide our country with the warning it would need for survival."

The fleet might serve to draw fire, I replied, but might it not also serve to provoke it—especially with these high-performance, heavily armed aircraft in such close contact with each other? "Well," the officer said, "it's true you've got these high-spirited, highly trained 22- to 24-year-old men out here in a position to take actions which would create an incident. Consequently, we look upon what they do as one of the most serious responsibilities we have. When a Badger is intercepted, it is a matter of standard practice for Admiral Holloway, the task force commander embarked in the carrier, to be present in the combat information center so that he is immediately available to radio communications in the event a command decision is required. If we said that on some occasions the admiral has actually talked with the pilots during an intercept, that would imply that our rules of engagement are no good. We won't say that. The point is that he's there if needed. We will also say that not long ago we very carefully reviewed these rules. They are very good rules and very logical."

The officer concluded by saying that he did not consider surveillance, interception, and escorting provocative. "In fact," he said, "I look at it in the reverse sense. The reason they are flying in our vicinity and we in theirs is a very valid one. We really want to know what the other guy is doing. In making this surveillance, we're checking the other guy's intentions to see if they're honorable. We don't want to be surprised. Because when you're surprised you may not act rationally. You don't have time to gather all the facts. If we intercept a Badger way out, we've got plenty of time to think of how to react—as opposed to having him break out of the clouds at 200 feet over the carrier. So we feel we're the peacemakers, instead of the reverse. The confrontation in the Mediterranean is under control precisely because we have surveillance."

CHAPTER 25

Undersea: The Silent Chase

Thomas B. Allen
and Norman Polmar

At the height of the Cold War, the nuclear submarine flotillas of the two superpowers were constantly soaring through "inner space" at unbelievable speeds, tracking, pursuing, shaking, feinting, and playing a potentially lethal game of cat and mouse with each other. The amazing thing is that, so far as is known, one of ours never collided with one of theirs. Or mistakenly zapped an adversary with a rocket-propelled depth charge.

So secret were these activities that the public had little idea of what was taking place.

Shortly after publishing their biography of the father of the nuclear submarine, Admiral Hyman Rickover, the naval experts Thomas B. Allen and Norman Polmar were granted a rare glimpse of this strange and dangerous world. This report appeared as a cover story in The New York Times Magazine in 1984.

Norman Polmar is a distinguished naval analyst and author of eleven books on naval affairs and strategic weapons. For ten years, he was the editor of the U.S. sections of Jane's Fighting Ships. *Thomas B. Allen, an author and editor, and formerly associate director of National Geographic Books, served in the Navy during the Korean War.*

The largest submarine in the world, a dark mass longer than the Washington Monument is high, rises through the frigid depths below the Arctic ice pack. The Typhoon-class ship, the newest entry in the Soviet underwater fleet, has almost half again the tonnage of the biggest American submarine. Beneath the double row of hatches on its forward deck nestle 20 intercontinental ballistic missiles. Slowly, carefully, the captain guides the Typhoon upward until its stubby superstructure nudges against the jagged ice ceiling.

In the United States Navy, this maneuver is known as "ice pick." It transforms the Typhoon into a floating strategic-missile base, just a few hundred miles from the Soviet mainland but within striking distance of any American city—and well hidden from pursuit. With twin nuclear power plants to maintain life-support systems, the Typhoon can hold that position for months at a time.

The U.S. Navy takes this new threat seriously: American attack submarines are increasingly engaged in war games beneath the ice pack, the hunter prowling in silence, its electronic sensors alert for the telltale sounds that will betray its prey. Navy officials offer few details about these exercises, but the world of ASW—antisubmarine warfare—has always been a secret place. And that has never been truer than today.

The stakes are rising. In November, Yuri V. Andropov, the Soviet leader, reacted to the scheduled deployment of American medium-range nuclear weapons in Western Europe by threatening to increase the number of strategic missiles "in ocean areas." Last month, Marshal Nikolai V. Ogarkov, the chief of the Soviet general staff, made the threat more specific: the Kremlin would see to it that missiles in submarines off the American coast could hit their targets as quickly as Pershing missiles launched from West Germany against Moscow. That could take less than 10 minutes.

The Russians have made a massive investment in their underseas fleet. They have 62 nuclear-powered strategic-missile subs, compared with the United States's 34. Their attack submarines, which can fire torpedoes or tactical cruise missiles against surface ships or submarines, number 280; the United States has 95. Their newest submarines are faster, dive deeper, and pack more firepower than their American counterparts. Within the last year, wide-ranging Russian submarines have been seen in the Atlantic, Pacific, and Indian Oceans and the Mediterranean and Caribbean Seas. (Perhaps the most dramatic sighting came two months ago when a Soviet Victor III was forced to surface off South Carolina after becoming entangled with an array of listening devices towed by an American frigate.) Meanwhile, the United States government's own commitment to the submarine has deepened, with the Navy now planning to spend $36 billion on a new class of attack submarines.

Out of this deadly competition has emerged a whole new kind of underwater weapon: Some submarines today can achieve speeds of 43 knots underwater, 10 knots faster than the fastest merchant ship afloat—and four times the speed of World War II submarines. And this destructive new weapon is forcing revolutionary changes in antisubmarine warfare. Both Moscow and Washington are spending ever more billions of dollars to find ways to detect and track and, if necessary, destroy each other's submarine fleets. Banks of ocean-floor hydrophones feed data to computer centers linked by communications satellites; hunter aircraft and attack submarines ceaselessly patrol.

According to most military experts, the United States is far ahead in the technology of detection, and that counts; American ASW forces would take a heavy toll of the enemy in the event of war. Moreover, the detection capacity is an element of nuclear deterrence. "We're part of the arms-reduction talks," says a naval surveillance officer. "The Russians have to know that we are good at tracking them."

There are some specialists who believe that advances in sensing and computer science may one day tip the balance in favor of the hunters, making the seas "transparent" to antisubmarine forces. But Admiral James D. Watkins, chief of naval operations, spoke for most authorities when he told a Navy audience last year that, far from becoming "more transparent," the oceans are getting "more opaque." In an opaque sea, the submarine has the edge.

From the cockpit of the turboprop Orion, out over the Atlantic, visibility is zero. Since early-morning takeoff from the Naval Air Station at Brunswick, Maine, the four-engine plane has been plowing through white fog. This November flight is a training mission, but the drill is realistic: The crew of the Navy patrol plane has been given a set of navigational coordinates that define an area of ocean where a Soviet submarine might be lurking.

Lieutenant Eric Haas, the tactical coordination officer, or TACCO, prepares to take over control of the mission. His fingers fly across a computer keyboard; a bright green circle appears on the pale green screen before him. A taciturn Haas nods toward the screen. "That's the FTP," he says. "The fly-to point." Once the Orion arrives there, Haas will run a simulated search for a Soviet sub.

The plane lumbers through the fog. "Every training mission is a real mission," says Lieutenant Phil Farrell, the pilot. Like the rest of the crew, he makes little distinction between a drill and a real hunt. "It's a semi-real world," he says. "We're doing something real—looking for Soviet subs and tracking them. But we just find them. In war, we'd find them and sink them."

Lieutenant Farrell's plane is one of some 400 Orions that pursue Soviet submarines, flying from bases in such places as Florida, Hawaii, Japan, Iceland, and the Azores. It is part of a worldwide detection network—what Admiral Wesley L. McDonald, commander in chief in the Atlantic, once described as "the application of a series of filters"—through which a Russian sub must pass.

The first of those filters, applied by the Russians as well as the Americans, are intelligence-gathering satellites. The Navy will not talk about them. A reporter's recent question, posed to an officer in the new Naval Space Command, elicited a terse reply: "I won't say one word about that." It is known, however, that the tracking starts when a sub leaves its berth. The sub must remain on the surface until it reaches deep water and submerges; meanwhile, it can be photographed by the high-resolution cameras of spy-in-the-sky satellites. According to a defense analyst who has seen such photographs, "You can tell if the guys on the bridge watch have their parka hoods up."

Once a departing sub has been spotted, information about it is added to the constant flow of data transmitted to Navy ASW forces through a global submarine-watch communications network.

The next antisubmarine filter is the Sound Surveillance System (SOSUS), thousands of hydrophones moored to the ocean floor to catch the noise coming from distant submarines. The reliance on SOSUS grows out of the fact that, from the submarine hunter's point of view, geography favors the United States. An American sub on either coast has a wide choice of routes to take to reach its deep-water destination; Soviet subs must pass through geographical bottlenecks to reach the open sea. Missile submarines based at Polyarny on the Kola Peninsula, for example, cannot get to the Atlantic without sailing past the hydrophones between Greenland and Britain. Submarines seeking to enter the Pacific from the Petropavlovsk base on the Kamchatka Peninsula may be detected by the SOSUS array along the Aleutians.

All sounds picked up by the hydrophones, whether produced by whales, oil rigs, or subs, are transmitted by cable to computer centers ashore. There, information provided by intelligence agencies—including the acoustic "signatures" of particular Russian submarines—is used in sifting through and analyzing the stream of sound. Interpreters can draw upon a library of Soviet underwater sounds gathered by SOSUS over the last two decades. The hydrophones can detect sounds produced by a submarine hundreds of miles away and can pinpoint its location within a radius of 50 miles.

Communication satellites speed word of the detection of a Soviet sub to naval forces around the world, and the Orion patrol planes pick up the trail. That is the kind of mission Lieutenant Haas is running as the fog-shrouded plane out of Brunswick reaches its fly-to point. Hunched over his computer keyboard in an alcove behind the cockpit, the TACCO produces on the screen a rectangle that marks off the area where the sub is thought to be. He speaks softly into a microphone. From the belly of the plane, a four-foot-long cannister—a hydrophone attached to a buoy—plunges toward the waves some 2,000 feet below. When the canister hits the water, the hydrophone begins to transmit what it hears to the aircraft overhead; a tiny, luminous triangle appears within the rectangle on Lieutenant Haas's screen. During an actual sub hunt, he would drop dozens of these sonobuoys with their hydrophones set to listen at specific depths. He would also put down a bathythermograph, a kind of submersible thermometer that provides the temperatures of various ocean layers. The theory: The submarine would probably try to hide in a layer of cold, dense water, where the noise of its machinery would be muffled.

The search for a submarine thus becomes a kind of three-dimensional video game. From the jumble of sounds transmitted by the sonobuoys, skilled sensor operators in the Orion pick out probable submarine noises; each such identification appears as a line on the computer display screen, a kind of arrow pointing from a sonobuoy toward the sub. As more and more sonobuoys are dropped and more and more lines intersect, the sub's track through the sea is revealed. Its probable depth is calculated with the help of the bathythermograph.

Now the TACCO is ready for the end game. He shouts, "Madman!" and the plane suddenly swoops to within 200 feet of the water to pick up the presumed track of the sub. Extending like a stinger from the Orion's tail is a MAD, a magnetic anomaly detector, which can locate distortions in the earth's magnetic field caused by large masses of metal. Submarines, for example.

Today, such tracking is a routine occurrence off the coasts of the United States, part of the system of filters laid down by American antisubmarine forces. In time of war, the scenario would change dramatically. The Orion would go for a kill, using Mark-46 torpedoes or depth bombs. And ASW surface ships, helicopters and attack submarines would be part of the protective screen around aircraft-carrier battle groups and other ships that the Navy labels "high-value targets."

Navy strategy calls for ASW forces to keep enemy submarines far from such targets. An essential element of this strategy, for example, is known as LAMPS—light airborne multipurpose system. LAMPS helicopters are carried by warships, including frigates that are specially designed to keep the copters flying in rough weather. A LAMPS copter, directed by computers aboard its mother ship, would seek out and torpedo enemy submarines; meanwhile the frigate, armed with torpedoes and depth charges, would launch its own attack.

But many critics question whether even the most modern defensive systems can stop a submarine determined to break through the ASW screen. According to Commander John L. Byron, a submarine officer in the Pentagon, "Operating a submarine against a carrier is too easy; the carrier's antisubmarine protection often resembles Swiss cheese." Writing in the Naval Institute *Proceedings*, the Navy's professional journal, Commander Byron reported that ASW attacks in fleet exercises are often not even begun until after the submerged "enemy" submarine has already dramatically signaled that it is in torpedo-firing position—until, as he put it, "green flares have startled the carrier's bridge watch."

The first actual combat test of modern ASW tactics and weapons occurred during the war over the Falkland Islands, the only major naval conflict since World War II. Among the NATO allies, the Royal Navy's antisubmarine force is generally rated second to that of the United States. Yet the British ships were unable to destroy an eight-year-old, German-built Argentine submarine that dogged the task force for five weeks. The Argentine submarine actually fired several torpedoes at British warships, which escaped without damage because of equipment problems aboard the submarine. The British made numerous attacks on suspected submarine targets, but their only kill was a thirty-eight-year-old former United States submarine, caught on the ocean surface.

In recent years, Norwegian and Swedish naval forces have attacked suspected Soviet submarines in their coastal waters without any apparent results. That happened in April 1983, for example, when a Norwegian antisubmarine frigate fired depth charges at what was believed to be a Soviet submarine in Hardanger Fjord. A Swedish parliamentary report has charged that Soviet submarines violated Swedish home waters at least forty times in 1982. A retired United States admiral, a world authority on military electronics, offered this comment after reading the report: "You'd be lucky to get fifty-yard detections even with twenty-thousand-yard sonars in those waters. The salinity, low temperature, and shallow, irregular sea floor—it all works for the submariner. It's a beautiful place to hide submarines." Similar conditions exist in favorite haunts of Soviet submarines off Japan and in the Mediterranean.

The ever-greater elusiveness of the modern submarine is spurring efforts to improve the ASW performance of attack submarines. For many experts believe that the ultimate weapon against a submarine is another submarine.

On a gusty fall day, a sleek, nuclear-powered attack submarine eases out of its berth at the Navy base in New London, Connecticut, and heads down the Thames River toward Long Island Sound. Sometimes a Soviet intelligence-collection ship will be waiting off Montauk Point, but today the sea is empty. The Russians have little interest in this familiar, Sturgeon-class attack submarine. They are after missile submarines and certain new attack submarines.

Below decks, the Klaxon blasts insistently, and the order "Dive! Dive!" sounds over the loudspeakers. In the control room, an officer methodically begins a series of commands: "Make your depth 200 feet. . . . Come right to course. . . ." As the ship descends, the deck tilts only slightly, and there is no change in the air pressure. The sub is quiet: the crew pads about in running shoes, the air-conditioning hums softly.

This test cruise will last only a few days. But when the Navy's attack submarines head out on patrol, they may be at sea for two months and spend virtually all of that time beneath the sea. On such a voyage, space is tight. Crates of food are stacked along the passageways. Of the 12 officers aboard, only the captain and his executive officer have individual staterooms, and the 115 enlisted men make do with only about 95 bunks. The space saved is committed—to the nuclear reactor, which has liberated the submarine from the earth's atmosphere, and to weapons and elaborate acoustic detection devices.

"There are really two driving issues in ASW," says one Pentagon research official. "Sensor performance and overall quietness." Attack submarines are designed to have both virtues, to be sensitive enough to hear a distant enemy, and stealthy enough to stalk it unheard. The hunt depends almost entirely on sonar.

In the sonar room of an attack submarine, technicians sit before three green luminescent screens. The ship's sonar is in a passive mode, and a parade of black electronic "spikes" crosses the screens, each spike representing a different frequency. The technicians are "listening" for the sounds made by other submarines or by surface ships—the noise of their machinery, the sound produced by water passing over their hulls.

When a possible target is discovered, an attack submarine will maneuver to get a clearer, identifying acoustic signal. The ship will move slowly, though, to minimize its own sounds. A submarine can also use sonar in an active mode, transmitting a beam of sound toward the target and listening for an echo. But active sonar announces the hunting submarine's own presence and exact location, and under current Navy doctrine submariners are not allowed to use it.

In a wartime sea, the contact with a Soviet submarine would become a duel to the death. Today, the captain of an American attack submarine might be under orders to close with the Soviet submarine to monitor its speed or acoustic "signature." The captain of an American strategic-missile submarine, however, would quietly head the other way. In peace or in war, his mission is to avoid detection and maintain his readiness to launch his missiles.

In wartime, United States ASW forces have a variety of weapons available to hit an enemy submarine once it has been ferreted out. One is called SUBROC, a rocket-propelled nuclear depth charge fired from a submarine; it has a range of about 25 miles. (Of course, the use of nuclear weapons requires Presidential authorization. That can be a problem for submarines, since radio communications may reveal their locations.) The ASROC—antisubmarine rocket—is fired toward a submerged enemy submarine from a surface ship; when the rocket nears the target, it ejects a depth charge or a homing torpedo. Another weapon, an ocean-bottom mine called CAPTOR, releases a homing torpedo when an enemy submarine passes over.

The performance of the United States's principal ASW weapon, the torpedo, is a controversial matter within the Navy. The controversy surfaced during congressional hearings when Senator Warren B. Rudman, a New Hampshire Republican, noted that new Soviet submarines of the Alfa class can travel at "forty-plus knots and could probably outdive most of our antisubmarine torpedoes." He asked what the Navy was doing about this problem. Vice Admiral William H. Rowden, then deputy chief of naval operations for surface warfare, replied that the Navy had modified the submarine-launched Mark-48 torpedo "to accommodate to the increased speed and to the diving depth" of the Alfa. As for the Mark-46, launched from aircraft and surface ships: "We recently modified that torpedo to handle what you might call the pre-Alfa." Many analysts point out that even if the Mark-46 could outrun and outdive a large, modern Soviet submarine, the torpedo's 95-pound warhead might be too small for a kill.

Gerald Cann, a deputy assistant secretary of the Navy and the Navy's top civilian ASW expert, comments: "We need to improve our weapons, but probably the single most difficult device to build is an effective ASW torpedo. I've been involved in several, and they're nightmares. Every part of the torpedo interacts with every other part. The noise of the torpedo—its propulsion system—interferes with the torpedo's own sensor. On the Mark-46, a while back, we solved the problem by a very simple process of slowing it down. And we gained a ten-fold increase in capabilities."

For an American attack submarine, the greatest challenge may be the new Soviet Typhoon-class missile submarine, operating beneath the Arctic ice pack. The Typhoon is well hidden from the eyes of antisubmarine surface ships and aircraft, and presents a difficult target for attack submarines as well. Sonar beams scanning the waters beneath the icecap, for example, have trouble distinguishing a hovering missile sub from the ice stalactites around it.

In some ways, America's newest attack submarines are actually less equipped for Arctic service than their predecessors. The United States Navy pioneered Arctic submarine operations. The U.S.S. *Nautilus*, the world's first nuclear submarine, arrived at the North Pole in 1958, and by 1962 the *Skate* and the *Seadragon* were playing war games under the ice pack some 300 miles from the Soviet mainland. Such under-ice missions were curtailed, however, and the

Los Angeles–class attack submarine, first launched in 1974, lacked even the reinforced superstructure needed to break through Arctic ice. Only recently has the Navy shown renewed interest in developing tactics and weapons for war under the ice.

Last winter, for example, the *Sturgeon*-class attack submarines *Aspro* and *Tautog* spent 40 days at war games in the Arctic. Commander Fred P. Gustavson, captain of the *Aspro*, later described the under-ice mission as "the most challenging and unforgiving operation a submarine can do."

Melvyn R. Paisley, assistant secretary of the Navy for research, engineering, and systems, sits in his office on the prestigious E-ring of the Pentagon's fourth deck. One wall of the room is dominated by a painting of a P-47 fighter plane—Mr. Paisley piloted a P-47 in World War II. As he fields questions about antisubmarine warfare, he has the air of a craggy, Ivy League professor conducting a tutorial.

"We have a lead on the Russians," he says at one point. "If you take what submarines are all about, it's the sensors and the noise level of the submarine. One could say it's the goodness product of those two things. And our goodness product is better than theirs."

Gerald Cann, who is seated at Mr. Paisley's side, elaborates on the point. Says Mr. Cann, who has served in four administrations: "I think one of the biggest breakthroughs in the sensor business was the ability to process lots of data. In some of the early sonars, you looked in one narrow direction at a time. We called it the searchlight sonar. Now you can look in all directions at one time, and that's largely the function of computer technology, because now we've shrunk computers from the size of this room to down to my wristwatch." Mr. Paisley's room is 30 feet by 20 feet.

Navy ASW research today concentrates on acoustics, and dozens of new weapons systems are also being explored. One example: An array of hydrophones, coupled with a torpedo, would be dropped from a plane in an area where an enemy submarine was suspected to be lurking. Upon entering the water, the torpedo would separate from the hydrophones, though remaining linked by a thin wire. If the hydrophones located the submarine, they would signal the torpedo through the wire and direct it toward the target.

The Navy is also working with what are known as "blue-green lasers." Mounted in an airplane, or possibly beamed from a satellite, a laser might theoretically be used to spot a submarine underwater. But lasers have difficulty penetrating far below the water's surface. Scientists have found that light from the blue-green portion of the laser's spectrum achieves the greatest penetration, and they are concentrating their research there.

Yet another area of major research seeks to detect submarines by discovering the minute changes in the water caused by their passage. The Navy is conducting studies, for example, of the weak radioactive emissions of nuclear submarines and of small, submarine-created increases in water temperature. Once such phenomena are understood, it may be possible to develop actual submarine detection devices. Whether the instruments would be borne by aircraft, satellites, or buoys would depend upon such aspects as the quantity of electricity the instruments required. It might not be feasible, for example, to use buoys if a large area of the ocean was to be scanned over a long period of time.

The Soviet Union has its own research and development priorities. Among other projects, the Russians are struggling to produce sonars and quiet submarines comparable to those of the United States Navy. In fact, there have been suggestions that the Russians have made American sensor technology a prime object of their industrial-espionage operations.

But the Russian submarines already have several advantages over American ships. "Our submarines are good," says one former nuclear-submarine commander, now in the Office of the Chief of Naval Operations, "but not as good as they could be and should be. Nor do we have enough of them." Most Soviet submarines, for example, are faster and dive deeper. Unlike their American counterparts, the Russian ships have double hulls, which provide an added safety factor, and their outer hulls are coated with a sound-absorbent (anechoic) material that can lessen the effectiveness of an enemy ship's sonar.

The United States Navy has ideas about upgrading its attack-submarine fleet. In November, Admiral Watkins, the chief of naval operations, was the host at a breakfast in the Pentagon for several congressmen and top congressional staffers in the defense area. The admiral informed his guests that the Navy wants a new class of attack submarine that will be larger and quieter and carry more torpedoes than the *Los Angeles* class. Navy officials report that plans call for thirty of the new submarines—for a total of $36 billion. A coordinator for the new submarine was introduced at the E-ring breakfast—Rear Admiral Bruce DeMars, assistant deputy chief of naval operations for submarine warfare. Like Admiral Watkins, Admiral DeMars is a former nuclear-submarine commander, a matter of some importance, given the internal politics of the Navy.

Last year, the Navy spent about 15 percent of its $75 billion budget on ASW-related items. Some of it went to buy fuel for Orion patrol planes at a cost of about $1,000 for an hour of flight. Three new nuclear-powered attack submarines cost $725 million apiece. But the responsibility for ASW resources—from helicopters to sonar arrays towed by surface ships to computer centers ashore—is scattered throughout the Navy. Possible solutions to antisubmarine warfare issues sometimes get lost within an organizational labyrinth.

Most of the Navy is organized into three communities, sometimes called "unions"—air, surface, and submarine. Officers tend to spend most of their time at sea or ashore in the service of one of these unions, to which they owe their promotions and prospects. Aviation and surface officers do not serve in submarines and submariners rarely serve in aircraft squadrons or on surface ships. Each union, or community, has built around itself a fence of tradition and self-interest.

There is no ASW community. Officers in the submarine "union" want Congress to buy more submarines, and officers in the other communities have their own ideas about how Navy funds should be spent. They have no desire to talk about the vulnerability of their ships to Soviet submarine torpedoes and cruise missiles, and that is what ASW is all about. This lack of an ASW "union" helps explain why no admiral would allow himself to be interviewed for this article on the record, and only a few would do so off the record.

The new class of attack submarines will meet some of the criticism of American underwater preparedness, but it will leave the United States far behind the Russians as to total number of attack submarines. Counting all types of submarines, including research and training ships, both nuclear- and diesel-powered, the Soviet Union operates about 380 submarines, almost three times as many as the United States Navy.

The official goal of the United States Navy, approved by the Defense Department, is a fleet of 100 attack submarines, but that goal seems unlikely to be achieved. Under current plans, older submarines are going to be retired faster than new ones will be built. Moreover, there are many defense planners who believe that the United States will actually need between 120 and 140 nuclear-powered attack submarines to counter the continuing Russian buildup of new attack submarines and surface ships.

The arguments within the Navy over these numbers are steeped in complex budgetary and strategic considerations. Thus, for example, some authorities propose building a small number of diesel-electric submarines; though not as efficient as the nuclear-powered submarine, the diesel could be useful for ASW training and for some combat missions. Its particular attraction: It costs about one-third as much as a nuclear submarine and has a crew one-third the size. However, the Navy's leadership contends that the United States need not pursue these diesel submarines because the diesels of our NATO allies would be available during a conflict. Diesel-submarine proponents counter that the NATO diesel-powered attack submarines are aging, generally lack modern sonars and torpedoes, and may not be made available by their governments.

Perhaps the ultimate ASW question concerns the strategic-missile submarine, central to the security equations of both the Soviet Union and the United States. Today, Moscow boasts 62 modern, nuclear-powered missile submarines carrying a total of about 950 missiles. (The United States's 34 missile submarines carry 568 missiles.) According to defense analysts, the longer-range Soviet missiles like those on the Typhoon are apparently aimed at American cities. Russian missile submarines could be positioned off the American coasts to strike rapidly at American bomber bases, command centers and, possibly, Washington. Some analysts believe that the threats by Soviet leaders to equalize the warning times permitted by Pershing missiles and Russian submarine missiles could be made real by firing offshore submarine missiles on a low trajectory—a so-called "depressed" trajectory.

If current Navy plans go through, the United States fleet of missile submarines will actually decrease in number in the late 1990s; the number may shrink to 16 or 17. The high cost of Trident submarines—now about $2.5 billion per submarine—is a major factor in that decision. But Navy officials also point out that forthcoming submarines will be quieter than today's ships and will carry more missiles, which will have a longer range. The theory is that the enemy will have a harder time finding fewer submarines operating in greater expanses of ocean.

The comparative strengths and weaknesses of the Soviet and United States antisubmarine forces are all but impossible to add up. The American submarines are quieter and the American surveillance and detection capabilities are currently superior. In a submarine-versus-submarine encounter, these advantages are thought to give the American ship an edge over the faster Soviet submarine. But that could be outweighed by the Russians' numerical advantage.

Just how a war might start and develop could entirely change the equation. Some Navy planners, for example, expect that United States and NATO submarines would be able to rush to the bottlenecks monitored by American SOSUS hydrophones; the theory is that the Soviet submarines could be detected and picked off as they sought to reach the open ocean. Other analysts insist that, just before a shooting war started, the Russians would send their submarines to sea and assign their large fishing fleet to disrupt SOSUS arrays.

And some experts believe that today's strategies are doomed to be outmoded by some future technological breakthrough that will make the oceans acoustically "transparent," with advanced sensors being able to easily locate submerged submarines. To date, though, there are no public indications that such a breakthrough is imminent. Submariners also like to point out that radar, which made the skies "transparent," did not eliminate the bomber.

On one point most ASW experts seem to agree. Whatever edge the United States may have, there is no reason to relax. Admiral Watkins recently recalled that when the first nuclear submarine he commanded was launched in 1960, "we were infinitely ahead of the Russians in nuclear-submarine technology. Later, about 10 years ago, we were about 10 years ahead of them. Today, we are only about five to eight years ahead and they are *still* in relentless pursuit."

THE
FALKLANDS
CONFLICT

The British frigate *Sheffield* after being hit by an
Exocet Missile in 1987.
(United Press International Photo/Bettmann Archives)

CHAPTER 26

The *Sheffield:* "Missile Attack! Hit the Deck!"

Admiral Sandy Woodward with Patrick Robinson

O n April 2, 1982, the military junta that had ruled Argentina for nearly a decade sent troops into the wind-blown Falkland Islands near the southern tip of Argentina where a British squadron had avenged the loss of Admiral Christopher Cradock's force in 1914 (see chapter seven). The token British garrison on the islands was quickly overwhelmed, and soon the Argentine flag flew over Government House.

In response, the British Prime Minister, Margaret Thatcher, sent thousands of troops 8,000 miles to recapture the Falklands. At first, it looked like an old-fashioned naval war shaping up. But soon, it became tragically clear that new and highly-sophisticated weaponry were at play—notably the sea-skimming, ship-killing, French-built Exocet missile that Argentina had purchased on the international weapons market.

What follows is the frightening experience of dodging such weapons—not quite fast enough.

Admiral Sandy Woodward entered the Royal Navy at the age of thirteen. As flag officer, First Flotilla, he commanded the South Atlantic Task Force Group in the Falklands war. Patrick Robinson is the author of five books.

They flew in radio silence, climbing to 5,000 feet above the white banks of cloud and fog which covered, partially, the rocky, almost treeless coastline they were leaving behind. The jet engines of the two single-seat naval attack aircraft were throttled back to a speed of around 400 knots to conserve fuel. They flew in close formation, headed due east, with radar switched on but not transmitting.

Disappearing swiftly with the slipstream was their last contact with their Argentinian homeland, the air control officer at the Rio Grande Air Base on the island of Tierra del Fuego, the legendary "Land of Fire" which sits south of the Magellan Straits—home of Commander Jorge Colombo's 2nd Naval Fighter and Attack Squadron.

The two pilots, Lieutenant Commander Augusto Bedacarratz and Lieutenant Armando Mayora, were members of a group of senior naval aviators specially selected to undertake these critically important missions, using the Etendard/Exocet system, a system regarded as the most serious and immediate threat to my aircraft carriers. Now, after a succession of technical problems, they were airborne, and on their way. . . .

It was ten o'clock in the morning on Tuesday, May 4, 1982. Britain was at war in the South Atlantic. . . .

In our case, on that morning, we fielded a picket line of three Type 42 guided-missile destroyers, quite small ships each displacing 4,000 tons. Far to my right, was the tall, rather patrician Captain David Hart-Dyke's HMS *Coventry*. Out to my left was HMS *Sheffield*, commanded by Captain Sam Salt, at five feet, four inches physically the opposite of Hart-Dyke but another experienced officer whom I had known, liked, and respected for many years. In the center was HMS *Glasgow*, placed to ensure the three ships presented a very wide surface-to-air missile defensive front. *Glasgow* was commanded by Captain Paul Hoddinott, the 40-year-old former commander of the Polaris submarine HMS *Revenge* and a man likely to make as few mistakes as any.

I trusted all three of them implicitly. I knew them all personally and professionally, and I knew what was involved in their unenviable task from my own time in command of the *Sheffield* five years before. . . .

All three of those picket commanders knew the risks they had to take. They knew that if the incoming enemy aircraft "popped up" and got a contact, the chances were that the Argentinian pilots would release their missiles at the first blip they caught on their radar screen. *Coventry, Glasgow,* and *Sheffield* had been carefully placed, and left to trust in their missile and self-defense systems almost alone. The only comfort in such a situation is to keep telling yourself that the chaff will work or, if not, that there are two other ships in the same position, and to hope fervently that it will be one of them that catches it.

But they knew, all three of them, Hart-Dyke, Hoddinott, and Salt, that their situation was very exposed. It remained to be seen how effective the Type-42 destroyer would prove in this situation. Stay alert; that's all they could do and all I could ask.

Some 18 miles to the east of the pickets lay my second line of defense; the frigates *Arrow, Yarmouth,* and *Alacrity* and the big, but older, destroyer *Glamorgan.* Behind them, there were three Royal Fleet Auxiliary ships *Olmeda, Resource,* and *Fort Austin*—placed as a further confusion factor for any enemy radar. Only beyond them could the Etendards hope to find their proper targets, the carriers *Hermes* and *Invincible,* each with their own "Goalkeeper" in the form of a Type-22 frigate. *Invincible* had, close beside, *Brilliant,* commanded by the dynamic and voluble Captain John Coward; *Hermes* had *Broadsword,* with Captain Bill Canning, an old and trusted friend, in command. These two 4,400-ton warships, primarily designed for antisubmarine work, had the remarkable antimissile system Sea Wolf fitted. This was new in service and its reputation was high. It had, in trials, actually hit the high-velocity 4.5-inch shell being used as the target. It was a short-range system, but with this performance we hoped it would find the bigger and slower Exocet relatively easy to deal with . . .

The two Argentinian Etendards were about 150 miles west of us when I left the flag operations room on board *Hermes* for a quick lunch. Bedacarratz and Mayora were just entering the clear air that surrounded us, and finding it not quite so difficult to fly right down at wave-top height. A few hundred feet above them, the sweeping beams of the British long-range radars were blind to the Etendards' high-speed approach.

The Argentinians' own search radar fitted to the Etendards was French-made, like the planes, and was code-named by us "Handbrake." If we were quick enough we could locate and recognize it. We could also deal with the subsequent missiles. If we were quick enough. . . .

It is now 1356. The two Etendards pop to 120 feet above the sea. They level out and Bedacarratz glances down to see a blip on his radar screen. His gloved hand moves less than a foot to the Exocet activate button. Mayora does the same.

Glasgow's ops room, like any other in the force, is packed with people sweating under their hoods. It is 1356 and 30 seconds. The air is hot, and the darkness seems to add to it. The battle group is still on "White Alert" when young Able Seaman Rose blows his whistle and calls the words which, Paul Hoddinott later said, "caused the hair on the back of my neck to stand on end."

"Agave radar!" snaps Rose.

Glasgow's air warfare officer [AWO], Lieutenant Commander Nick Hawkyard, reacts instantly, "Confidence level?"

"Certain!" says Rose. "I have three sweeps, followed by a short lock-on. Bearing . . . two three eight. Search mode."

Hoddinott swings around to stare at the big UAA 1 console. Both he and Hawkyard can see that the bearing line on Rose's screen correlates with two long-range air warning radar contacts 45 miles out on the AWO's display.

"Transmission ceased," reports Rose.

Hawkyard calls into the command open line: "AWO to Officer of the Watch—go to action stations, right now!"

And up on the bridge, Lieutenant David Goddard hits the intercom button broadcasting "Action Stations!" throughout the ship.

Hawkyard, staring at the picture on his big, flat table screen, switches to the UHF radio announcing to all ships "Flash! This is *Glasgow*, Agave . . . bearing two three eight . . . correlates track one two three four . . . bearing two three eight . . . range four zero . . . *Invincible*, over."

Invincible: "Roger, out."

Then Rose calls again: "Agave regained—bearing two three eight."

His electronic warfare supervisor, sitting next to him, confirms the second detection. The ship's radar operators, watching their air and surface warning radar screens, also confirm contact: "Two bogeys. Bearing two three eight. Range three eight miles. Tracking zero seven zero. Four-fifty knots."

Hawkyard to Hoddinnot: "That's two Super Es. Just popped

up for sure. May be about to launch missiles." And now *Glasgow*'s ops room really comes alive. They are 100 percent prepared for just this event. It was, after all, precisely what they were there for.

"Chaff!" calls Hawkyard, and across the room the hooded figure of Chief Petty Officer Jan Ames bangs his closed fists into the big, easy-to-hit-in-a-hurry chaff fire buttons.

Hawkyard again broadcasts on the radio circuit to the whole battle group: "This is *Glasgow* . . ." As he starts to speak he suddenly remembers he ought to have been saying "Handbrake," our code word for Agave radar. Hawkyard now corrects himself, hurriedly. "Handbrake!" he exclaims, "Bearing two three eight."

Simultaneously the fingers of the air-picture supervisor, Leading Seaman Nevin, are clattering away trying to release the full picture of the incoming raid, tracks 1234 and 1235 on the intership computer circuit, Link 10. Then, turning to see his relief standing at his shoulder ready for the watch change, the electronic warfare supervisor, Leading Seaman Hewitt, quickly hands over and fairly flies up the steep steps to the upper deck to help with the reloading of the chaff rocket launchers. "I had never," he admitted later, "moved at that speed my entire life."

As the Leading Seaman goes, Hawkyard switches back to UHF and tries to convince the force antiair warfare commander [FAAWC] in *Invincible* that this is real. But he is not succeeding. Hoddinott hears with alarm Hawkyard's voice rising in frustration, desperately trying to convince the FAAWC that this is deadly serious and not just another nervous "ghost". . . .

FAAWC, who has dealt with three or four such "panics" that very morning, wants more evidence. As far as he is concerned, the cry "Handbrake" has been heard more often than "Good morning" today, and he isn't going to commit the entire group to expenditure of our rapidly diminishing chaff stock without solid reason.

Invincible acknowledges: "Roger, out."

But at least he must know that *Glasgow* was sure of her own warning. Anyone listening to the air warfare net can hear *Glasgow*'s chaff rockets launch with that "whoosh" which is to become uncomfortably familiar to all of us.

Down at *Glasgow*'s electronic warfare console, Rose calls again: "Handbrake in lock-on mode."

Bedacarratz is on the point of releasing his missile and Paul Hoddinott feels the chill dread that hits you when you have incontrovertible evidence that a big missile is on its way toward you. For the next few minutes, the technique is for *Glasgow* to place herself carefully among the four clouds of chaff that are blooming around her, and which should decoy the missile off course to miss the ship. But chaff drifts with the wind. And you must stay in the pattern. Speed and position must be very quickly corrected . . .

At 1402, the pilots release their missiles and bank left. The Exocets fall away, locked onto their own targets. Neither pilot has the least idea what ship he has aimed at, nor are they going to hang around to find out. They know only that a radar contact has appeared on their screens in roughly the right bit of ocean. And they get out fast, diving back down, close to the water, beneath our radar beams, heading west.

We never detected them again.

Almost simultaneously, two amber dots, so small they can only be seen intermittently, appear on the radar of *Glasgow*, tracking their way fast across the screen.

"Zippo One! Bruisers! Incoming. Bearing two three eight. Range twelve miles."

Hoddinott orders his Sea Dart surface-to-air missile system into action to shoot them down.

Hawkyard calls again to Chief Ames, his missile gun director: "Take Track with twelve thirty-four and twelve thirty-five with Sea Dart." But it does not work. Unsuccessfully—nightmarishly—the fire-control radar cannot lock onto the small fleeting targets at that range. They keep trying, but the dots keep disappearing. Frustration mounts and the Captain fumes. Hawkyard again calls *Invincible* advising them to clear two sea harriers from the line of fire. But the ops room in the little carrier answers that they believe the raid is spurious.

Glasgow's AWO, now desperate, almost shouts on the radio circuit "Negative! The force is under attack! Raid twelve thirty-four and twelve thirty-five bearing and range correlate with Handbrake."

Invincible still does not agree.

Chief Ames, still furiously trying to engage the Exocet with Sea Dart, cannot help wondering how long the missile will take to hit, fearing it would strike *Glasgow* amidships where the ops room is. Like many others he begins to resign himself to his fate.

It is Captain Hoddinott himself who first realizes, with enormous relief, that *Glasgow* is safe. One of the missiles is heading toward *Sheffield*, and the other is going well clear.

Sheffield, with Captain Salt not in the ops room, has, for whatever reason, not got her chaff up yet. Hoddinott later recalled saying to Hawkyard, worriedly: "What the hell's happening to *Sheffield*?"

The only response he received was from his own operators, who said they could get no answer.

Twenty miles away, things were moving at a tragic conclusion in the small destroyer named after Britain's city of stainless steel. Problem number one was that she had been transmitting on her satellite communications system at the critical time when the Etendards' radar were used. This blotted them out in *Sheffield.*

The absence of the captain, incidentally, in his cabin directly after lunch, was bad luck, not bad management. He was perfectly entitled to be in his cabin. The captain must not try to stay alert and on watch indefinitely if he is to remain effective. He has to pace himself carefully and learn to rely on his watch-keepers.

The second problem was that the significance of the reports from *Glasgow* was not appreciated. There was some kind of gap in her ops room and no action was taken, nor were the aircraft or the missiles detected on *Sheffield*'s radars. It is tempting to conclude that if the *Glasgow*'s warning of the Etendard radar had been accepted in *Sheffield*'s ops room, chaff would have been fired and might have proved effective; or that *Sheffield*'s own radars might have detected both the Etendards and the incoming missiles. They were, after all, some four miles closer, albeit presenting a much smaller radar target to *Sheffield* than to *Glasgow.* And *Sheffield* had shown herself to be first class at this procedure only a few weeks previously in live missile-firing exercises off Gibraltar. Now, at war, how could their performance be less?

For whatever reason, at 1403 *Sheffield*'s chaff was not launched. Up on her bridge, Lieutenant Peter Walpole and Lieutenant Brian Layshon, looking out over the starboard bow, spotted a trail of smoke six feet above the sea, about a mile away and coming straight for the ship. There were only seconds left. One of them grabbed the broadcast microphone and shouted: "Missile attack! Hit the deck!"

The Exocet struck them at 1404. Amidships. Starboard side. A few feet above the waterline. There was some doubt that the warhead went off, but several men were killed instantly. A large fire was started, releasing great quantities of heat, smoke, and fumes which were to cause others to die, many of them in heroic circumstances. *Sheffield* was the first Royal Navy ship to be hit by an enemy missile since World War II. . . .

"*Sheffield* has suffered an explosion." Nothing more definite or descriptive than that. I take note, but permit business to continue as usual. . . .

The information continues to filter through slowly and methodically. Nothing of the "Hold the front page" variety. And although I can see that *Arrow* and *Yarmouth* and the helicopters are close to *Sheffield,* there is rising tension in *Hermes*'s flag ops room. Everyone can feel it, as if we were somehow helpless and that we ought to be doing more. One of my staff blurts out: "Admiral, you must do something!" Which is precisely what I should not be doing, I reckon.

I reply gently enough: "No . . . leave it be. . . ."

The fire appears to be getting out of control, Captain Salt's men are struggling for water, and they need pumps, which we fly over to them. The computer-room staff stayed too long at their posts trying to keep the ship's defense system working. They all died. Chief Petty Officer Briggs kept going back into the forward damage control section base to drag equipment out. Finally, overcome by fumes, he, too, died. . . .

In the middle of the afternoon, with the increasing danger of a major explosion, Captain Salt gave the order to abandon ship, and the remainder of the crew was taken off by helicopter and across to the frigates.

Sam Salt arrived on board *Hermes* soon afterward. I could see by the way he swallowed that he was close to tears, but he was no less brave for that, on this most terrible day. We did our best to speak in a matter-of-fact tone, to keep a hold on the situation, but I fear that in my worry, I was less than sympathetic. (Years later, Sam told me I said flatly: "I suspect someone's been bloody careless.") What I remember is being aware that I could not afford to let this situation get out of hand, any more than he could. . . .

Meanwhile, *Sheffield* continued to burn, her deck plates now getting very hot and her paint blistering in large patches over extensive areas. The fire was slowly gutting her, but still not getting to the magazine. Sam Salt wanted to go and assess the chances of saving her. This was put off until the next day as I did not want to risk losing a helicopter full of good men when we all knew perfectly well she could go up at any moment. Furthermore, poor *Sheffield,* supposing she could be saved, was now so badly damaged as to be of no military value, and not even much as scrap. . . .

That evening, with *Sheffield* still ablaze, we returned to some semblance of routine. The recce insertion went ahead as planned, the Special Forces men landing on schedule, all helicopters returning on time. All of the mundane business of running the battle group continued—everyone more alert now to the possibility of another

Exocet attack. I could start to plan ahead, not least because I was satisfied that the battle group was back in balance and that the *Sheffield* situation was being properly managed. . . .

And now I must try and sleep, which may be difficult, even tired as I am, since our next moves must be planned with care. The key word is control: control of our attacks; control of our defense; and control of ourselves in the face of disaster.

Whichever way you look at it, I had been training for this or something like it for most of my life, albeit in hopes it would never happen. This day, however, was elbowing its way into military and naval folklore. British warship hit by enemy missile. First major attack on the White Ensign in decades. I kept asking myself how I came to be in the middle of all this. I had never asked for a place in anyone's history book. Neither had the ship's company of *Sheffield*. And twenty of them were dead.

Copyrights and Credits

The editor and publisher of "*Fire When Ready, Gridley!*" are grateful to the following publishers, authors, and translators for permission to reprint many of the chapters in this volume. While every effort has been made to secure permission, we may have failed in one or another case to trace copyright holders. We regret any inadvertent omissions.

The United States Naval Institute, Annapolis, Maryland, for its consent to the inclusion of Chapter 3, "Port Arthur: The First Pearl Harbor," by William H. Honan, which originally appeared under the title "Nightmare at Port Arthur," by William H. Honan in *Naval History*, summer 1990, published by the United States Naval Institute. Reprinted from *Naval History* with permission; Copyright © 1990 U.S. Naval Institute.

Methuen London (Octopus Publishing Group Library) for its consent to the inclusion of Chapter 11, "Zeebrugge: Twisting the Dragon's Tail," by Sir Roger Keyes, which is a condensation of an excerpt from *The Naval Memoirs of Admiral of the Fleet Sir Roger Keyes, Scapa Flow to the Dover Straits, 1916–1918*, originally published by Eyre & Spottiwoode, London, in 1935, and E. P. Dutton & Co., Inc., New York. Reprinted by permission of Methuen London. Copyright © 1935 by Sir Roger Keyes.

The United States Naval Institute, Annapolis, Maryland, for its consent to the inclusion of Chapter 12, "U.S. Submarines: A Comedy of Errors," by Harley F. Cope, which originally appeared as "U.S. Submarines in the War Zone" in *Proceedings* of the U.S. Naval Institute, August, 1930. Reprinted from *Proceedings* with permission; Copyright © 1930 U.S. Naval Institute.

Curtis Brown & John Farquharson, London, for its consent to the inclusion of Chapter 14, "Oran: When the British Navy Fought an Ally," by Winston Churchill which, after being delivered as a speech in the House of Commons, appeared in the book *Blood, Sweat and Tears*, by the Rte. Hon. Winston S. Churchill, published in 1941 in Britain by Cassell & Company, Ltd. (now Cassell, London), and in the United States by G. P. Putnam's Sons, New York (now the Putnam Berkley Group, Inc., New York). Reproduced with permission of Curtis Brown Ltd., London, and the Putnam Berkley Group, New York. © Copyright by the estate of Sir Winston S. Churchill.

Hodder & Stoughton, Limited, London, and Lady Willmer and Ian Bremner for their consent to the inclusion of Chapter 15, "Merchant War: Freighters That Fought Back," by Sir Archibald Hurd, which is an excerpt from *The Battle of the Seas: The Fighting Merchantmen*, by Sir Archibald Hurd, first published by Hodder & Stoughton, Ltd., London, in 1941. © Copyright 1941 by Sir Archibald Hurd.

Peters Fraser & Dunlop Group, Ltd., London, for its consent to the inclusion of Chapter 16, "*Bismarck*: The Witches' Sabbath," by C. S. Forester, which is an excerpt from *Hunting the Bismarck*, by C. S. Forester, originally published by Michael Joseph, Ltd., London, in 1959. Reprinted by permission of Peters Fraser & Dunlop Group Ltd., London. © Copyright 1959 by C. S. Forester.

Little, Brown and Company, Boston, for its consent to the inclusion of Chapter 17, "Pearl Harbor: Hurling Monkey Wrenches in Exasperation," by Samuel Eliot Morison which is an excerpt from *The Two Ocean War: A Short History of the United States Navy in the Second World War*, by Samuel Eliot Morison, originally published by the Atlantic Monthly Press division of Little, Brown and Company in 1963. © Copyright 1963 by Samuel Eliot Morison. Reproduced by permission of Little, Brown and Company.

Koehlers Verlagsgesellschaft for their consent to the inclusion of Chapter 10, "Jutland: Blowing Up the *Queen Mary*," by Commander Georg von Hase, from *The Two White Nations (Die Zwei Weissen Völker)* by Georg von Hase, translated into English by Hector C. Bywater, published by (British) Admiralty, Naval Staff, Intelligence Division (I.D. 1220), May, 1920, © copyright 1920 by Georg von Hase and Koehlers Verlagsgesellschaft.

Paul Stillwell and the Naval Institute Press, Annapolis, Maryland, for their consent to the inclusion of Chapter 18, "Pearl Harbor: When the *Arizona* Went Down," by Paul Stillwell, which is an excerpt from *Battleship Arizona: An Illustrated History*, by Paul Stillwell. Copyright © 1991, Paul Stillwell. Permission granted by the U.S. Naval Institute, Annapolis, Maryland.

Stanley Johnston and the *Chicago Tribune* Company, Chicago, Illinois, for their consent to the inclusion of Chapter 19, "Coral Sea: 'Scratch One Flat-Top!'," by Stanley Johnston, which originally appeared as a news story in the *Chicago Tribune* in 1942. © Copyrighted 1942, *Chicago Tribune* Company, all rights reserved, used with permission.

Curtis Brown Ltd., New York, for its consent to the inclusion of Chapter 21, "Leyte Gulf: Kinkaid *vs.* Kurita, Etc." by Hanson W. Baldwin, which is an excerpt from *Sea Fights and Shipwrecks*, by Hanson W. Baldwin, originally published by Hanover House, Garden City, N.Y., in 1955. Reprinted here by permission of Curtis Brown Ltd., © copyright 1938 and 1955 by Hanson W. Baldwin.

Frank Harvey and Bantam Books, New York, for their consent to the inclusion of Chapter 22, "Yankee Station: Frantic Little Situations of Life and Death," by Frank Harvey, which is an excerpt from *Air War Vietnam* by Frank Harvey originally published by Bantam Books, New York, in 1967. Copyright © 1967 by Frank Harvey. Used by permission of Bantam Books, a division of Bantam Doubleday Dell Publishing Group, Inc.

Marilyn Elkins and *MHQ: The Quarterly Journal of Military History*, New York, for their consent to the inclusion of Chapter 23, "Vietnam: The Search for Lieutenant Elkins," by Marilyn Elkins which originally appeared under the title "MIA" in *MHQ*, Spring, 1992. © Copyright 1992 by Marilyn Elkins.

The New York Times for its consent to the inclusion of Chapter 24, "Mediterranean: Playing Chicken," by William H. Honan which originally appeared as "Soviet and American Pilots Play 'Chicken'," by William H.

Honan, in *The New York Times Magazine*, November 22, 1970. © Copyright 1970 by William H. Honan and *The New York Times*.

Thomas B. Allen, Norman Polmar and *The New York Times* for their consent to the inclusion of Chapter 25, "The Silent Chase," by Thomas B. Allen and Norman Polmar, which originally appeared as "The Silent Chase: Tracking Soviet Submarines," by Thomas B. Allen and Norman Polmar in *The New York Times Magazine*, January 1, 1984. © Copyright 1984 by Thomas B. Allen, Norman Polmar, and *The New York Times*.

Admiral Sandy Woodward and Harper/Collins, London, and the Naval Institute Press, Annapolis, Maryland, for their consent to the inclusion of Chapter 26, "The *Sheffield*: Missile Attack! Hit the Deck!" by Admiral Sandy Woodward with Patrick Robinson, which is an excerpt from *One Hundred Days: The Memoirs of the Falklands Battle Group Commander*, by Admiral Sandy Woodward with Patrick Robinson originally published in 1992 in Great Britain by Harper/Collins, London, and in the United States by the Naval Institute Press, Annapolis, Maryland. Reprinted with permission. Copyright © 1992 by Admiral Sir John Woodward and Patrick Robinson.

Chapter 1, "Manila Bay: 'Fire When Ready, Gridley!'," by Joseph L. Stickney is from *Life and Glorious Deeds of Admiral Dewey*, by Joseph L. Stickney, published by Chas. B. Ayer Co., Chicago, Illinois, in 1898.

Chapters 2 and 8, "Santiago: 'Don't Cheer, Boys. Those Poor Devils Are Dying!'," by John Richard Hale, and "Jutland: Blind Man's Bluff," by John Richard Hale, are both from *Famous Sea Fights: From Salamis to Tsu-Shima* (later entitled *Famous Sea Fights: From Salamis to Jutland*), by John Richard Hale, published by Methuen & Co., Ltd., London (now Methuen London) in 1911, 1916, and 1931. *Famous Sea Fights* was published in the United States by Little, Brown and Company in 1911.

Chapter 3, "Tsushima: A Whirlwind of Fire and Iron," by Capt. Vladimir Semenoff, is a condensation of *The Battle of Tsu-Shima Between the Japanese and Russian Fleets, Fought on 27th May 1905*, by Captain Vladimir Semenoff (one of the survivors), translated by Captain A. B. Lindsay, 2nd King Edward's Own Gurkha Rifles, by John Murray, London, in 1906.

Chapters 5 and 7, "Indian Ocean: *Sydney* vs. *Emden*," by Hector C. Bywater and "Coronel and the Falklands: Sweet Vengeance," by Hector C. Bywater, are both from *Cruisers in Battle: Naval 'Light Cavalry' Under Fire, 1914–1918*, by Hector C. Bywater, published by Constable & Co., Ltd. (now Constable Publishers), London, 1939. This book was also published by Macmillan Company of Canada, Ltd. (now Macmillan-Canada) in 1939.

Chapters 6 and 9, "British Submarines: Little Tin Turtles," by Rudyard Kipling, and "Jutland: Destroyer Work," by Rudyard Kipling, are both from *Sea Warfare*, by Rudyard Kipling, published in the United States by Doubleday, Page & Company, Garden City, New York, 1917.

Chapter 13, "Torpedo Boats: David *vs.* Goliath," by Hector C. Bywater is from "Their Secret Purposes: Dramas and Mysteries of the Naval War," by Hector C. Bywater, published by Constable & Co., Ltd. (now Constable Publishers), London, 1932. This book was also published by Macmillan Company of Canada Ltd. (now Macmillan-Canada) in 1939, and by Oxford University Press of Bombay, India, in 1939.

Chapter 20, "Midway: 'I Dive-Bombed a Jap Carrier,'" by Capt. Tom Moore as told to Frank Gervasi, was originally published under the same title in *Collier's Magazine*, April 10, 1943, published by the Crowell-Collier Publishing Co., of Springfield, Ohio, subsequently owned by the Macmillan Company, New York.

PHOTO CREDITS: All photographs are official U.S. Navy Photos from the Naval Historical Center, Washington Navy Yard, unless otherwise noted.

The painting reproduced on the jacket cover is used courtesy of the Lt. Charles Dutreaux Collection, Naval Historical Foundation.

The photograph reproduced on the endpapers is a captured German photograph showing the *Bismarck* firing at the *Prince of Wales* a few days before the *Bismarck* was sunk, courtesy of the Naval Historical Center, Washington Navy Yard.

In a career spanning more than two decades at *The New York Times*, William H. Honan has become recognized as a leading authority on naval history and affairs. He has written about naval matters for virtually every section of the newspaper from the Sunday *Magazine* to the *Book Review*. His articles on naval subjects have also appeared in *American Heritage, Reader's Digest, Naval History* and *MHQ: The Quarterly Journal of Military History*.

In 1991, Mr. Honan won wide praise for his book *Visions of Infamy: The Untold Story of How Journalist Hector C. Bywater Devised the Plans That Led to Pearl Harbor*, also published by St. Martin's Press.

John Toland, the Pulitzer Prize–winning author of *The Rising Sun*, wrote: "What makes Honan's book of historical importance is his proof beyond doubt that Yamamoto had not only carefully studied [Bywater's] 'The Great Pacific War' but later used it as the model for his own attack on Pearl Harbor. . . . Honan's stranger-than-fiction tale must be read by those who want the inside story of Pearl Harbor."

Harvard history professor Akira Iriye, the leading authority on twentieth-century Japanese history, called *Visions of Infamy* "a very important book," adding that "no study of Pearl Harbor (as well as of Japanese naval thinking prior to 1941) from now on can ignore the contributions made by Hector Bywater."

Writing for *The New York Times*, Professor Stanley Weintraub of the University of Pennsylvania called Mr. Honan's book "compelling," and concluded: "Part ingenious speculation, part detective story, part biography, *Visions of Infamy* adds another title to the few works of fiction that may have influenced history."

Reviewing *Visions of Infamy* for *Newsday*, Martin E. Weinstein, a professor of Japanese studies and international politics at the University of Illinois, called the book "one of the clearest and most readable accounts available of Japanese and American strategies in the Pacific war" which "focus[es] on the life and works of the convivial, pub-crawling British-American naval journalist Hector C. Bywater, and most especially on Bywater's best-selling 1925 work, *The Great Pacific War*."

Ronald Spector, author of *Eagle Against the Sun*, and a former director of naval history at the U.S. Navy Department, wrote: "Hector Bywater's life was so colorful and mysterious that it reads at times like an old-style spy thriller. *Visions of Infamy* is a highly readable account of one of the most fascinating and least-known figures in naval history."

Mr. Honan has lectured about Bywater's work at the United States Naval Academy at Annapolis and the Naval War College at Newport, Rhode Island, among other institutions.

Two of Mr. Honan's articles are included in this book—the first about the Japanese raid on Port Arthur in 1904, and the second concerning the United States–Soviet Union confrontation in the Mediterranean during the Cold War.

Currently chief cultural correspondent for the *Times*, Mr. Honan lives in Connecticut with his wife and three children.